THE RISE AND FALL OF THE ITALIAN COMMUNIST PARTY

STANFORD-HOOVER SERIES ON **AUTHORITARIANISM**

Edited by Paul R. Gregory and Norman Naimark

THE RISE AND FALL OF THE ITALIAN COMMUNIST PARTY

I communisti italiani e gli altri

A Transnational History

SILVIO PONS

Translated by
Derek Boothman and Chris Dennis

Stanford University Press | Hoover Institution, Stanford University
Stanford, California

English translation © 2024 by the Board of Trustees of the Leland Stanford Junior University. All rights reserved.

The Rise and Fall of the Italian Communist Party was originally published in Italian under the title *I comunisti italiani e gli altri*. © 2021 Giulio Einaudi editore s.p.a., Torino.

No part of this book may be reproduced or transmitted in any form or by any means, electronic or mechanical, including photocopying and recording, or in any information storage or retrieval system, without the prior written permission of Stanford University Press.

Printed in the United States of America on acid-free, archival-quality paper

Library of Congress Cataloging-in-Publication Data
Names: Pons, Silvio, author.
Title: The rise and fall of the Italian Communist Party : a transnational history / Silvio Pons ; [translated by] Derek Boothman and Chris Dennis.
Other titles: Comunisti italiani e gli altri. English | Stanford-Hoover series on authoritarianism.
Description: Stanford, California : Stanford University Press, 2024. | Series: Stanford-Hoover series on authoritarianism | Translation of: I comunisti italiani e gli altri | Includes bibliographical references and index.
Identifiers: LCCN 2023058054 (print) | LCCN 2023058055 (ebook) | ISBN 9781503638839 (cloth) | ISBN 9781503639256 (epub)
Subjects: LCSH: Partito comunista italiano—History. | Communism—Italy—History—20th century. | Italy—Politics and government—20th century.
Classification: LCC JN5657.C63 P6613 2024 (print) | LCC JN5657.C63 (ebook) | DDC 324.245/075—dc23/eng/20240222
LC record available at https://lccn.loc.gov/2023058054
LC ebook record available at https://lccn.loc.gov/2023058055

Cover design: Jason Anscomb
Cover art: Wikimedia and Jason Anscomb

For Leonardo

Contents

Introduction ... ix

PART ONE Genealogies: Internationalism and Cosmopolitanism, 1917–41

1 Revolution and Hegemony ... 3

2 Stalinism and Antifascism ... 41

PART TWO Influences: Internationalism and the Nation, 1943–64

3 The "New Party" and the Cold War ... 93

4 Polycentrism and Decolonization ... 153

PART THREE Transformations: The Twilight of Internationalism, 1964–84

5 Humanistic Socialism and the "Long 1968" ... 211

6 Europeanisms and Globalisms ... 259

Epilogue: The Dream of a New World Order ... 312

Notes ... 333

Index ... 379

Introduction

In April 1951, at the height of the Cold War, the CIA assembled a dossier of Italian Communist Party documents that dated back to 1923 and had been seized by the Fascist police.[1] The curators of these papers presented them as a rare source of information about communist organizations and their illegal conspiratorial activities, useful in general terms for gaining insight into their procedures and practices after World War II. For the CIA, the crucial aspect was the vast scale of communist networks documented; it was thought that they might provide suggestions about the investigative methodologies needed to combat the challenge of these "professional revolutionaries" during the Cold War. Shortly after founding their party, the Italian Communists had created bases and connections in Paris, Berlin, and Switzerland. The addresses possessed by a leader of the caliber of Umberto Terracini, and found in the documentation, pointed to a much wider "foreign organization" which, alongside Moscow, Vienna, Prague, and other European capitals, included cities such as New York, Buenos Aires, Melbourne, Cairo, and Alexandria. In actual fact, the American intelligence officials had attributed contacts belonging to Comintern, already in the early Twenties a global organization, to the Italian Communists. Their conclusions, though vitiated by their obvious Cold War psychosis regarding the threat posed by international communism's tentacular ramifications, unintentionally identified an essential historical element.

Rather than being a valid tool for analyzing a communist "conspiracy," usable in political warfare, these documents, produced in the early Twenties by a small, persecuted communist party, revealed the outlines of a global project.

This book aims to reassess from an international perspective the visions, connections, protagonists, and salient moments of the history of Italian communism. In other words, I analyze Italian communism as a case study in the global history of communism. This perspective is increasingly being adopted and discussed. Historians have, for example, examined the ambitions and ramifications of the "party of world revolution" between the two world wars, the relations between communism and anticolonial liberation movements, and the Soviet and Chinese strategies in the global Cold War and in the Third World.[2] In a similar innovative framework, there remained in the shadows the history of those communists who were not in power, though they too were an essential component of a worldwide presence, combining the roles of national and transnational nongovernmental actors. In particular, situating Western communism within the global history of communism implies reconstructing a multiplicity of relational and temporal contexts, ranging from the conceptions and practices of internationalism to the imaginaries and training of militants and leaders, and to the networks established not only in Europe but in the colonial and postcolonial world. It has been said that, given the very nature of their subject, historians of communism have practiced transnational history without realizing it. This is probably true in some cases. Yet it is a fact that for the most part—and until recently—they have approached this history without having really adopted such a perspective.[3]

The book reconstructs a well-delimited aspect among the possible approaches to the multidimensionality of global relations: the political culture expressed by personalities and leading groups via their visions of European and world order, their ways of making sense of the nexus between national identities and international connections, and their approach to the problems of peace and war. In this profile, a focus on political elites seems inevitable. Not only were questions of international policy the preserve of restricted groups in the last century (as they still are today), but any awareness of the global dimension only emerged with discontinuity, mainly in the context of elites who, for a variety of economic, cultural or political reasons, were themselves internationalized. At the same time, the communist movement constantly cultivated a pedagogical vocation, attempting an osmosis between the political discourse of its leading groups and the cultural development of its militants. In this light, contraposing the sentiments of militants and the strategies of their leaders, as has sometimes been done in studies, seems inadequate. The Soviet mythologies of world revolution, of actual socialism and of "peaceful power"—essential components of the internationalist culture of the communists—became widespread in very similar forms, albeit in different levels of awareness, among leaders, intellectuals, and simple militants.

Like many other leaders and militants, Italian communists saw in internationalism an essential part of their raison d'être. They had been formed between the two world wars, frequenting the milieus of the Comintern, mainly in Moscow and to a lesser extent in other European capitals. Antonio Gramsci, Palmiro Togliatti, Umberto Terracini, Angelo Tasca, Amadeo Bordiga, Ruggero Grieco, Mauro Scoccimarro, Camilla Ravera, Teresa Noce, Giuseppe Di Vittorio, Luigi Longo, Pietro Secchia, and Giuseppe Berti all spent more or less decisive parts of their political apprenticeships in the Moscow of the 1920s. They established contacts and relations with Bolshevik leaders and Comintern representatives, who formed part of a dense transnational network. For the Italians, the experience of exile started very early, in Paris and Moscow, where their leaders were joined by a conspicuous number of self-exiled militants. Togliatti became a leading member of the Comintern and its plenipotentiary in the Spanish Civil War, which was a crucial episode for many "professional revolutionaries" such as Longo, Vittorio Vidali, Velio Spano, Antonio Roasio and many others, including rank-and-file militants. After World War II, under Togliatti's leadership the internationalist generation of the Twenties became integrated with those emerging from antifascist militancy, and later from militancy in the Resistance movement. Among others, these leaders included Giorgio Amendola, Giancarlo Pajetta, Emilio Sereni, Celeste Negarville, Eugenio Reale, Pietro Ingrao, Paolo Bufalini, Mario Alicata, Armando Cossutta, Enrico Berlinguer, Giorgio Napolitano, and Alessandro Natta. Communist internationalism enjoyed continuity thanks to privileged relations with the socialist and anti-imperialist world, which was in expansion thanks to the transformations that war had wrought. The history of these relations and interconnections has often been reduced to a secondary issue, or merely to evidence of a constitutional "duplicity," with both views using the nation as the sole parameter for judgment. In actual fact, this history was part of a global project that gave rise to a source of identity, a connective tissue, and the guiding star of a vision of the world centered on the idea of politics as a demiurgic force.[4]

Unlike the French communists, with whom they were in close contact during the years of exile, the Italians did not participate in this project through the means of a European great power and an imperial metropolis.[5] They had experienced semilegality, clandestinity, emigration, and imprisonment in a country that had fallen to a Fascist dictatorship during the tumultuous years of the century's first postwar period. Between the wars, their profile in the Comintern was minor and peripheral, though the fact that they had lived through and analyzed the experience of fascism in Italy provided them with significant political credit. The original leading group dissolved as a result of both Fascist repression and the Stalinization of the Comintern. In this sense, Italian communists underwent a more lacerating destiny than did others, with the difference that their recognized leader, Togliatti, had been a member of the original group. The disintegration and uprooting peaked during the years of the Great Purge and the Pact between Stalin and Hitler, though the very conditions of marginalization that Italian leaders had been experiencing for some time spared them (but not their emigrant community in the Soviet Union) the more devastating consequences that afflicted other parties. Italian communism's international role assumed importance only after the war, thanks to the mass influence it had acquired in a European country that was of strategic importance in the bipolar world. It was then that the Italian communists carved out an important position for themselves within the global communist project, becoming the main communist party in the West.

For the Italians—as for many others—being communists meant adhering to a political project and at the same time making an existential choice, based on a radical critique of the existing societies. Their bonds with the Soviet Union were a fundamental component of that identity. Faith in the Soviet model of civilization as the embodiment of a just society, together with the consequent principle of loyalty to the socialist state, fueled from the outset a sectarian character. An element of strength during World War II, and a powerful vector of influence and of failures during the Cold War, the Soviet link would become the classic Achilles' heel. Nevertheless, Italian communists did not always mimic the ideological and political arsenal forged by the general staffs of international communism, its Marxist-Leninist axioms and its alternative project to Western globalization. On various occasions they acted as the critical conscience of an "imagined community" on a global scale. Their main particularity was the striking intellectual vocation of many of their leaders, which was extremely strong in the beginning and persisted despite generational turnover. This characteristic was recognized and appreciated not only by Lenin, Trotsky, and Gorbachev but also by figures such as Willy Brandt, Leopold Senghor, and Deng Xiaoping, and additionally by many Western and Third World intellectuals. In this way they achieved recognition as an independent voice in being national and antifascist, which increased their authority. But they were also capable of building networks of relation beyond the confines of that community, and this brought them to interact with a range of internationalist ideas and cultures. The coordinates of their political culture endured contradictions, mutilations, conflicts, and discontinuities, despite what their own narratives may describe. Such dynamics were inextricably interwoven with the rise and fall of international communism, but no less with events in Italy, culminating in the terminal metamorphosis of 1989.

To an empathetic and involved observer like Eric Hobsbawm, who assiduously frequented Italy and the milieu of the Italian left from the Fifties onward, communists and antifascists seemed the protagonists of a reaction to a sense of the country's cultural and political marginality, which Fascism had aggravated.[6] The socialist transformation of Italy was to remain a dream. Rightly or wrongly, however, the leading groups of Italian communism believed they had inherited a cosmopolitan tradition that was part of Italy's long history and which they had to adapt to the ideological and global conditions of the twentieth century. More or less consciously, they embraced an idea subject to a comment by Gramsci in prison:

> Italian cosmopolitanism has to become a type of internationalism . . . not the citizen of the world inasmuch as a *civis romanus* or a Catholic, but as a worker and a producer of civilization. One can therefore say that the Italian tradition is carried on dialectically in the working people and their intellectuals, not in the traditional citizen and the traditional intellectual. The Italian people is that people which "nationally" is more interested in internationalism. . . . Nationalism . . . is an anachronistic excrescence in Italian history, typical of those who turn their heads to look back, like the damned in Dante.[7]

The relation that Gramsci established between cosmopolitanism and internationalism could only circulate posthumously, after publication of the *Prison Notebooks,* when in the full flood of the Cold War and Stalinism the meanings of both concepts had undergone impoverishment. Yet the communists, more than any other Italian political culture, remained committed to a project that had its global influence, dimensions, and connections. The consequences were highly controversial. The heritage of communist internationalism left its mark on the original characteristics of the Italian Republic, forcing political adversaries to seek competitive international relations and designs that were integrated in the emergent Western world. The country's internationalization shaped and crystallized deep, lasting fractures within the nation, imposing the persistence of antagonistic social and political blocs, and requiring constant self-containment of leaders and leading groups on both sides. However, Togliatti and his successors inserted themselves into a furrow of a specific Italian interest for internationalism with no adjectives, which became the other side of the role of integrating the masses into society and the state. Protagonists of a "war of position" in the West, over time they also offered to act as interpreters and mediators between their own country and the socialist and anti-imperialist parts of the world. They forged links with the revolutionary constellations of the twentieth-century universe, they catalyzed critiques of Western models of development and consumption, and they performed liaison functions across fault lines in Europe and the Mediterranean. For several decades they created a community that included political elites, intellectuals, and the people, based on visions of the world variously conditioned by mythologies, but which also indicated an awareness of greater, superordinating realities into which national identity and its mutations should be inserted.

At the end of World War II, Italian antifascism contributed to eliminating the poisons of nationalism and to imagining a country inserted into relations of global interdependence more than it had been in the past. The communists feared the birth of international blocs, which Togliatti rightly saw as an unfavorable scenario for their hegemonic ambitions. It was the Catholic leader Alcide De Gasperi and the Christian Democracy party who made the fundamental choices regarding Italy's international position by adopting the Marshall Plan, joining the Atlantic Alliance, and participating in the European Community. This passage established the hegemony of the pro-Western forces. Togliatti's fundamental contribution was that of preventing an Italian civil war, thus leaving space for a scenario with a communist presence within a legal and parliamentary context. At the same time, the Italian example of a mass party presented implications and lessons for the communist movement, especially after Stalin's death. The communists' condition of being a minority on the Italian political scene turned out to be long-lasting. Nevertheless, their visions of the worldwide impact of decolonization and of the emergence of new actors outside the binary patterns of the Cold War exerted significant influence on a number of occasions. In particular, they contributed significantly to defining Italy's orientation toward international détente and the postcolonial Mediterranean, and to creating links with the protagonists of the nonaligned movement and various Third World liberation movements.

Later, under Berlinguer's leadership, the Communists were inspired by the humanist socialism of the "Prague Spring," reversing their opposition to European integration and indeed embracing the idea of Europe as a new subject in world politics. Thus, they gradually abandoned the old internationalism, opening a conflict with a large section of the political area to which they belonged, and reformulated it in a vision of a global role for Europe and relations between the North and South of the world as the horizons of meaning and political agendas in the context of a declining bipolar world order. This evolution was an essential component of the Communists' national consensus in the Italy of the 1970s. After the failure of their plan to accede to the governmental sphere and to create a Western communist alliance, they defended their acquisitions in terms of political culture. Italian reform communism chimed with Gorbachev's project and was one of his main interlocutors until the end. The national legacy of that political culture, especially as regards Europeanism, was to be anything but unimportant, even after the end of the Cold War and of communism.

In this light, the characteristics, contributions, and paradoxes of Italian communism become clearly visible. In their history, many of the communists in Europe and the world strove in their different ways, to translate their internationalism nationally. In this, the Italian experience was one of the most successful, even globally. The Italian communists maintained a permanent tension between their project of an alternative to liberal internationalism and their legitimization within the political nation, seen as a necessary integration of that project. From another perspective, an equally strong tension arose between their belonging to the socialist world, which exhibited a plurality of forms in reaction to the birth of the postcolonial world, and the idea of an Italian exceptionalism, bound up above all with Catholic and communist identities that were present in the life of the country. As Soviet socialism declined, this tension developed into one between the idea of Europeanization, based on the prospect of a political Europe and a new democratic hierarchy of values, and a claim to an identitarian diversity vis-à-vis the reformist and social-democratic political cultures of the continent, all with the aim of keeping alive the prospect of a radical transformation of society.

The Italian communists thus shadowed the changes of the century and entered into close contact with other languages and cultures, especially when they had to face up to the premature decline of the global communist project. They maintained a class-based vision of the world, imagining its unification under the banners of socialism and Marxism, yet they were capable of perceiving autonomous dynamics, interdependencies, and destinies common to humanity. Originally enemies of liberal democracy and proponents of the "dictatorship of the proletariat," they cooperated in writing the Italian Republican constitution. They conceived a mass democracy, and then became the defenders of the democratic state. They were adversaries of the United States and of Americanism, but reluctantly adapted to the consumer society. They constructed mythologies around Soviet socialism, but contributed to the subsequent delegitimization of that model; they ferociously criticized reformism, but themselves became reformers in their experience in government. Their ability to change themselves was perhaps their most significant trait. This ability did not go beyond the confines of their communist identity until the Berlin Wall tumbled; it never emancipated them completely from their existential bond with Soviet socialism, and was always hindered by their cultural difficulty in understanding the motives and driving forces of the "American century." Nevertheless, the Italian communists played an active role in redefining the original internationalist mission, and thus contributed to the final metamorphosis of the main revolutionary tradition of the last century.

The approach this book proposes takes into consideration various historiographies that do not always engage in dialogue with studies on communism. In particular, it considers those tendencies that reinterpret the history of internationalism and cosmopolitanism by analyzing visions of sovereignty, community, and identity that have emerged in multiple intellectual, political, and national contexts.[8] At the same time, it also takes account of the tendencies that reinterpret Italy's history, and does so with the aim of attributing accurate values to international factors and aspects, placing Italian history in global, transnational, and interdependent contexts that have been inadequately explored and considered in the past.[9]

The history of communism has often been reduced to an anomaly, in global history as well as in Italian history. In reality, the global agendas of communism interacted at length with the main changes, conflicts, and options of the last century, though they ended up succumbing to a hodgepodge of contradictions and antinomies. The exhaustion of the revolutionary project that had come into existence in 1917 and the failure of its predominantly statist dimension contributed decisively to liquidating the faith in politics that had animated the minds and hearts of millions of people. Communism was its most extreme manifestation: a source of awesome transformations and tragedies, of struggles for emancipation and repression of liberties, of hopes for the future and profound disillusionment. Thus in the end—involuntarily, and as a negative model—it fed the radical transformation of relations between the collectivity and the individual that took place at the close of the last century.

Today, however, we can see how the end of communist internationalism was not an isolated episode. It was also the prelude to a profound crisis of all forms of internationalism, a crisis that emerged in the new century and dissolved the illusion of a straightforward expansion of Western conceptions after the collapse of the Soviet Union. Our times have witnessed the unprecedented development of subjects, phenomena, and transnational networks that challenge the role of states. The proliferation of international institutions has, however, reproduced the intertwining and century-old tensions with national sovereignty, without offering effective responses to the main global challenges. In a world without a hegemonic order, prone to shocks and fractures of diverse types and stalked by neonationalist and fundamentalist tendencies, we seem to be seeing the waning of an essential element of political modernity: a vision of politics as the sphere of autonomous and transformative action, destined to unfold in the interaction between, and the compenetration of, national spaces and the international dimension. While we do not know whether the different versions of internationalism of the last century should be considered extinct, the transnational world is struggling to emerge. However, the cultural legacy of the older internationalism should not be written off too quickly. Perhaps it may still represent a lesson to be learned at a time when many heads are turned back toward the past, "like the damned in Dante."

This book is the fruit of work accumulated over time but finalized during the pandemic emergency that struck Italy and the world in 2020. The particularly difficult working conditions increased even further my indebtedness to numerous people, though it is clear that responsibility for the book's content rests exclusively with me. First of all, I am indebted to Giovanna Bosman, Dario Massimi, and Cristiana Pipitone for their permanent assistance in the Archive and Library of the Gramsci Foundation. I owe a special thank-you to Gregorio Sorgonà for his competent support and constantly available help. Francesco Giasi assisted me scrupulously and lucidly at various times and up to completion. I benefited greatly from the comments, advice, and suggestions of Leonardo Pompeo D'Alessandro, Michele Di Donato, Gianluca Fiocco, Bruno Settis, and Molly Tambor. I received useful and precise suggestions from Paolo Capuzzo, Alessio Gagliardi, Giovanni Gozzini, Nicola Labanca, and Sante Lesti. I am grateful to Michele Ciliberto and Giuseppe Vacca for their critical reflections. My gratitude must be extended also to many other scholars and friends who in more or less recent years have stimulated, enriched, and favored my experiences. Among them I would like to mention David Bidussa, Victoria de Grazia, Mario Del Pero, Juliane Fürst, Andrea Graziosi, Francesca Gori, Jonathan Haslam, Mark Mazower, Norman Naimark, Sophie Quinn-Judge, Federico Romero, Mark Selden, Stephen A. Smith, Andrei Sorokin, Antonio Varsori, Arne Westad, and Vladislav Zubok. Lastly, this book would not have been possible without the presence of Chiara.

PART ONE **GENEALOGIES**

Internationalism and Cosmopolitanism, 1917–41

1
REVOLUTION AND HEGEMONY

LENIN, WILSON, AND THE CONTESTED WORLD ORDER

Communist internationalism has often been considered a consequence of Vladimir Lenin's project to found the Third International after the dissolution of the Second; it had been conceived of before the October Revolution, and was implemented a little more than a year thereafter. Its genesis has been reconstructed with a focus on the actions of the political groupings, in particular the Bolsheviks, who met in Switzerland during World War I to affirm their rejection of nationalism, their opposition to the war, and their condemnation of socialist revisionism. However, many young intellectuals, leaders, and militants involved in the mass politicization of the war in Europe and the colonial world autonomously perceived the sense of the international dimension, intertwined with the national dimension, as inevitably representing the space for political projects and even identities. Their real and imagined contexts exhibited the most diverse roots, many beyond the ideological and political confines of Marxism and prewar socialism. Throughout Europe and globally, the conjuncture of the war everywhere disrupted the ways in which international vectors and communities were seen in relation to empires, national self-determination, and the nation-state. Lenin's project for a new International would bring into line and offer a common home for this diversified, heterogeneous set of radicalisms only well after the war had ended.[1] This is the light in which we should also see the main personalities who were to found the

Communist Party of Italy (PCd'I): Antonio Gramsci in Turin, and Amadeo Bordiga in Naples. This perspective is essential for a better understanding of a number of original aspects of communist political culture in Italy, which were destined to form, be transformed, or persist after the actual encounter with Bolshevism.

The comments made by Gramsci and Bordiga regarding the Russian revolutions of 1917 revealed a very limited and vague knowledge of Bolshevism, and were attempts to read events in the light of their respective ideas about the consequences of the Great War. Gramsci concentrated on the theme of mass consciousness and the birth of a new political subjectivity; Bordiga, on the antinomies between socialism and nation and between socialism and democracy. In both cases a generational tension emerged: a break with the tradition of the Second International, and an impatience with Italian socialism's provincialism. Here the analogies ended and the differences began, first because, as Giuseppe Berti classically observed, they were divided by the prospect of reviving an orthodox form of Marxism, embraced by Bordiga and extraneous to Gramsci.[2] Considering the most recent studies, it even appears misleading to draw a parallel between these two personalities, given Gramsci's unique position in the socialist debate of the period.[3] This uniqueness is evident, above all, in Gramsci's approach to world politics and the theme of internationalism. His celebrated article "The Revolution against 'Capital'," written shortly after the October Revolution, provides a decisive element for reconstructing his political thought and, at the same time, for casting light on the widespread perception of Lenin's arguments against evolutionary Marxism and concerning the transformative potential of politics: "Events have exploded the critical schemas determining how the history of Russia would unfold according to the canons of historical materialism," wrote Gramsci. "The Bolsheviks reject Karl Marx and their explicit actions and conquests bear witness that the canons of historical materialism are not so rigid as one might have thought and has been believed." And further: "Marx foresaw the foreseeable [. . .] but he could not foresee that the war would last as long as it has or have the effects it has had."[4]

From this time onward, Gramsci was distinct from Bordiga in this type of antideterministic sensitivity. Bordiga polemicized with Gramsci regarding his "idealistic" arguments, and praised the Bolsheviks for having detached themselves from Marx and Engels, but only in the sense of overcoming "the excessive importance" that they attributed to democracy.[5] The line of thought Bordiga and Gramsci instead shared was the idea of the "dictatorship of the proletariat" as a factor of revolutionary order in a society devastated by war. All followers of Bolshevism adhered to the separation between socialism and democracy practised by Lenin and the Bolsheviks, based on the presupposition that dictatorship was a necessary step and a transitory condition, and that liberal democracy did not provide an adequate response to the social earthquake and mass politics produced by the war. Albeit in very particular language, Gramsci expressed a shared thought, and at the same time an initial mythological construction, when he claimed that the soviets and the Bolshevik party were the integrated "organisms" of the new order, capable of overturning hierarchies and refounding them upon a "spiritual authority," a source of socialization and a responsible citizenship. "Dictatorship is the fundamental institution guaranteeing freedom," he wrote in July 1918. "It is not a method to be perpetuated, but a transitional stage allowing the creation and consolidation of the permanent organisms into which the dictatorship, having accomplished its mission, will dissolve."[6]

However, the first reactions to the news about October 1917 did not yet configure a precise internationalist vision. It was Woodrow Wilson's Fourteen Points that called for more definite visions, since they represented an ideal and political response to Lenin. The polemic around the figure of the American president had already developed widely among socialists, splitting pro-Wilson reformists such as Filippo Turati and Claudio Treves away from radical critics, including Bordiga. It was on this theme that Gramsci set himself apart from all others. He saw more clearly the worldwide scope of the challenge, and used the sharp weapons of his criticism to restrict the fortunes of Wilsonism in the socialist world, where what amounted to a cult was being created. He prophetically defined Wilson as the "triumpher of the peace," but held that "recognition of the historical usefulness of the Russian maximalists" would be "inevitable," because "history would reserve a front-rank place" for them, "as far superior to that of the French Jacobins as socialism is superior to bourgeois ideologies."[7] Here Gramsci transparently rejected the prewar European experience that had involved the socialist leading groups; but above all, he was drawn toward a new world scene contested by protagonists who were radically different from those of the past ("Lenin and Wilson are the two political geniuses that the war has placed in the front line, upon whose persons and actions is fixed the attention of the best part of the proletariat and the bourgeoisie of the world respectively").[8] Gramsci interpreted sentiments that were widespread in European public opinion, and perceived the dualism between two diametrically opposed innovative visions of a postwar order, which were spreading rapidly on a global scale, implying a choice between peace via socialist revolution and peace via liberal democracy. His view of Wilson was that of a figure who was progressive not for idealistic motivations but because he was linked to the new vector of the world represented by American power.[9]

The internationalist moment came at the end of the war, with the collapse of the empires of Central and Eastern Europe. Social unrest and the spread of the factory councils in Germany created the decisive change, alongside echoes of the Anglo-French intervention in the Russian Civil War in support of the White counterrevolution. At the end of 1918 and the beginning of 1919, it became a general conviction that a wave of revolutionary upheavals was possible, fueling hopes and fears. The collapse of the old European order was real, not imagined. The idea that the social revolution in Europe and self-government by workers were more urgent than the building of democratic states corresponded to widely held perceptions. A repetition of the events of a year earlier in Russia constituted a plausible scenario both for government forces and for revolutionary vanguards, re-creating in the heart of Europe an opposition between the constituent assembly and the "dictatorship of the proletariat." Repression of the Spartacist movement in January 1919 was a preventive action of the German government of Friedrich Ebert, born out of fear of losing control of the situation and destined to encourage the militarization and ideologization of the social conflict.[10] Identification with the revolutionary cause in Russia, or in Germany and Hungary, was motivated by the need for an international reference point, which until then had been lacking, for those political groups engaged in contesting socialist leaderships in Italy as elsewhere. However, the issue was far more radical and involved the existential foundations of politics. It amounted to a profession of faith, revealing how the Russian Revolution had—above all, among the youth of the time—an imaginary dimension that gave rise to orientations, passions, and identities. Narratives regarding the Russian Revolution had a rapid and divisive impact on the socialist universe of Europe; elsewhere, from the Middle East to Central Asia and from China to Latin America, they assumed the aspect of cultural mediations and transnational policies. Gramsci explored further the ideological reading of the Republic of the Soviets as an "organic state" and a factor for order in the chaos of the former Russian Empire. In his view, the original setup of the councils brought to life a solid and complex structure which in the historical conjuncture of the civil war was asserted by the force of the Red Army, but which also foreshadowed a nascent proletarian statehood.[11]

L'ordine nuovo in Turin, as much as *Il soviet* in Naples, manifested expectations regarding the birth of a new internationalism. There were, however, differing readings of the international order, and different evaluations of such a central figure as Wilson. During the triumphal trip to Europe by the American president, who was welcomed by vast crowds in Rome, Paris, and London, Gramsci remarked that Wilson was "the center of a social spell, which has elevated him to the top of a hierarchy of democratic prestige, and functions not only in the Allied countries, but also in the Germanic countries, in Hungary, and in the Slavic world subjugated to the destiny of the Central Empires. Many socialists, even among the Italian comrades, were unable to escape his spell." Wilson enjoyed an "authority over consciousnesses that has induced many socialists to unconsciously subordinate their own political conception, the internationalist conception of the history of the world—to his words." Thus Gramsci established a symmetrical relation and a clarificatory dialectic between Wilsonism and Leninism, a very fitting metaphor for the qualitative leap in the conflict between the capitalist world and the workers' movement. In his opinion, Wilson's League of Nations project announced "competitions for the economic conquest of markets to the production of the bourgeois industrial organisms" which could acquire "a wider scope of action, on a vast, worldwide scale." The way to combat the danger of subalternity to the new global order prefigured by American liberal capitalism was to hold firm the dialectical nexus between this process and the birth of a "proletarian International."[12] This approach was, however, alien to Bordiga, who thought Wilson's "utopia" an expression of the "extreme defense" of class domination, and simply a "distraction" from the socialist revolution.[13]

In actual fact, Wilson's internationalism expressed a new form of imperial power, endowed with an unprecedented capacity for expansion and hegemony.[14] The early months of 1919 saw the peak of the "Wilsonian Moment" on the world scene and revealed the "internationalization of nationalism" in the colonial world. The language of self-determination promoted by the American president, with all its genericity, was circulating far beyond the new nation-states of Central and Eastern Europe. Expectations that the principle of national self-determination might be applied to the British and French empires created a formidable vector of mobilization and internationalization in India, China, and elsewhere.[15] While to many, Wilson's project seemed the only authentic solution to emerge from the chaos of the Great War, the universalist proclamations of Bolshevism underwent a redimensioning in the theater of the Russian Civil War, which could have made the revolution implode within the border territories in Eurasia and Central and Eastern Europe. Even Gramsci saw a "compact Anglo-Saxon bloc" looming, inspired by economic liberalism and willing to use the League of Nations as the "juridical fiction of an international hierarchy of the bourgeois class," announcing a peace conference destined to achieve "the supreme revolution of modern society, the genesis of the capitalist unification of the world."[16] In this respect, it is no stretch of the imagination to claim that Gramsci's writings after the end of the war display a global vision, an essential element for the reconstruction of a political culture.

The Italian revolutionaries did not take part in the conference that set up the Communist International in Moscow in March 1919, and indeed they only received vague news about it. However, the simultaneity of the birth of the Comintern and the end of the "Wilsonian Moment" in the spring and summer of 1919 strengthened their arguments. Gramsci took advantage of the occasion to be ironic about the "iconoclasm" that had spread rapidly among Italian nationalists, but not only among them, when Wilson adopted a position against ceding the city of Fiume to Italy. This was only a minor episode in the decline of Wilson's fortunes at world level, caused by his refusal to apply the principle of self-determination to the colonial world. The League of Nations came into being with a strong Eurocentric and anti-Bolshevik design, aimed at marginalizing and containing the revolution in Russia.[17] In such a context, the dialectical nexus established between Wilson's and Lenin's internationalisms acquired new horizons of significance. The opposition between Lenin and Wilson exalted the cosmopolitical element of the "Ordine Nuovo" project. It is easy to see how the first issues of the newspaper *L'ordine nuovo* wove a fabric of constant interaction between the collapse of Italian society's traditional structure, the politicization of the working masses, the crisis of the European liberal order, and the problem of constructing a radically new international order. At a time when knowledge of Leninism was still indirect and entrusted to transnational mediators of the time, such as the American journalist Max Eastman, Gramsci for some months wrote a column entitled "Vita internazionale" (International Life).

The appearance of Gramsci's column emphasized a connection already established in people's consciousness between the national and international dimensions—so much so that it could be claimed that no individual existed incapable of understanding "how the destiny of every single man is linked to the form of the national state, the form of the international equilibrium in which states coordinate with and subordinate each other." Such a link marked, in a Marxist language sui generis, "the pillars of Hercules of the historical possibilities of the capitalist class," since it implied the collapse of the "organization of world civilization." "The metropolitan liberal states are falling apart internally," wrote Gramsci, "at the same time as the system of colonies and spheres of influence is crumbling." The main point of rupture would be the collapse of the British Empire, with the consequent "arrival of integral and permanent socialist civilization in the history of humankind."[18] The visionary aspect of his writing in no way excluded an analytic dimension. Although he used apocalyptic images, Gramsci was not depicting mechanical, inevitable scenarios. He was following the pattern suggested by the Comintern, which imagined an escalation of the contradictions of world capitalism that would create a tangle of ungovernable tensions; but he did not only see a destructive spiral. Resuming the thread of previous comments, he interpreted the Anglo-American choice of imposing a "punitive peace" on Germany as the genesis of a "hegemony of the Anglo-Saxon bloc in the world," which would not dissolve easily.[19] Indeed, "the unity of the world in the League of Nations" and the "global monopoly" exerted by British and American capitalism implied an epochal transformation, the end of the sovereignty of the nineteenth-century nation-state. Italy was, in his opinion, an obvious case of the "death of the state."[20] Rather than emphasizing the insoluble contradictions of the passage from British to American supremacy in the world, Gramsci glimpsed a new form of economic and geopolitical power. That is why he did not limit himself to denouncing self-determination as a trick to derail the class struggle. He believed instead that the idea was a dangerous illusion in the light of postwar global transformations, since these latter tended to clash with national sovereignty. In this sense, his vision could not be identified with the anti-imperialist vulgate that the Comintern was already emanating, and which Bordiga, above all, embraced in its catastrophic and deterministic aspects.

The birth of the Republic of Councils in Hungary confirmed the potentialities unleashed by the Russian Revolution. The Italian followers of Bolshevism also interpreted it in this way, and based their way of thinking on the alternatives of revolution and counterrevolution.[21] Gramsci's vision was centered on Europe, but it emphasized the connection with the unrest and rebellions in the colonial world. "The struggle is on a world level," he wrote, not failing to note that the Red Army had reached "the Persian and Afghan border" and controlled "the strategic communication nodes toward India, Turkestan, Asia Minor." It could stimulate "with significantly more effective persuasive power than the Germans a revolt of the Muslim masses against the exploitative merchants of Christendom."[22] At the time of the signing of the Treaty of Versailles, the canon of the "class struggle" on a world scale was widely established in the language of the communists. That is how they interpreted the conflict on peace between the Entente and Germany.[23] The international observatory of *L'ordine nuovo* developed in its hosting of writings by frontline personalities of the Comintern, such as Sen Katayama and Sylvia Pankhurst. However Gramsci's imprint continued to leave traces. His motivation for joining the Comintern was linked to the themes of social consciousness and statehood, implying a radical departure from the traditional institutions of prewar socialism. The new International was in fact not "a bureaucratic office of leaders," but "a historical consciousness of the masses" and "a network of proletarian institutions which from within express a complex and well-developed hierarchy." It was only in this way that it could truly oppose the coalition of the states of the Entente, now that the "social-democratic Reich" had been incorporated "into the economic and political system controlled by Anglo-Saxon capitalism."[24] In this sense, in Gramsci's view the "party of world revolution" was not automatically and at the same time the "party of civil war," as in the Bolshevik's formulation, but was rather the main force of deterrence against humanity sliding into an abyss.

The fall of Béla Kun's regime in Hungary and of the Bavarian Republic did not excessively weaken the communists' convictions, not least because the late summer of 1919 brought an end to the encirclement of the Bolshevik state in the Russian Civil War. The communists did not fully comprehend the reasons that had led to the failure of the Hungarian revolution. To them, nationalist mobilization and the rejection, by broad social strata, of the violence of the revolutionary powers, especially in the countryside of Central Europe, appeared to be just marginal aspects. The problem of the survival of the European social order was not part of their perspective. Incongruent aspects of the peace and the survival of the Russian revolutionaries contributed decisively to the consolidation of this attitude. The Comintern press underwent its first propaganda test precisely with the campaign against Versailles. Gramsci, however, read events in his own way. Without worrying too much about providing a Marxist interpretation, he observed the geopolitical scenarios from the perspective of previous influences and conflicts for European supremacy, linking them to the influence of Russia, even with regard to the outbreak of the Great War and its outcome, since the victory of the Entente had been favored by the unilateral exit decided by the Bolsheviks. At this point the Russian revolution had, "so to speak, taken the place of the war as the characteristic and dominant fact of the European situation," especially in Germany and the former Austro-Hungarian Empire. In this light, the edifice of Versailles seemed precarious to Gramsci, and lacked a credible setup in Central and Eastern Europe. The commitment of the European ruling classes to suffocating the revolutionary hotbed was itself the sign of its impact: "The revolt of the Ciompi, the French medieval Jacquerie, the Anabaptist unrest in Germany, or the Paris Commune of '71 are just innocent will-o'-the-wisps in comparison. The proletariat of the two worlds instinctively become aware of the absolute novelty and decisive importance of the Russian experiment." Unlike the Bolsheviks, Gramsci did not draw an analogy with revolutionary France, apart from mentioning the fear of the European ruling classes. He thought instead that revolutionary Russia would be "for proletarian Europe" what czarist Russia had been "for bourgeois Europe"—that is to say, a custodian of the new order.[25]

At the time of the first postwar socialist congress and the 1919 November elections, the antirevisionist polemic brought together the communist components, who distinguished themselves from the maximalists with regard to identification with Bolshevism. Even though the *ordinovisti* did not share Bordiga's antiparliamentary abstentionism, the shared idée fixe in polemic with the reformists was that a communist revolution was necessary in Italy primarily for international rather than national reasons.[26] The question was also generational, as Angelo Tasca observed, because the young, who had experienced war, were expected more than others to express a "creative energy" and a radical critique of the bourgeois system.[27] The rhetorical adherence of the Socialist Party to the Comintern and its electoral victory, which made it the largest Italian party, did not change the situation or heal the emerging fractures. The council's perspective remained essential and was even strengthened, despite the defeats in Central Europe. The factory councils movement came into being in Turin, corroborating the political and intellectual commitment of the "Ordine Nuovo" group. Indeed, it was perhaps the Comintern's influence and the wave of violence rocking Europe that persuaded the *ordinovisti* gradually to adjust their vision away from the themes of social consciousness and bottom-up initiatives, and toward the idea of relations of force and the consolidation of a new political order. As already noted, the latter represented "two underlying currents" of Gramsci's thought, which understood socialist revolution as, on the one hand, self-mobilization of the masses and individual liberation, and on the other, the cohesion and ordering of the social body, first of all via the presence and authority of the state.[28] The success of Bolshevik power tipped the balance away from civil war and toward the second of these two poles.

This is how Gramsci thematized the victory of the Bolsheviks in the Russian Civil War. In his eyes, the successes of the Red Army on the eastern and southern fronts of the war were "the greatest historical event of the first two decades of the century," since "a workers' state has arisen in Europe and in the world." He was convinced that the Bolshevik state incarnated "a vital principle, the wide-ranging scope of which is greater than that of any prior revolutions in the history of humankind; the principle that dwells and militates in the Russian revolution is the principle of the regeneration of the world, the principle of the unification of a regenerated world."[29] Gramsci's language depicted a mission far more palingenetic than was justifiable from the speeches of Lenin, who at the end of 1919 realistically defined victory in the Civil War as a "historic miracle." Gramsci was, however, in agreement with Lenin regarding the potential influence of the Soviet state in world politics:

> The system of the international proletarian revolution, which hinges on the existence and the development of the Russian workers' state as a world power, today possesses an army with two million bayonets [. . .]. The victories and the advances of the army of the Third International are rocking the foundations of the capitalist system, accelerating the process of decomposition of the bourgeois states, and exacerbating the conflicts within the Western democracies.[30]

In other words, he saw the revolutionary state not exclusively in its internal aspect as a party-state, but also in its international and power projection.

In March 1920, the coup d'état attempted by General Kapp in Germany brought about a sudden change in revolutionary perception and prospects following the failures of the first postwar year. The Bolsheviks interpreted it as a reopening of the prospects for a Western revolution, after having considered the alternative scenario of an "Asiatic revolution." There was a knock-on effect also among European revolutionaries. Gramsci's comment revealed a change of views regarding revolution in Europe. Kapp's attempt highlighted the fragility of the Weimar democracy, but also the strength of the German proletariat as an organized force, following a general strike that had blocked the military. In complete accord with the vision of the Bolsheviks and the International, Gramsci placed further hopes in Germany because "the balance of forces has shifted to the advantage of the working class." This claim ignored the fact that the workers' response had come mainly from within and not from outside social democracy; but Gramsci thought that after "the period of democratic stasis," the German proletariat would assume positions "enormously more favorable than in January 1919."[31] His expectations were set within a stance shared by the followers of Bolshevism, who were increasingly tending toward the prospect of civil war. Polemicizing with Tasca, he pointed to the analyses of the "theorists of the IIIrd International" regarding the finance capital that subtended a vision of revolutionary dynamics quite different from reformist culture.[32] For the first time, however, he reflected on the defeats suffered by European revolutions, recognizing that "in Germany, Austria, Bavaria, the Ukraine, and Hungary the revolution as a destructive act has not been followed by the revolution as a process of reconstructing society on the communist model." The underlying reason was the absence of a "conscious movement on the part of the proletarian masses tending [. . .] to substantiate their political power with economic power," such as to make "the factory the basic unit of the new state." The experience of European revolutions had shown how, "since Russia, all other two-stage revolutions have failed, and the failure of the second revolution has plunged the working classes into a state of prostration and demoralization. This has allowed the bourgeois class to reorganize in strength." The lesson he drew from this was the need for a higher and more aware level of political organization, in the first place via the "organic creation" of communist parties ("'Insofar as it can shape reality, the Party must create conditions in which there will not be two revolutions'").[33] Gramsci posed a similar objective shortly before the Second Congress of the Comintern, knowing that the construction of communist parties at that point was becoming a realistic project, and that the modalities would be the subject of debate and negotiation.

The birth of the communist parties in Europe launched in summer 1920 was affected by the shock created first by the revolutionary hopes triggered by the advance of the Red Army in Poland, and then by that army's defeat and withdrawal. The aim of capturing Warsaw, the expectation of a proletarian uprising in Poland and in Germany, and the prospect of exporting the revolution "on the point of a bayonet" inflamed the imaginations of the delegates at the Comintern Congress between July and August. The *ordinovisti* were not among them, despite the participation of a sizeable Italian delegation. However, Gramsci and his comrades obtained the sweetest of revenge when Lenin praised their positions, defining them as totally in accord with the Comintern's principles. Lenin was referring to the proposals of the *ordinovisti* for a radical transformation of the Socialist Party and the trade unions, but it is difficult to assume that he was not aware of the group's internationalist credentials, in comparison with those of all other exponents of the radical and maximalist wing. At the euphoric moment of the Red Army's western advance, Lenin imagined a workers' insurrection in Germany, and considered a possible "sovietization" of Poland and Lithuania. But he also believed, together with Grigory Zinoviev and Nikolai Bukharin, that it was necessary to "promote without delay the revolution in Italy."[34] His words on the *ordinovista* group must be seen in this light of intense revolutionary expectations in Europe and Italy.

Having learned of Lenin's endorsement, Gramsci again proposed the dual nature of his international vision as the Red Army's advance on Warsaw came to its climax. To his mind, the discipline and sense of hierarchy created by the workers' state coincided with the existence of a "national consensus" for the Bolshevik party and a "new hierarchy of the social classes" in which intellectuals, peasants, and the middle classes recognized the working class "as the leading class." He idealized the bases of consensus acquired by Bolshevism via the mass conscription of the Civil War, seeming not to realize the consequences of militarization for authoritarianism and violent practices. At the same time, he sketched out an analysis of the position that Soviet Russia had achieved "in the system of world powers." By building a mass army and waging war in Poland, Russia had become a "world power," endowed with "historic stature," capable of challenging "the entire world capitalist system" because it led "the system of real powers that are struggling against hegemonic capitalism." These "real powers" were for him the proletarian classes and the defeated nations, the rebel forces in the colonial world and the anticapitalist forces in the metropolises. These words did not just echo the proclamations of Bolshevik and Comintern leaders, at that moment marked by hubris and the expectations of a popular uprising in Poland and Germany in support of the Red Army. Gramsci shared a similar hope, which turned out very soon to be totally unfounded, but he also sensed a profound political and strategic mutation taking place independently of the outcome of the Polish-Soviet War. Soviet Russia had in any case "shattered the hegemonic system" of Versailles and the Entente, initiating a new global competition between states "in a form absolutely unpredicted by socialist thought."[35] The tone was far too emphatic, but he had grasped an essential aspect of the transition caused by the outcome of the civil war in Russia, which was destined to exert an influence on the political culture of the communists and on the postwar order.

Within a few days, Lenin's dream of tearing apart the Versailles system by capturing Warsaw faded under the pressure of Józef Pilsudski's counterattack. The prospect of an encounter between the victorious Red Army and the spontaneous uprising of the European working class vanished rapidly. A shadow was also cast over the factory occupations in Italy. Experienced by Italian revolutionaries as proof of the foolishness of the socialist leadership and of the need to disengage from reformism, the rapid defeat of the occupation movement in September 1920 was the last gasp of the "Biennio rosso" ("Red Biennium"), a period that was not only Italian but also European. The opposition between Lenin and Wilson had at this point waned: neither had the same significance, and reflected real or imagined tendencies, as they had in the immediate postwar period. No world upheaval had been inspired by Leninism or Wilsonism. Yet the communist project retained its relevance and still marked the conjuncture of the postwar period, via the creation of a revolutionary state and its role of giving rise to an organized movement. The communist parties were at the same time the offspring of a victorious revolution in Russia, a global project, and a historic defeat in Europe, which in Italy produced extreme consequences.

CONCRETE INTERNATIONALISM

The birth of the Communist Party of Italy (PCd'I) at the Livorno Congress in January 1921 took place according to the model of a resolute split from the socialist political world, via the rigid "twenty-one conditions" imposed by the Second Comintern Congress, which had already created two strong communist parties in Germany and France. Livorno, however, reflected the growing vicious circle encompassing the postwar Italian crisis, international political radicalization, and the instability of the European order, which the Versailles peace treaty had not solved. The dream of the Italian revolution, cultivated by Lenin, Zinoviev, Gramsci, and Bordiga, was peremptorily transmuted into an act leading the minority to split from the party. Comintern internationalism contributed to the breakup of a Socialist Party that was already paralyzed and divided after the failure of the factory occupations. Bordiga's dominant, intransigent influence interacted with the Bolsheviks' typical obsession with ideological purity, without the capability for maneuver they invoked, dispensing advice on the tactic to follow to include socialist maximalists into the Coummunist Party. The *ordinovisti* also contributed to a similar sectarian spiral by conducting an unyielding polemic against all socialists, reformists, and maximalists, who were branded as enemies of the working class. The PCd'I, with around forty thousand militants, was not an insignificant force, but its expansive capacity turned out to be limited. Instead of inspiring a new revolutionary impulse, the split in the workers' movement marked the end of the "Red Biennium." It was then that the violent and destabilizing ideological tail of the European postwar period revealed its extreme character in Italy, creating the space for a creeping civil war unleashed by Fascism, with its armed attacks against the workers' movement. Precisely in the months following the split, Fascism achieved national visibility, presenting itself as a force for order faced with the red threat, with the benevolent complicity of a ruling class in decline. Thus the Italian case was an exception to the capacity for resistance shown by bourgeois and liberal Europe, even in Germany, despite the destabilizing conflict between revolution and counterrevolution. But it also represented a paradigm born of the explosive mixture of the shock of war, endemic violence, mass politicization, ideological polarization, and nationalist reaction.[36] A few years later, Gramsci expressed a severe judgment on Livorno, noting that the communists had unwittingly been "an aspect of the general dislocation of Italian society."[37]

In the summer of 1921 the leading group of the new party found itself in the sights of the Bolshevik leaders and the Comintern. Concurrently with the new search for alliances and compromises launched after the failure of the "March action" in Germany, Lenin invited the Italian communists to rethink the Livorno strategy. At the third Comintern Congress, he accused Umberto Terracini of "ultra-leftism" and warned the Italian delegates that their revolution could not follow the model of the revolution in Russia. Lenin asked for an understanding with Giacinto Menotti Serrati to isolate the reformists in the PSI and a policy aimed at winning not only the majority of the working class but also the poor strata of the rural population. This initiated a trial of strength between Moscow and the entire leading group of the PCd'I, whose identity was founded on its split from the socialist world.[38] The honeymoon with the *ordinovisti* of the previous summer was now just a memory. The Comintern's influence increasingly became a factor of conflict as the change of direction desired by Lenin toward the "moderate" tactic of the "united front" became more apparent. This dynamic did not have a merely bilateral dimension, since it affected most European communists.[39] The activity of the Comintern's emissaries in Italy followed a disciplinary model also used elsewhere, which often produced effects that were the opposite of those desired. In the first year of life of the PCd'I, the bonds between Moscow and the Italian leading group were woven by the action of a range of Russian representatives who had been operating for a while in the country, under orders from the Comintern or directly from the Politburo.[40] In the context of the uncertain and sometimes improbable relations of the time, their action was often opaque, carried out via diplomatic, espionage, and variously informal channels, and this contributed to amplifying rather than reconciling dissonances. The presence of the Comintern, in any case, configured a dense transnational network. At different times and in the following years, high-ranking leaders such as Vasil Kolarov, Mátyás Rákosi, Otto Kuusinen, Dmitri Manuilsky, Jules Humbert-Droz, Osip Pyatnitsky, Béla Kun, and Karl Radek played roles directly in Italy or in Moscow.

The trial of strength around the "united front" was still ongoing when Gramsci left for Moscow in May 1922 to take up the position of party representative to the Executive of the Comintern. There was no easy solution. However, the period spent in Moscow turned out to be decisive for his political formation—first of all, for an unmediated acquisition of sources and ways of thinking, with important consequences for all other members of the leading group. The relations of Gramsci and his comrades with internationalism gained new meanings. Moscow in the early Twenties was a cosmopolitan crossroads, a crucial place for political meetings and cultural and ideological exchange, frequented by communists from all over the world. Almost two years later, writing to Palmiro Togliatti, one of the former leading personalities of the "Ordine Nuovo," Gramsci would remember this crucial moment of transition:

> Having gone to Moscow without being briefed on even a tenth of the questions of the day, I had to pretend to know, and had to carry out unheard of acrobatic feats in order not to demonstrate how irresponsibly representatives were nominated, without any provisions [. . .] other than Doctor Grillo's motto "May God send you all the best."[41]

These words probably applied to all communists who went to Moscow to take on responsibilities in the Comintern. Like many others, Gramsci needed time to navigate the Comintern environments and to weave relations, not least because of his precarious state of health. The most urgent problem consisted of the self-referential nature of those relations while in Italy the situation was escalating.

The sectarianism of the Italian Communists and the interminable diatribes about relations with the Socialists reflected an underestimation of Fascism and a tendency to see the conditions for a revolutionary occasion in the developments of the "reaction." The Comintern had greatly contributed to this dynamic, but then tried to correct it by laying all responsibility on local communists, as in Germany. However, the Italian case was the most sensational. It is emblematic that the March on Rome in October 1922 found the principal leaders of the new party in Moscow, where they were engaged in discussing the "united front" line and debating the formula of the "workers' government" while Fascism was taking power. Bordiga and Gramsci participated in the work of the Fourth Comintern Congress, defending the scissionist line of Livorno and underplaying the consequences of Benito Mussolini's coup d'état. They thus put themselves on course for a head-on confrontation with Lenin, Leon Trotsky, and the other Russian leaders. Bukharin pointed out to them that such a standpoint was unsuitable for creating opposition to Fascism among the working masses.[42] The trial of strength continued at length without a solution being found, mainly because of Bordiga's intransigence. Sent to Italy as an emissary at the beginning of 1923, Manuilsky wrote many alarmed missives to Zinoviev in light of the persecutions being perpetrated by the Mussolini government, confirming the need for a joint reorganization of the lines of communication between the leaders of the PCd'I and Serrati.[43] The letter of 20 March 1923, in which Zinoviev rebuked the Italian communists, is a classic example of the political tension between center and periphery, in which local leaders disobeyed the directives from above while at the same time professing their loyalty.[44]

The criticism by Comintern exponents of the Italian communists extended above all to the analysis of fascism. In particular, Giulio Aquila (aka Gyula Sas), a Hungarian communist sent to Italy, insisted on the nonephemeral mass character of fascism, capable of giving rise to popular consensus via a syncretic combination of socialism and nationalism, and even capable of achieving autonomy from the capitalist elite.[45] The notion of fascism's mass character was not unknown to the ex-*ordinovista* group. Evidence of this is provided by a report by Togliatti, which did not reach Moscow in time for the Comintern Congress and which outlined an interpretation centered on the weaknesses of the Italian liberal state and on the original traits of the Fascist phenomenon, unlike Bordiga's rigidly classist interpretation.[46] However, the nexuses between the analysis and the political line struggled to compose a coherent picture. Gramsci in Moscow performed a role of mediation, hampered by the weakness of a party decimated by police arrests and lacking a strong militant base. He accused Rákosi of adopting cursory methods that were contemptuous of the organizational capacity of the Italian communists, but conceded that the Comintern line needed to aim to conquer the mass of European socialist parties.[47] Shortly thereafter, however, Zinoviev sternly rebuked the Italian leaders, and criticized Gramsci for having made vague promises about upholding the fusion line, which he had not maintained.[48] Gramsci noted that the united front tactic had "in no country found the party or the men capable of concretizing it [. . .]. Obviously, all this cannot be accidental. There is something not functioning in the international field as a whole; there is a weakness and inadequacy of leadership."[49] After his first year in Moscow, he came to the conclusion that the entire strategic revision effected after the failure of the European revolution in the first two postwar years had been a frustrating and unconvincing experience, in part because of the Russian leading group's responsibility.

In Moscow, the visual field that opened up for Gramsci was much broader than the Comintern dynamics between center and periphery might suggest. Entering directly into contact with the Bolsheviks, and with the cosmopolitan environment of international communism, Gramsci put behind him the generic internationalism of the postwar European revolutionaries. His contacts with Trotsky, Bukharin, and other exponents of the Comintern leading group were significant. He was a participating witness to Bolshevism's reconversion to power after the Civil War. Precisely in November 1922, Lenin and Trotsky dilated the historical time of world revolution, originally imagined as an immediate, overwhelming event, while still claiming 1917 as their model. In a parallel fashion, Lenin presented the New Economic Policy (Novaya ekonomicheskaya politika, or NEP) as a strategic option, though his opinion oscillated between the idea of a "retreat" and a more long-term vision. The Bolsheviks followed the logic of consolidating their state power, which led them to privilege economic recovery and internal stability. Their revision after "war communism" was far more empirical than conceptual. The dual compromise constituted by the NEP in Russia and by the "united front" of the communist movement lent itself to different interpretations and took on a clearly asymmetrical aspect, because the theme of the "alliance" with the peasant world appeared to many to be more persuasive and necessary than that of the relationship with the social-democratic world. In any case, acceptance of a different time and place for the revolution than those imagined in 1917 was the subject on the agenda in the Moscow of 1922. Gramsci's meeting with Lenin, on 25 October 1922, was probably important in this connection. It is easy to believe that the dialogue with Lenin induced reflection on the failure of the factory occupations of two years previous, as would happen a little later in a meeting between the Russian leader and Tasca.[50] On the agenda was the problem of moving from a "war of movement" to a "war of position," destined to leave a long trace in Gramsci's thought, to the point of superposing ten years later his memory of the Fourth Comintern Congress, sanitized of its contingent aspects, and the retrospective theoretical elaboration he conducted in prison.[51]

The central element of Gramsci's reception of Bolshevism became the construction of social alliances, which he saw happening in the NEP and which constituted a chapter of the reading of the revolution as a new order, with international implications no less than national ones. This reading assumed the point of view of the Bolshevik leading stratum and added a gaze "from above" on Russian society, destined to produce mythological narratives about the "proletarian" nature of the regime and to postulate the existence of social consensus with little basis in factual data. Gramsci implicitly accepted the Bolsheviks' repressive government practices and the evident militarization of their language, which was transmitted to communist parties. Nevertheless, his vision was based on a real phenomenon: the adoption of an economic policy with effects on the reconstruction of the country, on the relations between the revolutionary state and society, and on the relations between the industrial metropolises and the immense Russian countryside. The NEP expressed the concrete exercise of power under the historical conditions of Soviet Russia after a long cycle of devastating wars, thus constituting a reference for reimagining the birth of an urban workers' revolution, especially in a country such as Italy. Thus, the very vision of interdependence between the Russian Revolution and the European revolution, which Gramsci had already conceived of in 1918, was transformed. He had considered the role of revolutionaries as a bastion against the dissolution of society, delineating a new world order after the Great War, which liberal internationalism was incapable of building. At the end of the Russian Civil War, he had defined Soviet Russia as a "power" in the postwar world. In his eyes, the NEP consolidated the Bolshevik state also in the world context, while the League of Nations represented a lame, limited organism. This vision predisposed Gramsci to combine the revision effected by Bolshevism in power with the sense of revolutionary internationalism, in a historical time that was no longer the time of the "war of maneuver" in Europe. The definitive moment of passage was marked by the failure of the "German October" in autumn 1923, and by the death of Lenin.

REFLECTING ON THE DEFEAT

At the end of 1923, Gramsci left Moscow for Vienna. This placed him in a visual field that induced him to reflect both on the reasons for the failure of revolution in Europe and on the prospects for the Russian revolution after Lenin. He accepted the official version about the German fiasco, which offloaded all responsibility onto the German communist leaders and on Radek, the Comintern emissary. To some extent, Gramsci was aware of the political divisions that existed between Trotsky and the other Bolshevik leaders. Indeed, he invited his successor in Moscow not to underestimate such divisions, observing that the situation in the Bolshevik party "is much more complicated and more substantial than Urbani [Terracini's pseudonym] thinks." At the same time, however, addressing the ex-*ordinovisti* exclusively, and excluding diehard leaders like Bordiga, Ruggero Grieco, and Bruno Fortichiari from his reflections, he suggested a way for them to comprehend the reasons for the Russian leaders' supremacy in the Comintern. "Their orientations" were founded, in fact, "on a material base that we could have only after a revolution, and this is what gives their supremacy a permanent and not easily assailable nature."[52] This realistic observation gave rise to a precise vision of internationalism that differed from Bordiga's. Gramsci challenged the contraposing of Russian backwardness and the historical "determination" of the West, thought to have constituted the authentic theater of the socialist revolution. In his opinion, Bolshevism had been formed not on a national but on an international terrain, and capitalist Europe was not simply proletarian but peopled by stratified classes of working people, influenced by social democracy. Hence, a differentiated vision of the revolution in the West: "The determination which in Russia was direct, and which launched the masses into the streets in a revolutionary assault, becomes complicated in Central and Western Europe by reason of all these political superstructures created by the greater development of capitalism." Only a strong internationalist bond could give a meaning and a future to the revolutionaries in the West, while cutting it would have condemned them. Therefore, Gramsci believed that, while Bordiga took the viewpoint of an "international minority," what was instead necessary was to adopt the point of view of a "national majority" integrated into the international movement.[53]

Among the founding elements of the internationalist vision elaborated by Gramsci was the idea of the fundamental unity of the Bolshevik leading group, "one of the great strengths of the Russian comrades," which was even more necessary given their political monopoly in the revolutionary state.[54] The Bolshevik state could express its potential only on the condition that political elites remained united. Gramsci's vindicatory obituary for Lenin implicitly expressed a similar point of view, together with uncertainty about the phase that was commencing. The creator of the "hegemony of the proletariat [. . .] conceived of historically and concretely" was lost, as was his central function in the leading group.[55] At the same time, Gramsci was fully aware of the mythological significance that emanated from the figure of Lenin and the revolutionary state. In a fragment of a letter written in early 1924, he described the cult of Lenin at the funeral of an agricultural laborer, remarking that the names of the revolutionary leaders "in a great part of the poor and backward masses, become almost a religious myth. And this is a force that must not be destroyed."[56]

Gramsci was writing in Vienna in the early months of 1924, during a period of reflection and of intense activity via his multiple relations within the Comintern organization.[57] It is easy to imagine that his thoughts were inspired precisely by his experience in the city with the best-organized workers' movement in Europe, dominated by social democracy in government, with the local communists reduced to marginality and numerically insignificant.[58] The fact is that in Vienna he elaborated a vision of revolution that was distant from or even contrary to the theories and practices of the offensive based on the 1917 model, which were identified largely with Trotsky's personality, though the entire Bolshevik leading group had subscribed to them in Germany in 1923. This vision, however, in no way meant separating the destiny of European revolutionaries from Soviet Russia. The problem of the "translatability" of revolutionary languages and practices was transferred to the interaction between the new Soviet statehood and the resilience of the European ruling classes, between the Bolshevik exercise of power within the NEP system and the conditions of hegemony in bourgeois Europe. At the same time, Gramsci was reflecting on the defeat suffered in the postwar period by the Italian revolutionaries. What had been missing was the capacity for "translating into language that could be understood by every Italian worker and peasant" the significance of the events of the "Red Biennium" of the years 1919 and 1920.[59] Gramsci used a notion of Lenin's, who in his intervention at the fourth Congress of the Comintern had stigmatized the difficulty encountered by the Bolsheviks' political language in Europe. Although he claimed that the "Ordine Nuovo" was capable of interpreting the political culture of Bolshevism in the Italy of 1919–20, his retrospective view on the birth of the PCd'I was severely self-critical, given the rise of Fascism.

Returning to Italy in May 1924, Gramsci soon had to take charge of the party, and found himself facing the crisis caused by the assassination of the social-democratic leader Giacomo Matteotti. In light of the crisis of the regime, he developed an analysis of the Fascist phenomenon as "a mass organization of the petty bourgeoisie," born in relation to the postwar "crisis of the middle classes." He called for prudence regarding the prospect of a popular revolutionary reawakening, despite the serious difficulties that Mussolini was experiencing.[60] At the same time, the leading group came to terms with all the possible contradictions of communist internationalism: it was under pressure from the logic of Moscow's diplomacy, and from the umpteenth criticism from the Comintern, this time with inverted roles. The establishment of diplomatic relations between Italy and the Soviet Union at the beginning of the year brought to the surface a tension that was unprecedented even in Germany. The notorious casus belli was the lunch of 11 July 1924 shared by the Soviet ambassador, Konstantin Iurenev, and Mussolini. Soviet diplomacy appeared to be offering support to Mussolini at the most critical moment of his international isolation and domestic predicament. Gramsci reacted harshly, and disavowed the ambassador's choice. Certain of the backing of the political counselor of the embassy, Aleksandr Makar, the Italian communists protested to the Executive of the Comintern, but no mollifying response was forthcoming.[61] This episode laid bare the risk of a collision course between Moscow's interests and the survival of the Italian party and other communist parties in Europe and elsewhere. At the same time, the Executive criticized Gramsci for his hesitations, and exhorted the Italian communists to set as their immediate objective "the toppling of the fascist regime," since the "entire Italian nation is about to rebel against fascism."[62] This view was, to say the least, simplistic in the Italy of 1924, as in Germany the previous year, just when Gramsci had taken on board the critical analyses of Fascism suggested by Bukharin and by exponents of the Comintern such as Sas and Clara Zetkin.[63]

An intervention by Maksim Litvinov, the deputy commissar for foreign affairs, became necessary. On 14 November 1924 he instructed Iurenev on the opportune manner to interact with "our political antipodes, the fascists." In the case of the Italian government, he explained, "we have a classic case of the dual nature of our policy toward fascism, as communists and as a state power." The "concrete relations" established with Mussolini were correct, but as for supporting Fascism "as a party and a political movement, that is obviously unthinkable." At the same time, Litvinov believed that the Matteotti crisis would lead to the end of Fascism; but so long as Mussolini remained in power, dealing with him was inevitable.[64] This line settled relations with the Italian communists in view of the opening of negotiations for a political treaty with Italy, in the form of a nonaggression pact, suggested by Rome on 7 November. The Soviet decision to carry on with negotiations followed shortly after a declaration by Mussolini, who brutally brought the crisis to an end by accepting political responsibility for the Matteotti crime. On 20 January 1925, Litvinov informed the Politburo about the conditions necessary to conclude negotiations with Rome. He pointed out that Gramsci and Grieco had also suggested "not to reject Mussolini's proposals, but only to hasten the start of negotiations," in the belief that after the elections there would be "an agreement between the Fascists and the oppositions." In the event of "a post-Fascist government in Italy," Litvinov observed, "it will be impossible to conclude an agreement." On 27 January the Politburo deliberated in favor of the treaty, tasking Bukharin to "prepare the Italian communists correspondingly."[65] In reality, negotiations dragged on for a long time without ever reaching a conclusion.[66]

The episode, however, remains of great significance. As can be seen from Litvinov's words, Gramsci did not limit himself to acknowledging the interests of the Soviet state. He even adhered with realism to a strategic line that allowed them to be favored, in this case via an agreement with the "revisionist" Mussolini which would integrate with the axis Moscow had already created with Berlin in anti-Versailles terms at Rapallo in April 1922. The dualism between the foreign policy of the Soviet Union, and the Comintern did not necessarily produce a dichotomy between reason of state and revolution in relations with the local communists. The latter were not characterized only by their loyalty. Precisely because Gramsci and his leading group, on a collision course with Bordiga, had set themselves the problem of a national "translation" of the teachings of Bolshevism, their vision of internationalism included acceptance of the Soviet raison d'état.

Trotsky's *Lessons of October* had in the meantime finally triggered the struggle for the succession to Lenin, evoking a strong impression among European communists.[67] Their perception of the "Russian question" turned out to be extremely imprecise. Many saw Trotsky as a "right-wing" leader who proposed delaying the revolution "indefinitely," yet he presented himself as the sworn enemy of the theory of "socialism in one country" outlined by Joseph Stalin and Bukharin, which he believed to be the renunciation of world revolution.[68] Gramsci, however, focused on the theme that for him was essential: Trotsky's visions represented a "danger" because "the lack of party unity in a country in which there is only one party will split the state."[69] Gramsci's second trip to Russia (March-April 1925) provided clarification, but did not dissipate his fear of the risk of a split in the Bolshevik leading group. He realized that it was Stalin's and Bukharin's majority that supported the thesis of the "stabilization of capitalism" after the adoption of the Dawes Plan launched by the United States and the stirrings of an economic recovery in Germany. Formally adopted precisely in March 1925, and immediately the object of ferocious polemics between the majority and minority of the Bolshevik Party, the "relative stabilization" formula integrated with the doctrine of "socialism in one country."[70] Gramsci found himself forced above all to defend his leading group from Manuilsky's accusation of "Carbonarism."[71] But he also expressed his own vision of the "relative stabilization of capitalism," referring to the period after 1921 as "characterized by a slowing down of the rhythm of revolution" which was the origin of the ideological weakness of the communist parties.[72] Gramsci did not accept Trotsky's (and Bordiga's) reading, which postulated a static opposition between "socialism in one country" and world revolution. Indeed, he saw a dynamic relation between the two notions. From his viewpoint, "socialism in one country" did not mean renouncing world revolution, as it could constitute a political and symbolic resource in its favor. The receding revolutionary prospects in Europe might, however, mean compromising the exercise of Bolshevik hegemony in Russia. Gramsci's lodestar was the unity of the leading group as the necessary condition for maintaining the authority of the Bolshevik state. In his confrontation with Bordiga, he posed as a "substantive" question the unitary conception of the Comintern as the "world party" of the revolution.[73] The nexus between the communist movement and the revolutionary state was the connective tissue linking the other strategic elements that separated Gramsci from Bordiga: "Bolshevization" as the organization and effort to build a mass party, the peasant question as a "national question," and the "relative stabilization" of capitalism.[74]

The Lyon Congress of the PCd'I in January 1926 left aside evaluations of the evolution of Soviet policy, as was requested by the Bolsheviks themselves. The Italian leading group concentrated on the prospect of reconciling the acquisition of "Leninism" with a national perspective and a reading of the historical dualism between North and South as the basis for the "alliance," inspired by the NEP, between workers and peasants. Under this profile, Italy could appear as the link between European revolution and world revolution, with the unique combination within its national perimeter of an industrialized North and a semicolonial South. The problem of the "translation" of revolutionary languages became even more crucial, and tendentially addressed a plurality of individuals who were not exclusively defined by categories of class.[75] In a conversation with the new Soviet ambassador, Platon Kerzhentsev, on 5 February 1926, Gramsci expressed his satisfaction with the outcomes of the congress, noting Bordiga's isolation.[76] However, the "Russian question" again became central immediately afterward, and Bordiga did not vanish from the scene. Indeed, he was part of the Italian delegation to the Sixth Plenum of the Comintern Executive, and his presence gave rise to a head-on confrontation with Stalin. Bordiga asked for "the questions dealt with by the Russian congress to be discussed"—that is, the development of the NEP and the problem of the opposition. Stalin rejected the request, arguing that the questions were "essentially Russian" and that the Western parties were "not yet prepared to discuss them." In this way he reemphasized the hierarchy existing between the Russian party and the others, speaking of a "privilege" that imposed precise "responsibilities" on the Bolshevik leading group. At this point, Bordiga provocatively raised the question of the relation between the Russian Revolution and world revolution, asking "whether comrade Stalin believes that the development of the Russian situation and of the internal problems of the Russian party is linked to the development of the international proletarian movement." This triggered an indignant response from Stalin: "Never until now has this question been put to me. I would never have believed that a communist could put it to me. May God forgive you for having done so."[77] It is clear that Bordiga had challenged a sacrality that was deeply rooted in Stalin, and had infringed a convention accepted by most communists. Grieco distanced himself from Bordiga, indicating that it was not possible to overturn the pyramid and establish an nonexistent "equality between communist parties," because "for the masses the revolutionary influence exerted by Moscow" constituted a factor of attraction toward communist parties.[78] However, the question expressed by Bordiga lingered in everyone's mind, starting with Gramsci's; and it would lead to some very different answers.

THE ULTIMATE SENSE OF INTERNATIONALISM

The general strike of 1 May 1926 in Great Britain once again brought attention to the vision of the European revolution. On 9 May, Togliatti, recently nominated the representative of the PCd'I at the Comintern, informed Rome that in Moscow the British strike was viewed as "the most important fact that has happened since the Russian Revolution." He did not neglect to mention that, as things stood, Trotsky had shown a more lucid capability for prediction than the other leaders by opposing the thesis of the "relative stabilization" of capitalism.[79] The ending of the strike and the immediate liquidation of revolutionary illusions caused the fierce antagonism existing among the Bolsheviks to explode, giving rise to a spiral that would not be settled between the Stalin and Bukharin majority and the united opposition of Trotsky and Zinoviev. Togliatti and the leading group in Rome, without sources of information beyond the Comintern press, came down in favor of the positions of Stalin and Bukharin, aimed at denying the pure and simple end of "stabilization." Scoccimarro wrote to Togliatti that "in general we agree with the directives and the attitude you have adopted." He cited the workers' strike in Britain, the financial crisis in France, and the coup d'état of Pilsudski in Poland as developments toward a possible revolutionary outcome, but specified: "We do not believe that we have already reached that point."[80]

Stalin and Bukharin decided to involve the communist parties with the objective of limiting the possible influence of Trotskyism. Togliatti made this known with caution ("I have been told that it would be desirable for the PCd'I to take a position on the questions now being debated in the International. From a Russian comrade. We need to examine the matter a little").[81] Indeed, on 15 July he intervened at the Plenum of the Russian party in support of the majority, accusing the opposition of "revolutionary impatience."[82] Then he sent detailed information to Rome about the standoff between the Bolshevik leaders. In his summary, he agreed with the definition of the opposition as "an unprincipled bloc," and acknowledged as inevitable the conclusion of the Plenum with "a sanction of an organizational character against the opposition" (that is to say, the exclusion of Zinoviev from the Politburo). Togliatti maintained that the choice of a head-on confrontation made by Trotsky might "exert consequences on the life of the RCP (Russian Communist Party) that at the moment are incalculable, but are certainly very serious." At this point, he expressed the opinion that the decision of the Fourteenth Congress of the Soviet party not to allow European communists to discuss the "Russian question" had been overcome. The Comintern would necessarily have to face the problem, because it was experiencing "an essential moment in the development of a proletarian state and of its policy."[83]

We have no direct knowledge of Gramsci's point of view regarding the developments of the "Russian question" in the spring and summer of 1926. However, his report to the Central Committee of the PCd'I of 2 and 3 August provided a particularly detailed and unconventional international analysis. He took no position in the heated debate among Lenin's successors. His judgment was that the "stabilization" of capitalism had not reached its endpoint, and that the notion itself needed rethinking and adapting to a differentiated analysis that distinguished between the center and the periphery of the capitalist system. Returning to the red thread of a thought already outlined two years earlier, he observed that in the countries of advanced capitalism. "the ruling class possesses political and organizational resources which it did not possess, for instance, in Russia," and that therefore "even the most serious economic crises do not have immediate repercussions in the political sphere." His remark implicitly referred to a European situation that had undeniably transformed in the preceding two years, following Germany's exit from the cycle of crises of the first five postwar years. The German Revolution had failed, but so had reaction on the fascist model in the heart of Europe. Instead, in the peripheral countries, such as Italy, Spain, Portugal, and Poland, where "the state forces are less efficient," the movements of the intermediate classes, "which seek to carry on, and to a certain sense succeed in carrying on, policies of their own," presented a different influence and either a reactionary or a revolutionary potential. The periphery of Europe in the postwar period had gone through transitions similar to those in Italy, which remained the "classical and exemplary" form. Now however, the time had perhaps come for a "molecular" shift of the intermediate classes from reaction to revolution. If so, Gramsci argued, "we are entering a new phase in the development of the capitalist crisis."[84]

Scholars have dwelled above all on this illusory prediction of Gramsci's, in the light of the criticism in terms of realism leveled at him at the time by Tasca.[85] Certainly the analyses of Fascism as a mass movement based on the middle classes had not diluted the expectations of a destabilization of the regime, even after the end of the Matteotti crisis. It is likely that the hopes for an imminent crisis of Fascism were induced by, among other things, the need to counter the influence of Bordiga. Revolutionary visions were not a monopoly of Trotsky and his followers. The differences among the leaders of world communism regarding greater or lesser realism were much more blurred than is usually thought. In particular, the Chinese Revolution raised transversal expectations. All the Bolshevik leaders, despite their political divergences, continued to believe that the scenario of a revolution in Asia destined to destabilize the British Empire was still open.[86] Gramsci's specificity consisted, rather, in believing that revolutionary prospects were still a possibility in Europe, but only in the peripheries and not in the metropolises of advanced capitalism. Thus, his framework did not follow the revolutionary visions of Trotsky and Zinoviev. He did not think that the England of 1926 was like the Germany of 1923. On the subject of the English strike, he accepted the positions of the majority of the Russian party, that the conditions for giving rise to autonomous action by the communists were not present. Gramsci was looking elsewhere, not at Germany or Great Britain, but not even at China. His vision was directed not toward imaginary interconnections between the Chinese Revolution and the British Empire, but at the fault lines on the European continent, which assigned Fascist Italy a role as laboratory.

Gramsci's differential analysis implied attention toward the diverse national situations and a distancing from integrally classist readings of the international dimension. Comintern canons and languages did not prevent the acknowledgment of a certain autonomy to international dynamics and their multiple connections with national contexts (which led him to stress, among other things, the peculiarities of some countries of the capitalist center, like France). Gramsci was moving between the coordinates suggested above all by Bukharin, but with an important difference. The theoretician of the NEP had some time earlier already explained that the doctrine of "socialism in one country" and the notion of "capitalist stabilization" did not liquidate "world revolution," because only the latter could protect Soviet Russia from the threat of an attack by the capitalist powers. Gramsci's notion of an "intermediate" phase and his distinction between national realities implied dissent about the idea of "two stabilizations" that mirrored each other. His idea was that the thesis of the "relative stabilization" of capitalism offered scant analytical aid, and that the revolutionary movement's raison d'être could not be reduced simply to defense of the Soviet Union. Within this framework, he was well aware of the role of the United States, albeit in broad terms. In particular, he stigmatized the Fascist government's "complete subservience" to American capitalism, a central argument in the press polemics against Treves and the socialist reformists, in line with the visions of the principal Bolshevik leaders. Trotsky, Zinoviev, and Bukharin more than once had emphasized the overwhelming American economic supremacy and the significance of the Dawes Plan in Europe as an instrument for the reorganization of world capitalism. The Plenum of the Comintern of February-March 1926 had equated "Americanization" in Europe with a reactionary phenomenon that profited from the presence of the governmental social democrats and had launched the watchword of the "United Socialist States of Europe."[87]

Gramsci, however, did not use the theory of "inter-imperialistic contradictions," which led the Bolsheviks to imagine a scenario of war between Great Britain and the United States. As he had already done just after the war, he emphasized the influence of American economic power, which now was clearly eclipsing the European powers. On Europe's periphery, global capitalism's tendency to limit the national sovereignty of states was not always a factor for stability. Also in this respect, he adopted a Eurocentric vision of global dynamics, which did not seek circumvention strategies in Asia in order to destabilize the Western empires. He envisioned instead a more realistic and subtle analysis of European societies and their contradictions, with the objective of identifying the weak points of the international order constituted by the Dawes Plan, the Locarno conference, and the entry of Weimar Germany into the League of Nations. Questions about effective stabilization were being widely floated in mid-Twenties European politics, in particular because the Locarno Treaty had outlined a geopolitical scenario centered entirely on Western Europe that was inadequate regarding Central and Eastern Europe and the role the United States would effectively play.[88] Gramsci interpreted this theme in his own way, while in Moscow it was mainly understood as being a threat to Soviet security, or as suggesting even more a strategic turn toward China in an anti-British key.

The conflict in the Soviet Communist Party was becoming increasingly intense. For Togliatti, the involvement of the European communists was "of fundamental importance for the prospects and the tactic of the vanguard of the proletariat at the present time."[89] On 26 September he announced the convocation on 15 November of an enlarged Comintern Executive destined to discuss the question.[90] The tensions in Moscow were reflected in public discourse, since the Italian press did not fail to propagate alarming news and polemic barbs about the lacerations in the revolutionary leading group. Gramsci undertook a defense of the revolution in Russia, centered on the NEP. He upheld Bukharin's thesis that the historical dynamic between the industrial and agricultural strata of the nineteenth century was being replicated in the twentieth century by workers and peasants, and that the bond between these two classes gave rise to a revolutionary experience destined to build a socialist society.[91] The apologia of "socialism in one country" was in these terms an ideal reference for the Gramscian leading group. Up to this point, it had to some extent distinguished itself from the sectarian logic that pervaded the Comintern. Yet the circumstances of 1926 engendered a discontinuity. Put under pressure by the request for alignment from Stalin and Bukharin, the Italian leading group divided itself in a conflict that was irreconcilable and full of implications for Gramsci and Togliatti.

Part of this dynamic was, in all probability, the reading of the integral text of Lenin's "testament."[92] Probably dictated by Lenin to his secretaries between late December 1922 and early January 1923, and read out to the delegates at the Thirteenth Congress but kept secret by the Bolshevik leaders, Lenin's "letter to the Congress" (or "testament") was like a unexploded bomb for the communist politics of the time, even though its authenticity was uncertain. The call to remove Stalin from power was its most serious and recurrent aspect in the no-holds-barred struggle for succession. The existence of this document, and some of its contents, became known to European communists from the spring and summer of 1925, when the American communist Max Eastman (well known to the ex-*ordinovisti*) quoted selected passages from it in a pamphlet, with the aim of putting Trotsky in a positive light.[93] Stalin forced Trotsky to distance himself from Eastman because of his nonchalant manipulation of a document that all the Bolshevik leaders had agreed not to make public; yet he did not deny its existence. After a long series of controversies and mentions of the document by the opposition, Stalin himself quoted widely from it in the Plenum of the Central Committee of July 1926, open to Comintern representatives, in an attempt to blunt a weapon of the opposition, pointing out the opinions Lenin had also expressed about them, which were anything but flattering.[94] The integral text thus became a classic open secret. In one of his missives from Moscow, on 4 October 1926, Togliatti hinted at the opposition's intention to demand "a referendum on Lenin's testament."[95] He mentioned the document without emphasis, evidently taking for granted that it was familiar to his comrades. In other words, it is likely that the Italian communist leaders (and not only they) had read Lenin's "testament" before its publication by Eastman in the *New York Times* of 18 October 1926.[96]

This casts particular light on the letter Gramsci sent on 14 October 1926 to Togliatti in Moscow so that the latter could forward it to the Soviet leading group, in reply to a request from the leaders of the Bolshevik majority for support against the opposition. Gramsci declared at the beginning of the letter that he perceived a "different and much more serious" situation than in the past, because "we are seeing a split taking place and widening in the central Leninist group." He ended by indicating Trotsky, Zinoviev, and Kamenev as "the people most responsible for the current situation." The term "split" was common currency in the communist movement, and Gramsci himself had used it more than once in referring to Bordiga and Trotsky. However, he was now using this notion in a different way—that is, as denoting the poisoned fruit of a conflict with an "organic character" in which all were responsible, including Stalin. Such a split endangered "the principle and practice of the hegemony of the proletariat" and "the fundamental relationships of the alliance between the workers and the peasants," and thus "the pillars of the workers' state and of the Revolution." Criticism of the Trotskyist opposition centered on the argument that they had betrayed the idea that the proletariat could not "maintain its hegemony and its dictatorship" without sacrificing its own "corporative interests," and had thus resuscitated "the whole tradition of social democracy and syndicalism," the Western proletariat's main obstacle to "organizing itself as a ruling class." However, Gramsci's main preoccupation was that the Stalin majority intended "to triumph," and thus to favor a split that would cause "irreparable and lethal" damage. "In these last nine years of world history you have been the organizational element and driving force of the revolutionary forces of all countries," he declared. "But today you are destroying your own work; you are degrading and running the risk of nullifying the leading role that the CP of the USSR had gained through the impetus of Lenin."[97]

It is fair to think that this vision was influenced by, among other things, the reading of Lenin's "letter to the Congress." This document stated that the risk of a "split" in the party came, to a great extent, from the personalities of Stalin and Trotsky. Indeed, that was its central aspect, much more so than the appeal to remove Stalin from power, which was linked to a contingency that had already passed. In autumn 1926 this warning could be read as a prophecy that was being fulfilled, and it suggested avoidance of the logic of excessively rigid alignments.

We know that Gramsci prepared the letter carefully and announced it on 6 October to Kerzhentsev, who mentioned it to Stalin on the same day:

> Com. Gramsci, member of the CC and of the Political Bureau of the Italian party, informed me today that the CC will send to our party conference a letter containing an indication of all the damage caused by the opposition to communist work abroad. He asked for my opinion (in the form of a private, friendly conversation). As a member of the VKP(B) [All-Union Communist Party (Bolsheviks)], I told him that sending that letter would bring support for our party, since effectively the opposition is destroying the cause of communism not only in our country but everywhere. Gramsci said that the letter will be sent in the next few days. This is for your information.[98]

By clarifying in advance his loyalty toward the Bolshevik majority, Gramsci evidently thought of placing himself within a dynamic that was still uncertain in Moscow, for a truce appeared likely during those same days, as was announced by Togliatti in a communication on 11 October and subsequently officialized in *Pravda* on 17 October.[99] Gramsci's conceptual framework was not restricted to the "testament," but was based on Lenin's last writings. He referred to the NEP as the great postrevolutionary challenge. His profound conviction, expressed using the same language as that of the Bolsheviks, was that the proletariat would be able to maintain "its hegemony and its dictatorship" only by sacrificing "corporative interests" in the name of the "general and permanent class interests." It was around this narrative, destined to become a guide for his reflections in prison, that Gramsci centered his personal vision of internationalism. The unity of the Bolshevik leading group was for him at the same time a necessary condition for "proletarian hegemony in the NEP regime"—that is, for "the fundamental relationships of alliance between the workers and peasants," and for "the development and triumph of the world's revolutionary forces." From this viewpoint he pronounced the harshest accusation: "In our opinion the violent passion of the Russian questions is making you lose sight of the international aspects, [thus forgetting that] your duties as Russian militants can and must be carried out only within the *framework of the interests of the international proletariat*."[100]

In his reply, Togliatti ignored the connection established by Gramsci between the systems of power based on the NEP and their international implications. He indicated the "essential defect" of Gramsci's argument as that of having placed the fact of the split in the foreground, and "the problem of the correctness of the line" followed by the majority in the background. He reprimanded Gramsci for not having made any distinction between the majority and the opposition in the Soviet party, adding that "probably from now on the unity of the Leninist old guard will no longer [. . .] be realized in a continuous fashion. In the past, the greatest factor of this unity resided in the enormous prestige and personal authority of Lenin. This element cannot be replaced." Togliatti denied that there was a link between the unity of the Bolshevik leading group in its present form and the historical function of the organization of world revolutionary forces which was absolved by the Soviet Communist Party.[101]

At this point, on 18 October, the bombshell of the publication of Lenin's "testament" in the *New York Times* exploded. The news immediately went global, and Gramsci learned of it from the *Corriere della sera* of 19 October.[102] On 21 October, Manuilsky wrote to him to reassure him about the stability of Soviet power and the utter defeat of the opposition. It is likely that these two statements sounded contradictory to Gramsci and did not fit his idea of the stability of the state. Manuilsky also claimed, like Togliatti, that the Italian comrades had an inadequate perception of the real state of affairs in Moscow, and he promised to remedy this by sending an emissary to Italy, in the person of Humbert-Droz.[103] However, this was not the real point of the question. Gramsci certainly understood that the situation in Moscow was getting worse, also and above all in the wake of the publication of the "testament." He found confirmation of this in Togliatti's statement on 25 October about the drastic decisions made by the majority against the minority on 23 October, and about the request of the delegation of the Executive of the Comintern to remove Zinoviev from his position as president.[104]

Gramsci's reply to Togliatti on 26 October must be understood in this context. He admitted that unity could not be maintained "at least in the form it has had in the past." Nevertheless, he described it as the "existential condition" both for parties of the International and for "the hegemony of the prolet[ariat], that is to say, the social content of the state." This, too, would appear to be a nod to Lenin's last phase, and to the theme of the stability of a state founded on two classes. Clearly, Gramsci thought that the unity guaranteed by Stalin was more a problem than a solution, because it produced a loss in terms of ideas and personalities. For this reason he stated that it was "our objective to contribute to maintaining and creating a unitary plan in which the different tendencies and different personalities may once more come closer together and fuse together even ideologically." Even reformulated in this way, the unity of the "Leninist core" represented in his view "a question of utmost importance in the international field," and indeed, *"from the point of view of the masses,* [. . .] the most important question in this historical period." This led Gramsci to formulate the theme of hegemony in international terms:

> Today, nine years after October 1917, it is no longer *the fact of the seizure of power by Bolsheviks* that can revolutionize the Western masses, because this is already taken for granted and has had its effect; today the conviction (if it exists) is politically and ideologically active that, once the proletariat has taken power, *it can build socialism*. The authority of the P[arty] is bound up with this conviction, that cannot be inculcated into the broad masses by the methods of scholastic pedagogy, but only through revolutionary pedagogy, in other words, only through the *political fact* that the R[ussian] P[arty] as a whole is convinced and is fighting in a united fashion.[105]

In other terms, Gramsci extended the notion of hegemony that he had acquired from Bolshevism to the "international field." In so doing, he offered a version of hegemony that differed from how that term was used by the Bolsheviks themselves. It presupposed that hegemony and the symbolic force of the revolution were distinct from the political and strategic leadership's military conception. In this sense, his words revealed a resistance to the assimilation of Bolshevik language, and to the militarization of political culture.

Gramsci's hope may have been anachronistic, given the escalation of the political conflict in Russia, and even an overestimation of the Bolsheviks' cultural dimension. It is reasonable to wonder whether he remained tied to a mythical conception of the Soviet party that was incongruous with its evolution.[106] His idea of the unity of the Bolshevik leading group seemed to ignore the party-state's repressive logic, even within the political elites, which Lenin had increased and not relaxed after the end of the Civil War when he launched the "state capitalism" of the NEP, and which Stalin followed faithfully.[107] Gramsci's vision, however, presented not only the aspect of a tardy or illusory intervention, but also another more realistic aspect. Unlike Togliatti and the other Comintern leaders, he sensed that the fracture between Lenin's successors put at risk the precarious political and social equilibrium of the NEP. Indeed, such equilibrium was broken a little more than a year later, when Stalin finally dropped his moderate mask, initiating the turn toward a gigantic and violent transformation of Russian society that in 1926 was not even vaguely on the cards: a "second revolution" destined to have crucial impact of the international choices of the Soviet Union and the Comintern. In this sense, Gramsci's letters of October 1926 were a prophecy and a testament, which followed the last sense of the cosmopolitan internationalism of the Twenties.

Gramsci's stance was highly atypical in the context of Western communism, while that of Togliatti constituted unreserved compliance. Gramsci's intention was not only to affirm reasons of principle and of the PCd'I's national policy, and Togliatti was not simply invoking reasons of discipline. The correspondence between the men shows their full awareness of being part of a world movement, and the arguments they used both started from that point of view. In practice, it was their respective ideas on internationalism that diverged, despite their shared stock of experiences accumulated over the previous years. Put on the spot by circumstances, Gramsci became convinced that the fracture of the Bolshevik old guard might compromise the symbolic resource represented by the Soviet state, seen as an essential condition for international hegemony. Togliatti did not share this conviction, and bet instead on the concrete solidity represented by the strength of the majority gathered around Stalin. Gramsci's arrest removed this question from the field of vision of the Italian communists. Their political culture continued to be based on the notion of the interdependence of the international and national dimensions, which they applied to the analysis of Fascism and its transformation into a totalitarian regime, while no longer including questions about the role and destiny of the Soviet Union in their analytic and strategic framework.

2
STALINISM AND ANTIFASCISM

THE CENTRALITY OF THE SOVIET STATE

The arrest of Gramsci, the outlawing of the PCd'I, and the rise of Stalin were the prelude to the disintegration of the leading group, which had been laboriously formed over the previous period. The cohesion that had been forged in the former "Ordine Nuovo" group and its enlargement at the Lyon Congress, the culmination of a long and conflictual interaction with Bordiga, was found lacking precisely on the terrain of internationalism. The October 1926 conflict between Gramsci and Togliatti did not have immediate consequences, but at the same time it marked a turning point, which put an end to the attempts to find an intermediate position among the various attitudes in international communism and implied a divergence that was destined to become wider. Over the next two years, the end of the alliance between Stalin and Bukharin had reverberations in all communist parties; the Italian party was no exception. The Italian leaders were completely taken by surprise by Stalin's turn toward a radical transformation of Soviet society and the adoption of an extremist line in the Comintern, after they had supported him—for opposite reasons—in his fight against Trotsky. Their various responses were a source of further disintegration. Unlike other parties, however, the Italians did not undergo a total purge of their own leaders. The figure of Togliatti represented a continuity with the previous era, albeit with a thousand contradictions and adaptations. His personality became the dominant one and ended by establishing a hierarchical relation with the others, in a dialectic of challenge and co-optation of the younger generation, making use of the role played in the leading organs of the Comintern. This particular dialectic between one single personality and the other leaders would deepen and continue right up to the end of World War II.

Before Mussolini's turn to totalitarianism at the end of 1926 outlawed the PCd'I and drove into exile or imprisoned its leading group, Togliatti's internationalist training had undergone a decisive change. The choices he made left a lasting trace, and turned out to be fatal in the light of the headlong rush of events in Italy. As soon as he had been nominated the PCd'I's representative at the Comintern, Togliatti found himself having to adopt a line of conduct when faced with the escalation of affairs in the Russian party. He was certainly not unaware of the evolution of Soviet politics, nor was it a disadvantage to know Comintern leaders such as Manuilsky personally. But like all the European communists, he ran up against the limits of selective and approximate information. His activity was almost entirely absorbed by the happenings in Russian politics, which defined the boundaries of internationalism by establishing ever narrower and stricter confines. Bukharin became Togliatti's main interlocutor when to all intents and purposes he took over leadership of the Comintern.[1] As appears evident from his correspondence with Rome, Togliatti took note of the logic of alliances that the Soviet protagonists themselves were suggesting in their inflamed political conflict, and became the spokesman for the lines of conduct as indicated by the majority grouped around Stalin and Bukharin. At the same time, he consolidated the role played by the Italian communists as analysts of fascism. In the Comintern press, he rejected generic definitions of fascism that attributed "too general and too abstract a sense" to the term. His intention was not to present fascism as an exceptional phenomenon limited to Italy, but to draw out its specific social complexity and ideological eclecticism. He indicated the distinction at the analytical level between the aspects linked with the historical particularities of the country, beginning with the weakness of the liberal state and the especially deep crisis of the immediate postwar period, and those which could on the other hand also have a significance for other national realities. Togliatti was thereby indicating in fascism an international problem, not only an Italian one, but at the same time he warned that only a differential analysis could provide the tools for understanding it.[2]

However, in October 1926, as we know, the leading group split on the question of internationalism. The forcing of affairs by Gramsci, who in the name of higher unitary and hegemonic principles and values criticized all Lenin's successors, also forced Togliatti to express his own point of view more clearly. From here divergent visions emerged, not because doubt was being shed on the strategic option of "socialism in one country," or on the basic elements of the analysis of fascism and the international situation, but because different adaptations could be found for the need to reconcile the interests of the security of the Soviet Union with the world revolution. Togliatti's choice of following and justifying without reservation the line and conduct of the Stalinist majority was an irreversible fact. It was then that his personality emerged fully. He became the head of a group of political émigrés who worked between Paris and Moscow, but also became recognized as a leader of international communism. As from his interventions at the Seventh Plenum of the Comintern in November and December 1926, he proposed a vision that developed the main analytical and strategic aspects shared in common by the leading group of the Italian party, aligning himself closely, however, with Soviet reasons of state. His insistence on capitalist "stabilization" and on the historic defeat of the workers' movement did not stop him from following in the footsteps of Gramsci regarding the scenarios of fascism. "The Italian experience has an international value," he declared, insofar as it demonstrated that the attempt to "stabilize capitalism" by mobilizing "some of the middle strata on the basis of the fight against the working class and as the basis of a new regime" was generating contradictions that were "much more serious than the advantages that it was procuring." He even evoked the return to a revolutionary situation comparable to that of 1919–20. At the same time, he asserted the "identity between the Russian revolution and the world revolution"— quoting quite precisely, without mentioning it, the letter Gramsci had sent him on 26 October 1926 on the need to keep active in the consciousness of the masses the conviction that in Russia, "after having taken power, the proletariat can build socialism." However, he followed the priority of the defense of the Soviet State. Even in Italy, he declared, "when we organize our party illegally," the result of such work was to "indirectly help the Russian proletariat in the construction of socialism."[3]

Togliatti thus developed the essential point of his reply to Gramsci of 18 October 1926, namely the dissociation between the problem of the unity of the leading group of the Soviet party and the vision of internationalism. In April 1927 he provided the Italian cadres with a reconstruction of Bolshevism totally centered on the notion of the "hegemony of the proletariat" over the peasants, presenting it as an infallible guiding principle of Leninism. The condition for exercising this hegemony was, he indicated, in the "correct inner-party regime," going on to censure the Trotskyist opposition both for its tendency to construct "factions" potentially leading to a disintegration, and for its mistaken inclination to postulate "the return to an immediate revolutionary situation."[4] His vision of the revolution as a process that reflected the inequalities of capitalist development was squarely placed in the furrow traced by Gramsci. The notion of hegemony was not, however, the Gramscian one: even if it referred back to the capacity of leadership, it was not applied to the international role of the leading Soviet group. In this way, Togliatti thereby adapted to the link with the Soviet state much more closely than in the past. He continued, however, to present the analysis of fascism as the primary contribution of the Italians, insisting on the specificity of the phenomenon, but also on its more general consequences. On his arrival in Paris to construct the foreign center of the party at the beginning of 1927, he wrote that fascism was a factor that was intensifying the tensions in capitalist Europe and driving it toward war. Mussolini's Italy was "a capitalist country which is tending with all its might to resolve its internal contradictions through war."[5]

As we have already seen, the vision that Togliatti proposed went outside the strictest canons of the Leninist theory of imperialism, and was not very far from that of Rudolf Hilferding and other leaders of European social democracy in arguing that the international threats were being generated more by Fascist Italy than by the great Western powers that had emerged victorious from the war.[6] At the same time he drew a picture of Europe as an "immense field of trenches," emphasizing the danger of war which instead rejected the social-democratic theses and once more relativized the "stabilization" of postwar capitalism. "Socialism in one country" in

Russia, and the growth of the revolutionary movement in China, became the two main directives of a perspective of the crisis of world capitalism.[7] Here Togliatti did nothing other than follow the theses of Bukharin, in whose view world capitalism would not be able to encircle the Soviet Union and at the same time contain the "anti-imperialist national revolution" in China, destined to accelerate the decline of the British Empire.[8]

The scenario of a Chinese revolution destined to redeem the failure of the European revolution suffered a mortal blow in April 1927. The massacre of the Communists in Shanghai at the hands of Chiang Kai-shek was immediately recognized as a dramatic defeat. The vision of the "three levers" of the revolutionary movement proposed by Bukharin (the British working class, the Chinese revolution, and the Soviet Union itself) did not stand up to the facts of the situation. With the collapse of the scenario of world revolution that all the Bolsheviks had imagined, albeit in different tones and accents, the subject of the defense of the Soviet Union was destined to become ever more impelling. The leaders of the Stalinist majority launched a veritable war alarm, shared by the opposition. In the absence of the fundamental premise of a revolutionary movement acting as a deterrent to imperialism, the isolated Soviet Union risked acts of aggression, even more so after the breakdown of diplomatic relations with Great Britain and the co-optation of Germany into the League of Nations. Trotsky attributed the responsibility for this situation to Stalin, but it was the latter who profited from the war alarm, using the accusation of defeatism to liquidate the opposition once and for all.[9]

From this time onward, the priority of defending the Soviet Union underwent a brusque acceleration. Togliatti interpreted the new internationalist canon in his own way. Among those who immediately drew the more general implications of the failure of the revolutionary movement in Asia, he stood out for the argumentation put forward at the Eighth Plenum of the Comintern in May 1927. Here he in fact proposed to put at the center of Comintern strategy the "struggle for peace," arguing for the capacity this would have for creating a "direct link" between the "policies of the workers' state" under threat from the "united front of the imperialists" and the "deep-felt sentiments against war of the masses."[10] While Bukharin himself had put this subject on the agenda, he rejected the Italian delegation's proposal using the argument that it could not be applied to China, where a "revolutionary war" was taking place.[11] Bukharin continued to place hopes in the Chinese revolution despite the disaster in Shanghai, while Togliatti's position was different. The Italian leading group had never put much trust in the scenario of the "revolution in Asia." Togliatti proposed instead to challenge the European socialists on the terrain of their international "peace" agenda, which after the Locarno Accords centered on the subject of disarmament, linked to the League of Nations, with strong contrasts and disagreements between the main parties.[12] Communist "peace" perspectives could be linked to the interests of the Soviet Union, which had adhered to the Briand-Kellogg initiative for disarmament, and thus seemed to open the way to convergence between different internationalist cultures.[13] It also implied a nonexclusive vision of communist internationalism and the aim of challenging social democracy for the consensus of the working masses, liquidating the minority of European communist parties. Both perspectives would remain a distinctive feature of Togliatti's personality.

In the conjuncture of the end of the 1920s, the picture that became dominant was the vision of the inevitability of war, based on the Leninist theory of imperialism. Communists had to mobilize against an impending war, while the idea of prevention was illusory and impracticable. The campaign against the danger of war intensified with the collapse of the global revolutionary scenario in summer 1927 after the definitive rupture between the Comintern and the Guomindang, the Chinese nationalist party, and the bloody repression of the workers' strikes in Vienna. Stalin at this point enunciated the principle of the identification between internationalism and the defense of the Soviet Union. At the end of the year he put the stress on "capitalist encirclement," foreseeing a new crisis, risks of war, and the fascistization of bourgeois governments. His was not a revolutionary prophecy, but rather an unprecedented emphasis on the centrality of the Soviet Union as a "factor of disintegration" in world imperialism. In so doing, he detached his own political figure from the moderate conception of "socialism in one country."[14]

Togliatti followed the coordinates laid down by Stalin. In his report in January 1928 to the Second Conference of the PCd'I, held in Basel, he liquidated the ideas of "organized capitalism." "If Russia is developing toward socialism, the capitalist world cannot become stabilized, since a part of itself is missing," Togliatti now argued, without taking into account the very fact that the revolution represented a "factor of disintegration of the capitalist economy through the authority that Russia has on the working masses of the whole world." Togliatti drew a picture of a world dominated by two types of explosive conflict: that between the capitalist states, in which he put the bellicose nature of Italian Fascism, classically destined to end up in colonial and general wars, and the fundamental one between the imperialist powers and Soviet Russia. The watchword of the communist movement was now that of the "struggle against war," which meant closing ranks around the Soviet Union by placing agitational work above politics.[15] Following Stalin's example, Togliatti did not alter the idioms and vocabulary of the communists, but used them in a selective and simplified fashion. His trajectory thus came into line with that of all the leaders of international communism. In the case of the Italian leading group, the discontinuity was particularly important. Gramsci had in fact always avoided catastrophic determinism, and in essence ignored the theory of the inevitability of war. The approach of a "differential analysis" still was defended by Togliatti, as well as by Tasca, in his contributions on the simultaneous presence of modernization and backwardness in the Italian economy, on the narrowness of the bases of Fascist imperialism, and on the financial role of the United States.[16] This approach, however, risked being compromised to a great extent by the undifferentiated vision of the capitalist powers on a war footing.

The Sixth Congress of the Comintern, in July 1928, took place under the insignia of the danger of war and the defense of the Soviet Union. Bukharin adopted a radical line that liquidated some of his own previous positions on "organized capitalism." Following the evolution of the leading group of the Bolsheviks, Togliatti appealed to the "awareness of the inevitability of war" and followed Stalin's theory of the "intensification of the class struggle."[17] The sole element of a "differential analysis" that Togliatti defended was his invitation not to generalize the phenomenon of fascism and to avoid analogies between fascism and social democracy that were too facile. He recalled that fascism "as a mass movement" brought together the interests of the middle classes and the big bourgeoisie, while social democracy maintained its majority influence in the European working class. On this terrain he continued to exercise his realism, despite the image of war that dominated communist rhetoric without any real foundation in international dynamics.

Togliatti's alignment did not go so far as to accept the theory of "social fascism" which, from the summer of 1928 onward, had held sway in communist discourse. Stalin had theorized the analogy between social democracy and fascism as early as 1924, and had shown a substantial misunderstanding of the Fascist phenomenon.[18] To accept the theory of "social fascism" was equivalent to jettisoning the elaboration over previous years of the Italian leadership group regarding the specificity of fascism.[19] Togliatti stigmatized the tendency to designate as fascism "every form of reaction," whereas it actually represented "a particular, specific form of reaction." The specificity of Italy lay in "the political unity" that the various components of Italian capitalism had sought in fascism in order to remedy their own historical limitations. This had produced a transformation of the movement into a regime with a mass basis, directed toward the construction of a totalitarian state. In the wake of Gramsci two years previously, Togliatti maintained that it was improbable for fascism to develop in an advanced capitalist country, and that its potentialities for spreading internationally were limited to the periphery of Europe, as, for example, in Poland. More so than in the past, he limited fascism to Italy. This was above all a line of defense against the ever stronger tendencies to identify the development of capitalism and of social democracy into an outcome of fascistization.[20]

At the Congress, in his role as a leader of the Comintern, Togliatti was charged with intervening with a report on social democracy and the "colonial question"—an unusual subject for him, even though in the past he had been involved with the questions of China and Latin America. The Latin American countries could not be put under the heading of the "colonial question," but all the same they constituted an analytical and strategic *trait d'union* at the global level. In particular, Togliatti saw Brazil as the theater of a possible "alliance" between workers and peasants, along the lines of the Lyon Theses.[21] *Lo stato operaio*, the new review of the PCd'I, published in Paris as from March 1927, had from the start devoted attention to the question of the anticolonial struggle, in particular with a comment of Tasca's at the Congress of the League against Imperialism, founded by Willi Münzenberg.[22] In July 1928 Grieco presented a report on the Comintern's "Near East Commission," in which he recognized that the thesis on the "colonial question" approved at Lyon had remained a dead letter, but relaunched the possibilities of activity by the Italian communists in Tunisia, with the support of the French, and in Libya.[23] In actual fact, Togliatti's perspective in his report to the Congress was centered much more on Europe than on the colonial world.[24] He dealt with the question as a weak point of the social democrats as a force subaltern to the European imperial system. The argumentation reflected the bitter polemics of the past decade, but brought out the ambiguities of the Socialist International, oscillating between the prevailing demands for reform of the colonial system and the idea of national independence. At the end of the Twenties, the anticolonialism of the Comintern had put the European socialists on the defensive, marginalized as they were from the lively anti-imperialist circles active in the imperial metropolises of London and Paris.[25] Togliatti, however, also criticized the insufficiencies of communist practices and analyses, despite the consciousness of the potential link between the Soviet experience, anti-imperialist activity, and the European colonial systems.[26] This type of vision had no outcome because of the unexpected fall of Bukharin and the marginalization of Münzenberg, which was to signal the end of the line for Lenin's idea of an alliance with the colonial elites in the name of self-determination.[27] To all effects this road was not followed, but was destined to reemerge, like rivers in a karstic region, only many years later, and then in the context of decolonization.

Togliatti charged Tasca with representing the PCd'I in the Comintern and suggested that he should collaborate with Bukharin, whom he judged to be "the only one who thinks [. . .], who tries to see the new elements of the situation."[28] Both soon realized, however, that the Sixth Congress had marked a very fragile compromise between Stalin and Bukharin. The news that Tasca sent to Paris indicated the growing tension between the two Bolshevik leaders that was splitting the Politburo and paralyzing the Comintern. At the beginning of December, Tasca claimed among other things that the Executive was "very far" from deserving the definition of the "general staff of the revolution," since it was not playing any leading role. Togliatti invited him to restrain the judgment of great insufferability he expressed regarding the now dominant climate of conspiracy. But the problem was also created by the perception of a political change that was imposed by Stalin, aimed at radicalizing the line of the Comintern, and destined to have repercussions even on the German party and all the others. Tasca ended by declaring that his disagreement could not be healed, and that there was no longer any reason for his stay in Moscow.[29] On 17 December, Togliatti wrote to him after a meeting of the Central Committee held in Switzerland in the presence of Manuilsky, to say that the position of the Italian communists remained bound to the line of the Congress and that the political problems had to be placed in "the front line" even if the subject of the "internal regime" had its importance. He said he was, "in essence," in agreement with Tasca, and informed him that no one had concurred with Manuilsky on the impossibility of recomposing differences in the German party, for months at the center of accusations against the "right."[30]

The radical turn took place two days later when Stalin launched a fierce attack against the. "right deviation" in the German party, which heralded a vast purge in its ranks. On this occasion Stalin, among other things, strongly attacked Humbert-Droz and Tasca, accusing them of "opportunism."[31] This side of Stalin was irreconcilable with that of the balanced realist, which he had cultivated up to a short time before, but was instead consistent with the extreme choices made in adopting "exceptional measures" and violent requisitioning against the peasants, which compromised the city-countryside relationship of the NEP. The linkage between the shift in the Comintern, the crisis of the NEP, and the growing conflict within the former majority of the Soviet Communist Party thus emerged perceptibly. From that moment onward, a decline came about in the role of the Comintern and a deterioration of its cosmopolitan environment as a consequence of the liquidation not only of the left opposition but that of the moderates. This meant a sharp loss in terms of political personalities and minds, but above all a rapid slide toward forms of intolerance, disciplining, and censure that until then had been unknown. The launch of the "revolution from above" in the Soviet Union, with the turn toward a forced industrial modernization and a violent collectivization of the countryside, led to an escalation of verbal extremism in the communist movement, of sectarianism and of catastrophism, rhetorically directed toward declaring the continuity of the concept of world revolution, but entirely oriented by state priorities and by the "danger of war."

The break between Togliatti and Tasca followed the model of the purge of moderates that took place in other parties. It was, however, a source of great anguish. Togliatti had already criticized Tasca harshly at the end of December, telling him that if his judgments were correct, there remained no alternative but a "reconstruction of the International from the bottom up."[32] He did, however, try to avoid drastic decisions. At the beginning of January 1929, Manuilsky wrote to Stalin that the measures taken regarding the Communist Party of Germany (KPD) would help the Italians, explaining their "hesitations" by the fact that they "live rather outside the great path of the communist movement." He then informed Stalin of the events at a meeting of the Italians and Germans on 12 January 1929, held in the presence of two Comintern representatives, Kolarov and Georgi Dimitrov. In Togliatti's estimation, his intervention had been "affable," with the aim of avoiding a real discussion and of "diplomatizing" the problems. Togliatti had been very insistent on putting off until a meeting of the PCd'I the question of a clarification with Tasca, who was guilty of having broken the canon of unanimity and of having criticized the repressive method used by the Executive Committee of the Communist International (ECCI) toward the German party, and who in his turn had received a severe reprimand from Stalin. Togliatti had also observed that he himself, Tasca, and Grieco represented what remained of the "old guard." It was precisely these words, according to Manuilsky's letter, that had inflamed the confrontation and led the Soviet delegate to say that the Italians were slipping out of his hands "like a wet fish." He maintained that the problem was represented by their loss of contact with the "mass movements," and suggested that should move to Germany and not to Switzerland.[33]

Togliatti's argument about the "old guard" of the party, which he knew would be unacceptable and even counterproductive, revealed a raw nerve—perhaps also at the emotional level—and showed a real preoccupation about an irreparable political and generational mutation. This did not stop him from coming into line with the Stalinization of the Comintern. The critical path chosen by Tasca, precisely at the time when the leading group was hesitating, made the situation untenable. In a letter of 20 January, he drew a picture of Stalin as pitiless and realistic, outside any acceptable canon after 1927 ("The whole situation revolves around Stalin. The CI does not exist; the Soviet CP does not exist; Stalin is the 'lord and master' who moves everything").[34] Like Trotsky and many others, Tasca was probably underestimating the political qualities of Stalin, here presented as a mediocrity who "regurgitated ideas" and did not rise to the height of the problems of the revolution, to which he would cause fatal damage.[35] Tasca's judgment of Stalin as a despot and an autocrat put the finger where it hurt, and made any recomposition impossible. Having to choose between Stalin and Tasca, Togliatti could only opt for the former. Togliatti's indictment at the party's Central Committee in March 1929 put an end to any hesitation, and marked a point of no return. He adopted an unmistakable code, indicating in the "danger of war" the convergence of "all the contradictions inherent in the capitalist world at this current time."[36] The subtext was that the juncture between the war plans of the capitalist powers and the influence of the "right" in Moscow and in the communist movement was to be avoided. As he himself had revealed in his correspondence with Tasca over the previous few months, in the absence of a revolution "in Europe or in the colonies," the pressure from the "right" as expression of the petty and middle "bourgeoisie" in the countryside and the cities of the Soviet Union was destined to grow.[37] Togliatti had been cautious as possible, but he had arguments at his disposal to justify Stalin's turn of the screw in the Soviet Union and the end of the NEP, which thereby liquidated the positions on the "alliance between workers and peasants" sanctioned at the Lyon congress.[38] On 22 April, Stalin launched his definitive attack on Bukharin at the Plenum of the All-Union Communist Party (Bolsheviks), accusing him of having the same positons as the social democrats on the "stabilization of capitalism"; he also attacked the Germans and Czechoslovaks, but spared the other parties.[39] The signal was obvious to all.

At the Tenth Plenum of the Comintern in July 1929, Togliatti made amends for the delay on the part of the PCd'I in condemning the "opportunism" in its ranks. He followed a double register. On the one hand, he unreservedly supported the turn taking place in the Soviet Union, declaring that it would have been useful to "link more closely the debates on international questions and those on the political questions in the Russian Communist Party," and quoting Stalin ("On the sharp turns there is always someone who falls and remains behind on the ground").[40] On the other hand, his line of defense, together with that of Grieco, was based on a reluctance to accept the thesis of "social fascism." Togliatti accepted Comintern discipline while at the same time defending the difference between a theory of "exceptionalism" and an analysis of national specificities. He declared that "since we cannot be stopped from thinking, we shall keep these things to ourselves and limit ourselves to making general statements."[41] Immediately afterward, in a letter to Ernst Thälmann, the new head of the Stalinized KPD, he confirmed the full alignment of the Italian delegation against "conciliatory" attitudes.[42] This conduct has usually been interpreted as an attempt to salvage what could be salvaged of the national line, giving way on international questions, as a consequence of the serious difficulty created by the fall from grace of Bukharin, Togliatti's main point of reference.[43]

But it should perhaps be seen in a different light. Togliatti's difficulties in fact stemmed not just from the fall of Bukharin, but also from a radical political shift by Stalin, perceived until a short time before as the guarantor of the "realists," but now the promoter of ultraradical visions in domestic policy as much as on the international scene. Thus, the fact that Togliatti had given way was much more important, and was not limited to the contingency of 1929. His programmatic declaration of dissimulation made at the Tenth Plenum appears to us now as a methodology whereby the greater or lesser conviction in a political line had to remain different from constitutive, ideological, and institutional loyalty. The problem was not that of consideration of the political line, as Togliatti had suggested first to Gramsci and then to Tasca. Stalin was the central personality of the Bolshevik state, and showed himself to be the architect of policies that were very different from one another. The position expressed by Togliatti between loyalty and dissimulation did not reflect the internationalism of previous years with its oscillations of conformism and dissent, but the adhesion to new unwritten rules of the game—a qualitative leap of blind faith in the party-state and in its leader, destined to last a long time.

With the expulsion of Tasca in September 1929, the endpoint was reached in the disintegration of the leadership core of the PCd'I formed in the struggle against Bordiga, legitimized by Moscow, and consolidated around the mid-Twenties. This also meant an impoverishment and dispersion of a political and intellectual heritage. With Gramsci, Terracini, and Scoccimarro in prison, Togliatti as the main political survivor had to carry on as the undisputed head without really having presided over the formation of a new leadership group for the decade of turmoil to come. The Italian Communists long remained in the Comintern's line of fire. Their interaction with Moscow caused new wounds and failures, exacerbating their condition of exile. Togliatti himself found he had to face harsh personal criticism, perhaps because he remained the only leader of an important European communist party not directly nominated by Moscow. Certainly, for generational and intellectual reasons, he was not to be numbered among the blindest of Stalin's followers. The new younger generation, forged after the death of Lenin, and then in the context of the "revolution from above" in the Soviet Union and the Great Depression in the West, presented different characteristics, effectively illustrated by Eric Hobsbawm in his memoirs. Their postrevolutionary formative experience implied not only a choice of life and the adhesion to a principle of loyalty, but a mentality centered on ideological dogmatism, on militarized operationality, and on the "drama of sacrifice."[44] This generation was represented in Italian communism by Luigi Longo and Pietro Secchia, who had grown up in the national and international youth organizations. From 1928 they had both advanced on the scene as members of the new Stalinist holy writ. Togliatti was able to keep his distance from the new generation in the hierarchy, avoiding the formation of an authentic leading group capable of supplanting even him. This did not mean that he did not share with them the main perspectives that came down from Stalin's choices, which implied a vision of the world centered around the existence of the Soviet Union as a socialist state, as a great power, and as a noncapitalist society under construction, besieged by Western imperialism. Togliatti's peculiarity consisted in avoiding a mere deduction of political orientations from ideological motivations, and in keeping together mutually contradictory elements.

Having the attack on Tasca as a starting point, Longo and Secchia were involved to the hilt in the political radicalization imposed by the Stalinized Comintern, and in the perspective of an imagined "third period" which would have opened the gates to revolution even in Italy. They became the bearers of the idea of a "return to Italy" from the end of 1929 onward, persuaded as they were that, whatever the price, an organized link within the country had to be re-created. Togliatti supported them, overturning the positions he had held previously.[45] The human cost was justified at the time by the aim of contact with the country, a controversial argument that was destined to remain in the memory of communists, and which was relaunched retrospectively in the light of the Resistance.[46] What appears evident is that, at that immediate moment in time, the drive to construct a clandestine network in the country, following the fantasy of revolutionary upheavals, was equivalent to suicide for the few thousand militants that still remained, making the PCd'I into a party of prisoners rather than a party of conspirators. Those who opposed this policy, like the "three" (Alfonso Leonetti, Pietro Tresso, and Paolo Ravazzoli) and like Ignazio Silone, were expelled from the party in 1930. The Stalinization of the party was so complete that, in the context of a wide-ranging international purge, it struck leaders of the caliber of M. N. Roy.[47] Togliatti was one of the few to be spared among those who were near to Bukharin. His position emerged as strengthened by the identification of the dissidents as followers of Trotsky.

A very similar shadow was cast by the dissent expressed in prison by Gramsci and Terracini regarding the "class against class" line, which took definitive shape in summer 1930. Terracini wrote a long letter making clear the entire difference between the moment of the "turn" and the previous political practice ("up to the end of 1926 there had been at the Center an element of coordination and inspiration represented by Antonio who, in his periodic talks with each of us, almost inadvertently operated so as to keep a common line of thought"). In his estimation, the tendency to identify fascism and capitalism reproposed "Bordiga's concepts, which have already been intensely combatted."[48] Gramsci stigmatized his marginalization in a meeting in July 1930 with his brother Gennaro. He then clearly expressed a vision of fascism opposed to that put forward by the Comintern. In his report for the party, Gennaro wrote of having hypothesized, in answer to a precise question, that the possibility of him and his brother seeing each other under conditions of freedom would come soon, given the international and Italian "crisis." Antonio, who said he was well-informed through his reading of the press, replied that he was very pessimistic ("I do not think that the end is so close at hand. Instead, I would say to you that we have still seen nothing, the worst is yet to come").[49] For the first time, he also advanced very grave doubts about the attitude of his own comrades, referring in particular to a letter of Grieco's dating to 1928 which could have damaged the prospects of his liberation, by writing that such event would happen in the short term.[50] From here a gradual but irreversible detachment of Gramsci from the party was to begin. At the same time, his ex-comrades chose to isolate him in order to avoid the repercussions of his opposition to the Comintern, and in all probability to save themselves as much as to save the prisoner. The Fourth Congress, held in Cologne in April 1931, canonized the figure of the martyr and icon of the struggle against fascism, drawing a veil over his dissent. The campaigns for his liberation carried on by the PCd'I made him an antifascist hero, but in his eyes they prejudiced the possibilities of an authentic negotiation or an amnesty. In other words, the divisions in the leading group of the Italian party were not simply a consequence of Mussolini's Special Tribunal, but the fruit of a series of political conflicts generated by the relationship with Bolshevism and with the Comintern while still remaining in the context of a common belonging and identity.[51]

The most slippery ground for Togliatti was created by his attempts, however cautious, to keep elements of realism firm in his political judgment. It is indicative that immediately after the Cologne Congress, held under the auspices of orthodoxy albeit without too much emphasis on the prospects of an imminent revolution, he was harshly attacked by the ECCI representative, Leon Purman. In a report to Manuilsky and Pyatnitsky in Moscow, Purman accused Togliatti of having used arguments that were "dangerous in the extreme"—in other words, of having brought to mind the 1923 discussion on Germany without taking into account the "new international situation." The report was sent to the head of the Comintern,

Vyacheslav Molotov, a loyal follower of Stalin.[52] The criticism evidently alluded to the insidious analogies that could be drawn between the failure of the "German October" and sectarian radicalism of the present, which in the Germany of the Great Depression was being put to the test and was giving rise to results that were even worse than in the earlier period. Perhaps having had wind of these criticisms, Togliatti yielded to the pressures from Moscow, though reluctantly, expressing support for the choices made by the KPD to participate in the plebiscite in Prussia in 1931, which to all intents and purposes signposted a convergence between communists and Nazis against the regional social-democratic government.[53] In his analysis he accentuated the distinction between Italian Fascism and German National Socialism. Indeed, at the Twelfth Plenum of the Comintern in September 1932 he maintained that it was mistaken to see in Italian Fascism the model to be considered "a classic line, obligatory in all countries." This differentiated vision was already part of his makeup. But in this case he aimed most of all at avoiding putting the situation in Germany on the same footing as that in Italy. In other words, Togliatti was following Comintern imperatives regarding the imminent revolutionary crisis in Germany, but not doing the same for Italy.[54]

The political trait of Togliatti's personality is reflected in the bareness of his autobiography, written in August 1932 following the practice adopted by the Comintern as a procedure of bureaucratic and ideological control. He conceded nothing to motivations regarding ideas, illustrating his personal path through a series of selective points of information. These were significant above all for the striking omissions, which mutilated the very identity and heritage of the leading group of the previous decade. He cited the name of Bordiga, recognizing that he had been under his influence at least up to 1922 and claiming that he had then fought against it; but he avoided mentioning the name of Gramsci and the Lyon Congress of 1926. He did not, however, omit to mention the criticisms he had undergone in 1929 during the struggle "against the opportunistic errors of Tasca," making it clear that he had recognized the "complete correctness" of these criticisms.[55] The tone and format of the biographies of the younger leaders was different, in giving a detailed account of their youthful formation, political careers, and ideological preparation, as in the case of Longo.[56] Everyone seemed to know well what aspects, moments, and names had to be avoided or underlined in order to fit in with the Stalinist canon, whose aim was to obliterate the memory of having belonged to the socialist world, but also to make amends for or to cancel the differences and dissents of the previous decade in the communist movement. In this way, there was unleashed a formidable mechanism of self-discipline and self-censorship.

At the same time, the narrative of the existential choice annulled the boundaries between the private and political spheres, combining between them elements of a religious order with the vocabulary of modernity, destined to leave a long trail in the practices and imaginations of the communists.[57] The very notion of a "professional revolutionary" implied a control over the emotions and a strict vigilance over private life, even among the militants who had had their internationalist apprenticeship in the Lenin School.[58] The experience of a younger figure than Longo, like Giorgio Amendola, was completely different. Amendola, coming from a family of the high bourgeoisie, the son of one of the most prominent personalities of liberal antifascism, joined the party as late as 1929, only to be arrested three years later. Under the influence of Emilio Sereni—the two were born in the same year—he became a member of what in his view was the most consistent antifascist force. Reconstructing his biography years after becoming a member, however, he accented the fact that the party was "internationalist, therefore strong through the influence (and the indispensable discipline) of a great world movement." In particular, Amendola recalled having read Togliatti's report on the colonial question at the Sixth Congress, which he saw as one more reason for a differentiation from the social democracies of the time.[59] Internationalism continued to be a unifying characteristic, and a constitutive factor of identity and of the communist "imagined community," even for those who had never been to Moscow.

ANTIFASCISM AS INTERNATIONALISM

Through Stalin's forced modernization, the Soviet Union raised itself to the level of a socialist power in a world thrown into turmoil by the Great Depression. In communist eyes, this new chapter of the revolutionary mythology made the horrendous human cost of the "revolution from above" and the collectivization of the countryside negligible. These upheavals were inserted into the narrative of a necessary "second revolution" imposed by a class and anticapitalist logic, but also by the perceived threats of an imminent counterrevolutionary war. The end of the gigantic and violent transformation of Soviet society coincided with the dramatic change in the European scenario caused by Hitler's rise to power in 1933. This event could justify the methods used by Stalin to build Soviet power and strengthen the idea that fascism constituted the authentic destiny of liberal and democratic capitalism. All this exalted the Soviet state's universal and redemptive mission, whose propaganda expression would be found in the 1936 Constitution.[60]

All the communists, apart from a small number of dissidents excluded from the movement at the end of the 1920s, shared a similar vision of the future, composed of mechanical laws and catastrophic prophecies. Under this aspect, the leading groups were bound even more than before to a political faith that, by definition, did not concede any benefit of the doubt and yielded an unconditional investiture to the figure of the leader. Their messianism made it possible to see in the sphere of politics the privileged realm of the highest cynicism, as long as it was subordinated to a fatalistic conception of history that materialized in the power of the state.[61] Gramsci alluded to a similar conception, and branded it with the term "statolatry" in his prison writings. Togliatti instead adopted it, accepting the primacy of Soviet power. Both believed in the "construction of socialism" in Russia, and shared this faith with all the other leaders, cadres, and simple militants as a spiritual support for the hardships of prison or exile. But Gramsci saw in Stalin's modernization a primitive phase of an "economic-corporative" nature, and asked himself about its future in the light of the violent rupture of relations between city and countryside.[62] This was a problematic vision that was inadmissible from 1928 onward in the communist movement, and was destined for future generations. Unlike Gramsci, Togliatti avoided constructing mythologies about the Soviet Union. His references to the "construction of socialism" were always concise and essential, even if they fully adhered to Stalin's "revolution from above." Probably he was of the opinion that the strength of the Soviet myth was gifted with its own proof and capacity for reproduction. His writings took it for granted, and limit themselves to the sphere of politics.

Stalinist state-centrism fed off a formidable factor of persuasion, that is to say "capitalist encirclement" and its presumed or real threat to the existence of the Soviet Union. From the start of his stay in Moscow in 1926, Togliatti had witnessed the escalation of the perception of an external threat in the leading group of the Bolsheviks. This was the condition for assimilating a code that had not belonged to the Italian communists: a reading of international relations under the sign of the doctrine of the inevitability of war. More than once, Stalin made it clear that "capitalist encirclement" was not only a geopolitical notion but a class strategy applied to international politics irrespectively by all the main powers. It is probable that Togliatti accepted more for reasons of opportunity than out of conviction this doctrine of the inevitability of war, whose importance for the Soviet state he well understood. It is an observed fact that he applied it in numerous of his writings from 1929 onward, fully assuming responsibility for it together with the leaders in exile in Paris. From his polemic with Tasca at the Tenth Plenum, he presented the danger of war as incumbent and directed against the Soviet Union, expressing in the wake of Stalin the prophecy of a war of the capitalist world united against Bolshevism.[63] This code would long exert its influence even in the attempts to dissociate from it some years later. He went as far as reneging on the subject of the "struggle for peace" which he had unsuccessfully proposed in 1927, criticizing the opening of the French and German communists toward the campaign against the war conceived by Münzenberg, who in the course of 1932 had involved personalities of the caliber of Henri Barbusse and Romain Rolland.[64] At this point, the elements of distinction that the Italian communists had developed were reduced to a minimum. Togliatti's insistence against the analogies between the German and the Italian situations defended an element of past analyses, but at the price of expressing a mistaken prophecy on Germany, as he himself had later to recognize.

Hitler's rise to power had the immediate effect of increasing the conviction, not only in international communist circles, that war was inevitable. It was easy to foresee that the days of the Versailles system were numbered, and that by now a slope was forming that would slide Europe and the world into a second catastrophe. Like many others, Togliatti asked himself not whether there would be a new great war, but "where this war would be fought, when, by whom, and against whom."[65] In this context he emphasized afresh the role of Italian Fascism as the instigator of war, precisely through its nature of a "weak imperialism," directed toward destabilizing the international system. For the communists, the scenario of the inevitability of war constituted an unchallengeable doctrine, and also implied an interpretation of the coming to power of Hitler as a possible prologue to revolution. Togliatti contributed to fueling the fatal illusion that, unlike that of the German Social Democratic Party (SPD), the KPD's role would be that of a mass mobilizer in the Germany of 1933 and that, had it been up to such a task, it would have exploded the contradictions of the nascent dictatorship. He pronounced words of confidence regarding Germany, in the light of the "construction of socialism" in the Soviet Union, even at the Thirteenth Plenum of the ECCI in November 1933. In February 1934, following Stalin's perspective, he saw in the bloody repression of the workers' demonstrations in Vienna the announcement of the outbreak of a war between the imperialist powers, under the pressure of the fascistization of Europe. In his view, even the workers' and democratic protests then taking place against the fascist threat in France were an insufficient counterweight, and "to hope that the march of fascism [could be] halted by the armed resistance of the 'democratic' State," as the liberal-socialist leaders of Giustizia e Libertà did, would be a "pure reactionary utopia."[66]

This was one of the most shortsighted judgments that Togliatti made in his political career. It was precisely the repression in Vienna and the simultaneous popular demonstration in Paris against the danger of the right that were a turning point for the birth of a transnational antifascist space. The threat that Nazism represented in Germany imposed a political response that could not be reduced to prophecies of war. In the course of 1934 the communists liquidated the theory of "social fascism," even though they did not make amends for their contribution to the rise of Hitler, and they joined the antifascist arena in an attempt to construct a new legitimation in Europe after the failure of the world revolution. Stalin encouraged and brought under control the antifascist change. He favored the new policy and at the same time defined its boundaries. The Comintern no longer had pride of place in his priorities. However, his presence made itself more than felt in 1934, and he gave back a role to international communism, linked to the foreign policy of the Soviet Union. His choice as head of the Comintern was Dimitrov, the Bulgarian communist who had survived and emerged from the Leipzig trial, where he had defended himself brilliantly from the Nazi accusations of having set fire to the Reichstag in March 1933. Dimitrov arrived in Moscow at the end of February 1934 famous in Europe as an antifascist hero. Stalin met him little more than a month later and invited him to take on the responsibility of leadership, harshly criticizing the leaders who had formed the "quartet" which from 1929 had been blindly loyal to him (Pyatnitsky, Manuilsky, Kuusinen, and Knorin).[67]

Togliatti took part in orienting the Comintern in a much more direct fashion than he had done at the end of the previous decade. Dimitrov immediately co-opted him into the leading group that was being reconstructed under his leadership. The name of Togliatti appears for the first time in Dimitrov's *Diary* on 27 May 1934, when he was inserted among those who were to give reports at the imminent Seventh Congress, together with Pieck, Manuilsky, Wang Ming, and Pollitt.[68] Evidently, his choice represented a recognition of the role being played in the analysis of fascism by the Italian leader, whom he had met in Berlin. Togliatti arrived in Moscow a few months later, probably in August. In his first intervention at the Comintern on 29 August, he asserted that it was necessary to draw up a "balance of the fascist dictatorship in Germany and in Italy," and that on this basis the Comintern could "speak to the masses."[69] The main implication of these words was the invitation to leave behind illusions regarding the fragility and instability of Hitler's regime, illusions which had been nurtured in the past in the case of Mussolini. On this crucial point, Togliatti had something to teach the main participants in the debate on Nazism in the Comintern, such as Varga, Knorin, and Manuilsky, who were inclined to see in Hitler's dictatorship a transitory form of power subjected to the domination of finance capital. The great obstacle to overcome in order to effect a credible revision was the declaration approved in December 1933 at the Thirteenth Plenum of the Comintern Executive which codified fascism simply as a "terrorist dictatorship," the direct expression of finance capitalism, ignoring the analytical elaborations regarding its mass base that had been carried out in the 1920s. Paradoxically, fascism's breakthrough in an advanced capitalist society, which had been excluded by communist analyses at the time of the Weimar Republic, fueled a class scheme because it could be read as confirmation of the predominance of capitalist interests in the fascistization of Europe.

The meeting with Dimitrov restored a political orientation to Togliatti which he had lacked in the previous years. For a few months, the question of a new congress remained in suspension, but Stalin approved the antifascist political course in France, sanctioned by the action pact between communists and socialists in July 1934. Meanwhile, Togliatti assumed the role of Comintern emissary, going on missions to France and Belgium with the aim of verifying and orienting the new alliance policies of the left that were taking shape in the popular front. It is not clear whether he himself was persuaded by the possibility of unreservedly launching a similar political initiative, which saw Maurice Thorez and the French Communist Party (PCF) in the front line. However, on his return to Moscow at the end of the year, he devoted his energies to the preparation of the Congress and put at the center of his interventions the fight for "democratic rights" in countries under fascist dictatorship, and for their defense in the other European countries.[70]

Togliatti's "course on adversaries," a series of lessons held between January and April 1935 for Italian cadres, is collocated in this context. The course was part of the activity for cadre education and training, which from the beginning of the 1930s had undergone great expansion in the Stalinized Comintern and constituted an authentic system of "total pedagogy," aimed at discipline and ideological loyalty.[71] But Togliatti's analysis revealed the attempt to safeguard forms of critical surveillance, and allowed one to see to the work underway to circumvent dogmatic formulas and prepare the way for a political change. Without openly denying Stalin's 1933 formula, Togliatti constructed a more complex analytical framework regarding the relation between the popular masses and the Fascist regime, a foretaste of which was already contained in an article of his in the Comintern press. The conceptual sources for Togliatti's analysis may be traced to the elaborations made in common with Gramsci and Tasca in the 1920s. The basic point, as in the past, was to carry out a specific analysis of Italian

Fascism while adopting perspectives and categories with more general implications, which were becoming an indispensable element with the advent of Nazism in Germany. It is obvious that Togliatti's thought, albeit within the pedagogic code of the language employed, referred to the impact of World War I on mass politics and to the responses provided by the fascism and Bolshevism in Europe and in Russia. The 1933–34 analyses of Tasca, by now a fierce adversary of communism, were no different regarding the question of the relationship between the masses and fascism as subject of antiliberal modernity.[72] Togliatti, however, made a number of selective choices. He first of all rejected the category of Bonapartism, which in the meantime had been a starting point for the analysis of fascism developed by Gramsci in prison.[73] This distancing may be explained by the fact that the category of Bonapartism had been used by Trotsky, among others; and just for this reason the matter was becoming incandescent. The point, however, is that Togliatti was avoiding fixing his attention on categories dealing with defining the autonomy of the regime from the influence of all social classes.

Togliatti developed an attentive and clear analysis of the architecture and social bases of the Fascist regime as a form of modern mass politics that had the aim of making understood the complexity of the task of fighting against the dictatorship and for "democratic liberties."[74] In particular. he analyzed fascism's response to the Great Depression, as a passage from the "disorganization of the masses" and of class institutions to the choice of "leading the masses into its organizations" in order to broaden its own social bases. His analysis steered clear of a comparative dimension in Europe. In light of the rise of Hitler, Togliatti recognized it as an "error" to have thought that fascism was solely a "regime specific to countries of weakly developed capitalism," but he did not omit to underline once again the historical peculiarities of Italy, beginning with the fragility of the political organization of the bourgeoisie. He observed how National Socialism, unlike Fascism, had conquered mass bases already before taking power, and this had made it easier for its leaders to generate forms of "rebellion" "against the open dictatorship of the big bourgeoisie" and internecine struggles within the regime in rapid evolution, as had happened in the "night of the long knives."[75] But Togliatti went no further than this.

In the lectures, one may also note a mutual reflection between the Fascist state and the Bolshevik state in the new phase that opened after 1929.[76] If, however, the "course" did implicitly really bring together the experiences of Fascism and Stalinism under the profile of the state and the organization of the masses, it must be asked how little its author was aware, or reluctant to recognize, that the consensus around Mussolini or Hitler was much more extensive than the fairly limited one enjoyed by Stalin, especially after the war against the peasants and the mass deaths caused in the countryside by his regime.[77] This was a possible sign of the influence exerted even on Togliatti by the cult of personality, and the mythological narratives regarding the birth of a classless society in the Soviet Union. Certainly, Togliatti was extremely sparing in his use of the term "totalitarianism" itself, which lent itself to defining the mass organization of the Fascist regime, but also presented implications that were too open regarding the subjection of society in its entirety by the state. In this respect, Gramsci in prison was freer than Togliatti in applying the category of "Bonapartism" and totalitarianism even to Soviet reality.

Togliatti's interpretation of Hitler's rise to power can be reduced to the reading of Stalin: a defeat of the workers' movement, the responsibility for which was to be laid exclusively at the door of the social democrats. The consequences of the disaster in Germany, in his view, would lead to a broadening of the "front of antifascist struggle" in a series of European countries, and a thoroughgoing crisis of social democracy. There was foreshadowed in this passage the preparation of the Comintern's antifascist turn. Togliatti legitimized the perspective of defending democratic institutions against fascism, presenting it as a way of finally prevailing over social democracy. He utilized a scheme of antinomies based on the coupling reaction-restoration, and placed the emphasis on the dualism between fascism and communism in Europe. His approach in this regard was realist and did not hide the genuine state of the communist movement in Europe, which would have been able to confront fascism only by showing itself able to overcome its own "weaknesses" and win over the majority of the working class.[78]

Togliatti's vision excluded the role of other protagonists and presupposed that Soviet socialism and the communist movement were the sole vector of transformation in world politics. It is not difficult to see the distance of such a posing of the question—centered on the dichotomy between revolution and counterrevolution, and emblematic of the imagined "European civil war"—from the analysis that Gramsci in his prison devoted to the question of Americanism as the transformative phenomenon at the global level, intertwined with the influence of fascism in Europe, thus forging the category of "passive revolution."[79] The difference in the two visions does not connect back solely to the respective realities—distant from each other and noncommensurable—of the two protagonists, but also to divergent thematizations and hierarchies of meaning. In particular, the presence or absence of interrogatives regarding the Soviet Union, quite transparent in Gramsci and removed or censored in Togliatti, presented an evident reflection of augmenting or simplifying the complexity of the visions and analyses of the world order.

Gramsci's vision in prison and that of Togliatti at the Lenin School in Moscow for a long time would not enter into the cultural consciousness of the Italian communists, right up in fact to the postwar period and afterward. The juxtaposition between them makes sense above all for understanding the continuity and discontinuity between the two major personalities of the PCd'I, who for years had woven a common web but had unexpectedly found themselves in political conflict in 1926. That conflict was not reconciled but, on the contrary, widened over the succeeding years. The years of the "class against class" line and of "social fascism" had marked the moment of most radical divergence in the strategic conceptions, contributing to the marginalization of Gramsci and the final dissolution of the Italian leading group. This laceration bore its weight even after the antifascist turn had reassessed in real terms the reasons for the dissent of a few years previously. In this light, the historical analysis of the ruptures of the 1920s onward, including the cultural ones, gives the lie to the continuist self-representation constructed many years later by Togliatti himself, which long influenced historiography.[80] But most of all, it contributes to shedding light on a change of era and a fracture of the trajectories of the communist political elites between the two wars. The ideas and visions shared in common even by the most lucid and intellectually organized leaders, such as Togliatti, burned the bridges not merely through conceptions of the oppositions of the previous decade, but also through substantial components of a mental and conceptual universe that would be dissolved once and for all by the Great Terror. The absence of interrogatives concerning the road taken by the postrevolutionary regime in Russia did not merely constitute adherence to a conformist canon. With the liquidation of the political problem of the "construction of socialism" and of internationalism as hegemony, a political culture took final shape centered on the primacy of the socialist state, on discipline, and on self-censorship.

The antifascist period opened the way to some very serious rethinking, but those bridges can be reconstructed only with difficulty because of the sedimentation left by Stalinism. Some years later in 1938, from the spatial and temporal distance of internal exile, Terracini wrote a very eloquent letter to Grieco on this question. He did not hide his disappointment at the detached attitude of the party, and he recalled severely that those in internal exile were not "buried alive" but continued to cultivate politics as their sole passion ("They are not 'sportsmen' or just people curious about the revolutionary movement but dedicated militants who have devoted their life and sacrificed their freedom"). Terracini supported the antifascist turn, and recalled having been "classified among those in opposition" after 1929, together with Gramsci, above all for having refused the simple identification between fascism and capitalism. He complained that dealing "by conditional and indeterminate hints" of a subject like that "of the thought of Antonio about the policy of the Party over the course of the last decade" was continuing. He was not satisfied, however, in seeing the recognition of his own reasons, which he had continued to uphold in prison, but noted the limits of the political change. It was no surprise that the new line met with passive or visible opposition among leaders and cadres, he wrote, because "a wide-ranging self-criticism" was lacking, as was a clear distancing from previous positions.[81]

This conduct was a choice made by Stalin, who met with Dimitrov and Togliatti on 9 July 1935, on the eve of the Seventh Congress of the Comintern. In a letter to Molotov at the moment of the Congress, Stalin gave a positive judgment on it, noting that its work would be "even more interesting after the speeches of Dimitrov and Ercoli" on the tasks of the fight against fascism and the "struggle for peace" respectively.[82] It is obvious that this assessment expressed approval for the antifascist line but limited it to a change of tactics. Stalin had some time earlier warned Dimitrov to avoid critical references to the previous years, including the thesis of "social fascism."[83] The new aspect of the report consisted in the indication of fascism as the "main enemy" of the working-class movement and the Soviet Union, and in the invitation to carry out a differential analysis of the "capitalist world," aimed at underlining the differences between the fascist state and "bourgeois democracy."[84] The subject of the "struggle for peace," entrusted to Togliatti, was more controversial despite the obvious parallelism with the "collective security" foreign policy identified in the personality of the commissar for foreign affairs, Litvinov. It was easier to indicate in fascism the "main enemy,'" two years after the advent of Hitler and while the Italian aggression against Ethiopia was being announced, than it was to superimpose a "peaceful" language on that of the "international civil war," a move that had already showed itself a failure at the end of the 1920s.

Togliatti's analysis represented a cross-section of the world as seen from Moscow in the mid-1930s. He adopted a global vision that saw not only the end of the Versailles system in Europe but also that of the Washington system in the Pacific. In his vision, Nazism in Germany now foreshadowed a "Balkanized" Europe, Japanese militarism and the Italian war in Ethiopia put the question of an "indivisible peace" on a world scale, and the conflicts between the great powers could no longer be negotiated. Fascistization was the central phenomenon in this scenario, while the role of America was lodged within the Marxist-Leninist scheme of the "antagonism" between Great Britain and the United States. Togliatti implicitly regarded the meaning of the New Deal as unimportant, and downgraded to mere power politics the analysis of America's world role carried out by Gramsci and Tasca in the first post–World War I decade. He did not represent the contempt contained in the assessment of "Rooseveltism" expressed less than two years previously, when he had juxtaposed it with fascism on the political and ideological levels, but neither did he deny or modify it.[85]

Togliatti's language revealed not only his astuteness but also a basic contradiction between the doctrine of the inevitability of war and the politics of preventing it. He oscillated between two different registers. He indicated fascism and war as the sole outlet of capitalism in "putrefaction" within the shadow of the Great Depression while at the same time socialism was asserting itself in the Soviet Union. A catastrophic perspective was becoming widespread in European political and intellectual circles which went beyond the communist world, and which in Moscow presented highly stringent implications for doctrinal orthodoxy. He propounded a fight against catastrophism and a struggle for peace and the defense of the Soviet Union, using among other things the "contradictions" of the capitalist powers. The consequence of such an oscillation was that he was depicting the communist movement as a "great army which is fighting for peace" but presented the outcome of war as an unavoidable fact. He spoke of the "prevention of war" but maintained that the situation was one of a "second cycle of revolutions and wars". He posed the minimum objective of "delaying war" while making it evident that "in given circumstances even the avoidance of war is possible and attainable."[86] In other words, Togliatti was operating within the constraints of the theory of the inevitability of war, while seeking to hold out the prospect of a positive policy oriented toward the avoidance or spread of the conflict, which brought back into play his idea of the "fight for peace" going back to 1927. On this posing of the question there weighed the unresolved aporias of previous years and the constraints posed by Stalin, whose ultrarealism was by no means separate from an ideological conception of the world but, rather, presupposed precisely the prophecy of the inevitability of war.[87]

The constraints of Stalinist realpolitik emerged immediately after the Seventh Congress when, in a letter to Molotov and Kaganovich, Stalin rejected Litvinov's proposal to impose unilateral sanctions on Italy because of the nascent conflict in Ethiopia. In his view, the real conflict was not between Italy and Abyssinia (as it was then commonly known) but between Great Britain and Italy.[88] The question, as posed by Stalin, was separate from the subject of fascism and, together with London, contributed to the ineffectiveness of the intervention of the League of Nations. His vision regarding politics and power would also have a decisive influence on the communist movement. Notwithstanding this, the question of Fascist

Italy's war in Ethiopia precisely at that moment found a worldwide echo and became a testing ground for the birth of an antifascist and peace-oriented opinion in Europe.[89] Despite its anachronistic nature, Mussolini's war enterprise made European imperialism converge with colonialism in the form of Fascism. As a side effect, albeit for a limited temporal conjuncture, it allowed the Italian Communists to emerge from their marginalized position. The confirmation of the link they had established between Fascist revisionism and the danger of war favored an internationalist action, the first of any substance for many years. In a conference in Brussels in 1935, Grieco, together with the socialist Pietro Nenni, launched an appeal for resistance against war operations and prophesied the deep crisis of Fascism.[90] Togliatti called for caution and realism, hypothesizing, if anything, a gradual detachment of the masses from identification with the regime.[91] The successive mission of Velio Spano in Egypt did not give rise to significant consequences, though it did have the sense of linking European antifascism to anticolonialist feelings brought to the surface by Italy's invasion of Ethiopia.[92]

The Ethiopian question gave rise to an oscillation between the use of the anticapitalist motif and the question of "popular liberties" in the propaganda directed toward the country and to the Fascists themselves. This dual register emerged in the first half of 1936. The defeatism outlook was predominant in the Comintern, together with the idea of appealing to the material conditions of the Italian population, which the war would have worsened instead of resolving—an argument whose reference point lay in the failed realization of the Fascist program of 1919. In his lectures to the Italian cadre forces in March 1936, Togliatti argued that the Italian Communists should gather the popular material aspirations but direct them to the question of democracy, since "for us the problem of freedom is not an expedient." This posing of the question constituted in his view a necessary updating of the Lyon Theses, which he returned to quoting. Still more insistently than in the "Course on our Adversaries" of a year earlier, the typescript that summarized Togliatti's interventions reported the need for a struggle "for a democratic Italy" and to articulate a program of "democratic demands," since "at the moment when the masses begin to move, they move to fight for freedom."[93]

When the empire was proclaimed in May 1936, the question of Ethiopia had already lost some of its cutting edge for mobilizing antifascist opinion in Europe, which had turned to the threat represented by German rearmament in the Rhineland. Hitler represented a more than sufficient reason for strengthening the Eurocentric optic that from the start had distinguished the communist interpretation of the conflict in Ethiopia, though its global repercussions were amplified instead in the colonial world, particularly in the pan-African movements.[94] The hope placed by the Italian Communist leaders in a political and military fiasco that could destabilize the Fascist regime was frustrated. They maintained the contradictory idea of promoting an "anticapitalist and democratic movement" which superposed two motifs in mutual conflict and gave credit to the demagogy of the original program of Fascism. The result was an "appeal to our brothers in black shirts," approved by Togliatti himself, which used the watchword of "national reconciliation" at the moment of Mussolini's triumph, and was harshly criticized by the other antifascists. The document also implied, however, a realization of the mass bases of the regime, and a vision of the Popular Front in a national framework.[95]

INTERNATIONALISM AND TERROR

The Seventh Congress did not mark a U-turn in the tendency to downgrade the Comintern that had started in 1929. Choices and decisions continued to be the result of informal meetings and personal relationships more than the exercise of institutional activity. The leading group represented a centralized and sectoralized oligarchy, with intermittent channels of communication with the central sphere of Soviet power. The foreign communist leaders' custom of frequenting and interacting with the members of the Politburo no longer existed, not to mention the possibility of openly expressing one's own opinions. The political elites of the Soviet state formed an inaccessible circle, and the Comintern apparatus became a bureaucracy closely integrated with and subordinate to Soviet apparatuses, beginning with political police. A dense curtain of secretiveness had fallen on all the activities of the communists, governed by rigorous rules of "conspiracy" in the relations between center and periphery, not only where the parties were clandestine. In this sense, the cosmopolitan environment of the 1920s was a far-off memory. The foreign communist community in Moscow, increased due to the wave of political immigration from Germany, was a transnational presence in a mistrustful and hostile environment. The practice of internationalist hospitality had by now been terminated and the system of controls over foreign citizens had become far more stringent, meaning for some that they had to take out Soviet citizenship, and leading to the dissolution of the clubs and schools of the emigrants. Shortly after the murder of Sergei Kirov in December 1934, the increase in persecution against the former or presumed oppositionists would involve all levels of the Comintern. Political emigration circles were explicitly indicated as a possible channel of infiltration for espionage activity. Antifascist internationalism and the wave of terror in the Soviet Union thus underwent an intertwining and a short-circuiting.[96]

Togliatti found himself involved through his role as vice-secretary of the Comintern, entrusted with supervising the most sensitive area: that of Germany and the Central European countries.[97] The idea of governing the "periphery" of the parties from the center contributed to fueling a spiral of tensions, given that the principle of loyalty and respect for hierarchies did not stop the local leaders from following visions and strategies that were incoherent or discordant with the desires expressed in Moscow. The "struggle against Trotskyism" now figured as a central task of the entire organization and was embarking on a dangerous path. In December 1935, Togliatti held a lecture for teachers of the International Leninist School centered on the importance of this struggle for the political training of the cadres.[98] In this circumstance, he made a distinction between "Trotskyism" in the Soviet Union, where it was regarded as the fight against the "counterrevolution," and that in other countries, where it threatened only the formulation of a "correct policy" freed from residues of social democracy. In this way, Togliatti was probably trying to keep at a distance from the Comintern circles the policing practices that elsewhere were widely present. But this type of distinction was fated to show itself untenable within the space of a few months. Togliatti also indicated the correct way to refer to Stalin by harshly criticizing the review by Otto Bauer of Boris Souvarine's biography of the Soviet dictator, because it introduced a comparison between Stalin and the "fascist leaders." This was being done naïvely he remarked, by recent émigrés to the Soviet Union, not understanding that Stalin was giving a correct political and ideological orientation, not only as the architect of Soviet modernization but as leader of the international communist movement. It is obvious that Togliatti was not only praising Stalin, but depicting him in a light that he himself considered as conforming to reality. Under this aspect, his vision of Stalin was identical to that of Dimitrov.

The personalities of Dimitrov and Togliatti stood out in the leading group of the Comintern for their effort to open up a political perspective, even if their influence was limited above all by Manuilsky and by Mikhail Moskvin, the latter an agent of the political police. The two Comintern leaders interpreted antifascism as a form of political realism, which considered the defense of peace as a question of priority, rejecting fatalism and the perception that the international crisis unleashed by Nazi Germany was inevitably a prelude to a repeat of 1914. The idea that such a repetition was inevitable continued, however, to weigh enormously on the mentality and visions of the political elites in Moscow. The subject of the "fight for peace" came over immediately in concrete terms at the moment of the Rhineland crisis in March 1936. Togliatti then supported the idea of sanctions against Germany with the aim of containing Hitler. He opposed "fatalism," arguing that "on the basis of the relations of force in Europe" there were the conditions for the "prevention of war."[99] In short, he was proclaiming the watchword of the "maintenance of peace" as the strategic task of the communist movement, while conveying to the Italian cadres, as we have seen, the suggestion of the defense of democracy.[100] His viewpoint showed itself to be in the minority. The leading group of the Comintern continued to issue generic denunciations of the "war danger" which ignored the fragile innovations of the Seventh Congress. Togliatti and Dimitrov's attempt to present the "struggle for peace" as a revolutionary objective foundered with the outbreak of the Spanish Civil War in July 1936.

The war in Spain immediately came over as the testing ground for a mass antifascist mobilization, which up to that time had not really been promoted but only invoked. The failure of Weimar experience was turned into success. The main task for the communists was the defense of the republic. Dimitrov agreed with Stalin on the first instructions for the Spanish communists, which ordered them not to go beyond "the struggle for a genuine democratic republic,"[101] an orientation which remained a fixed point in communist policy. Dimitrov and Togliatti justified it by arguing the idea that the Civil War would generate a "democracy of a new type" and an "antifascist state," not a 1917-style revolution. Togliatti explained that the Spanish Republic could not be reduced to "a common type of bourgeois democratic republic," since it was being forged in the "fire of a civil war" in which the working class was becoming the "leading part" and was being born in a historical era whose protagonists were fascism "in a series of capitalist countries" and socialism in the Soviet Union.[102] This vision introduced into communist language a notion that was different from liberal democracy, then experiencing its darkest hour, and also from the Soviet model, although this latter remained the lodestar.

Dimitrov and Togliatti sought to define the role of the communist movement as protagonist of a policy supporting "collective security" and indicating practicable political goals, downplaying the anachronistic theme of the "dictatorship of the proletariat." They were aware that the watchwords of a "struggle for peace" and a "people's democracy," necessary for expanding the influence of communism, contained the premises for a revision of concepts. The former watchword implied the possibility of stopping the outbreak of a war, and therefore the abandonment of the theory that wars were inevitable and that civil wars were the aim of the revolutionaries, while the latter shed doubt on the unique nature of the state form created by Bolshevism and the universal nature of the Soviet experience. Neither revision was really developed, however. On this question, it is not difficult to agree with Eric Hobsbawm that the problem of the relation between antifascism and socialism in communist thinking should remain there, and that the "fog surrounding the debate on this question will never be lifted."[103] The same may be said for the relation between antifascism and war in the 1930s. As Giuliano Procacci has noted, even after the Seventh Congress the doctrine of the inevitability of war remained a constraint that was incompatible with the possibility of asserting unambiguously the goal of preventing conflicts.[104] The language used by Togliatti and Dimitrov could not constitute a reform of communist cultural policy, but its ambiguity did make sense. It allowed the justification of an internationalist mobilization of communists within the political space of European antifascism.

Communist antifascism thus had many faces; it was at the same time a form of political realism and an identity superposed on the classist and anti-imperialist tradition. Antifascist mobilization in Spain created a widely shared raison d'être, though with different implications as to its ultimate objectives. The internationalization of war imposed by Hitler and Mussolini soon created a unifying experience of feelings and belonging, experienced as a redemption for the illusions and the defeats of the post–World War I era and as a promise for the future, whatever the outcome of the struggle taking place. The communists were fully involved in a similar melting pot, from the "professional revolutionaries" to the simple combat fighters, even though not all shared the same romantic impulse. They felt the sense of being connected to a world movement that gravitated around the Soviet Union, but which had ramifications everywhere, as was shown by the International Brigade volunteers. The mythologies surrounding the Russian Revolution had an influence even on noncommunist combatants and were fueled by a considerable military, political, and cultural presence on the Republican side. The languages of internationalist propaganda even found a reflection in the private letters of the combatants.[105] After the disappointments of the Ethiopian War, the Italian antifascist militants found new motivations in the conflict with fascism, which reached its climax in the battle of Guadalajara, and in the armed conflict between Italians on the two opposite sides. Among the communists the question of "fraternization" then substituted that of "reconciliation," thereby proposing a national idea that was clear and consistent with antifascist internationalism.[106]

Spain was not, however, a laboratory capable of removing fractures that had been consolidated over time. It gave a formidable impetus toward coalescing the antifascists but did not cancel the divisions among them, fueled above all by the state interests of the Soviet Union and by the international fallout of the Great Terror. The antifascist mobilization was based on the refusal to sacrifice the struggle in Spain on the altar of diplomatic agreements, especially in light of the fragility of the "nonintervention" pact signed by the European powers and also by Moscow. Dimitrov pursued the aim of obtaining recognition for the international nature of the challenge represented by Spain, clearly in the conviction that a Republican victory would consolidate the prestige of the communists and the strength of antifascism in Europe. This position was opposed to that of Litvinov, who argued that it was necessary to end intervention in order to reestablish the conditions for a credible diplomatic initiative by the USSR. Stalin chose a third alternative. The Soviet Union supported the Republic without, however, abandoning the "nonintervention" pact, a two-sided policy whose inspiration was the logic of keeping hands free and of not being tied down by choices that were too binding. It was precisely the war in Spain that induced Stalin to see the dangers more than the advantages of a coherent antifascist orientation, namely a break with the Western powers and a possible collision with Nazi Germany. The first signal of this vision appeared in a conversation of his with Dimitrov, Togliatti, and André Marty, the head of the International Brigades, on 14 March 1937. They considered the option of dismantling the International Brigades in case of an understanding among the European powers on the withdrawal of foreign forces from Spain.[107] The dead hand of power politics would weigh heavily on the whole experience of communist internationalism in Spain.

It is probable that in this circumstance they considered the idea of sending Togliatti on a mission to Spain, which he himself had proposed to Dimitrov in November 1936. Dimitrov considered it unwise, and suggested that Togliatti go to Paris to speak with Thorez and Jacques Duclos, but without crossing the Spanish frontier. Togliatti went to Paris only in June 1937, and his mission to Valencia began about two months later. Dimitrov wrote to the Spanish communist leader, José Díaz, that Togliatti would be with him for a long time. Togliatti found himself in an ambiguous position in that he had neither legal status nor precise directives, while his presence became immediately known in antifascist circles. He complained of this to Dimitrov, but such was Stalin's wish.[108] Togliatti's aim right from the start was to consolidate the alliances of the Popular Front, so he proposed to dispense with Victorio Codovilla, then the Comintern representative, and to put a limit on Marty, head of the International Brigades, both of whom in his view were inclined to militarist methods. He himself trusted ruthless coworkers such as Vittorio Vidali—"Comandante Carlos"—a symbolic figure of the "professional revolutionary" and the protagonist of cruel purges in Spain as a close collaborator of the Soviet military advisers.[109] However, Togliatti did not identify with the militarized ethos that widely pervaded the militant armed experience. This was true, above all, in the case of Luigi Longo, who became the emblematic figure of internationalist solidarity and strategic leadership in the International Brigades.[110] Togliatti maintained a more political profile, responding to Soviet interests and to the choice of moderation made from the start by Stalin in opting for the defense of republican democracy. It is certainly not by chance that among Togliatti's numerous pseudonyms of that time, on top of the classic "Ercoli" and "Alfredo," there also figured "Kautsky," a self-ironic reference to the firmest opponent of Lenin in international socialism. Without ever appearing publicly, he was a highly important figure of influence in the republican context, as shown by his constant presence in top-level meetings, confirmed by his work diaries.[111]

Among Togliatti's tasks were the aim of isolating the "Trotskyists" in Spain who on the whole were identified with the Workers' Party of Marxist Unity (POUM) of Andrés Nin, a cosmopolitan figure of a militant in the Soviet Union in the 1920s and a supporter of Trotsky until his expulsion from the country in 1929. Nin's assassination in Barcelona in June 1937, probably commissioned by the Soviet emissary Aleksandr Orlov, resulted in a once-and-for-all rift between the communists and the radical left.[112] By this time the Comintern was already involved in the throes of the Great Terror, and the "fight against Trotskyism" had taken a ruthless turn. Togliatti himself had made a report on the question in September 1936, immediately after the trials mounted against the former opposition in Moscow, which ended with a serious accusation against the German communists, among those most heavily hit by the purges.[113] In a February 1937 conversation with Dimitrov, Stalin irreversibly crossed a threshold by accusing the Comintern of being a nest of spies. The main leaders of the Stalinized Comintern of the early 1930s were arrested, and over the next few months the political and human community of the Cominternist leaders housed at Moscow's Lux Hotel was torn apart and dispersed. The repressions quickly acquired a mass character, fueled by xenophobia, and struck a vast area of cadres and émigré communities.[114]

Dimitrov's *Diary* shows that he approved and underwent the basic motivations of the essential characteristics of Stalinism, even if he probably did not share all the consequences and feared being a victim of them himself. There is no reason to believe that Togliatti's thoughts were any different. He had, among other things, entrusted Vidali with developing the question of the "fifth column," a formula that alluded to the conspiracy against the Republic in Spain but also against the Soviet regime, in a series of articles in the latter half of 1937, which contributed to the reputation of "Comandante Carlos" as a sworn enemy of the Trotskyists.[115] Togliatti's mission to Spain allowed him to escape the darkest and, for his safety, the most dangerous phase of the Terror, even if it did not absolve him from further responsibilities. But it made him live to the utmost extent the contradiction that had now opened up between internationalism and the xenophobic direction being taken by Stalin's regime, which was inclined to see in antifascism and cosmopolitanism a reason for suspicion much more than a virtue. He was a figure at the crossroads of that destructive tension. He remained an éminence grise of the Republic right up to the end, undertaking a constant role in the anti-Trotskyist witch hunt.[116] This did not stop him from making autonomous political judgments, as for example in February 1938, when pronouncing in favor of participation in the Negrín government, going against Stalin's directives. Togliatti allayed matters by sending Stalin a telegram that took note of the Soviet leader's counsel as a spur to essential reflection; even the Spanish party then acted differently.[117] This was not a secondary question. Stalin's preoccupation with avoiding any possible friction with the Western powers had already caused the French communists to withdraw from the Popular Front government in May 1936. Togliatti insisted at length, like Dimitrov, that there should be increased recruitment by the International Brigades, but in the end he had to accept the logic of disengagement dictated by Soviet security interests. Upon temporarily going back to Moscow in August 1938, he took part in a meeting with Dimitrov, Manuilsky, Moskvin, and the Spanish communists which ratified the withdrawal of the Brigades from Spain.[118]

At that selfsame moment, Togliatti found himself involved in a new chapter of the Terror with regard to the Polish communists. He signed the act of dissolution of the Polish Communist Party, whose leading group had been decimated by the purges. In that sort of climate the fate of the Italian communists was precariously balanced. The Foreign Center in Paris had never had the status of an authentic leading group in exile, but as an operating nucleus under the command of Togliatti, who was simultaneously acting as leader of the Comintern. From 1934 onward this mode of organization began to lose out, despite the new injection of confidence from the French Popular Front. The Parisian leaders, without Togliatti's mediation, found themselves exposed to Moscow's criticism while the attempts to organize an underground network in Italy were to a large extent unsuccessful. In March 1937 the leaders were put under surveillance at the arrival in Paris of the Comintern plenipotentiary, Giuseppe Berti, an exponent of the younger generation of Stalinist communists. Berti had replaced Grieco as representative of the PCd'I in the Comintern in 1930, and from 1932 onward he had divided his activity between Paris and Moscow. In completion of his inquisitorial task, he presented a final report containing very serious judgments on the workings of the entire Paris group, and in particular on Grieco.[119] In April 1938, a PCd'I delegation arrived in Moscow to respond to accusations that were similar to those which in the previous months had already caused the arrest and violent repression of the leaders of other parties, namely violation of the rules of conspiracy, a lack of "revolutionary vigilance," and culpable inefficiency in regard to the "fight against Trotskyism." In the absence of Togliatti, Berti took measures equivalent to putting the leading group under strict control, and on 14 June 1938 Manuilsky formally charged the Italian party with inadequacy. This was the nth chapter of an infinite story that many times had seen Manuilsky in the role of inquisitor, but this time it was a possible prelude to a violent repression.[120] In August, the Parisian Foreign Center was dissolved, but the presence of Togliatti ensured that the Italian leaders were not dispersed to the four winds. The leading group of the PCd'I thereby avoided the tragic end of the Italian émigrés in the Soviet Union, who were decimated by violent purges; and perhaps it was the leading group's salvation that aggravated the émigrés' fate.[121]

Among the central elements in the investigation threatening the Italian leading group was Gramsci's letter of 14 October 1926, in which from an internationalist stance he had criticized the leading group around Stalin no less than the Trotskyist opposition. The highly controversial nature of the document, which was evident from the first moment and which remained in memory as a clear sign of the dissent that marked Gramsci in prison, was becoming a very dangerous precedent. And Tasca had thought well to refresh everyone's memory by publishing the letter in April 1938 in France. Manuilsky had read the document when it arrived in Moscow, and was certainly aware of its publication by Tasca. In his accusation he did not omit citing it.[122] A year earlier, Togliatti had celebrated the memory of Gramsci immediately after his death, paying homage to him with a tribute that aimed at consecrating him as a symbol, and which at the same time established a red thread of continuity, with the goal of dispersing shadows and dissent.[123] The operation was not fully successful, even though it laid the basis for a construction of the communist identity in the longer term. In the Moscow of 1938, the spectre of Gramsci returned to threaten unwelcome contiguities with the demon of "Trotskyism." By then, it was no longer only former oppositionists, or their suspected sympathizers dating back to the 1920s, who were now branded as Trotskyists, for the term had undergone an arbitrary and uncontrollable semantic expansion. The most disparate, even mutually contradictory, accusations could be molded and manipulated according to the circumstances by using any antecedent whatsoever that offered its flank to the suspicion of a plot, independently of its real or presumed political ends. In other words, this was a spiral with no decipherable code, destabilizing the architecture of communist identities that had been constructed over time, in a mixture of rational logics and indisputable beliefs, forcing everyone into an excess of blind obedience.

On 26 August 1938, Togliatti had a meeting with Stella Blagoeva, Dimitrov's secretary and the endpoint of the police apparatuses at the top levels of the Comintern. Blagoeva's notes relating to the "opinion of comrade Ercoli" contain her personal and political judgments on the leaders of the Foreign Center. In essence, Togliatti recognized that the center had shown itself incapable of observing the rules of "vigilance," but avoided drawing more general conclusions. At the same time, however, he exempted himself from past or future responsibilities, adding clearly that his political advice had not been accepted by the PCd'I leaders, and making it explicit that they should not count on him.[124] In this way Togliatti defended the leading group from more serious dangers, while his line of conduct also had the sense of a personal defense. In the previous few months there had been at least a sinister signal of the possibility that the crisis between Moscow and the PCd'I could hit not only the Paris Center but also himself; this was the arrest in March 1938 of his brother-in-law Paolo Robotti. Although Togliatti was involved in the affairs of the PCd'I more as a leader of the Comintern than as being the directly interested party, this sort of situation urged the most extreme caution.

He forced himself to bring attention back to the matters of political importance by indicating, in essence, two orientations that were characteristic of an antifascist inspiration: to remain firmly on the "line of the Seventh Congress" and not to ignore "the differences in the bourgeois camp regarding foreign policy."[125] These positions expressed once more the link between Togliatti and Dimitrov and a clear difference with Manuilsky, who had ignored the subject of antifascism in his accusation against the PCd'I. Togliatti argued his own vision in his report on the Fascist regime, made in Moscow on 23 August to the organs of the Comintern. His analysis took up again the elements of the "course on our adversaries" held in 1935, while also providing points for an understanding of the international conjuncture. The main point was that the *Anschluss*, Germany's forcible annexation of Austria a few months earlier, and the consequent "descent of Hitler on the Brenner" constituted the "grossest national question that has presented itself since the end of the Great War." In Togliatti's view, this was giving rise to "anti-Hitler tendencies" in Fascism, in opposition to the pro-Hitlerite ones that were dominant within the regime, as well as to a widespread unease most of all among Catholics, and it meant it was possible to mount an agitation "for national independence" against the policies of the Rome-Berlin Axis.[126] The situation of the Italian leading group was, however, totally inadequate for realizing this political inspiration.

The tendency of the Italian Communists to make amends for their past culminated in the proposal to Togliatti to make a public criticism of Gramsci's 1926 letter. Togliatti's reply was clear in its opposition: "It is not advisable to use this method to speak of all these things of the past. It would be an error to tie down the future life of the party on this basis. Things that happened in the past cannot be canceled; they remain. But one cannot tie things of the future to these."[127] Words of this type expressed a much greater astuteness than had been shown up to then by the other leaders of the PCd'I, and a consciousness of the infernal mechanisms of the Stalinist purges. The position of Togliatti and the other Italian leaders remained precarious, however, and their profile emerged considerably weakened from the Terror, even though there were no worse consequences. A letter written to Togliatti two years later by Armando Cocchi, the founder with Gramsci of the Italian "Émigrés' Club" in 1923 and a person who then joined the ranks of the Red Amy, furnishes dramatic evidence of the climate of the era. Cocchi confided to Togliatti that during the period of his arrest, from August 1938 to January 1939, "they wanted to convince me that you had been arrested and shot," but that he had refused to sign a confession written in advance. After his release, he had drawn up a memorandum for the PCd'I representative at the Comintern, Rigoletto Martini, protesting his innocence and faith in the party, but had lacked the courage to send it off. Now he sent it to Togliatti and was happy to know that he was alive, after having seen Togliatti's signature on a document of the Comintern in the press.[128]

THE END OF THE PCD'I

A short while later, the war in Spain came to its tragic end for the Republicans. Being well aware of Moscow's withdrawal, Togliatti worked for a defense of the Spanish Republic even after the fall of Barcelona, but without supporting a defense at all costs. At the end of February he telegraphed Moscow from Madrid, asking for instructions regarding the possibility of the communists' "forcibly taking" all the levers of power and the "direction of the war," with the aim of preventing a mutiny of the military and the collapse of the government. Dimitrov's reply was that the conditions for further Soviet military assistance were lacking. Before going to France after the military coup against the Republic and the catastrophic outcome of the Civil War, on 12 March Togliatti wrote a letter from Valencia to the Spanish leaders accusing Negrín of treason, but recognizing that the Communist Party had lost the confidence of the masses. The letter was delivered to Stalin by Dimitrov a month later.[129]

The weight of the defeat in Spain was of such import as to involve the ruin of the protagonists. On his return to the Soviet Union in June 1939, Togliatti found a voluminous and threatening dossier of accusations and suspicions hanging over his head, which would hold him in a viselike grip for two years until the outbreak of war. The main problem was his role in the epilogue to the Spanish Civil War. On 7 April 1939, Stalin in person criticized the lack of a strategy and the Spanish communists' retreat without a fight, which obviously brought in the responsibilities of the Comintern. The dictator rejected Togliatti's retrospective argument regarding the impossibility of opening a front to overthrow the counterrevolutionary junta in Madrid, holding up as a model the tactics, successful according to him, that he himself had employed at Tsaritsyn during the Russian Civil War.[130] In May 1939 Manuilsky wrote a letter to Stalin in which he accused Togliatti of having kept hidden the loss of the Spanish Party archives. This was a serious accusation, equivalent to shedding doubt on Ercoli's capacity for "vigilance" in the demobilization following the end of the Civil War.[131] At the same time, there hung over Togliatti the still open enquiries relative to the ideological reliability of the Italian leading group and the "Gramsci question." Between April and June 1939, Robotti was repeatedly interrogated by the Narodny Komissariat Vnutrennikh Del (People's Commissariat of Internal Affairs, or NKVD) with the intention of extorting details that could be used for charges.[132] Togliatti found himself involved in an investigation of Blagoeva's, consequent on the accusation by Yulya Schucht and her sisters at the end of 1938 regarding responsibility for the lack of success in freeing the prisoner.[133] Immediately sent to France by Dimitrov, Togliatti avoided the consequences of this situation, though many problems were merely put off until his return.

Stalin's decision in favor of the pact with Hitler, signed on 23 August 1939, liquidated in just a few days the antifascist internationalist experience of the communists. Stalin's attachment to the Soviet policy of "collective security" had ended with the fall of Litvinov, replaced by Molotov in May 1939. Stalin went for the option of unilateral security, maintaining that Hitler's recognition of Moscow's sphere of influence in Eastern Europe, above all the partition of Poland, was a concrete and useful fact in view of the possibility of a future war. He saw the pact as the authentic recognition of the Soviet Union's status as a great power, as well as the application of the Bolshevik line of dividing the "capitalist front" by avoiding the mortal danger of an anti-Soviet war of the imperialist states. At the beginning of September 1939, immediately after the German invasion of Poland and the outbreak of World War II, he dictated to Dimitrov the lessons that had to be drawn from the events: namely, the end of the opposition between democracies and fascisms as the criterion of political orientation, and the relaunching of the undifferentiated vision of the capitalist world, dating back to the pre-Hitler era.[134] Dimitrov reluctantly fell into line, abandoning the naive hope of being able to maintain a distinction between the line of the Comintern and the strategy of the Soviet Union.

The effects of the pact were disastrous for all the European communists, first in France. Togliatti, on a par with Thorez, deluded himself for a few days that it was possible to safeguard the antifascist line, as Celeste Negarville would recall three years later in his diary.[135] His arrest in Paris on 1 September contributed to increasing the disorientation. The exiles found themselves at a loss and without any bearings, above all at the moment when the PCF had been outlawed and Thorez had to leave the country. A "total dissolution" resulted, as Amendola recalled.[136] Some top-ranking leaders dissented, Giuseppe Di Vittorio being a case in point. Di Vittorio was immediately marginalized, though he was a particularly authoritative figure, protagonist of a unique combination of long trade union activity, bringing him to the leadership of the Italian General Confederation of Labor (Confederazione Generale Italiana del Lavoro, CGIL) in exile, and to an internationalist experience in Paris, in Moscow, and in the International Brigades in Spain, right up to editorship of *La voce degli italiani*, the journal of the antifascist émigrés in France. Camilla Ravera and Terracini too, in internal exile on the prison island of Ventotene, rejected the cancellation of the distinction between democracies and fascisms, upheld by Scoccimaro and Secchia. In a memorandum written in the autumn of 1941, Terracini confirmed and argued his positions, maintaining that the choices made by the Comintern after the pact were the expressions of an "extremism" which saw the Soviet state "once again elevate itself to a position looking down on the undifferentiated world of imperialism" when instead its enemy remained Nazi Germany.[137] In consequence, he was expelled from the party, probably with the agreement of Longo, who was also a confinee after his arrest in France. In hindsight, Terracini recalled it as the concluding episode of a dissent dating back to the "turn" of ten years previous.[138]

After the start of the war, the Foreign Center of the PCd'I was transferred from Paris to New York, under the leadership of Berti. The circumstances surrounding this change remained unclear and were never fully clarified. Togliatti considered Berti the main person responsible for his arrest, being marked with "almost criminal negligence," as he wrote to Dimitrov in March 1940 after coming out of prison.[139] The decision to shift the Foreign Center to New York was in any case made in Moscow. At the beginning of June 1940, in a meeting with Dimitrov, Blagoeva noted that the financial resources with which Berti had been provided served to cover nearly a year's work, and that the change was confirmed. Such information was conveyed to the secretary of the US Communist Party, Earl Browder.[140] The dispersion of the leading nucleus was completed after the Nazi attack on France. Leaders such as Amendola, Dozza, and Sereni were transferred to the south of Vichy France, while Togliatti and Grieco returned to the Soviet Union. Togliatti fell into line with the politics of undifferentiated anti-imperialism in his *Lettere di Spartaco* (*Spartacus Letters*), though he was sceptical about whether the pact between the Soviet Union and Germany would be long-lasting.[141] His identification with the antifascist line during the previous years had been a reason for personal exposure at the height of the alliance between Stalin and Hitler.

The enquiries hanging over Togliatti remained open. Shortly after his return to Moscow, a note of Blagoeva's repeated that a dossier of suspicions still surrounded him. In particular, the note reported the judgment of the Schucht family on him, as well as mentioning Gramsci's letter of 1926 and Togliatti's "uncertainties" in 1929. In December 1940, Gramsci's widow wrote a letter to Stalin containing the definitive and most serious accusation against Togliatti, considered guilty of treason. Stalin referred the question to Dimitrov, who took on the task of finding a reconciliation and avoiding police measures.[142] At the same time, Dimitrov urged Togliatti and Vincenzo Bianco to write about the situation in Italy and on Mussolini's war in the light of the military disaster in Greece, maintaining that not enough had appeared in the Comintern press.[143] Rather than a reproof, this was a sign of attention, which was a prelude to taking on again in the Comintern the joint analysis of Germany and Italy, which had been made at the beginning of 1941. In the *Lettere di Spartaco* an article appeared taking up again the reason for the possible destabilization of the regime, going back to the war in Ethiopia; but it looked at the "antifascists or a-fascists" who could be activated in the country through the first military defeats.[144]

Dimitrov involved Togliatti in a number of strategic decisions, such as the choice of interrupting the link between the Comintern and the US Communist Party, with the aim of avoiding its being outlawed, and the correction of the French Communist Party line of compromise between Paris and Vichy.[145] But above all, on 21 April 1941 Dimitrov brought to Togliatti and Thorez's attention the question of the possible dissolution of the Comintern, posed the day before by Stalin, with the invitation to follow the example of the US party in order to better root the parties in their own countries, maintaining their identity but "not with their look turned toward Moscow." Togliatti and Thorez expressed their agreement with the idea of putting an end to the activity of the Executive and substituting it with "an information organ of political and ideological support for the communist parties."[146] In other words, the question of the relation with the nation, posed by the Popular Fronts, had not been canceled by the Molotov-Ribbentrop Pact but, rather, was artificially separated from antifascism, as was evident in the case of France.[147] The "deradicalization" itself of the aims of the movement, limited to the defense of republican institutions in Spain and to the national revolution in China, was an overall direction remaining substantially unchanged. Even the silence that had fallen in Stalin's post-1934 speeches regarding the notion of world revolution was not interrupted, and instead implied a negative judgment on the strategic perspective of the civil war in Europe from the time of Lenin onward. This continuity represented a card to be played by figures like Togliatti or Thorez, even if the question of the end of the Comintern remained suspended and for a time had no followup.

The day after the German invasion of the Soviet Union, on 22 June 1941, Dimitrov formed a "permanent leadership of the Comintern" with Manuilsky and Togliatti.[148] The announcement of an immediate return to national and antifascist watchwords was a much more congenial terrain for Togliatti. This notwithstanding, he was equally equally to a veritable misfortune which seems even to have attacked his relation with Dimitrov. The shadows hanging over him regarding the Spanish question had never been dispersed. The Spanish leaders began once more to fuel suspicions immediately after the outbreak of war. Díaz let Dimitrov know, through Blagoeva, that he no longer had confidence in Togliatti. On 19 July he repeated this assessment, together with Dolores Ibárruri, who went one step further in her assertion that in Togliatti she discerned "something extraneous, not belonging to us." Dimitrov noted the decision to exclude Togliatti from taking part in "strictly secret questions."[149] In effect, Togliatti ceased to exercise the role he had played from 1935 onward as a top-ranking leader of the Comintern, while the Italian leading group, or what remained of it, was dispersed and divided.

The leaders of the PCd'I had failed in their tenaciously pursued objective of building significant contacts within the country; they were torn apart by personal conflicts, but had fortunately found themselves outside the sphere of the purges. The ransom sought in the internationalist struggle had given rise to moments of exaltation, but in the end was resolved in a burning defeat. After the start of the war, the PCd'I leaders were in essence a rootless group, detached from the reality of Italy. Antonio Roasio recalls how in France, then under Nazism, they were a "small shipwrecked group, at the mercy of the fury of the waves," perceived as double enemies through their political and national identity.[150] But others were also destined to marginal positions and repression in the "socialist fatherland," including the veterans from the Spanish war. The pact between Stalin and Hitler had declassed the protagonists of the Popular Front in Moscow as elsewhere. The anguish on account of this reality, which involved even the private sphere of the "professional revolutionaries," is well illustrated in the diary that Negarville kept in occupied Paris and in the constant thoughts he sent in letters to his loved ones living in Moscow.[151]

The personal balance sheet covering more than a decade was for Togliatti very controversial. He had followed Stalin in the name of realism, only to find himself totally disoriented by the extreme consequences of the "revolution from above." He had reluctantly fallen into line with the ultraradical theses of the Stalinized Comintern on "social fascism," but had also suffered its effects: the liquidation of personalities like Gramsci and Tasca, and the setting aside of the essential part of the intellectual heritage constructed in the 1920s. He had found his redemption in the role undertaken at the time of the antifascist conversion of the Comintern, and had provided a contribution in ideas to the analysis of fascism, to the "struggle for peace," and to "antifascist democracy." But in Spain he had followed both the line of the Popular Front and that of the politics of persecuting "Trotskyism," strongly divisive of antifascist internationalism. On the eve of war, Togliatti's position seemed threatened by various sources of tension and police-type investigations, which, as in a distorting mirror, reflected the ambiguities of his choices and responsibilities. Among these there continued to figure the question of Gramsci, full of personal, political, and symbolic implications. After Gramsci's death, Togliatti was involved in covering up the dissent and in depicting him as the head of Italian communism, with the goal of deflecting from the party any threatening suspicions, but also constructing a source of mythology. He now knew that his old comrade had rebelled against the ritual of sacrifice in the name of the higher interest of the party, and had reached the point of suspecting Togliatti of having abandoned him to his tragic fate.

Under the pressure of the investigation that had sprung from this and was still pending, Togliatti read the notebooks Gramsci had written in prison, which had reached Moscow in 1938 while he was in Spain. On 25 April 1941 he informed Dimitrov that he had studied "almost all of them scrupulously." He expressed his opposition to leaving a copy of Gramsci's manuscripts with the family, since they contained "materials which may be used only after carefully re-elaborating them," in the absence of which "the material cannot be utilized and [. . .], should certain parts be used in the form in which they are currently found, [. . .] could turn out not to be useful to the party."[152] Togliatti sought to turn the disagreement with the Schucht family to his advantage, using the well-tried argument of political and ideological control, if not actually censorship. The allusion to the inconvenient nature of Gramsci's writings was highly transparent, however cautious Togliatti's language was. Togliatti was well acquainted with the narrow confines of what was legitimate in the Soviet Union. And yet it is precisely his argumentation that reveals his awareness of both the heterodox nature and the value of Gramsci's writings. That material reconnected him with an intellectual heritage and an analytical way of thinking that certainly were not alien to him, though their original political meaning was by now lost.

A similar duplicity of material, between Stalinist political culture and the Gramscian legacy, would reemerge years later in historical conditions that were different and incapable of being predicted on the eve of war. We may easily argue, however, that the duplicity was evident to Togliatti from that moment. Italian communism had known defeats analogous to those of the other European parties without being able to boast authentic moments of glory—unlike the French and Spanish parties. There remained the first origins of an intellectual heritage that no other communist movement possessed in Europe and which, at the world level in highly different circumstances and languages, perhaps only the Chinese communists had more recently accumulated under the leadership of Mao Zedong. Like all the communist leaders after the Nazi German attack on the Soviet Union, Togliatti was free to thematize the question of the nation, with the difference that his cultural instruments were decidedly more solid than those of the others. Now that Hitler's war on the Eastern Front prefigured the possibility of a redemption, the visions, analyses, and identities bound up with antifascism were an essential resource.

PART TWO **INFLUENCES**

Internationalism and the Nation, 1943–64

3
THE "NEW PARTY" AND THE COLD WAR

THE "NATIONALIZATION" OF THE COMMUNISTS

The dissolution of the Comintern in June 1943 was the prologue to a mass dimension that was unprecedented for many communist parties. A new legitimization emerged from the combination of the Soviet war against Hitler and the efficacy of the national and anti-imperialist appeal on a global level. The interaction between the Red Army's counteroffensive after Stalingrad and the growth of antifascist resistance movements favored the recruitment of a new generation of young communists. Their internationalism no longer needed a "world party of revolution," because it combined with a national mission imposed by the struggle against fascism, and handled with self-assurance the concepts of class and nation. At this point, the words and meanings of the internationalist vocabulary had changed. Stalin had not performed a simply cosmetic operation when in May 1943, in support of the decision to dissolve the Comintern, he claimed that it was necessary to prevent enemies from presenting communists as "agents of a foreign state," and to strengthen the parties as "national workers' parties," thus consolidating "the internationalism of the popular masses, whose base is the Soviet Union." The idea of "nationalizing" communist parties was not a rhetorical but a political project, which made use of lessons learned from the Comintern's failures.[1]

Togliatti's role must be understood in this context. In propaganda operations promoted after the Nazi invasion of the Soviet Union, initially from Moscow and then, after the evacuation of the Comintern apparatus, from Ufa in central Asia, he had, like everyone else, used the language of "national unity," adapting it to Italy's history and culture. This propaganda, which also targeted Italian prisoners and the soldiers of the Fascist army that had invaded the Soviet Union, began to show plausible efficacy, with Mussolini's war effort showing signs of crisis, popular discontent, and the turn in the war brought about by the battle of Stalingrad. In a letter to Vincenzo Bianco in February 1943, Togliatti supported a punitive line toward Italy, in the hope that the Anglo-Americans would be welcomed as liberators despite the bombing of Italian cities. He portrayed the hard lesson of the invading army's rout in Russia as a necessary moment of awareness, going so far as to display cruel indifference to the tragic destiny of Italian prisoners. He is thought to have discussed with Stalin the use of prisoners to form an armed antifascist contingent, but that did not happen. Togliatti participated in the decision to dissolve the Comintern in June 1943, knowing well that Stalin had proposed a similar operation two years earlier, with almost identical motivations about strengthening parties' national rootedness.[2]

The Italian Communists were among those who benefited most from the events of 1943, despite their lack at the start of any strong popular rootedness, their long period of illegality in the recent past, and the influence left on society by Fascist anticommunism. There were multiple reasons behind their upturn, but they can only be understood in the light of the profound discontinuity which took place in Italian history between the fall of Fascism on 25 July and the armistice on 8 September. The collapse of the state; the territorial split between the South, liberated by the Anglo-Americans, and the North, invaded by Nazi Germany; and the new eruption of mass politics channeled by the Resistance and by antifascists against Nazism and Mussolini's collaborationist republic—all of these marked a point of no return. For the first time in the history of united Italy, wrote Claudio Pavone, "Italians lived, under various forms, an experience of mass disobedience," which presented implications of freedom amid the country's disintegration.[3] Institutional breakdown, fractured territorial integrity, and the outbreak of civil war created extreme fluidity and social and existential uncertainty, which impacted the forms and the very foundations of authority, giving rise to a need for new individual and collective structures of meaning.[4] In this context, it is difficult to overestimate the international conjuncture that in some ways made Italy a laboratory for the final phase of the war in Europe. The collapse of Italy also meant the elimination of a border between the national and the international dimensions. The presence on Italian territory of the Nazi and Anglo-American armies suggested radically opposite models for the postwar period, easily decipherable even by an exhausted civilian population that had fallen back on a day-to-day defense of its survival. Gradually, the material and symbolic influence of the Allied great powers, including the Soviet Union, imposed itself, alongside the Catholic Church, as a factor for order and a promise of reconstruction, interacting in controversial ways with the mobilization of resistance.

The end of the Fascist regime in Italy suddenly forced Communists and antifascists to transform their appeals into a policy. The events of the war thus put Togliatti in a unique position. He was the first European communist leader, in his Moscow exile, to formulate the lines of a concrete national policy for the postwar period. Togliatti wrote to Dimitrov immediately after the fall of Mussolini, on 27 and 30 June 1943, to solicit his own return to Italy. He had already outlined a prospective policy: abdication of the king, formation of a provisional government to "restore democratic freedoms," and convocation of a Constituent Assembly. However, he thought it would be wrong to seek a head-on confrontation with the monarchy, despite its responsibility for the catastrophe caused by the Fascist regime.[5] Thus, immediately after the dissolution of the Comintern, the formulation of a national policy became a real fact and not just rhetoric for the Italian Communists. Togliatti had to wait a long time, however, for a response from the highest Soviet authorities. On 14 October, after the Italian declaration of war on Germany and on the eve of the Moscow Conference between the Allied Powers' foreign ministers, he protested openly about the fact that the question of his return to Italy had not been solved. He also solicited a decision regarding the question of the Italian Communists participating in the Badoglio government. In his opinion, in case of an official invitation from Badoglio himself, it would be difficult for the Italian Communists to justify a refusal.[6] In other words, Togliatti proposed a translation of the "national fronts" theme into the choice of a moderate policy of cooperation with all the forces that intended to combat Nazism and Fascism.

The Moscow Conference, in October and November 1943, saw the Soviets assume a strong position that went beyond the principle of eradicating Fascism as the fundamental objective of Allied policy in Italy, as stated in the final declaration. They insisted on the creation of an Allied advisory council on Italy, with headquarters in Algiers. Moscow expected to exert its influence in the country via this organism, to which Andrei Vyshinsky, a high-level personality and Molotov's deputy, was nominated, with a view for the "reorganization" of the Badoglio government "via the inclusion within it of representatives of antifascist groups."[7] This position was fully consonant with that expressed by Togliatti. On 2 November, he wrote to Manuilsky that his continued stay in Moscow was against "the interests of my party and our general interests, and makes no sense."[8] He also sent him the names of a "small group of activists" for whom he requested a immediate return to Italy. Besides his own name, there were those of Grieco, Bianco, Edoardo D'Onofrio, Teresa Mondini, and Rita Montagnana. It was not the nucleus of a leading group, either past or future, but rather the sign of an urgency concerning the personality of the leader.[9]

The reconstruction of a leading group was yet to be achieved after the disintegration of the previous fifteen years; and it was to happen, as before the war, by co-optation under Togliatti's leadership.[10] The diaspora of Communist leaders caused by the war would be only partially reunited. The Foreign Center, reconstituted in New York under the direction of Berti and Ambrogio Donini, had kept *Lo stato operaio* alive, distributing it among the Italian communities even in Latin America. Togliatti was in contact with the Foreign Center.[11] But the New York group had no claim to the political leadership under reconstruction. Very different was the importance of the Communist leaders who had been released from prison or had returned from exile in France—like Scoccimarro and Amendola, who in the autumn of 1943 led the party's first moves in the South and in Rome, and Longo and Secchia, who in the Resistance in the North explicitly referred to the model of the Spanish war and performed a crucial function of leadership and organization of the liberation movement.[12] These two centers highlighted the vitality of the Communists vis-à-vis the challenge facing all antifascists, that of entering into contact with the real country; but they also risked entering into conflict with each other, as in fact they did.[13] In any case, the Italian Communists very soon presented themselves as an extremely important force in the Resistance, placing themselves within the already outlined global tendency, whereby the communist parties were protagonists almost everywhere in Europe and Asia thanks to their militarized ethos, their traditions of clandestinity, and their ability to make the sense of national liberation their own.[14]

In the speech he gave on 26 November 1943 at the Trade Union headquarters, Togliatti established the essential points of the political line to be followed, as they had emerged from the Moscow Declaration: postponement of the institutional question until the end of the war, with a proposal to convoke a Constituent Assembly, and the focus on the unity of the nation and of the democratic forces. These coordinates were in the spirit of the first encounter between the three great powers, which took place in Tehran a few days later, and inaugurated the scenario of the antifascist coalition. However, the effective application of this line was subordinated to a complicated political game that commenced between Soviet diplomacy and the antifascists in Italy.

The Kremlin's decision to send Vyshinsky to Italy in December 1943 and January 1944, immediately after the Tehran meeting, sent the clearest of signals regarding the importance of the competition in which the great powers had engaged in the country. The position reached by Vyshinsky after his meetings with local Communists who took part in the Committee of National Liberation (CLN) in the South—Velio Spano and Eugenio Reale—and with the general secretary of the Italian Ministry of Foreign Affairs, Renato Prunas, is known to us now via a letter the Soviet emissary sent to Molotov from Algiers. Vyshinsky thought Italy was clearly passing under the influence of Great Britain—despite, in his opinion, the preference for the Americans expressed by "the Italian powers"—and that this would strengthen the monarchy, thus limiting the actions of the left. He therefore judged it necessary to "ensure our influence within the Committee of National Liberation."[15] In a nutshell, Vyshinsky suggested not a diplomatic move by the Soviet Union toward the Badoglio government, but the exercise of influence on the country via the Communist Party's role within the CLN. Thus Vyshinsky's diplomatic mission was interwoven with Communist policy options, seriously influencing them.

On 24 January 1944, Dimitrov wrote to Molotov, submitting a "draft reply to the Italian comrades," which he had written with Togliatti. Dimitrov was already aware of the information transmitted by Vyshinsky after his meetings in Southern Italy. The document called for the antimonarchist stance to be maintained, and excluded participation in the Badoglio government.[16] This position liquidated the collaborative opening put forward earlier by Togliatti, accepted the intransigent positions of the local Communists, and followed the idea of consolidating Communist influence in the CLN, as suggested by Vyshinsky. Molotov approved the document a few days later, on 29 January.[17] Thus, the intransigent option was encouraged by the head of Soviet diplomacy, who was also the personality closest to Stalin. A month later, under the supervision of Dimitrov and Manuilsky, Togliatti drew up a document "on the present tasks of the Italian Communists," which accepted this intransigent policy line. Its essential points were the proposal to form a "provisional democratic government" led by Sforza, the demand for the king to abdicate, the refusal to take part in the Badoglio government, unity of the antifascist forces represented in the CLN, and a Constituent Assembly.[18] The document was written after Vyshinsky had returned to Moscow and had met with Stalin and Molotov. We can therefore conclude that, contrary to what has been claimed more than once, Vyshinsky's mission opened no prospects for a diplomatic agreement and indeed played an important part in determining a toughening of Moscow's position and an inversion of the tendency regarding the line of collaboration put forward in the final months of 1943.[19]

On 1 March, Dimitrov asked Molotov to receive Togliatti before the latter's departure, planned for 4 March 1944.[20] In reality, the meeting took place between Togliatti and Stalin, in the presence of Vyshinsky and Molotov, during the night of 3–4 March. The decisions made marked a new reversal of strategy. It was in fact decided to allow the Communists to take part in the Badoglio government, and to drop the demand for the king to abdicate. The motivations provided by Togliatti to Dimitrov the day after the meeting centered on the need to avoid a split in the camp of the forces opposed to Hitler and Mussolini and to hinder the influence of Great Britain. As Dimitrov wrote in his diary, "The existence of two camps (Badoglio–the king, and the antifascist parties) weakens the Ital[ian] people. This is advantageous for the English, who want a weak Italy in the Mediterranean Sea. If also in the future the struggle between these two camps continues, it will bring ruin upon the Italian people." On the basis of the information he had received from Togliatti, Dimitrov also noted that "the Communists can join the Badoglio government with the aims of pushing for an intensification of the fight against the Germans, proceeding with the democratization of the country and achieving the unity of the Italian people."[21] From this moment on, the influence of Italian communism was seen by the protagonists in both a national and a geopolitical perspective, as shown by the mention of the role of Italy in the Mediterranean with an anti-British function. In other words, the role of the Italian Communists was linked to the allocation of interests in Europe and the Mediterranean between the Soviet world and the capitalist world, in the context of new power relations. Their mission maintained this character, even in the multiple metamorphoses of the postwar period.

The meeting between Stalin and Togliatti marked a joint change of course in the strategy of the Soviet Union and the political line of the Communists, which to a great extent represented positions that had already emerged at the end of 1943. Until the last, all the protagonists oscillated between different options. Whether or not to collaborate with the Badoglio government depended on the Soviet decision about whether to intervene in the Italian theater via a politico-diplomatic initiative, or to react with an intransigent line against being marginalized, thus indulging the positions of the local Communists. In the end, Stalin decided for a collaborative orientation, choosing between two options that had both been delineated by Togliatti: the former by him alone, the latter under the influence of Vyshinsky and Molotov. This choice was consistent with the move of recognizing the Badoglio government and thus creating difficulties for the Anglo-Americans. It was probably also the choice most congenial to Togliatti, given the positions he had adopted autonomously in the final months of 1943.[22]

Togliatti found himself in a position of key responsibility, as the leader of the European communist party which before all the others had to formulate a concrete policy. The implications of the decision-making process that involved him went far beyond the Italian question, because they concerned the application of the "national fronts" formula, the visions for the reconstruction of Europe, and the nature of the relations to be established among the Allies in a postwar perspective. His return to Italy was to enable the function of European communist leaders exiled in Moscow, who were destined to benefit from an unquestionable investiture almost everywhere, with the exception of Yugoslavia and Greece, where the leadership was held by personalities linked to the experience of Resistance. Following Stalin's indications, Togliatti acted as pathbreaker for the realist line, which aimed at reining in the radicalism of local leaders of the national liberation movements. But he was also an interpreter endowed from the very beginning with his own vision of the dynamics between national and international policy, who cannot be seen as a mere enforcer of Stalin's directives.[23]

The declaration of willingness to enter the government, made by Togliatti at Salerno on 30 March 1944 immediately on his return to Italy, thus represented the launch of a strategy by the communists in Europe. As Stalin had suggested, in his public discourse Togliatti suppressed the nexus with the Soviet Union's strategy, but it was obvious to and well understood by both his followers and his adversaries. Benedetto Croce noted in his diary that the "Salerno turn" was "a skillful blow dealt by the Republic of the Soviets to the Anglo-Americans."[24] In Italy the consequences were immediate, leading to the formation of a new Badoglio government and the elimination of the antifascist camp's preliminary condition regarding abdication. Once the Communists were guaranteed participation in the coalition government and the question of the monarchy was momentarily set aside, the line to be followed could be subject to various interpretations: either as a tactical retreat in view of a revolutionary crisis and the breakup of the international coalition between the USSR and the Western powers or as a strategic choice aimed at a peaceful and democratic conquest of power with the intention of continuing the alliance when the war was over. Both positions were represented among European and Soviet leaders. During his first months in Italy, Togliatti sometimes seemed uncertain, and checked with Moscow regarding the limits to be respected when criticizing the Anglo-Americans. Moscow's response, agreed upon by Dimitrov and Manuilsky with Molotov at the beginning of June, was to continue to follow the line of broad antifascist alliances.[25]

In the last year of the war, Togliatti followed more and more strictly a strategy that aimed at maintaining national unity, avoiding a civil war, and ensuring that the Communists had an important government role for the first time in their history. The idea that a social revolution was not inevitable in Italy contradicted an opinion quite widely held even among Socialists and members of the Action Party. How to be "national" from this moment on created fault lines within the communist movement, running transversally across parties and leading groups. In this panorama, the "Salerno turn" and Togliatti's subsequent political action constituted a political model not limited to the conjuncture of the war. It implied an internationalist alternative to the revolutionary dreams cultivated on the model of the first postwar period, a search for influence linked to the new world role of the Soviet state, an attempt to establish the role of the Communists as a legitimate component of a national community to be reinvented after Fascism, and a version of mass politics oriented toward social integration.

In September 1944, however, the "national unity' line followed by Togliatti came under fire from the intransigent criticism of Aleksandr Bogomolov, the Soviet representative in Europe. Bogomolov accused the secretary of the newly renamed Italian Communist Party (PCI) of not having a political program aimed at mass mobilization, given the approaching end of the war.[26] Bogomolov's vision was not isolated. He was the mouthpiece for transnational radical tendencies in the communist movement, with their epicenter in the Yugoslav leading group under the guidance of Josip Broz Tito, but perhaps also with support from Moscow. At the same time, very similar sentiments were cultivated by the leaders of the Resistance in the North, such as Secchia, who had found the "Salerno turn" hard to digest and who, unlike Togliatti, saw the Italian war of liberation as fully in continuity with the "democracy of a new type" of the war in Spain.[27] Thus different visions emerged of the significance of the preponderance of power established by the Red Army in Eastern Europe after the summer of 1944: as the foretold prologue of a realistic allocation of spheres of influence among the allies, or as the possible beginning of a revolutionary escalation in the Balkans and Northern Italy.

In this context, Togliatti played a role that did not concern Italian politics alone. He maintained a long-distance understanding with Stalin, who was resolutely contrary to revolutionary actions in the countries under Anglo-American control, as they might have endangered the formation of the Soviet sphere of influence and relations with the Allied powers. In the meeting with Winston Churchill in October 1944 on the repartition of the spheres of influence in southeast Europe, Stalin reassured the British leader regarding the perspective of the Italian Communists, saying that Togliatti was not a politician who was inclined to take part in doomed "adventures."[28] The replacement of Bogomolov with Mikhail Kostylev as Soviet ambassador in Rome from October 1944, was a sign of Stalin's support for Togliatti. The latter declared that he was against the "class against class" line, for reasons that concerned the internal and international situation. His conduct showed a decisive opposition to the more intransigent tendencies, and rejection of any hypothesis of armed insurrection. He expressed himself in this sense, for example, in his meeting with Edvard Kardelj, one of Tito's principal collaborators, in October 1944.[29] He knew that Thorez would return to France from Moscow after having agreed with Stalin on a line of policy analogous to that established in the "Salerno turn," which already had been imagined in relation to the French situation.[30] In December 1944, Togliatti imposed on the leading group a clear option for the national unity line, warning that this choice also had international significance. In this way he blocked the intransigent tendencies represented explicitly by Scoccimarro, but which were present, though silent, in the party.[31]

Togliatti considered the continuation of the war alliance to be in the interest of the Soviet Union for its economic reconstruction, but also a requirement for eliminating the prewar isolation and sectarian character of a large number of communist parties—the legacy of a minority condition now to be consigned to the past. The collaborative international context was above all a condition for defining a profile of Italy embedded within the bipolar world and freed from the ambition to carry out power politics of its own, something one section of the country's leading class still desired. In this way, Togliatti combined the PCI's internationalist bond with the national profile that he had started to elaborate after 8 September 1943. This theme was not just pedagogy aimed at restraining the revolutionary potentialities of Resistance mobilization, as it is sometimes interpreted. Rather, it provided a code that was easily deciphered by all, connected with the messianic expectations of moral and social redemption that had been spread by the partisan struggle, and which wove together the theme of national redemption and the Soviet myth of the just society. The theme of internationalism as an antidote to nationalism and as an unrenounceable dimension for a country like Italy was to redefine the very meaning of the nation. Under this profile, Togliatti's vision belonged to a context of internationalist ideas broader than the communist one, the product of reactions to the catastrophe of nationalism and oriented by the prospect of profound social change.[32]

Togliatti did not go as far as Browder in seeing postwar political reconstruction as a renunciation of the Communist Party's centralism. He did not lay himself open to the fatal accusation leveled at the US Communist leader, first of all by Dimitrov and then publicly by Jacques Duclos, of abandoning class principles, thus transforming the party into a movement of opinion.[33] Indeed, Togliatti used the party form as an instrument for modernizing politics in Italy, modifying constitutive elements of Cominternist practices. At the time of the "Salerno turn," he announced that "our politics is a mass politics," with the objective of giving "new content" to the life of the nation, and accusing Fascist imperialism and the leading classes that had been accomplices of the regime of having been "antinational." The lesson Togliatti made his own was that "the nation [could not] limit itself to acknowledging the catastrophe and identifying those responsible," but had to find its "road to salvation." With a self-critical allusion to the part played by the Communists in the first postwar period, he claimed that "our duty is to indicate this road concretely and to direct the people toward it." Putting into practice this vision meant that "the character of our party must change profoundly," and that it was necessary to build a "mass party" and not just a "narrow association of propagandists of the ideas of communism and Marxism."[34] Two months later, after the liberation of Rome, Togliatti informed Dimitrov that the party was growing everywhere: a large proportion of party members consisted of religious believers, and there were many "Christian communists."[35] The "new party" project challenged the other forces that were protagonists of reconstruction, and in particular the Catholics, given that it presupposed respect for religious freedom. In principle, this implied a conception of the political nation which excluded only Fascists and thus was more inclusive than the conception prevalent in the official world of Catholicism, which inclined to exclude also communists.[36] This openness toward believers was closely linked to a strategy for involving women within a perspective of emancipation that had emerged during the Resistance experience, and aimed to broaden female participation in politics. Under this profile, the PCI contributed to an awakening of gender awareness that would go beyond the perimeter of the membership of parties and make itself independent of their control.[37] The "feminization" of politics had an impact on the sphere of democratic citizenship, though far less on the sphere of internationalism.

At the end of 1944, Togliatti's vision had definitively won acceptance within the leading group of the PCI. Its key international calling was fully embraced by Giancarlo Pajetta, who was a member of the directorate of the Comitato di Liberazione Nazionale Alta Italia (National Liberation Committee for Northern Italy, or CLNAI) and an exponent of the Resistance, alongside Longo and Secchia, who in the past had spent a short but intense period of activity in Moscow in the Youth Communist International before spending a decade in Fascist prisons.[38] Pajetta maintained that it would be wrong to imagine "the subsequent contraposition of two absolutely antithetic worlds: the democratic-Soviet world and the capitalist-imperialist world" and the idea of "zones of exclusive influence." For this reason he rejected "a simplistic conception" whose objective would be to "extend by a few square kilometers the surface directly and explicitly under the Soviet government."[39] This vision acknowledged the emergence of a bipolar order after the war, but placed the accent on interactions and not on antinomies. The birth of a bipolar world did not inevitably imply irreducible antagonism, as the Yugoslav leaders believed. This revealed an evident polemic against their expansive territorial ambitions. Even the most reluctant communists had to come to terms with Togliatti's vision. It presented an alternative to radical tendencies, and a way to provide a constructive channel for the ethic of sacrifice and for the enormous popular potential accumulated thanks to the struggle for liberation, thus avoiding a catastrophic destiny.

The political leadership of the insurrectional movement in the early months of 1945 met under the sign of such a vision of the postwar world.

However, the possibility of a worsening of the precarious domestic and international situation loomed. Conversations between the Italian Communist leaders and the Soviet ambassador revealed several times a concern that dramatic events might take place. The worst fear was that of a coup d'état and of the PCI being made illegal, although various opinions were expressed. Togliatti confided to Kostylev his fear that reactionary forces might move with the aim of a coup d'état on the Francoist model.[40] The Italian Communists hailed Yalta as a highly positive event, since it confirmed the coalition of the three great powers. But they also thought that the results of the conference might mobilize those who interpreted it as a Western concession to Stalin. Togliatti did not rule out the anticommunist forces provoking a conflict with the objective of destroying the organization of the PCI.[41] At the same time, the Trieste crisis severely tested the harmonious framework of the connection between the coalition of the great powers and the national identity of Italian Communists.

The question of Venezia Giulia had been the subject of a generic agreement between the Italian and Yugoslav communists in October 1944, which postponed the more delicate territorial questions until the end of the war. Togliatti met with Kardelj and Milovan Đilas (Djilas). He avoided taking any binding positions regarding Trieste, but probably underestimated Yugoslav ambitions. From the beginning of 1945, the obstinate behavior of the Yugoslav leaders forced him to appeal to Moscow to intervene as arbiter, insisting on the serious problem that an eventual de facto annexation would create for Italian communism as a credibly national force. Togliatti insisted on a solution with direct Italo-Yugoslav negotiations and the internationalization of Trieste, while acknowledging Yugoslav ambitions as legitimate.[42] Moscow took its time in replying to the questions raised by Rome, while Tito did not hide his annexationist intentions. A strong tension was thus created between the Italian and Yugoslav communists.

In the question of Trieste, an important role was played by Reale, who was performing a side-by-side activity with Togliatti in both party and government, where he held the position of undersecretary for foreign affairs. Coming from a tormented series of events, including incarceration and emigration to France, Reale had no prior Cominternist experience. Togliatti gave him a role with international responsibility in the context of the generational turnover within the PCI. At crucial times, he absolved a delicate function in relations with the Soviets. On 17 April 1945, Reale conveyed to Kostylev the concern of Togliatti about the risk of the Communists being isolated and a possible split in the party, alluding to the need to avoid a fait accompli in Trieste.[43] Moscow, however, maintained a wait-and-see attitude in its relations with the PCI even for some time after the Yugoslav occupation of Trieste, which started on 1 May. On 4 May, acting on orders from Togliatti, Reale asked Kostylev about the credibility of the rumor that Stalin had promised Trieste to Tito at their meeting in mid-April.[44] Clearly, the Italian Communists thought it was at least plausible. But at the Directorate meeting of 13 May, Togliatti reaffirmed that the PCI's line had not changed: "No acceptance of faits accomplis. Need for collaboration with Yugoslavia. Defend Italianness of Trieste, not compromise future of Trieste, respect will of Yugoslav populations."[45] In the meantime, Togliatti forwarded a new request for clarification to Dimitrov, and strongly criticized Tito's unilateral conduct, judged to be in contrast not only with the interests of the PCI but with those of the Soviet Union.[46]

In the end, Stalin accepted Dimitrov's proposal for the annexation of Trieste to Yugoslavia. Togliatti was informed with a message sent on 28 May.[47] On 31 May he met Kostylev and told him that only a short time earlier he had been in contact with Tito, and admitted that the port of Trieste would be more useful to Yugoslavia and the Danubian countries than to Italy—the same argument with which he had been informed of Stalin's decision.[48] In the meantime, the Yugoslav armies confirmed the most pessimistic predictions regarding the consequences of the occupation, initiating systematic terror actions and summary executions against the Italian population in Trieste, Dalmatia, and Venezia Giulia. This gave rise to an unsustainable situation for the national credibility of Italian communism, which could have jeopardized Togliatti's project. Not too paradoxically, it was Stalin who provided a solution. Realizing that Western reaction might provoke a conflict with unpredictable consequences, within a few days he changed his mind and withdrew his support for Tito's claims. In short, between the end of May and the beginning of June 1945, Stalin put the

Italian Communists before the fait accompli of his decision in favor of the Yugoslavs, and then withdrew the decision.

The Trieste incident thus highlighted how fragile the PCI's "nationalization" was within the ever-changing geopolitical dynamics at the end of the war. The relation between "national unity" in Italy and the interests of the Soviet Union, established a year earlier, remained standing, however, thanks to the unwritten principle of the spheres of influence, which Tito had attempted to violate. Shortly thereafter, at the beginning of August, Togliatti asserted at the Directorate that "relations between Yugoslavia and Russia will change," and he even went so far as to indicate the objective of "avoiding the risk of a war between Yugoslavia and Russia."[49] Such an extreme and surprising thesis was an eloquent sign of the lacerations perceived in the Trieste crisis. He foresaw a fracture destined to emerge spectacularly three years later. His was an implicit warning to hold onto the perspective of the unity of the "socialist camp" in formation, but it was also obvious that, should relations between the two states plunge dramatically, there was only one side the Italian Communists could choose. Sent to Moscow in August 1945 as the general secretary of CGIL to negotiate the distressing issue of prisoners of war, Di Vittorio presented Stalin with a proposal for mediation on Trieste, which envisaged a transitory status of autonomy to be negotiated between Italy and Yugoslavia. He took advantage of the occasion to praise the project of the mass party, which at that point already counted a million and a half members. He also restated the intention to avoid a drift toward a civil war like the one that had broken out in Greece, having in mind the elections for the Constituent Assembly, which were destined to be a "historical turning point."[50] The determination to continue in the spirit of Salerno became an essential deterrent to the rampant violence and vendetta killings which had occurred in various areas in the country after the end of the war, and which provided a glimpse of the dangers of a new civil war.

THE PROBLEM OF INTERNATIONAL AND NATIONAL "BLOCS"

In his speech at the Fifth Congress of the PCI on 29 December 1945, Togliatti illustrated his vision, which centered on the rejection of the "blocs" as the main interest of democratic Italy, and on the relevance of avoiding speculation about conflicts between the great powers. The rejection of Fascist power nationalism, with the aim of rethinking the country's place in the world, constituted the main perspective and the contribution of antifascism to defining the foundations of the national interest. In his opinion, however, this perspective was an objective yet to be achieved, not something already obtained. Italy's independence, he stated, "must be reconquered with slow, careful political action, navigating around numerous obstacles and dangers." The world order emerging in the postwar period did, in his opinion, allow engagement in such political action, because the age of empires—which at this point had reached "the critical moment of their existence"—was coming to an end.[51] Togliatti did not go into a detailed analysis of international politics, but the implications of this argument were important, as they alluded both to the predicted end of European colonial empires and to a crisis and transformation of the very idea of imperialism in the postwar world. The measured tone used by the Communists regarding the United States was linked to the construction of national credentials and even to an attempt to leave the door open to an appreciation of Roosevelt's legacy and "democratic capitalism."[52] The rejection of "blocs" as an Italian interest brought together the language of the Communists and that of the Christian Democrats, although with a different degree of internationalization in their respective visions. In the case of the Christian Democrats, the idea of keeping Italy out of a binary logic followed a neutralist inspiration that was very present in Catholic political culture, combining a universalist vocation with a moderate nationalism, while the international bond with the United States was still weak. Communists and Socialists followed the Soviet Union's collaborative strategy, in the hope that the spheres of influence would remain open.[53] The common denominator consisted of an awareness of the fragility of the nation's unitary fabric.

Togliatti renewed most of the leading group for the "new party" project, but also in the light of post-Cominternist internationalism. His choice was to promote, alongside the Longos and Secchias, the generation that by different routes had become antifascist and communist in the Thirties and in the Resistance, that was no less bound to the Soviet myth, and that was better disposed to connect "nationalization" with an up-to-date international vision. This was the logic that presided over the co-optation into the Directorate of figures such as Amendola, Pajetta and Sereni, who had intellectual personalities of their own. However the apparent consensus in the leading group of the PCI fragmented when confronted with the growing tensions between the Soviet Union and the Western allies after Stalin's speech of February 1946. Stalin appeared to belittle the role of the coalition by speaking of the "imperialist" character of World War II, while at Fulton the following month Churchill spoke of an "Iron Curtain" descending across Central and Eastern Europe. In April, Togliatti fell victim to a public attack by French communists that was not episodic and which marked a change of climate. In a strong letter to Thorez, defending the PCI's positions on the "essentially Italian character" of Trieste, he claimed to see the question of the eastern border and the "spheres" that existed in Europe differently from the "terrible schematism" of the Yugoslavs. It was his opinion that "spheres" existed in every country, "that is to say, democratic and reactionary forces struggling to get the better of each other." He believed that the game was not yet over in various European countries and the decisive "national" card would be compromised by a territorial and ideological conception of the "spheres of influence." Togliatti recalled that the Yugoslavs had manifested this vision from the end of 1944, thus infringing their agreement with the CLNAI, which had postponed the question of Trieste until the end of the war.[54] Under this profile, there was a reemergence of a transversal divergence of sensibility and inclinations within the European communist movement, which had remained below the surface during the final phase of the war but was now destined to deepen.

The success of the republic over the monarchy in the June 1946 referendum was a turning point that assigned primacy to the left in the division of the country into two political blocs delineated by the result of elections to the Constituent Assembly. The very idea of a republic was an essential part of the political capital of the antifascist left, which in the Resistance had kept alive the symbolism of the Spanish experience and filled the power vacuum that arose after 8 September.[55] Founding the republic was an outcome that Communists and Socialists had pursued with clarity in comparison to the moderate forces. Even though the topic was very controversial, the Communists could claim that the "Salerno turn," criticized for an excess of caution, was the origin of a weakening of the monarchist option; and they could affirm that they were the force that had contributed most intelligently to the founding of the republic. This notwithstanding, the electoral result, which listed the PCI as the third party behind the Christian Democracy and Socialist parties, gave rise to new polemics regarding Togliatti's strategy.

Secchia considered the result of the elections unsatisfactory. He expressed himself based on the logic of the "professional revolutionary" disappointed by the scant impact of the "wind from the north" after the end of the war, and drew strong attention to the discontent of the working class for the lack of a "more energetic struggle" against "the most reactionary section of the Christian Democracy party and the clergy," and for the concern that "within our party a sort of national-communism" might develop. His role as the person responsible for the party organization, a position that was central for the construction of the "new party," lent particular authority to his words. In national politics his power was only partially balanced by the presence of Amendola, a convinced supporter of the "Salerno turn."[56] Secchia did not limit himself to the electoral question, and at the same time he introduced an internationalist argumentation. "We are internationally isolated," he complained, since communist parties had "contrasting positions on a series of 'national' questions" and engaged in "polemics among themselves." In his opinion, "this is certainly not an element that is positive and favorable to us." Secchia used language very similar to that of the French and Yugoslavs, and it was not difficult to interpret it as a broadside against Togliatti.[57] The first fracture in the PCI's leading group in the postwar period thus immediately presented various implications regarding the international nexus. The respective visions of Togliatti and of Secchia presented themselves as two opposing paradigms, since Togliatti feared a separation between internationalism and the question of the nation, while Secchia invoked one.

Secchia was expressing a vision circulating among the leaderships of various communist parties that had never really digested the "nationalization" project after the dissolution of the Comintern. Nobody openly proposed the Comintern's reconstitution, but some, like the Hungarian

Rákosi, floated the idea of reorganizing the movement at the international level. At the beginning of 1946, Stalin and Tito discussed the constitution of a new organism of the international communist movement, different from the Comintern. In that circumstance, the two leaders appeared to liquidate the ill feelings left over from the Trieste crisis of the previous year. Stalin is even thought to have invested Tito with the role of his heir—expressing, among other things, a contemptuous judgment of Togliatti ("He's a theorist, a journalist, he writes a good article, he's a good comrade, but gather people together and 'guide' them, I think not").[58] Such a personal judgment might also have alluded to a negative assessment regarding the institutional and parliamentary priorities of the line followed by the Italian Communists. In other words, the transversal split of European communism between realists and radicals that emerged before the end of the war was still there, with the difference that Stalin seemed to shift the weight of his authority toward the latter after having sensed the probable collapse of relations with the Anglo-Americans. Togliatti could hardly look with favor upon the idea of a new international communist organization, given that it implied an antagonistic bipolar vision that set militant internationalist spirit in opposition to the project of the "nationalization" of the parties.

In parallel, concern reemerged regarding a destabilization of the political situation immediately after the outcome of the institutional referendum. Reale reported to Kostylev that Togliatti did not exclude a civil war breaking out, given the king's ambiguous attitude after the victory of the republic.[59] Expressing such a fear also fulfilled the function of confirming a moderate line and avoiding isolation. Togliatti's speech on 29 June to the parliamentary group elected to the Constituent Assembly followed this priority.[60] He predicted a "profound crisis" linked above all to the international situation. "Harsh peace conditions" were expected, with an obligation to "pay for fascism." Togliatti confirmed that it was necessary to explain to Italians that the country had avoided "the fate of Germany," but feared "a campaign of a nationalist and fascist type." The political point was, therefore, to pose the problem of "national independence" but prevent this formula from becoming the banner of reactionary forces. Abandoning the foreign policy of two years earlier had, in his opinion, deprived the country of the Soviet Union's support, leaving it "without international backing" and exposed to the strategies of Great Britain, which preferred a weak Italy so that it could "dominate the Mediterranean unopposed." Clearly, Togliatti was reproposing almost verbatim one of the main coordinates of his meeting with Stalin before the "Salerno turn." Times had changed, however, in part because of Stalin's choice. Togliatti cited the unresolved question of Trieste, for which he imagined an autonomous status "within an Italo-Yugoslav condominium." He avoided mentioning that Moscow supported Belgrade, as Molotov had clarified to Reale ten days earlier in Paris, thus frustrating the hopes of the Italian Communists of repeating the coup de théâtre of March 1944.[61] Togliatti's position was therefore more complicated than how he himself presented it. But in any case, he maintained the aim of a political agreement to enable coalition governments and the work of the Constituent Assembly to continue, even amid the increasing international difficulties.

In many ways, Togliatti's was not an obligatory choice but an option meditated in light of his experience in Italy, Germany, and Spain during the interwar years. More than once he had observed at close quarters the disastrous effects that using political violence and the bugbear of a "European civil war" had on projects of social emancipation. Seeking legitimization, he inserted the choice of "national unity" into a long sequence that had started at the time of the Popular Front, glossing over the fact that in the previous decade the attempt to "nationalize" European communist parties had finished dismally in France, under the shock of the pact between Stalin and Hitler. His political action actually reflected the profound discontinuity created by the war. Togliatti held onto the idea that Italy's slide into a national catastrophe in September 1943 had been the origin of its fundamental moral and political redemption, but that a second catastrophe of equal intensity would have destroyed it. The lesson of the Greek civil war, which broke out in December 1944, played a very serious role. Togliatti's bête noire became what he himself called the "Greek prospect"—that is, social conflicts turning into an armed struggle between the forces of the "antifascist front" and the army. Therefore, he saw the bipolar division into international blocs as a threat and not an opportunity, and imposed this vision on leaders and cadres who might have followed indications inspired by the nexus between war and revolution. He was aware that the interdependence of national and international politics would be accentuated in the postwar world, and that therefore the dynamic between the great powers was a decisive element in Italian politics.[62]

The nexus between the rejection of the "blocs" and Italy's interests was hard to contest, and was no monopoly of the Communists. Additionally, this vision made it possible to imagine hybrid and transitional modalities between capitalism and socialism. Togliatti's discourse on "progressive democracy" echoed the notion of "people's democracy" as a form of state distinct both from the Soviet model and from liberal democracy, legitimized by Stalin in Central and Eastern Europe on more than one occasion.[63] All communists were profoundly convinced of the "superiority" of the Soviet system over all forms of capitalism—an essential element of Stalinism which, in their eyes, had been totally confirmed during the war. Togliatti and his group were no exception. Their "progressive democracy" formula alluded, however, to the possibility of creating intersections and intermediate zones between the two dominant social systems, which the antifascism experience had enabled. A world order founded on the anti-Hitler coalition would be able to oversee postwar reconstruction and allow progressive economic and social choices in Europe, despite the existence of the spheres of influence. Italy was in a particularly suitable geopolitical position to benefit from such a perspective, which allowed the choices of a socialist transformation to be deferred to a future date.

However, the effort to combine the various aspects of the PCI's role was subjected to irreconcilable pressures. The failure to conclude peace on the German question put the theme of "blocs" at the center of international politics after the Paris Conference of the summer of 1946. Togliatti declared that "to accept the definition of competing blocs means already placing oneself in a certain sense on the terrain of an adversary, an enemy." The problem was not, in his judgment, that of the "two blocs," but that of two "conceptions of international politics," because "today, internationally, two blocs about to fight a war do not exist."[64] On this basis Togliatti devised the prospect of an Italian "autonomous international policy," which would have its say on the main questions regarding the European situation. But that implied the expectation of an active and benevolent policy of the Soviet Union toward Italy, which did not materialize for any of the most important aspects of the peace question, including that of Trieste. Indeed, the Soviet policy of manipulation, control, and repression in Central and Eastern Europe was contributing to a division into blocs, and revealed the influence of conceptions never abandoned, founded on an integrally classist vision of international politics.[65] In other words, Togliatti played his cards with his trust placed in an international stability that Stalin in reality did not believe entirely practicable. In this light, Togliatti's adverse visions of the antinomy between the two "worlds" could be likened to those of Litvinov. At this point, olding no official role and dissenting from Stalin's choices, Litvinov was convinced that the Soviet Union, after having won the war, was losing the peace, because the idea of an inevitable conflict between the communist world and the capitalist world was again becoming prevalent.[66] The Italian leader, however, had never had a vocation for dissent—more likely, one for dissimulation. Stalin took the spheres of influence more seriously than he did antifascist democracy. Togliatti consequently had to adapt, holding firm to the principle of loyalty without giving up his project of a "new party."

The decisive tesserae in the strategy inspired by the "Salerno turn" did not all fall into place. The national and the international elements of the initial strategy separated from each other as the spheres of influence consolidated. Yet the vision and practice followed by Togliatti up to that point had achieved unexpected results. The rejection of the Greek solution was not only a question of a more or less convincing strategy for all leaders and militants, but also the adoption of a legalitarian and parliamentary perspective. The vote for the Constituent Assembly of June 1946 was a decisive passage, because it assigned an institutional role to the Communists, making them the defenders of democratic citizenship and legitimizing them as components of the political nation. The "new party" was the engine behind this strategy. When the Italian Republic was founded, the PCI already exhibited the character of a very well-rooted mass organization, above all in those regions where the workers' and Socialist movements had traditionally been present in the early twentieth century. Even more than the slogan of an "Italian road" to socialism and a vague idea of "progressive democracy," it was this mass character, which aimed to penetrate the various strata of society without excessive vigilance over its ideological purity, that characterized Togliatti's project.[67]

The core of this project was the attempt to reconcile internationalism with the "nationalization" of the party. This implied the construction of an idea of a nation that embraced essential political legacies of Italian history.[68] After the war, Togliatti thus developed a discursive register that fitted into the national tradition, and at the same time, an alternative historical grammar addressed to the intellectuals and the people, emphasizing the role of the workers' movement in the rebirth of the democratic nation. The constituent moment filled with real meaning the narrative of a "second Risorgimento" which would unify the divided experiences of World War II. However, the legitimization of the Communists was obtained not solely by the creation of a shared institutional and patriotic fabric, but also through an ideal and symbolic division. The "second Risorgimento" was a contested idea, soon destined to show the limits of shared memory within the republican space. In fact, unlike the Catholics, the Communists assigned a central place to the mythology of the Resistance as a national and democratic rebirth, aimed at changing the face of Italian society.[69] The image of the Soviet Union integrated the Resistance narrative and endowed the Communists with a singular mixture of the national and the international. The myth of Stalin, reinvigorated by World War II, played a divisive role, as either hope or fear, in the collective imagination; but it concentrated the Communist identity and fueled its messianic elements.[70] The repressive and authoritarian practices already introduced in Central and Eastern Europe at the end of the war did not impact excessively on Italian Communists, who were not alone in interpreting them as a process for eradicating the old pro-Fascist ruling classes. Their democratic credentials were fragile, but for many it was more important that they had fought for freedom against the Fascist dictatorship. None of the mass political forces of the Italian postwar period presented impeccable international points of reference regarding the liberal and democratic tradition. The Soviet Union was, to a great extent, the shared mythical and political point of reference for both Socialists and Communists. There was, however, an evident problematic relation between the Catholic tradition and the United States, not to mention the conceptions which in the Catholic Church saw Francoist

Spain as a model state. At the end of the war, Togliatti's irony about the fact that the Anglo-Americans could show diffidence toward a Catholic foreign minister like De Gasperi was not unfounded.[71] Unlike the others, the Communists boasted an iron bond with a great power that had been victorious in the war, and brought with it a social model that presented a radical alternative to the failures of prewar capitalism.

Togliatti's mass party project was not at all the foundation of an Italian anomaly in the postwar European panorama, though it has often been presented in this light. If anything, it represented a significant national variation of an expanding global movement, endowed with new social and state dimensions. The Italian Communists convinced only one-fifth of the electorate—a significant result, but far from the success of the Czechoslovak Communist Party, for example, and lower numerically than that of the French Communists. Yet the critical mass of more than two million people was an unprecedented resource. The Italian Communist Party could be seen as a sui generis variant in the postwar reconstruction of communist parties, which offered a highly variable panorama even though it was oriented by the Leninist archetype of the revolutionary vanguard, the practices of "democratic centralism," and the primacy of organization.[72]

For all its national particularities, the reconstruction of Italy in the second postwar period did not represent a case apart, and indeed was, much more that in the past, a part of international dynamics.[73] The rootedness of a left that was closely tied to the Soviet Union was a part of those dynamics, although it took the unpredictable form of a massive communist force. The reestablishment of the Italian national community in the second postwar period was at the same time consolidated and divided by the Communist presence, which contributed to the avoidance of conflict within the antifascist camp and represented a possible alternative for the country's future. To obliterate one of these two aspects, as so often has been done in historiography by representing the Communists as either an endogenous or an alien subject, is to preclude one's comprehension of the multiple reasons for the resilience and fracture of the Italian nation in the "long postwar era" of Europe. It is instead essential to understand the dual fracture along the communism-anticommunism and fascism-antifascism axes, which today is still suppressed or explained with unilateral narratives that are exclusively centered on national history.[74] Experienced by Italians since the last year of the war under not only a political but a cultural and existential profile, this dual fracture shaped the perceptions and expectations of a society that was scarred by the experience of civil war, thus anticipating, rather than simply reflecting, the divisions of the Cold War.

In the new Europe that was rising from the ashes of a thirty-year-long catastrophe, the progressive ideas that found inspiration in a social and political modernization of democracy seemed to have the wind in their sails.[75] The communists benefited from the new public consensus—antifascist and open to the theme of a centrally planned economy—which in various countries allowed them to enter into competition with the Socialists, unlike in the first postwar period. While their acknowledgment as a legitimate component of European political nations was contested in various ways, they renewed their popular bases in France, Czechoslovakia, and even Germany, and they acquired new ones elsewhere, as in Yugoslavia and Greece, but also in Belgium and Finland. Antifascist democracy could be seen as a new form of political modernity characterized by a multitude of variants and experiences which did not necessarily reproduce the dualism between liberal capitalism and Soviet socialism. Thus Italian communism presented the face of a peripheral reality, scarred by the legacy of the Fascist regime and civil war. Yet it also revealed the character of an experience which aimed to invert the sign of that catastrophic perspective, cultivating the image of a national popular party, which in the bipolar world could liquidate the original nexus between civil war and revolution without renouncing its own identity. Divisions within the national community were not new in Italian history. The real problem was whether or not a catastrophic spiral like the one of the interwar period would reappear in the second postwar period.

THE MARSHALL PLAN AND THE COMINFORM

Bipolar confrontation began to directly condition Western European politics by the end of 1946. In Italy, hypotheses emerged about a breakup of the governing coalition. Togliatti did not exclude a change of direction of a nationalist type, but soon abandoned it.[76] De Gasperi's trip to the United

States in January 1947 showed how the anticommunist forces intended to oppose Communists with a more stable and recognizable international bond of their own, not yet a prelude to a logic of alliances, but destined to have repercussions on national politics. The promise of an American presence in the Mediterranean given by the Truman administration in the month of February fueled the sense of a passage from antifascism to anticommunism among the priorities of the European leading classes. In May and June 1947, the coincidence between the end of national coalition governments in Italy and France and the launch of the US plan for the economic reconstruction of Europe inaugurated a new season, which put paid to the objective of preventing the formation of blocs. In Italy, where they had already come into being, the interrogatives very soon became dramatic. Immediately after the government crisis and the exclusion of the Communists and Socialists, there was a meeting of the PCI Directorate, which took place at the beginning of June. Togliatti argued that the PCI should continue to act as a "government party" and "prevent the party and the masses that follow us from sliding into positions that lead to armed struggle and insurrection."[77] The other members of the Directorate approved this line. Togliatti did not mention the international aspect; but a little later, during a conversation with the Soviet emissary, Dimitry Shevlyagin, he expressed his conviction that "the majority of the questions of domestic policy in our country are questions of an international character."[78]

The launch of the Marshall Plan reinforced this opinion. In his report to the Central Committee on 1 July, Togliatti presented an interpretation of the Italian situation as a consequence of the offensive of the "forces of imperialism." He observed that the United States had conquered a decisively greater position of strength than "all the other imperialistic" powers and had set itself the task of "the conquest of world domination." At the same time, Togliatti believed that the "expansionism" of the United States was provoked by the "threat of an economic crisis," which in his opinion was advancing inexorably and was the origin of American "nervousness." He perceived America's hegemonic design, but did not acknowledge the Marshall Plan's potential to be the driving force behind European reconstruction. His vision of US supremacy was linked to categories of the past, which had gained the upper hand over the timid and implicit hints at revision emerged in the previous two years. The "risk of war" with the Soviet Union returned to center stage, evoking an obvious analogy with the decade before the war. In this context, however, Togliatti reproposed his personal anticatastrophist inclination: he asked himself if the prospect of a "third war" was "a real, imminent prospect," and answered in the negative, since that tendency was "restrained by a series of factors," the principal of which was "the existence of a democratic movement in all European countries." His gaze was also retrospective, with the objective of claiming that the strategic choices made since the end of the war were right. "If we had accepted the challenge of civil war at certain moments, and above all when the challenge could have been accepted—that is, between July and October 1945," he asked himself, "what result would we have obtained?" His reply was that the only result would have been a division of the country. One part of the country would have had "more advanced economic and political development" because it was occupied "by non-Anglo-American troops," but at the price that the rest of Italy would not have been "a united country, free and independent."[79] In other words, Togliatti suggested that national unity was preferable to transforming the North into a "people's democracy."

Togliatti avoided making forecasts about the national and international consequences of the new political situation. His prudence was also dictated by the synchronicity between the PCI meeting and the Paris Conference on the Marshall Plan, which saw the participation of a Soviet delegation led by Molotov. At the conference, Molotov questioned Reale about the ousting of the Italian Communists from the Italian government, pointing out with annoyance that their declarations made no mention of the interference by the United States in the matter.[80] The Soviet minister for foreign affairs was already suggesting a strong internationalization of Italian politics, despite Washington not having played a direct role in the government crisis.[81] The problem, as Molotov confided to Djilas, was not the national policy of the Western communists (attacked, however, by the Yugoslavs), but the fact that it was not coordinated with the "people's democracies" and the Soviet Union.[82] The decision of the Soviet delegation to abandon the conference and reject the US plan was no bolt out of the blue, but it promised a serious heightening of tension. This compromised the Italian

Communists' opportunity to regain a role in governing the country by not opposing the US recovery plan. It soon became clear that the Soviet choice precluded such a possibility, thus pushing them toward positions that were incompatible with the profile of a government party. In his conclusions to the Central Committee on July 4, Togliatti changed his tack. Contradicting his own claims of a month earlier, he considered the possibility that "progressive democracy" might not be a peaceful path.[83]

Yet his political conduct changed little. He presented his personal choice of permitting ratification of the Italian peace treaty by abstaining in parliament, despite Moscow's silence, as an act of national responsibility and an attempt to curb the spiral created by international politics. His speech to the Constituent Assembly on 29 July was an indictment of the Western tendency to divide Europe, considered "a first step toward new conflicts and perhaps toward a new war." He declared, however, that war was not "destiny," and emphasized that he had defended this thesis in 1935 "against extremist positions that claimed war could in no way be avoided." Togliatti avoided any reference to Leninism, and linked back to a more distant tradition, remembering that "as socialists, we know the great truth of those words of one of our greats, Jean Jaurès, when he said that capitalism bears war within itself like the cloud carries the storm." Change in the postwar world was revealing a decisive nature, because there existed sufficient forces "such that by uniting, they can prevent a war." Among these, the crucial role clearly belonged to the Soviet Union. What induced greater hope was, therefore, the relation of strength with the capitalist world. Togliatti's vision did not openly include the new dimensions taken on by the question of war after the US atom bombs dropped on Hiroshima and Nagasaki.[84]

It was not difficult to foresee that Stalin's decision to reject the Marshall Plan would imply a turn of the screw in Central and Eastern Europe and an anti-American mobilization of communist parties in the West. On 8 August 1947, in a conversation with Dimitrov, Stalin criticized the French and Italian communists for their weak conduct in the respective government crises.[85] What Togliatti and the other European leaders could not know was that the Soviets were secretly planning the creation of a new organism of international communism, which was destined to exacerbate an already dismal, dangerous scenario. Around mid-August, Secchia was informed by the Polish leaders Władysław Gomułka and Bolesaw Bierut that a conference was being planned with the generic aim of creating an interparty coordination.[86] The agenda of the conference, to be held in Poland in the last third of September, was unknown even when it was time to send delegations. Togliatti sensed the political climate and instructed the Italian delegates Longo and Reale accordingly, recommending that they defend the vision and strategy followed up to that time. Togliatti's words are reported by Reale in his memoirs, written after leaving the PCI: "If they reproach you because we were unable to take power or that we let them kick us out of the government—he told us in sending us off—well, tell them we couldn't transform Italy into a second Greece. And that is not only in our interest but also that of the Soviets themselves."[87]

The proceedings of the conference confirmed Togliatti's forecast. The representatives of the Central and Eastern European parties, the Italians, and the French performed their ritual communications, but immediately thereafter the Soviet delegation staged a coup de théâtre. Without any warning, the head of the delegation, Andrei Zhdanov, presented a report on the international situation, carefully prepared with Stalin. It could not go unnoticed to those present that for the first time since the end of the Twenties, one of the main Soviet leaders was giving such an important speech before an assembly of communist parties, albeit behind closed doors. It was easy to interpret the event as an internationalist relaunch which to some extent reversed the choice of dissolving the Comintern made four years earlier. The thesis enunciated by Zhdanov about splitting the world into "two camps," imperialism and anti-imperialism, led respectively by Washington and Moscow, was a response to the Marshall Plan and a challenge aimed at reinforcing the Eastern bloc while destabilizing the process of formation of the Western bloc. The formula of dividing the world between capitalism and socialism was not new and indeed dated back to the Twenties. Its use at this point, however, presupposed reading World War II as the genesis of an antagonistic bipolar order. Its most obvious corollary was the removal of support for the realist and parliamentary line followed by Western communists, the restoration of forms of control over their moves, and a call for extraparliamentary actions against the American presence. Zhdanov's target was "parliamentarism" and the legalitarian strategy. He took very good care to avoid recalling that such a strategy had been decided in Moscow, and that its first formulation dated back to the March 1944 meeting between Stalin and Togliatti.[88]

The Soviet delegates reported to Stalin in detail about the progress of the conference, manifesting among other things, the impression that the PCI, "thanks to the errors and the lack of resolution of the Directorate, does not know what to do and is waiting to see how events develop."[89] Zhdanov's indictment of the Western communists was amply backed by a barrage of interventions from the leaders of Eastern Europe and above all by the Yugoslavs, following a script prepared behind the scenes. Kardelj accused Togliatti of harboring the illusion that a legal path to power and a peaceful transition from capitalism to socialism were feasible in the capitalist countries. He affirmed that at the end of the war, a revolutionary opportunity had been lost in Northern Italy, an opinion certainly shared by many PCI leaders and cadres. The most logical consequence of this thesis would lead toward reversing the realist suggestion made by Togliatti to Longo and Reale. According to Kardelj, it was necessary to regard the civil war in Greece as the example to be followed in Italy and France. Longo accepted Zhdanov's criticism, manifesting his own internationalist discipline, but glossed over the ultra-radical theses of Kardelj.[90] The distinction between mass mobilization and the Greek model had become crucial, though it was easier to express it in words than in practice. The founding of the Cominform thus seemed to mark a significant rise in the consensus for militant rather than moderate orientations within the communist movement. Nonetheless, Zhdanov did not address his criticism about the "missed revolutionary opportunity" to the PCI, which would have called into question the orientations decided by Stalin at the end of the war. The Greek Communist Party had not been invited to the constituent conference of the Cominform because Stalin, faithful toward the spheres of influence, did not believe that an internationalization of the civil war was in the Soviet interest. In his concluding speech to the conference, Zhdanov did not express his opinion regarding insurrectional prospects. This did not escape the sharp notice of Reale.[91] Thus, the ultimate aims of the change imposed on the strategy of the communists in the West, and perhaps also the limits of that strategy, remained unclear.

The Cominform forced the Italian Communists onto the front of the nascent Cold War in Europe. Their belonging to the "socialist camp" exposed them to a conflict with potentially catastrophic consequences and pushed them toward political isolation, despite their significant social strength. The criticisms leveled at them confirmed a basic reservation, never overcome since the time of the Popular Front, regarding the significance of democratic institutions as the terrain for political action, and the expectation of new crises and upheavals in capitalist societies. But the new "class against class" turn also stimulated animal passions and identitarian motivations that "nationalization" had relegated to second place. The appeal to give priority to extraparliamentary mass mobilization touched heartstrings in the psychology and culture of all communists. In this way, the fracture between realist and intransigent elements that had surfaced during the war reemerged, with the difference that the latter could now aspire to the leadership of their parties with the benediction of Moscow, and under the pressure of political polarization in Europe.

On 7 October 1947, Longo informed the Directorate about the criticisms suffered at the founding Conference of the Cominform, acknowledging the need to modify the political line "above all in consideration of the fact that today there are two blocs in the world, and that it is not only about preventing their constitution." It was also necessary to avoid the error of believing that "only on a legalitarian level is it possible to achieve certain political results."[92] Longo repeated the defensive strategy already adopted during the work of the conference, which entailed strict alignment with Moscow on the thesis of the "two camps," without giving in to the more extreme Yugoslav criticisms. Secchia, however, made no similar distinction. He called for "a profound change" of the political line through mass mobilization and a search for new social alliances. The distinctive trait of his intervention at the Directorate was the acknowledgment of a "weakness" in the PCI's policy: "I believe not so much now as in 1945, until 2 June and also later, when we had an outstanding position of strength which we did not perhaps exploit." Similar positions did not identify with head-on criticism of "parliamentarism," but neither were they a defense of

Togliatti's fundamental choices, which was instead undertaken by Reale. Terracini was something of a black sheep, expressing reservations on the very meaning of the Cominform and observing that a brusque radicalization would expose the party to losing contact with the middle classes.[93] His intervention received numerous criticisms in support of international discipline. Togliatti set the limits for the inevitable toeing of the line. He proclaimed the need to side "with the Soviet Union's policy of peace," and to acknowledge that "dissolution of the Communist International has not put an end to the leading function of the Bolshevik Communist Party." But he was openly doubtful about the insurrectional scenario. Indeed, he affirmed that a communist could not exclude it "forever"; but as for putting forward "an immediate prospect" of that type, he felt that it was not right "to put the question in this way."[94] The measures to be taken at the organizational and conspiratorial level were probably debated but not reported in the minutes. A little later, Reale told Kostylev that in the North the partisans were reorganizing and creating "paramilitary formations"; but he also affirmed that he did not know the details about what he defined as "necessary measures."[95]

Zhdanov's report was made public on 22 October 1947, with the passages explicitly critical of the Italian and French communists removed. The thesis of the division of the world into "two camps" was perceived in the West as a declaration of cold war. Though formulated by an entirely selected Eurocentric organism, the Cominformist challenge presented clear global implications, gathering the "democratic and anti-imperialist" forces around Moscow. Italy found itself at the center of a similar challenge. Despite censorship of the criticisms about "parliamentarism," public opinion immediately perceived pressure of a conflictual and dangerous nature. What is more, a veritable "case" developed around Terracini. Readmitted to the party in 1944 after his expulsion following dissent over the pact between Stalin and Hitler, Terracini maintained a freedom of expression which reflected his personal and biographical distance from the cult of the Soviet state.[96] His position as president of the Constituent Assembly endowed him with particular authority. In an interview, he asserted his position of nonalignment with the blocs, stating that in case of war, the Italian people should stand against aggression, wherever it came from. The party secretariat obliged him to issue a partial correction.[97] In reality, Terracini was following a logical thread that was consistent with the views held up until a few months earlier by the PCI. He claimed that while the formation of the two blocs was "objectively contained 'in the bud' in the actual ending of the war," the correction of spontaneous tendencies was precisely "the raison d'être of politics." Togliatti clearly saw the strong core of the argument, and accused Terracini before the Central Committee on 11 November of having presented the policy of the Soviet Union as a "series of actions provoked by the policy of the Western countries," implicitly denying that Moscow had "its own peace policy."[98]

The Terracini case was a litmus test for the consequences of the nascent Cold War. Banning his criticism of Soviet conduct and adhering unreservedly to the struggle against the Marshall Plan meant weakening the credibility of communists as defenders of the national interest. His marginalization symbolically wiped out an essential element of the Italian Communists' national image. He was not punished, however, and was able to sign the new Constitution a few months later. Substantially, the birth of the Cominform laid bare the profound contradiction for communists between absolute fidelity to the Soviet Union and the construction of a national and democratic identity. Togliatti's PCI maintained a slim but decisive margin for maneuver, thus excluding an overturning of the project of a "new party." The scenarios opened up in Italy by the Cold War were, however, dramatic and unpredictable.

THE CIVIL WAR SCENARIO

The birth of the Cominform put back in play the antagonistic visions that had animated the forces and the people most inclined toward revolutionary solutions during the final years of the war and toward the challenges of an inevitable conflict between capitalism and socialism. Right or wrong as prudence may have been after the war's end, it now became superfluous. The political culture of the Communists, including the new wartime generation, was predisposed to embrace such a Manichean vision of the world order. The influence exerted by the militant components of the individual parties, especially in the Western ones, was potentially more significant than it appeared from the positions expressed by the leading organisms. That is how the role adopted by Secchia should be understood. He was in agreement with the Cominformist inspiration of a renewed internationalism based on the Soviet Union's preponderance of power. His role became increasingly important with the sense that Togliatti's moderate trajectory had reached the end of the line. At the beginning of December, Secchia told Kostylev not to exclude the possibility of the United States halting the evacuation of its troops from Italy "if they only just thought that a new world war would inevitably break out." But on this subject, he added that "the Americans are not alone in the world, and if they decide to keep their forces in Italy, other forces could also be kept in other countries."[99] His words were uttered in a national context already deeply shaken by the strikes against the Marshall Plan and by growing political tensions. In those same days, the leading group of the Christian Democrats met to examine concretely, as the Communists were doing, the hypothesis of dealing with a civil war, mobilizing all the resources available to the state apparatus.[100]

Secchia went on a mission to Moscow in mid-December 1947. Unlike Thorez, Togliatti avoided taking a similar step. The choice of sending Secchia was an acknowledgment of his influence in the party, but it also exposed him to the risk of failure. Togliatti was perhaps aware that at the meeting with Thorez a month earlier, Stalin had spoken of the French situation in a much more cautious way than might have been expected, given the harsh Cominformist criticism; and there was no reason to believe that his vision of Italy would differ by much. Togliatti's move was perhaps risky, but it was a winner. Already at his meeting with Zhdanov, Secchia raised the central question, asking about the opinion of the Soviets regarding insurrectional prospects and the possibility of a civil war breaking out in Italy. He explained that Togliatti refused to pose the stark alternatives of "insurrection" or "peaceful parliamentary development." Togliatti's argument, reported by Secchia, was that only a direct threat of war could make civil war inevitable, but that the international situation had not yet reached that point, and that therefore the idea that it was not possible to continue along the "democratic road" would have been wrong. However, Secchia did not limit himself to providing Togliatti's position, and presented an alternative vision. He claimed that a violent clash was on the horizon in Italy, and that to avoid repeating the errors of the past, it was necessary to take the counteroffensive. It was up to the Soviets to decide whether the international situation suggested the avoidance of a civil war or, otherwise, whether "a decisive struggle in Italy is useful and necessary." It would then be necessary to impede "the enemy from deciding whether to maintain the struggle on a democratic basis or to take it onto the terrain of an armed struggle at a moment convenient for him." He added, "We ourselves must choose the moment that is convenient for us." Zhdanov took no position, and left the matter for the Italian leader's meeting with Stalin.[101]

Stalin disavowed the alternative proposed by Secchia, but did not totally exclude it. "We believe that an insurrection should not be aimed for," he said, "though we must be ready if the adversary attacks."[102] In actual fact, Stalin was agreeing with Togliatti. The impact of the founding of the Cominform therefore turned out to be less devastating than had initially appeared possible. Togliatti had understood Stalin's orientation better than anyone else.[103] Indeed, Stalin chose to avoid any kind of exposure in Italy, even of a peaceful nature. Secchia presented in Togliatti's name a proposal to prepare an official meeting, to take place on the eve of the elections, at which the Soviet side would promise economic aid to Italy should the left win. The request aimed to counterbalance the impact of the Marshall Plan on public opinion. Zhdanov passed on Stalin's reply, stating that with a similar step, the Soviets would seem "too similar" to the Americans, giving rise "to a violation of national independence and sovereignty."[104] Thus Moscow abstained from any kind of intervention in Italy, evidently in order to avoid repercussions in the Soviet sphere of influence.

Secchia gave a speech in Moscow on 16 December in which reproposed his own option. He presented Italy as the central geopolitical focus for the "attack" prepared by the Americans against the Soviet Union and the countries of "new democracy." He criticized "parliamentary illusions" with his gaze turned toward the past, claiming that the party had "very lightly" renounced the instrument of the Committees for National Liberation "when it would have been necessary to expand them over the entire Italian territory." He reminded those present that the struggle for "the extension of democracy" was taking place in a country "where the positions of reaction are still strong," and that consequently the party had to be "ready to take up the armed struggle if it proves necessary."[105] The option of the PCI in favor of a "'progressive democracy" based on civil peace was thus conditioned by a different future evaluation of the objective conditions, as Stalin himself had suggested.

In this profile, it was even possible to contest the construction of the mass party. Secchia explicitly asked for Stalin's opinion about whether it was opportune to maintain the mass character of the party or to create a party of cadres. Stalin replied that "wherever there are other parties, the Communists cannot restrict party membership because people would join these other parties. [. . .] Therefore the Italian Communists cannot limit party membership, but they must strengthen political activity among its members."[106] Criticism of the mass party had been a hobbyhorse of the Yugoslavs at the Cominform Conference. Stalin and Thorez had dealt with the issue a month earlier. The French leader expressed perplexity about the PCI's mass dimension, which in his opinion at times led the Italian Communists "to renounce their own views regarding problems of principle." Stalin appeared to liquidate the question with a reference to the particularities of Italy, displaying perspicacity about continuity between the mass politicization achieved by Fascism and that of the postwar period. Indeed, he observed mischievously that "Mussolini taught them something. If there had been a Mussolini in France, he would have taught the communists something there too."[107] But this stance did not remove a sense of serious perplexity.

To sum up, Secchia's mission to Moscow did not weaken Togliatti's leadership, but it lent him credibility as a top-level international leader. On Stalin's indications, Secchia brought back substantial Soviet financial contribution to the PCI's electoral campaign, stopping over in Yugoslavia, where he met Kardelj and Djilas. Shortly thereafter, he was nominated vice-secretary of the PCI.[108] The sixth Congress of the PCI, in January 1948, saw an escalation of Cold War tensions in Italy and in Europe. The Italian election campaign promised to be a life-and-death battle which both sides fueled with inflammatory tones. Togliatti limited himself to presenting an international vision based on the "two camps" thesis. The Soviet representative, Pavel Yudin, relayed to Moscow a private conversation with

Togliatti, from which Yudin concluded that the Italian Communists were seriously preparing for the possibility of an armed conflict analogous to the war that had broken out in Greece.[109] However, Togliatti's reply to the Yugoslav delegates' insistence that he should take the road toward an "open revolutionary struggle" was, "When it comes to revolution in Italy, leave it to us."[110]

In February 1948 the communist coup d'état in Prague completed the establishment of one-party dictatorships in the whole of Central and Eastern Europe and exacerbated the reciprocal perceptions of danger. The United States viewed it as an operational modality that could be replicated in Italy, at this point the key country for the American presence in Europe. This led George Kennan to suggest that the PCI should be banned and elections canceled, even at the cost of military intervention, and that mass violence should be used to split the country in two, as the North was likely to fall into the hands of the communists, aided by the Yugoslavs. Such a scenario was also considered by Ambassador James Dunn and the US National Security Council.[111] The interventionist hypotheses that emerged within the Truman administration were based on the perception of the fact that Moscow would not risk a war to aid the Italian left. In retrospect, Stalin's prudence seems clear. In a letter sent to Kostylev in early March, Vyshinsky accused the ambassador of superficiality for having argued that the tasks of the Popular Front—the alliance of the left—were similar to those of the CLN at the end of World War II, this time with the aim of avoiding "at all costs" Italy's entry into the "Western bloc." According to Vyshinsky, it was naive to think that Italy's destiny could not be separated from that of Central and Eastern Europe.[112]

The views of the Italian Communists reflected, as in a mirror, scenarios of a bloody outcome, revealing strategic uncertainties and diverse visions. It was possible to establish a certain analogy between Czechoslovakia and Italy as regarding the strength of the workers' movement and the Soviet myth. For some components of the party, Prague represented a temptation and an option to be considered.[113] The crucial difference was that in Italy, the anticommunist forces had a monopoly over the military and security apparatus. In a conversation with Kostylev in mid-March, Secchia considered an armed attack against the victorious Popular Front likely, and possibly destined to take place on the same day as the elections or on the following day. He even went so far as to outline several scenarios. He observed that "if there is no American intervention, the armed workers will succeed in getting hold of almost all of northern and central Italy," while the remaining national territory would certainly remain in the hands of the "reactionary forces." In his opinion, an American intervention—and thus an "international conflict"—could in no way be ruled out.[114] Less optimistic about the predicted election results, Reale used a different tone and confided to the Soviet ambassador that the Italian leading group wondered whether an armed intervention by the Americans would "turn into a world war, or [whether] war in Italy would have a local character, as in Greece." But, he added, "Italy is not Greece, and there is no scarcity of progressive forces in Italy."[115]

The decisive moment was a secret meeting between Togliatti and Kostylev on 23 March 1948. According to the ambassador's summary, Togliatti declared that he could not exclude serious provocations, before or after the election, against the Popular Front, which in his opinion would foreseeably prevail, and that he believed the Communist Party should prepare for all eventualities, including an armed insurrection in Northern Italy. Indeed, Togliatti requested, as he had done three months earlier through Secchia, the opinion of the Soviet leaders on the prospects for armed insurrection. He now seemed to take far more seriously into consideration the possibility of a sudden worsening of the situation in Italy. He affirmed, however, that even in the case of a positive response from Moscow, the Italian party would go into action only if extreme circumstances arose. Above all, he advised taking into account the fact that a step of this kind might lead to a new world war, in which the countries of "new democracy" plus the Popular Front, and the Western countries including the United States plus the Christian Democrats, would find themselves on opposite sides. Moscow's response was immediate. On 26 March, Molotov cabled Kostylev, asking him to inform Togliatti that the Kremlin's advice was to engage in an armed struggle only in the case of a military attack from reactionary forces, but that it was of the opinion that an insurrection at the moment would be totally inappropriate. Molotov took care to warn the Italian Communists not to heed the advice of the Yugoslavs, pointing out that they were not informed about the Soviet stance, even though they claimed to be.[116]

Togliatti therefore acted, with approval by Stalin, to prevent an Italian catastrophe. The account of his meeting with Kostylev reveals a climate of great apprehension and uncertainty, but also the precise determination of the secretary of the PCI. He intended to avoid a violent outcome unless extreme conditions arose, and tried to exert a moderating influence on the opinion of his Soviet partners, in protection of their interests. The argument that a civil war in Italy might light the fuse of a third world war was clearly intended to feed Stalin's caution. Unlike what the intransigent members of the PCI and the Yugoslavs believed, this argument was a powerful dissuasive factor in Moscow. Togliatti had always avoided statements of principle about the nexus between "progressive democracy" and civil peace. He had expressed himself solely in terms of political realism, insisting on the still remaining possibilities for democracy and legality in national society. Put to the test, however, he firmly reiterated this choice. His principal compass was the need to prevent Italy's political conflict from degenerating into a second civil war, like that of 1943–45.

Thus the role of Togliatti's personality in the Italian and European conjuncture of 1948 should not be underestimated. There was very real possibility that an uncontrollable spiral might occur. The willingness to use violence was spreading among components of the left and former partisans, who were frustrated by the lack of an insurrection at the end of war; but it was also contemplated on the international level by the Americans and the British. The Catholic Church depicted the political conflict in Italy as a clash of civilizations, and communism as a menacing form of modern atheism. Togliatti and De Gasperi were the most moderate and realist figures in an incendiary panorama.[117] When making crucial political decisions, Togliatti showed that he had come to terms with the doctrine of the inevitability of war, much more than in the Thirties. Ever since the end of the war, his memory of the prewar decade had implicitly guided his choices; he viewed that decade as a disaster never to be repeated, rather than as the internationalist legacy of the war in Spain.

The election triumph of the DC and the ruinous defeat of the Popular Front on 18 April 1948 presented obvious international effects, in the sense of a stabilization of the blocs. From Washington's point of view, with the worst forecasts now dispelled, Italy could become a winning model for political warfare motivated by anticommunist ideology, and designed to exploit any means available—including "covert" operations and propaganda campaigns—save recourse to war.[118] The election defeat caused no significant reactions in Moscow, where it would not have been difficult to use it as proof of the pernicious effects produced by "parliamentary illusions." Stalin acknowledged the results of the election and probably considered it, as did the Americans, a turning point in the formation of blocs in Europe. On 26 April, Togliatti pointed out to the Soviet ambassador that Washington could not be satisfied with the results of the vote, because now the hypothesis of replacing the Christian Democracy government with "a different reactionary government" became much more difficult to achieve.[119] In reality, this was a blunder. The DC's landslide victory was greeted enthusiastically by the Americans who considered it the prologue to a season of reforms and modernization in Italy via implementation of the Marshall Plan.[120] However, Togliatti's words meant that he considered De Gasperi and the DC as a bastion against the occurrence of a reactionary solution with American approval.

After April 1948, the PCI was no longer in the Cominform's line of fire. The scenario of an international action aimed at preventing the formation of a Western bloc had dissolved. Instead, clouds were gathering over the parties of Eastern Europe. Togliatti and Secchia formed a high-level delegation at the second Cominform conference, unlike at the first. A little beforehand, the Italian delegates were informed that the conference had been convened to pronounce the sensational excommunication, called for by Stalin, of the Yugoslavs, with obvious consequences for the disciplining and the sovereignty of the other communist states of East Europe. In his confidential discussions with the Soviet delegates at Bucharest on 20 June 1948, Togliatti did not hesitate to accuse the Yugoslavs of having played a dangerous game, referring to the question of Trieste.[121] At the conference, the rituals of communist liturgy were respected and sentences without appeal were pronounced even by those who must have experienced the break between Moscow and Belgrade as the shattering of a revolutionary dream. Secchia was probably among these. Togliatti did not limit himself to the liturgy, however. He took the opportunity to defend the construction of a mass party, and declared that it had been "politically right after World War II to use the development of the democratic and workers' movement to create mass parties."[122] As we know, it was not the Yugoslavs alone who turned up their noses at the choice of mass recruitment and the resulting dilution of ideological vigilance. Tito's condemnation did not mean a change of course on the question, and indeed heralded a tightening of the screw in Eastern Europe. Togliatti went ever further, explaining how the internal and international polarization of the Cold War obliged neither a reversal of the "new party" option in Italy, nor a step backward in the development of the "people's democracies." Clearly, the consequences of such a stance were not restricted to any national specificity. Togliatti believed that it was possible to claim the case of Italy as the example of a choice that was still correct for the communist movement, thus overturning the negative vision the Cominform had adopted less than a year earlier.

The attempt on Togliatti's life on 14 July 1948 dramatically revived the scenario of civil war in Italy, and its internationalization. The proclamation of a general strike and a spontaneous popular mobilization led to the risk of political leaders losing control, and to a relaunch of insurrectional prospects after the frustration of the election defeat. The experience of the preceding months, when Togliatti's vision had overcome the militant tendency and had received the support of Stalin, turned out to be decisive. Following an appeal launched by Togliatti himself from his hospital bed, conduct aimed at preserving legality prevailed among the highest leaders of the PCI. Di Vittorio's moderate conduct and influence on the trade unions were particularly important in avoiding an "insurrectional strike."[123] In the hectic hours after the attempted assassination, Secchia told Kostylev that "according to the leadership of the PCI, and on the basis of recent analyses of friends of the Italian communists," the time had not come for an armed uprising.[124] He was obviously referring to exchanges between Moscow and Rome going back to March, aware that the appeal for moderation made by Togliatti alluded to that crucial choice. We are not informed about the nature of the PCI leaders' discussion, but it is easy to imagine that the confidential words pronounced by Secchia reflected the orientation of a majority. It must not be forgotten that the striking split between Moscow and Belgrade was also a significant factor of deterrence for an Italian insurrection. The backing promised by the Yugoslavs ever since the end of the war for a revolution in Northern Italy had suddenly vanished, and that objectively strengthened the positions of the realists.

In a speech delivered to the Central Committee in September 1948, Togliatti, having returned to the political stage, confirmed his choice of self-containment. In his judgment, the situation was "in the whole world and in our country a situation of class struggle," but those communists who conceded "victory to their adversary" by claiming that the time had come to "prepare for war," were in the wrong. Progressive democracy might "also mean civil war," but to consider the possibility of sliding into illegality and to think that war was "already on the doorstep" amounted to putting oneself "in a cul-de-sac."[125] In other words, Togliatti believed that the Italian Communists could fight a "war of position" in the international system under American hegemony, on the condition that they maintained the fundamental choices made at the end of World War II, which tied together legality, sovereignty, and mass politics. As Norman Naimark has observed, in the context of the "post-war struggle for sovereignty" in Europe, Togliatti can be viewed as a leader who pursued postfascist sovereignty and the construction of democracy in Italy despite his indisputable loyalty to Moscow.[126] This presupposed a vision of the bipolar order and the Cold War as not being a necessarily catastrophic prospect, a vision that Togliatti maintained even in the final years of the Stalin era.

SOVIETIZATION AND PACIFISM

Between 1948 and 1949, antifascism gave way to anticommunism all over Western Europe, while in Central and Eastern Europe it became an ideology of the regimes. The emergence of Christian Democracy as the dominant force in Italy and Germany was the main sign of the conservative stability created in the West by the division of the continent. American containment put the Italian and French communists in a minority position, though it could not drain the pool of their social base. The American reforming and modernizing inspiration was tempered and mediated by Christian Democracy using anticommunism as the instrument of its political centrality.[127] Togliatti perceived that the power of the DC could ensure a profitable position for the Communists in a polarized political system. But he underestimated the consequences of the Marshall Plan for the consensual stabilization of Western Europe. Europe's division placed the Italian Communists in the difficult position of being an outpost of the "socialist camp" in the country most exposed to the enemy bloc, and considerably weakened their political influence. The splits in the trade unions, which took place simultaneously at international and national levels, were the most deleterious consequence after the expulsion from the government sphere.[128] Stalin's strategy, centered on geopolitical spheres of influence, left meager prospects to communists in the West, not to mention the devastating effects on Central and Eastern Europe and their international impact. The strategic defeat suffered by the communist movement rendered arduous any prospects of a "war of position."

The Cold War required rigid operational modalities and covert channels for security. The transnational bonds of the Italian Communists, which had strengthened after the founding of the Cominform, were largely oriented by a conspiratorial legacy dating back to the interwar years. Their connections with the Soviet intelligence apparatus and that of the "peoples' democracies," designed to adopt paramilitary defense measures, interacted with the presence of secret anticommunist organizations such as "Stay Behind."[129] In his role as the person responsible for the organization, Secchia was the main weaver of, and terminal for, connections and sensitive information. Shifted to Bucharest from its original seat in Belgrade after the break between Stalin and Tito, the Cominform set up a permanent secretariat which was the main liaison structure between the socialist bloc and Western communists. Links with Prague were particularly important. Militants involved in violence and bloody revenge attacks after the war in the so-called red triangle area, who had become a possible focal point for civil war, were expatriated, in order to avoid criminal indictment, to the Czechoslovak capital, where a small Italian communist community formed.[130] Repositories of materials selected from the current archive and dating from the eve of the elections in 1948 were transferred to and stored at Prague and Moscow—a revisitation of a practice much used during the interwar period in relations with the Soviet Union.[131] In this way the archives were safe from possible confiscation by the police, while at the same time being very real instruments of control by the Eastern party-states over the Italian party. However, the main factor of dependence remained the finance distributed to communist parties, with privileged quotas being assigned to the Italian and French parties, thus playing an essential role in supporting the costs for strong apparatus, the periodical press, instruments of the cultural Cold War, and election campaigns.[132] In addition, in continuity with prewar practices, there was a reprise of cadre training in Moscow, which now integrated the political schools set up in Italy and implied exchanges and meetings with communists from various parts of the world.[133] In the bipolar order, this all constituted structured, hierarchical relations rather than a transnational network comparable to the Cominternist mobility of the interwar years. The resources fielded by such relations were a factor for survival, but added little to the autonomous strength of the Soviet myth and to the vision of a socialist destiny. Consciously or instinctively, Italian Communists knew that spreading the myth could depend on their discursive and agitational ability much more than the stereotyped Soviet and East European propaganda, which was often just ineffective ballast.[134]

The nature of the connections with Eastern Europe reflected a precise vision of the bipolar order. The "two camps" doctrine expressed an antagonist outlook, merely the evolution of the reciprocal siege between capitalism and socialism that dated back to prewar times. The new hegemony of the United States and the reconstruction of European capitalism were increasingly read through the lenses from the Thirties, with the prospect of economic collapse, fascistization and war. In the "socialist camp," the model of Sovietization and auto-Sovietization practices became imperative, sweeping away the idea of intermediate areas and making uniform the differences between individual countries.[135] The end of "national roads" in Eastern Europe had obvious repercussions for West European communists, who found themselves asserting their national sovereignty against American imperialism, while the notion itself was losing meaning in the "socialist camp."

In essence, the creation of the Cominform marked the end of the "nationalization" model of the European communist parties, which had come into being with the dissolution of the Comintern. But it launched no well-defined internationalist strategy, and even less did it exhume the Bolshevik tradition of the "civil war party." The most dangerous immediate consequences, represented by the possible end of the legal existence of the mass parties of Italy and France, were defused. What was lost, at least for an entire historical phase, was the possibility of increasing power shares in national societies, and the potential international influence of the Italian mass model, which presupposed a cooperative order that had never really come into being. However, communist influence in Italy had absolutely not been liquidated. The Cold War placed a limit on the communists' influence in Europe but provided them with resources that the Italians exploited to the full. On the mythological level, the Sovietization of Eastern Europe might have appeared as a "revolution from above" aimed at expanding socialism in Europe and confirming its unstoppable forward march in the postwar world, provoking fears or hopes as it had half a century earlier, but conferring legitimacy to the communist project. On the ideological level, recourse to anti-Americanism became a strong instrument for mobilizing the masses, and a new source of cohesion for communist identity after the end of Fascism. On the level of strategic visions, the choice of the struggle for peace, despite its openly unilateral and pro-Soviet character, turned out to be favorable terrain for exerting social influence far beyond the boundaries of the left. These three levels were closely intertwined and flowed into a strategic conception of the cultural Cold War, which was not simply a propaganda instrument but involved the identitarian structures of both leaders and militants.[136]

Togliatti designed the PCI's peace strategy in close coordination with Stalin's indications for Western communists.[137] In an extremely harsh parliamentary speech against Italy joining the Atlantic pact, on 15 March 1949, he compared American hegemony to Hitler's plan for domination.[138] Little different was his speech in private to the leading group, in which he stated that the Atlantic pact should be considered "an act of war," and warned of the risk of a new conflict provoked by the policies of the West.[139] The Italian Communists presented themselves as part of a pan-European movement, with the aim of crossing the borders of the "Iron Curtain." In Italy this framework presented more incisive political potentialities than in France, given the uncertainty that reigned among the ruling classes about that country's place regarding the nascent Atlantic Alliance. The Communist campaign against Italy joining NATO was conducted in the hope that splits in the moderate and conservative front caused by the siren calls of neutralism, especially in the Catholic world, would have been capable of producing the desired result. In reality, the argument about defending sovereignty against American imperialism might touch still vibrating nationalist strings, but for a large section of public opinion it lost credibility given Stalin's tightening of the screw in Eastern Europe. De Gasperi's highly incisive action on the international level finalized Italy's entry into NATO, an outcome that was not at all assured at the time. The result was a second severe defeat for the left after that of the previous year's election and a realization that the political scenario had definitively crystallized. The leader of the DC in this way kept a firm grip on the decisive choices regarding Italy's international position, and forced the left into a subaltern position. The nexus he established between joining the Atlantic Alliance and the choice of European integration for Italy was the keystone of a political supremacy with long-term implications.[140]

The communists could only undertake propaganda actions, though that they did with remarkable efficacy. They used the international conjuncture to deploy an incisive peace campaign, which appealed to the widespread antiwar sentiment in the country. The birth of the "Partisans of Peace" (also known as the World Peace Council) configured a mass movement capable of reaching broader social sectors and sections of public opinion than their usual voter pool, exploiting the widespread and justified fears present in public opinion. Peace propaganda achieved no influence on government agendas in Italy and France, but was highly pervasive and effective at embracing universalist appeals against the specter of an atomic holocaust. The ideal leader of the movement was Emilio Sereni, an emblematic figure of Stalinist internationalism, bearer of an unshakable Marxist-Leninist faith, and a renowned intellectual capable of organizing and connecting various interlocutors on a European scale.[141] The peace mobilization of Western communists caused alarm in the United States because it was much more incisive than anticapitalist propaganda.[142]

At this point a narrative was adopted that was destined to persist at length among the communists, but also in various environments of the Italian left, based on a Manichean scheme which presented Soviet policy as a defensive reaction to the aggressiveness of the Western bloc. This pattern was not new; indeed, it was a reprise of propaganda going back to the Thirties. But the idea of the Soviet Union as a "peaceful power" was renewed after the war as an essential component of the Soviet myth, and it contributed to containment of the most bellicose spirits. The vision of the United States as the new "chief enemy" of progress and socialism eliminated any nuance or attempt at differential analysis. Above all, it precluded comprehension of the intertwining of economic liberalism with the New Deal model as key to Americanism and its influence in Europe after World War II. In Western Europe, the struggle for peace represented where the Soviet myth and the American antimyth fused together. It was a discourse that lent credibility to the objectives of contesting liberal capitalist modernity, strengthening the communist countersociety, and supplying the sense of a community separate from the lifestyle and sentiments of Western societies. These symbolic and ideological resources were employed to contrast the penetration of American cultural models among the young generation and incorporate their material aspects into a different universe of values which proposed the identity of the public and private spheres, a collectivist ethos, and the condemnation of individualism. The prevalent symbologies were often extraneous to the national dimension and were linked instead to the "imagined community" of international communism.[143]

Under this profile, Italian Communists expressed no specificity. If it existed at all, their specificity resided in the fact that the forms of a "political religion" and the self-representation of a "community of believers," fed by myths and antimyths about the dichotomy between socialism and capitalism, were late in coming into being in Italy in comparison to other experiences of European communism. The long period of illegality had coincided with the founding moment of the sacralization of politics in Stalin's time, which had been embraced by a few thousand exiles, largely deracinated from their society and scattered by emigration. This does not mean that Soviet myths were less strong in Italy. Indeed, the conjuncture of the final war years, with its effects of political and social disaggregation and existential disorientation, was fertile terrain for the birth of new identities and horizons of meaning. In this light, the Soviet myth had been far more a spontaneous factor than the product of an organization, a symbolic and syncretic resource which during the apocalypse of the war shaped messianic sentiments and even traditional beliefs in popular culture.[144] For this reason too, almost invariably, a political choice continued to have, above all, an existential motivation that came before membership and ideological instruction, both for rank-and-file militants and for the intellectuals.[145] The moment of political choice, however, was a passage full of ambivalence. For many young people, the choice of antifascism stemmed from disillusionment with fascism as their "political religion," which might imply a search for a different and opposing credo, but also a more secularized, internationalist, and antinationalist vision of politics. A similar ambivalence was reproduced in the encounter with Catholic power and ideologies in postwar Italy, and was destined to create among communists sentiments of emulation both in the moral sphere and in the hierarchy of values, and at the same time a drive to become interpreters of the secularization of Italian society. Thus Italian communism's dimension as a subculture met with and became diluted within the mass of militants, becoming permeable to the transformations of Italian society.[146]

The peculiarity of the Italian Communists gained ground in their variegated expression of visions and ideas that did not adhere to the ideological leveling of the Cold War. In the first place, the conquest of the intellectuals was used to counterbalance the political hegemony of the Catholics, and centered on an exclusive cultural resource: Gramsci's prison writings, published between 1948 and 1951 under the careful editorship of Togliatti. Gramsci's writings immediately turned out to be a formidable instrument of national legitimization in the world of culture, despite the polarization of the Cold War. The communist strategy of attracting intellectuals that was exerted by a "national-popular" reading of Gramsci presented a strictly national horizon and implied little openness toward the social and cultural transformations that were taking place, and which were destined to change the face of society and the function of the intellectuals.[147] Nonetheless, it consolidated interaction between a leading nucleus who were capable of tailoring their different styles of expression to the cultured classes: on the one hand, to the workers and peasants, and on the other to a wider environment of politicized intellectuals who felt capable of being in contact with the popular classes.[148] Secondly, the mass mobilization from 1950 on was also carried out in defense of the Constitution of the Republic, understood as an expression of the Resistance myth, a programmatic document which was intended to change the face of the Italian society, and an antidote against reaction. The symbolic investment in discourse regarding the constitution was directly proportional to its genericity.[149] In this way, the PCI could present itself as an antigovernment but not antisystemic force, even though its international connections and its own reference to "people's democracies" created abundant impetus in the second direction.

In both cases, it was the national profile of the party that was exalted, in coexistence with representations of the transnational "imagined community." However, such national peculiarities would have been inconceivable outside the perspective of an international "war of position" based on the presence of the "socialist camp." Togliatti took care to outline a historical profile of the PCI as a progressive and "necessary" force of the Italian nation, but steered well clear of reducing the international nexus. His 1951 essay "Appunti e schema per una storia del Partito comunista italiana" (Notes and scheme for a history of the Italian Communist Party) provided a historically credible version, albeit one crammed with mythological narratives. Published in a *quaderno* of *Rinascita* dedicated to the thirtieth anniversary of the PCI, this writing had a notably wide distribution. Togliatti was addressing a unitary audience based on the idea of "a broad democratic national front of culture."[150] In his argumentation, the Gramscian national canon and the international Marxist-Leninist canon intersected. The former called for a reading of Italian history shared by many, centered on the narrowness of popular bases in the unitary state and the chronic weakness of the bourgeois ruling classes. The latter accepted without reservation the coordinates of Stalin's *Short Course*, widely distributed among the party militants, about the inevitability of the historical processes set in motion by the October Revolution, the cult of the Soviet state, and the mutilation of revolutionary history.[151] Togliatti's skillful directing thus managed to hold together two apparently disassociated narratives, both of which were as valid for the leaders and cadres as for the militants without any hierarchical separation or distinction. As already noted, the conceptual division of communist political culture into an elite sphere linked to Gramsci and a mass sphere linked to Stalinism now appears, to a great extent, misleading.[152] The symbolic bond constructed in communist iconography around the joined figures of Gramsci and Togliatti performed the function of a strong reference to the origins and represented the sole legitimizing cult not exclusively restricted to the Stalin epoch in the panorama of European communism.[153] Instead, the cosmopolitan genealogy represented by Gramsci, particularly regarding the questions he had posed about the nexus between the Soviet experience and world revolution, was glossed over. Formulated in a past that was now buried, these questions maintained their present relevance in the world of the Soviet superpower and of the Chinese Revolution, but they could not be expressed.

THE LIMITS OF STALINIST INTERNATIONALISM

Togliatti's personality continued to appear imposing even after the birth of the Cominform. At the end of 1949 he received another investiture from Moscow. He was the rapporteur for the third Cominform conference, held in Budapest from 16 to 19 November, which marked the de facto birth of the Soviet bloc. Here Mikhail Suslov, the rising star among Stalinist leaders, presented the "struggle for peace" as the key watchword in Moscow's repertoire, thus in reality launching the prospect of impending war, with an evident allusion to a return to the scenarios of the eve of World War II, ten years earlier. Togliatti delivered a flat, aligned speech, which referred back to the moments of most ferocious conflict with the social democracies. Besides justifying the spiral of Sovietization with his very presence, he attacked "Europeanism" and the "cosmopolitanism" of social democracies as a "propaganda weapon of imperialism" which had nothing to do with socialist internationalism. His denunciation included without reservation all the European socialist leaders, which he accused, among other things, of favoring "atomic diplomacy" and of converting Western Europe into a "colonial" market of the United States. Neither did he spare the UK Labour Party's nationalizations and welfare, which in his opinion had not undermined the power of the "financial oligarchy." All of the foregoing, in his opinion, favored mass mobilization by the Communists, particularly on the question of peace.[154] It was already clear that the struggle against Tito, conducted with the most venomous expedients of Stalinist propaganda, would produce a drift toward suspicion and persecutions in the "people's democracies," which commenced with the removal of Gomułka in Poland and continued in Hungary and Bulgaria with the cases of László Rajk and Trajčo Kostov. Togliatti accepted fully aware responsibility for positioning himself on the front line in the Stalinist internationalism of the Cold War. This choice certainly left him open to the accusation of privileging a compromising loyalty that was irreconcilable with his national image. Yet he seemed not to care about the repercussions in Italy, and led a delegation consisting of exponents who were hand in glove with Moscow, such as D'Onofrio and Cicalini. After the division of Germany into two states, and of the European continent into two blocs, this type of legitimization seemed to be an irrenounceable element of exercising communist leadership. Anti-Titoist persecutions were committed also in Italy, affecting leaders of a certain importance in Emilia and in the peace movement, such as Valdo Magnani and Aldo Cucchi.[155]

On 26 December 1949, Togliatti met Stalin for the first time in five years, on the occasion of the celebrations for the dictator's seventieth birthday, and at the height of the communist movement's worldwide expansion. The prospect of a revolutionary relaunch in Asia, following the proclamation of the People's Republic of China, linked up with the scenario of an impending war, although for communists the Soviet atom bomb was a reason for reassurance. According to notes taken by Togliatti himself, Stalin mentioned the project of extending the Cominform into Asia, which would, however, incur the resistance of Mao Zedong with the argument that it raised the risk of infiltration by spies.[156] It is not without significance that Stalin confided such sensitive information to Togliatti. The question of an "Asian Cominform" was extremely controversial. Beijing might see it as an opportunity to institutionalize its own role as the internationalist hub of Asia, in a geopolitical division of roles already delineated before the revolution. Moscow could instead see it as a way to exert more control over the Chinese communists, limiting their sovereignty. In any case, Stalin once more acknowledged Togliatti's prominent role in international communism.

The talk between Togliatti and Stalin revolved around the theme of "national roads," at this point reserved solely for the Western parties. Stalin confirmed his ambiguity. On the one hand, he was not inclined to encourage a violent conflict in Italy, because of the dangerous international implications, and indeed he suggested an improbable "bourgeois government" with Communist participation. On the other, however, he stressed the importance of extralegal action as an instrument for preparing the party for future battles, although this scenario did not refer to the immediate future. The sparse notes taken by Togliatti during his talk with Stalin focused on the fundamental theme of the contradiction between the legacy of the "European civil war" and the prospect of a "war of position." In general, Stalin emphasized tactical openmindedness rather than any strategic principle. His words on the theme of religion provide the most eloquent example: "Do not attack religion; you can even believe in the cat-god, like the Egyptians."[157] Perhaps this was his way of commenting on the choice of the Italian Communists to open the party's doors to religious believers. But the subject of the mass party remained delicate and controversial, more so than ever in the approaching scenarios of war.

In April 1950, Togliatti sketched out for the Central Committee a scenario of "confusion and disintegration of the Western world" that might hasten war, and he presented the Christian Democracy bloc as a mere "political and social device" that would lead toward a catastrophe. His reference to the role of the communists in the Resistance was nothing new, but it announced a mobilization that was particularly intense given the growing "war psychosis."[158] A week later, Secchia reported to the Secretariat of the Cominform about the conspicuous effort of mass mobilization carried out by the PCI on the theme of peace.[159] An anti-atomic campaign was imminent, which represented the peak of peace mobilization and saw all the main exponents of the leading group in the front row for the first time. The outbreak of war in Korea on June 1950 suddenly brought tension to an even higher level, proposing the scenario of a global militarization of the blocs. The darkest predictions of war spread with an opinion that went beyond the borders of the areas of social influence of European communism. Catastrophic prophecies multiplied in the communist press. Togliatti, however, kept his anticatastrophist guard high. In a meeting of the Directorate on 12

July 1950, while acknowledging that greater alarm was justified, he reportedly claimed that despite everything, war was not inevitable, and that the government would not ban the PCI.[160] Continuity with the positions held since 1947 is evident. In a public speech, he invited the Christian Democratic ruling class to understand the lesson of the pre–World War I liberal leader Giovanni Giolitti, to appreciate the progressive role of the workers' movement instead of repressing it. But that very same speech was also a message to his own side, when he recollected that the ferocious attacks on Giolittism had benefited only the nationalists and the right.[161]

The two blocs' reciprocal perceptions of threat gave rise in Italian politics to the same dynamic as two years earlier: the impact of international tensions, a tendency to identify the danger as a new "fascism" or "totalitarianism," the preparation of paramilitary measures, and the stubbornness of leaders in search of a political solution. De Gasperi went so far as to define the PCI as a Soviet "fifth column" in the Western bloc, and had the interior minister, Scelba, launch exceptional measures; but overall, his behavior was moderate.[162] This time, however, Togliatti's moderation risked isolation. In September, the extralegal option was presented by Secchia and Longo as a very real possibility requiring adequate organizational preparation.[163] Shortly thereafter, the progress of the war in Korea worsened significantly, thus delineating a pitched battle between the People's Republic of China and the United States. In November the Secretariat of the Cominform met in Sofia to examine a plan, attributed to Stalin's wishes, to relaunch the international organization with the aim of consolidating centralized control from Moscow over the European parties. On this occasion, the Italian delegates Pietro Ingrao and D'Onofrio supported the plan, yet the PCI was accused of still indulging in its legalitarian activities and scarce ideological vigilance.[164]

This was the climate in which Stalin asked Togliatti to take over the leadership of the Cominform in Prague. Stalin's choice of Togliatti made sense. After the defection of Tito and the death of Dimitrov, he was the most important personality in European communism. The Cominform Conference of November 1949 had confirmed this recognition. As the leader of the largest communist party in the West, Togliatti's exposure in such a role would assume the meaning of a mobilization against the

Atlantic Alliance but no longer limited to orchestrating peace movements. At the same time, figures like Secchia and Longo promised, thanks to the removal of Togliatti, to steer Italian communism toward extraparliamentary practices that chimed with the prognosis of an imminent international conflict. What followed remained cloaked in secrecy at the time, but its implications were of great importance for the PCI and the Cominform. A guest in Moscow after a suspicious car accident, Togliatti was almost Stalin's hostage for several months. We are aware only in limited terms of the content of his meetings with the dictator.[165] In any case, he turned down the proposal to become secretary of the Cominform without consulting with his comrades, and commenced an unforeseen tug-of-war with Stalin. Togliatti's motivations in his letter to Stalin of 4 January 1951, sent after an informal conversation between the two, were of a national and personal character, but were also linked to a different vision of Cold War scenarios. Togliatti declared that he preferred his own position as secretary of the Italian party, and restated the reasons that kept the road open to the party putting down roots in national society. He claimed that the possibilities for legal action by the PCI were not exhausted, and that indeed it was possible to "extend its influence." He also raised doubts about the actual usefulness of the Cominform, which he saw as a "clandestine organization" as compared with the mass politics dimension ensured by the "Partisans of Peace" movement.[166] His message to Stalin was essentially that the Cold War would not necessarily degrade into an armed conflict, and that militarized bipolarism would in any case not hinder legal mass struggles in Europe.

Stalin did not accept Togliatti's arguments, and turned to active persuasion, supported by the most senior leaders of the PCI. At the end of January he met Togliatti in the presence of Secchia and Longo, who in the meantime had been summoned to Moscow. The Soviet leader claimed that war could break out from one moment to the next, and that the European communist parties would soon be plunged into illegality. He maintained that it was necessary to consolidate the Cominform as the organizational center of a clandestine communist network that also included the Western communist parties. With this bleak prognosis, Stalin resolved the dilemmas of 1947–48 in his own personal way. There was no insurrectional option on the ground; but with the prospect of war, the option of extralegal action gained strength. In Stalin's mentality, with an inclination to read the present as reiteration of the past, the scenario of the end of the Thirties was repeating itself. When on 1 February Secchia and Longo reported the terms of the Moscow meeting to the PCI Directorate in Rome, the majority supported Stalin's proposal, with only Terracini, Di Vittorio, and Noce voting against, and Longo and Pajetta abstaining. Sent back to Moscow, Secchia and Arturo Colombi transmitted on 12 February an informational note to Stalin on the favorable decision of the Directorate, signed also by Togliatti, which proposed his temporary return to Italy for the Party Congress.[167] Even though he had been boxed into a corner by his own leading group, Togliatti obstinately refused to change his mind. Stalin played his last card in February 1951 at a further meeting with Togliatti and Secchia, inviting them to put aside considerations of a personal nature, and ignoring the political stance that Togliatti had taken in favor of legal action. Togliatti got out of the situation with a compromise: a generic commitment to accept the proposal only after the seventh Congress of the PCI.[168]

Thus, for the first time in his life, Togliatti openly dissociated himself from Stalin. At the same time, he was forced to cross swords with the most important members of his own party. The support given to Stalin's proposal by the PCI's leading group revealed the effect of discipline but also, very probably, a plan to remove Togliatti from leadership of the party, after the opportunity to do so had vanished in 1947–48. The confidential revelations made by Togliatti to Luciano Barca ten years later support the hypothesis of an authentic plot headed by Secchia. Togliatti confided to Barca his belief that even before he left for Moscow, Secchia and D'Onofrio had arranged with Beriya the plan to send him to Prague and oust him from his role as secretary of the PCI. The operation was very likely presented to Stalin as a PCI proposal. That, in Togliatti's eyes, explained both Stalin's unusual visit to him at the dacha after his arrival, and the dictator's "surprise" at his refusal. To convince Longo, it would have sufficed to say that the directive came from Stalin. Togliatti admitted his surprise at the majority vote by the Directorate against his will. He recalled that in the end he had managed to convince Stalin that "the question was political" and had nothing to do with his "personal safety," thus demolishing Beriya's argument.¹⁶⁹ The essential part of Togliatti's retrospective revelations to Barca are corroborated by a note written by Secchia and preserved among his papers—this too written after the events. Secchia denied that he was motivated by personal ambition, but acknowledged his responsibility, and involved Longo—indeed, presenting him as the one most convinced that it was opportune to do without Togliatti. Secchia claimed that he and Longo were both driven by "political considerations" and, to be precise, by the fact that the party under Togliatti "would have continued to develop as a socialdem[ocratic] p[arty]." This opinion dated back to 1945. Using an argument already adopted in the past, he recalled a bitter conversation with Longo in June 1945 about the "devalued" Resistance. Secchia also mentioned the compromise eventually reached with Togliatti in Moscow, making Colombi responsible for it. The Soviets understood immediately that Togliatti would never go to Prague. Stalin ended the matter by declaring that "the situation is clear. The Italian com[rades] are afraid of offending T[ogliatti] and T[ogliatti] is afraid of offending us."¹⁷⁰

The episode caused an irreparable fracture between Togliatti and Secchia, and a serious split in the party's leading group.¹⁷¹ Feeling betrayed, Togliatti shrewdly gathered the generation of the Amendolas and Pajettas to his side. Yet the question was "political" in a deep sense, as Togliatti affirmed, because it brought into play both leadership and political culture. He defended the anticatastrophist option that had inspired his political action after the war, and enforced it as a limit to the application of blind internationalist discipline. The episode marked a divergence between the opinions of Togliatti and Stalin on the evolution of the Cold War, and also on how to conceive of the role of a mass communist party in Western Europe. The catastrophist visions presented by Stalin, on the other hand, made easy inroads among the senior PCI leaders, laying bare long-simmering dissent toward Togliatti. At the height of the Cold War, Secchia and Longo revealed not only a sense of unconditional belonging to the Soviet Union but a link to the prewar tradition of expecting war. Secchia was close to creating a new majority that was ready to regiment the mass party in a more robust structure of cadres and "professional revolutionaries," which would have amounted to a normalization of the PCI in the European panorama. His plan aimed not to unleash a revolution, but to prepare for a war scenario. Such a mutation of the mass party in Italy would have been per se a factor for militarization and conflict, aggravated by the fact that its most popular leader would have operated beyond the "Iron Curtain." In this way, the PCI would have inevitably put itself on a collision course with the changing American anticommunist strategy in Italy and France, which had become more aggressive since the beginning of 1950, with the objective not only of keeping the Communists out of government but of realizing measures of psychological warfare.[172] In other words, the eventual success of Secchia's plan would probably have had grave and irreparable consequences for republican democracy itself.

With all the pedagogy and energy invested in reconstituting a new leading group after the conflicts and breaks of the interwar years, Togliatti found himself almost alone when the time came to question total loyalty to Moscow in order to save the "new party." Only outsider figures demonstrated that they had profoundly understood the lesson of the civil war avoided during the postwar period. The keystone of Togliatti's arguments was an appeal for a continuity of vision which tied the national to the international element. The reference to the "struggle for peace" went back to a tradition that was solidly linked to the Soviet Union. The problem posed by Togliatti in counterposing the mass movement of the "Partisans of Peace" and the conspiratorial practices of the Cominform remained suspended, to be solved only after Stalin's death. But it is no exaggeration to claim that Togliatti's refusal contributed to the definitive downfall of the Cominform, which played no significant role in Stalin's final two years of life. Thus Togliatti's project of the mass party had an unpredictably crucial international impact.

In April 1951, at the seventh Congress of the PCI, Togliatti claimed that the legalitarian and constituent choice made at the end of the war was right, despite the Cold War spiral. His speech linked the mass dimension of the "new party" to the struggle for peace, constitutional loyalty, and the defense of "parliamentarism." Secchia expressed a different point of view, asking what the point was of a mass party if it counted for little in the political life of the country.[173] But the difference between Togliatti and Secchia was not limited to this point, decisive though it was. Togliatti's idea of the Cold War was not that of a conflict that was fatally destined to break out, but that of a long-term "war of position." The PCI's mass occupation of the democratic space in the Italian Republic was based on the continuity of such a vision of bipolar antagonism, and a consequent political praxis, destined to make its way empirically and gradually. The choice of legality was also a form of resistance against the American inclination to push for a ban on the PCI, which found support in the conservative anticommunism of the DC. As Togliatti well knew, from De Gasperi's point of view, any attempt to eradicate Italian communism would be not only risky and dangerous but counterproductive, because it would have produced a political earthquake destined to compromise the very foundations of the DC-dominated political system. The Catholic party based its own function not only on anticommunism but on constitutional recognition of the PCI within the republican space.[174]

From Togliatti's point of view, his biographical link to Stalin remained a fundamental point, beyond dispute. This was the main meaning of his speech on the death of Stalin, on 6 March 1953. All communists without exception, Hobsbawn recalls, saw in Stalin the "commander of the disciplined army of world communism in the global Cold War," admired him "as the leader and embodiment of the Cause," and felt a "sense of grief and personal loss," sentiments shared "undoubtedly by hard-bitten leaders like Palmiro Togliatti, who knew the terrible dictator at close quarters."[175] In two key passages, Togliatti defined Stalin not only as the standard-bearer of peace and antifascism but as "the founder and head of the socialist state," and he publicly revealed the most significant moment of their long partnership, saying that it had been Stalin "who in the terrible year of 1944 was the first to reach out his hand to our people," and recalling "the conversation with him in that year, before my return to Italy." Togliatti concluded by declaring that Stalin's legacy was "too profound for it to be left behind."[176] He would remain faithful to these words in those terms, even after the denunciation of Stalinist despotism pronounced by Nikita Khrushchev three years later.

What Togliatti left unsaid was the extremely controversial character of Stalin's legacy even within the communist world. The vision of inevitable war between the "two camps," the violent Sovietization of Central and Eastern Europe, and the creation of a supranational conspiratorial and police organism like the Cominform constituted a series of problematic issues. Togliatti had constructed the project of the mass party in democratic Italy while in close contact with the geopolitical choices made by Stalin at the end of the war. His legalitarian and self-containment strategy had contributed decisively to the avoidance of a possible Italian catastrophe, despite the pressure of the intransigent components of his own party. But at various times, especially after the division of Europe, Togliatti found himself defending his own vision by resisting the impetus triggered by the Soviet Cold War, in a precarious equilibrium of loyalty and dissent that involved his own leading group. His choice of democratic legality turned out to be a conquest, obtained by playing a difficult game with his international partners, and by moderating the most dangerous dynamics that were active in national society.

In Italy, the bipolar world order thus consolidated identities founded on the antagonism between two large political aggregations positioned permanently in government and in opposition. Each based an essential part of its identity on a mirror image of the enemy. Their reciprocal siege triggered dynamics of long-term political delegitimization.[177] The image of communism as totalitarianism conveyed by Catholic propaganda was often matched by a pre-political vision that aimed to depict communism as a form of barbarism and an aggression against Christian values. The paradox of Catholic hegemony was that while it constituted the political architrave of Italian reconstruction and of republican democracy, its clerical component contributed to the creation of a new division within the nation. The image of anticommunism as portrayed by communist propaganda was more political but no less antinomic, often aimed at labeling it as a new fascism and at denouncing membership of the Atlantic Alliance as a loss of national sovereignty. The main ideas of the Western world held by communist militants replicated Stalinist dogmas about the proximity of economic collapse, mass poverty, and inevitable war, suppressing or denying the dictatorial nature of the communist regimes of Central and Eastern Europe. The defeat suffered in 1948 created the myth of an externally imposed betrayal of authentic popular will, which led to ambiguous promises of future revenge to be exacted, or resistance to be resumed.

At the end of the Stalin era it could be claimed that Italian communism was both a factor that fractured the political nation, though not the only one, and a component of the Republic, albeit one banned from the government sphere. Togliatti spoke both languages, but his role was decisive in stabilizing and giving meaning to Italian bipolarity. He exercised his leadership to construct a political vision of the adversary, which was aimed at mediating the antinomies of the blocs in the life of the nation, and suitable for the prospect of a long international "war of position." The international dimension not only implied moral, existential, and ideological irreconcilability but crystallized the national divide, creating a form of stability in the sense of a permanent truce. The nexuses established between national politics and international politics constituted, in this profile, both a vehicle that imported the Cold War into Italy and a factor for the containment of its worst implications, thus configuring a political model which would exist for a long time to come. Internationalism, however, was not a static given or a permanence of the past. It was a central pillar of imaginaries, practices, and political culture which after Stalin's death would experience serious transformations, going beyond the limits of the organic bond with the socialist world.

4
POLYCENTRISM AND DECOLONIZATION

DE-STALINIZATION AND CRISIS IN EUROPE

Immediately after Stalin's death, the communist world recognized for the first time the legitimacy of a reform from above. Even though the first measures undertaken by the Soviet oligarchs took place in the opaque and contorted context of the struggles for succession, they outlined an immediate detachment from the Stalinist terror, and led to an easing of the worst tensions of the Cold War through ending the war in Korea. At the same time, the popular protest that was repressed in East Berlin in June 1953 revealed the potential for social revolt against Sovietization. The distancing from Stalin came across as a contradictory phenomenon: as a necessary search for stability on the one hand, and as a source of destabilization in the "socialist camp" on the other. The easing of international tension was in any case a favorable development for Western communists. De-Stalinization offered them the promise of a counterpoint internationally in accordance with the choice they had adopted of legality and a mass politics, unlike in previous years. The transnational change had its political and cultural implications as well as its generational and organizational ones. Togliatti established a good relationship with Georgii Malenkov, regarded at that time as the main successor to Stalin, and with his appeal for "peaceful coexistence" against the threat of a nuclear war. On 12 April 1954 Togliatti made a speech on the danger of the destruction of humankind represented by nuclear weapons. Indicating the aim of the "salvation of civilization," he turned to the Catholic world, making it clear that the idea of "peaceful coexistence" was as valid for international relations as it was for the "relations inside a single state."[1] Secchia drew his consequences and is said to have commented acidly, "First we talked of 'class,' then of the 'fatherland,' and now we've arrived at 'mankind'... where will we end up?"[2]

In fact, Togliatti was breaking the canon of class and posing a question of political culture destined to reform and divide the visions of the communists on a world scale. As ever in his conduct, a declaration of this type was linked to political positions. In a letter to the Secretariat of the PCI, written at the time of Alcide De Gasperi's death, he brought out the need for inserting "the movement toward détente in Europe ever more effectively" into the "conflict" between the Western powers that had emerged over the question of the European Defense Community.[3] Togliatti's valedictory article on De Gasperi, based on the language of the Cold War, was particularly harsh, probably with the intention of both sending a message to De Gasperi's successors and closing ranks within his own party.[4] He refused to acknowledge in the Christian Democrat leader the capacity to create national spaces of maneuver in the context of transatlantic relations, while he himself had followed a logic of self-defense against the pressures exerted by his own partners and international constraints. His conduct did, however, reveal a precise orientation. The Secchia affair, and Secchia's replacement as the party's chief organizer by the "national communist" Giorgio Amendola in November 1954, put an end to any suggestion of action outside the law, which at the previous year's general election had already been weakened by the failure of De Gasperi's project of a protected democracy.[5] Secchia remained deputy secretary, but lost his influence once and for all, and was quite aware of having been defeated in the long tussle with Togliatti.[6] The latter had certainly been preparing such a move, and finally was able to exploit the opportunity afforded him by the scandal associated with the name of Giulio Seniga, Secchia's assistant, who in July had fled with the party funds. It is worth noting, however, that Togliatti's choice was made at a precise moment in time. When De Gasperi died in August 1954, American pressure to outlaw the PCI reached its height, inducing the interior minister, Mario Scelba, to prepare and present at the end of the year a packet of legislative provisions that if implemented would have destabilized the constitutional equilibria in Italy.[7] The Christian Democrats did not follow this logic to the letter, given, among other things, that Togliatti's decision to dismantle Secchia's apparatus had doused the flames of the domestic cold war.

Togliatti operated within the perspective of a gradual and silent de-Stalinization. However, Malenkov's fall and the rise to power of Nikita Khrushchev led to an incontrollable situation which was to produce a shock wave at the international level. In February 1956 the Twentieth Congress of the Communist Party of the Soviet Union (CPSU) was the occasion for launching the doctrine of "peaceful coexistence," which consolidated the gradual lessening of the worst tensions and created a broader space for maneuver for Western communists. From the point of view of Togliatti and the PCI, a cycle was closed in the best of ways: the cycle of the double register between the "fight for peace" as a mass mobilization campaign and the conspiratorial and police activity of the Cominform that had begun in 1949. Togliatti took part in the decision to liquidate the Cominform, taken while the congress was in session.[8] The Soviet leaders sanctioned the end of the organization shortly afterward, on 13 April 1956, with the view of establishing new forms for the relations within the communist movement, without any critical mention of the Stalin era.[9]

The Twentieth Congress opened an unforeseeable and explosive front. The impact of the "secret speech" that Khrushchev made behind closed doors led to a shake-up for all communists. In Moscow, Togliatti was informed of the contents of the document, as were other heads of delegations, but, in scrupulous observation of the undertaking with the Soviets that the document should remain confidential, he steered clear of discussing it even with his own leading group. He justified himself in retrospect, saying that he had informed the Secretariat "on the basis of his notes" but that he had not considered himself "authorized to inform the Executive Committee of the Party."[10] The leaks circulating in the Western press about the "secret speech" gave rise, however, to a growing restlessness.

It was Amendola who brought up the question on 5 April 1956, at the meeting of the National Council of the PCI, demanding clarity but also indicating the liberatory nature of Khrushchev's revelations, which had freed the PCI "from all shackles." Luciano Barca noted in his diary that for the first time, an open split had surfaced in the leading group of the party.[11] Togliatti defended his choice of silence and invoked the "bond of iron," using an inflamed autobiographical rhetoric ("This was our side, this was our cause, our banner, our life").[12] Aware of the explosive nature of the attack on the myth of Stalin, and probably in dissent against the choice made by Khrushchev, he avoided taking up a position for as long as possible. The denunciation of Stalin's crimes struck at the credibility of the communist movement and at an essential part of Soviet mythology, including that of the "Great Patriotic War," offering in return some vague moral redemption and the narration of a "return to Lenin," of use in defending the legitimacy of revolution but in contradiction with the idea of uninterrupted continuity in the "building of socialism." Togliatti had committed himself in person to an out-and-out defense of the historical figure of Stalin, and not only at the moment of the dictator's death. Khrushchev's "secret speech," however, liquidated the prospect of turning the page gradually with respect to the legacy of Stalin.

On 1 June 1956 Togliatti met Tito, thereby reestablishing the relations that had been brusquely interrupted eight years previously, and beginning a bilateral relationship destined to become ever more important for the PCI, even as compared with its relations with the single-party states of the Soviet bloc. Togliatti shared with the Yugoslav leader the judgment that Khrushchev had not "fully clarified" how "the extremely serious errors committed by Stalin" had been possible. In his opinion, Stalin had to be criticized "on questions of political importance" while avoiding the "moral destruction of his figure and neglect of the positive side of his activity." Tito placed the accent more on the "processes of bureaucratization." In other words, Togliatti established with Tito a general agreement in favor of de-Stalinization but aimed at containing iconoclastic tendencies.[13] A short time later, he gave an interview to the journal *Nuovi argomenti* which saw the light after the *New York Times*'s full publication of the "secret speech" on 4 June 1956.[14] Togliatti declared that his interview had been already prepared before the *New York Times*'s publication; but as a matter of fact, after having hesitated and kept silent for some month, he was put on the ropes.[15] He decided to publicly criticize the limits of Khrushchev's criticism of Stalin's "cult of personality," and advanced the thesis of a "bureaucratic degeneration" of the Soviet system, a position obviously inspired by Tito. Togliatti was thus able to remedy Khrushchev's weak thesis and to offer an interpretation more consonant with Marxist culture. It was in this perspective that the interview was accepted by the leaders of the PCI. All of them, not least Secchia and Scoccimarro, recognized that Khrushchev may have been wrong in the method but right in the substance. Only a few of them, in particular two figures as different as Amendola and Terracini, emphasized how the denunciation of Stalin had cleared the way for the "Italian road" to socialism.[16] The thesis of a "bureaucratic degeneration" caused a harsh reply of resentment from the Soviets. On arrival in Moscow, Pajetta and Negarville encountered irritation and resistance to admitting such a formula, which brought into play an interpretation of Stalinism that went back to Trotsky, although Khrushchev had skated over the issue.[17] Togliatti could, however, count on the consensus of his own leading group, though this consensus was accorded him with very varied motivations, which ranged from a sense of liberation to the sheer impossibility of remaining silent after Khrushchev's revelations.[18]

The most significant question Togliatti raised was, however, something else, which under the circumstances passed almost unobserved. He used the formula of "polycentrism" to uphold the need for a new articulation of the international communist movement after the end of the Cominform. This notion implied the recognition of a growing complexity in the world order, as there were no longer "two camps" but "three groups" taking account of the movements for colonial liberation, which he maintained were heading for socialism.[19] In this way Togliatti raised the stakes regarding the new forms of communist internationalism. Khrushchev was ready to recognize the plurality of roads of "transition" to socialism, but not eager to give up the primacy and centrality of the Soviet Union. Togliatti's formula of "polycentrism" constituted an evident alternative, because it did not represent a simple regionalist option and remained silent about the new role assigned to Moscow. Togliatti shed doubt on whether the maintenance of a "single leading role" was opportune, and pressed for more articulated relations in the "socialist camp" and the international communist movement. His was also an analytical assessment of the changes that were being generated by decolonization. He looked favorably on the emergence of a global third force at the Afro-Asian Bandung conference held the previous year in Indonesia, which had seen the participation of communist China and taken on the aspect of a symbolic moment of self-determination and anti-imperialist sovereignty.[20]

Within the party's leading group, Togliatti presented the questions arising from the relation between socialism in the world and the anticolonial orientations of national extra-European leaders such as Nehru, Nasser, and Sukarno.[21] In his meeting with Tito he had shown his understanding for the choice made by Yugoslavia to avoid any participation in new organizational centers of the communist movement, as they would have lessened the role of Belgrade "in the international socialist and democratic movement."[22] He even publicly adopted a lexis analogous to that of Tito, using the notion of "active coexistence" at the Central Committee meeting of 24 June, and argued that "the new initiatives aimed at modifying the course of international relations" and at "putting an end to the Cold War" were entirely due "to the socialist countries or to the new states that have emerged from the collapse of the colonial system."[23] Paradoxically, it was precisely the denunciation by Khrushchev, so distant from what he felt, that induced Togliatti to regain the role of strategist of international communism, overshadowed by the Cominform. In the interplay for the reorganization of the communist movement after Stalin's death, Togliatti put himself forward as a protagonist, aiming at interpreting the wave of global changes caused by the Chinese Revolution and by the decay of the European empires, all of which called into play a historical time longer and deeper than that of the Cold War.

The dramatic crisis opened up by the popular revolts in Poland and Hungary substantially modified the terms of the question which Togliatti had posed in the *Nuovi argomenti* interview. The workers' protest in Poznan in June 1956 demonstrated that the 1953 revolts had not been an episode linked to the death of Stalin, but heralded a deep fracture. The popular movement in Hungary revealed the transnational dynamic of de-Stalinization and the discredit of the Stalinist establishments of Eastern Europe after Khrushchev's denunciation. Togliatti changed his tone radically. He clarified that the priority lay in the unreserved defense of the "socialist camp," even before that of its reform, and he used a language that again echoed the darkest moments of the "European civil war." Whatever the political orientation was, it could not be separated from the stability of Central and Eastern Europe, which he saw threatened by the "enemy presence" lurking behind the popular protests. Following this logic, Togliatti interpreted the extreme attempt at reform by Imre Nagy, at the end of October, as unwarranted and as representing a mortal danger. On 30 October 1956 he expressed to the Soviet leaders his extremely firm stance against the "reactionary orientation" of Nagy, which underwrote the opportunity of intervening with force in Hungary, at the moment when the Soviet leadership was divided and undecided in a choice between repressive action and the relaxation of tension. He appealed for firmness before the unfolding of events, which in his view threatened the unity of the party both in Italy and in the Soviet Union. The Soviets replied, declaring that they fully shared his pessimistic judgment of the situation in Hungary, and reassuring him of the unity of their "collective leadership," thereby attributing a significant recognition to him.[24] Expressed in other words, Togliatti contributed to defining the limits of de-Stalinization drastically. His dour and sullen definition of Nagy went to extremes, and even implicitly constituted a manifest lack of confidence in Khrushchev's leadership.

Togliatti used the expedient of aligning himself against "two opposed tendencies," both of them "mistaken," meaning those who hankered after Stalinism and, opposed to them, those who claimed that the PCI should have supported the popular insurrection. His key phrase at the Party Directorate of 30 October was: "One remains with one's own side even when that side makes mistakes." But he also warned that one must "not put oneself on the terrain of pure liberalism."[25] Among the PCI leaders, only Di Vittorio exposed himself, even publicly, by refusing this logic and arguing that "not all those in revolt are enemies of socialism." Di Vittorio claimed that democratization was a "condition for the salvation" of the socialist system, and saw in the scenario of Soviet repression in Hungary the end of the line for de-Stalinization as political reform.[26] His was an authoritative voice as head of the CGIL and also of the World Federation of Trade Unions (WFTU), so much so as to make him appear an alternative to Togliatti. But it was an isolated voice, destined to reenter the ranks under the blackmail threat of party discipline. The other leaders lined up with

Togliatti's position, with no distinction between generations.[27] Many expressed their dismay at the popular protest and at the lack of any support for the first intervention by the Red Army a few days earlier. They were thus showing how a mythological idea of the "people's democracies" had created a veil over their eyes, and how deep within them the Cold War had penetrated. The unity of the leading group was thus assured at the moment of the invasion, and succeeded in stemming dissent within the party.

The defections were notable, however, especially among the intellectuals, who were little inclined to let themselves be influenced by the myth of the "people's democracies" and by the Manichaean languages of "counterrevolution" dating from the assumed "international civil war." It fell to Antonio Giolitti to express in clear terms the refusal of these visions in his speech at the Eighth Congress of the PCI, with the authority that had come to him from his participation in the antifascist Resistance and from the party and institutional positions he had held after the war. He shed doubt on the democratic and socialist legitimacy of the Hungarian regime, and laid bare the contradiction in the Italian Communists claiming a democratic role in Italy while defending communist dictatorships in Central and Eastern Europe.[28] A short while afterward, Giolitti left the Party, amid great polemics. Eugenio Reale also left the PCI after having been on the margins for some time because of a crisis of conscience caused by the violence of Sovietization.[29] Togliatti maintained that the defections were the price to pay when faced with the danger of a catastrophic domino effect in the "people's democracies" and, in consequence, among the Western communists.[30] As in the cases of other European communist leaders, his main motivation was to avoid the threat of the collapse of a system of reference regarded as necessary for the very existence of communism in Europe and in the world.

Socialist Central and Eastern Europe were similar factors in the scenarios of the polycentric world. Such was Togliatti's reading of the temporal coincidence between the Suez crisis and the Hungarian one. This was the nexus evoked by Khrushchev at the moment of the fatal decision to invade Hungary, and used instrumentally in the political polemic. It then took on a symbolic and political nature, since it linked the decline of the European empires with the Cold War in Europe.[31] In his speech to the Eighth Congress of the PCI on 8 December 1956, Togliatti began by denouncing the intervention of Britain and France in Suez, which in his view had brought the world "to the edge of the precipice" of a "third world conflict." He placed in this context the action of the "counterrevolutionary forces" in Hungary, at the same time admitting that the "mass uprisings" had revealed a crisis of Hungarian communism. He placed the accent on "mistaken political directions," but also on the "presence of the enemy," which without the intervention of the Red Army would have led to a fascist regime. In the first position he put internationalism as the "basic duty" and premise for a "unity that is created in the diversity and originality of single experiences [. . .], the prefiguration of the international society for which we are fighting."[32] These words constituted not only a rhetorical exercise but the definition of a nonnegotiable principle. Togliatti's interpretation, as ever, was characteristically and exclusively political. He maintained that there had been no change in the aggressive character of imperialism, and argued that "you can put a straitjacket [on imperialism] but you cannot change its nature."[33] It was from this viewpoint that he incriminated the forces of imperialism, Atlanticism, and social democracy, which he regarded as solely attempts to put a brake on the movements for national liberation, and to return to the Cold War. International relations of strength admitted the prospect of socialist progress without war. Even after Stalin's death, Togliatti's vision of the "war of position" was based on the idea that American capitalism was not a vector of global transformation, and that the United States was the final heir of a declining civilization, albeit still able to express military and geopolitical supremacy. Expressed in other terms, Togliatti imagined a future already moving in precise directions even though they still remained to be firmly defined, and did not contemplate the possibility of a transformation realized by the ruling classes in what in Gramscian terminology would have been called a "passive revolution." It is worth noting that Togliatti's reading of Gramsci did not take into account the reflections on "Americanism and Fordism," crucial to the formation of this political category in the *Prison Notebooks*.[34]

Togliatti did not move exclusively within the perspective of a bilateral antagonism. He asserted, rather, that "the world has become polycentric" insofar as the growing collapse of the colonial system offered new possibilities for relations and created a plurality of subjects. He indicated once again the "socialist camp" as a vector of human progress, but within a vision that recognized the positive significance of the emerging postcolonial world and which crossed the confines of bipolarism. In this context, he made one precise element explicit. It had been "a limit," he argued, to present the pattern of legality, parliamentarism, and the mass party as a solely "national" fact at the end of World War II. That model possessed ever more transnational characteristics, given that the very affirmation of the revolutionary and anticolonial movements created the conditions for a democratic and peaceful "way."[35] In reality the idea that the project of a mass party was not limited to a national particularity was always implicit in Togliatti's outlook after the war. His discourse was never framed as praise of Italy as an exceptional case, but as an invitation to the consistent application of strategies and practices having their origin in the most expansive moment of the communist movement, with the aim of liquidating minority sectarianism. At this moment, when the birth of a "polycentric world" was opening different international scenarios in the new horizon of meaning provided by the anticolonial liberation movements, he relaunched his vision. His objective was not to present Italy as a political laboratory, but to demonstrate the value of the experience of the Italian communists in the new global perspective of international communism.

Togliatti knew that the space for the influence of such a vision was still wholly to be conquered in the relations with the "socialist camp" and within the sphere of Western communism. The potentially strategic understanding with the French communists was almost nonexistent, despite the attempts to establish collaboration. Thorez refused to accept Togliatti's proposal to sign a common declaration that, while emphasizing the support for Soviet intervention in Hungary, recognized the popular nature of the protests, the lack of foresight by the Hungarian party and the Soviets, and the need for a loyalty based not solely on class solidarity but on "peaceful coexistence." The head of the PCI's foreign section, Velio Spano, observed after a mission to Paris that "we and the French comrades speak different languages," and he could have extended this assessment to many other communist parties, East and West.[36] The French and the East Germans did not spare their criticism of the gradualism and "pacifism" of the

Italians. The episode demonstrated how difficult it was to politically found the notion of Western communism and to distinguish it from the party-states of Eastern Europe. However, the "Italian road" and its more general ambitions were by now firmly established. Togliatti completed the changes initiated two years previously by marginalizing members of the old guard such as Secchia and Scoccimarro, who were opposed to de-Stalinization, and replacing them with a younger group no less representative of the Resistance, especially in the persons of Amendola, Ingrao, and Pajetta. In actual fact, the change went much further in all the leading organs, marking the advent of a "new generation" that would govern the party right up to the end, in a difficult relationship of continuity and discontinuity with the heritage of Togliatti.[37]

INTERNATIONALISM AFTER STALIN

After having put the shock of 1956 behind them, the leaders of the PCI turned to the Soviets to define an international agenda, consistent with the "Italian road." In January 1957, Longo and Spano met with Khrushchev, Suslov, and Boris Ponomarev to discuss the project of installing a "system of encounters for the exchange of opinions and experiences" and creating an international "press organ" of the communist parties. Khrushchev informed them of a possible meeting of the socialist countries agreed with the Chinese. He agreed on the fact that no attempt was being made to exhume the Comintern or Cominform, but one had to remember that "the social democrats have their International, the Western powers have NATO, SEATO, the Baghdad Pact and so on." In other words, the Soviet leader and the Italian Communists were arguing that communist internationalism had lost ground as compared with the Western international system, and could regain it only by creating new forms and rules of the game. The request of the Italians, made in the name of Togliatti, for a discussion of "the causes of the Hungarian events" and "how these had been possible after twelve years of the existence of system of popular democracy" remained, however, a dead letter. Khrushchev asserted that the Soviet leaders had not yet considered the question, but that one could say that there were similarities between Hungary and Poland, where the party "did not have links with the masses" and its leading group was "in the main composed of Jews"—an anti-Semitic argument that had already been used in the past by Gomułka. To a specific question from Spano regarding the role of the Yugoslavs in fomenting the revolt, the Soviet leader replied in the affirmative, indicating Moscow's concern about the influence of Belgrade on the "popular democracies." The Italians underlined their support for the decision to send the Red Army into Budapest, but did not receive the response they had requested.[38] In his report to the Party Directorate, Longo limited himself to outlining the intention of the Soviets to "put a brake on the centrifugal forces set in motion by Yugoslavia."[39]

The aim of containing the activity of the Yugoslavs against the Cold War blocs and reconstituting an international architecture for the movement was common to both Moscow and Beijing, albeit with different interpretations. At the start of 1957, Zhou Enlai undertook a long journey to the USSR and Eastern Europe, during which he openly attacked the "revisionism" of the Yugoslavs. He also made a veiled criticism of the Soviets' inability to prevent the crises of the previous months. Mao leaked his own mainly negative judgment on de-Stalinization, which implied his reserve regarding "peaceful coexistence."[40] The Italian Communists agreed with the criticism of the failure to foresee the Hungarian crisis, and with the attack on "revisionism," which could have been struck at them; and they especially shared the reserve regarding "peaceful coexistence." Togliatti knew that the first meeting of international communism after the death of Stalin would have to face intricate problems, beginning with the "leading" role more or less recognized as belonging to the Soviets.

A meeting of the thirteen communist parties holding power was held in Moscow on 14–16 November 1957, followed by another meeting attended by delegates from about sixty communist parties, including the Yugoslavs and the Italians. The restricted conference approved a declaration which for the first time put forward the doctrine of the "socialist camp." The document was founded on the idea that decolonization and the expansion of socialism were processes that converged in causing the decline of imperialism. The choice between "war or peaceful coexistence" was the key problem of world politics. As for relations in the "socialist camp," the path followed was that of the declaration made in Moscow on 30 October

1956 during the Hungarian crisis, about the principles of sovereignty and noninterference, given the lie to immediately afterward by the Soviet invasion. But pride of place was given above all to "mutual fraternal assistance" and the close unity of the communist states, which was equivalent to delineating a doctrine of limited sovereignty in the "socialist camp" in Europe. The scenario of a "peaceful road" was counterbalanced by one of revolutionary violence, a point on which the proposals for redaction of the text advanced by Mao were concentrated.[41] The wider conference released a "manifesto on peace" that rhetorically reconciled the principle of "peaceful coexistence" with the multiform perspectives of the world communist movement.[42]

All the delegates recognized the "leading role" of the Soviet Union in the "socialist camp" and in the communist movement. The most exposed in his support of this formula was Mao, and the most cautious were Gomułka and Togliatti. On 18 November, Togliatti devoted a large part of his speech to illustrating the "Italian road." He observed that after the end of the Comintern, only a few parties had been able to exploit the possibilities of "developing as great political mass forces." In Western Europe in particular, many of the parties had gone back to "being small-scale propaganda organizations." Togliatti thus emphasized the project of a mass party, which in the Italian situation had demonstrated its best potentials, and the recognition of which he proposed regarding its international implications. Among other things, he did not hesitate to preach the possibility of "structural reforms" within capitalism, using a reformist language that a large part of the delegates found hard to digest. In this way he gave a valid lesson to the entire movement.[43] His was not so much a strategic proposal, aiming at elevating the "Italian road" to the position of a model in a highly differentiated panorama. His scope was, rather, to consolidate the internationalist implications of "peaceful coexistence." He knew from experience that a force like Italian communism could exert its influence on the condition that it avoided contrapositions in terms of models. In the report Togliatti made on his return to Rome, he explained that he had attempted to present "the profile of our political positions," and to offer "that contribution which it behooved us to make toward clarifying the present-day problems of the movement."[44] He did not use the term "polycentrism," which had been coined the previous year. In light of the fractures that had come to the surface, he had probably set aside the more ambitious scenario of a "flexible" relation between the center in Moscow and its peripheral parties and states, which might even have thrown into doubt the notion of a "center."

Mao's intervention outlined a vision that differed widely from Togliatti's. The Chinese leader famously launched his image of a world in which "two winds" were blowing, a "wind from the East" driven by the forces of socialism and now stronger than the "West wind." He argued that a "counterrevolution" had been put down in Hungary, that the USSR had prevented a "war of occupation" in Suez, and that the launch of Sputnik had thrown the whole of the West into "a state of anxiety." Mao used the same arguments as the Soviets regarding the prospects for economic development, which in his view would bring the Soviet Union to surpassing the United States, and China to reaching Great Britain, within fifteen years. These considerations led him to formulate the prediction that the socialist powers would by then be "invincible," and to insist on his well-known metaphor that the imperialist powers were a "paper tiger," no longer be able to prevent the advent of "peace on earth." He did, however, draw the delegates' attention to the "worst-case scenario"—namely, that a nuclear war could be unleashed in the meantime. In that case, he said, he was less pessimistic than Nehru, declaring that he had told the Indian leader that the whole of humankind would not be annihilated, but only a third or even a half, and that imperialism would thus be "razed to the soil," and the "whole world" would become socialist.[45] In essence he was presenting himself as the consistent interpreter of the Leninist doctrine on war and of militant anti-imperialism, using tones far removed from the diplomatic ones that Zhou Enlai had used two years earlier at the Bandung conference. While upholding Moscow's leading role, he subtly undermined "peaceful coexistence" as a unified platform for the communist movement.[46] Mao's speech was particularly discordant with the interventions of a number of European communist leaders, and especially with that of Togliatti, who had declared that a thermonuclear war bore the danger "of the destruction of all civilized values," and had proposed to relaunch the movement for peace. "Peaceful coexistence" and decolonization thereby risked dividing rather than unifying the international communist movement. The polyphony imagined by Togliatti showed itself impracticable, the more the Maoist conception of the linkage between decolonization and world revolution asserted itself.

Despite this, Mao's speech apparently did not give rise to public or private reactions even from Togliatti. The Chinese leader's prestige was unquestioned. His speech of 18 November took up significantly more space in Togliatti's notes than all the others he made during the conference proceedings.[47] Ingrao recalled that Togliatti was "sparing with his comments" and avoided making "any remark of formal assent."[48] In his report back to the leading group of the PCI, Togliatti mentioned having met Mao twice, "observing that there was full agreement on all questions touched on."[49] Even on the hypothesis that Togliatti was keeping his perplexities about the Chinese leader's radical tones hidden, we still have to assume that the implications of Mao's speech left no significant traces. Most likely, Togliatti ascribed those accents to the division of duties established between the USSR and China in Europe and Asia, maintaining in any case the view that Moscow would exert a moderating influence. He was, beyond doubt, aware of the difference of views with Mao. Before the start of the conference, during the consultations on the conference declaration, he had met with the Chinese leader and with Thorez, expressing his option for the peaceful road and dissenting from the emphasis placed on revolutionary violence.[50]

The most visible tensions at the conference were caused by the attack on Togliatti by the French delegate, Jacques Duclos. Feeling they were the target of the Italian amendment denouncing "sectarianism" as a vice that had prevented many parties from acquiring a mass base, the French delegates provoked an authentic incident by opposing the idea of leaving parties freedom in how they gave their accord to the final conference document.[51] The question was smoothed over through the intervention of the Soviets, who confessed to the Italians that they had not been made aware of the French intentions.[52] The question of the mass party hiding behind the cryptic reference to "sectarianism" was no marginal aspect, and went back to the first years of the postwar era. With its implications in terms of social alliances, cultural hybridization, and relative ideological tolerance, it confirmed a difference in political culture between the leading groups of the French and Italian parties, which was coming out again despite the common support expressed for the Red Army's intervention in Hungary. But the criticisms made by the French were not isolated. According to Vidali's recollection, the praise of the mass party made by Togliatti in Moscow gave rise to icy reactions, not to mention the widespread impression that the Italian Communists were attempting to "give a lesson to all and sundry."[53]

However, the center of gravity in the Moscow conference did not lie in the alternative between centralism and polycentrism, but between "peaceful coexistence" and world revolution. Both the Soviets and the Chinese showed indifference, if not hostility, to any idea of a more flexible articulation of relations between communists. In this aspect, they shared the same political culture, modes of command, institutions, and totalitarian practices. But their visions and languages diverged when it came to the meaning to be attributed to the global role of communism. The alternative between coexistence and revolution was firmly denied by the Soviets, who saw no opposition between the two terms, while it was thrown into relief by the Chinese, who alluded to the problem of the potential contradiction between the interests of the Soviet State and the anti-imperialist role of the movement. The two pillars of world communism were identified in divergent scenarios of world revolution and tended to impose them, thereby generating a dualism at the practical level. Togliatti unreservedly plumped for "peaceful coexistence." It was precisely the need for such a clear choice and the perception of a possible line of fracture of the movement generated by decolonization, not less than that of de-Stalinization, that constituted one more reason for not insisting on the question of polycentrism.

The visions of communist internationalism in contention in Moscow in November 1957 remained substantially unaltered over the next three years. The Soviets maintained that they had fixed a point of equilibrium, but the consensus arrived at on the formal level was fragile and fictitious. Even Togliatti thought that the compromise reached at the conference was sufficient to configure a new season of international communism, including within it the legitimation obtained for the "Italian road." In an apparently simple way, he put aside the disagreement with Duclos. In reality the episode left its mark and was used as a pretext for the "old guard," to a great extent marginalized, to find a counterpoint in Moscow and reenter the game. In the summer of 1958 Robotti, at the behest of D'Onofrio, sent the international department of the CPSU a memorandum containing an accusation against the new generation of the PCI, which had the support of Secchia, Colombi, and Vidali. The accusation, made above all against Amendola and Pajetta but also against Ingrao, Mario Alicata, Paolo Bufalini, and Enrico Berlinguer, was that of overestimating parliamentary activity at the expense of cadre organization, and of inoculating the PCI with a form of "revisionism" influenced by Yugoslavia, which would have led to a separation from the Soviet Union. The criticism was also directed, albeit more cautiously, against Togliatti and the interview he gave to *Nuovi argomenti*, which had given rise to breaches in relations with the Soviets that had not yet been repaired. The authors did not spare Nilde Iotti, considered to have a negative influence on Togliatti in that she ensured the link with the "younger generation." This could open up the road, in the authors' view, to a removal of Togliatti himself, leaving the party under the formal leadership of a diarchy composed of Longo and Amendola; this would be an expedient for the effective leadership to be consigned into the hands of the latter. The attempt by the signatories to find a hearing in the CPSU evidently fell into the void after Longo and Amendola's talks in Moscow in September 1958.[54] Above all, then, the document was a testimony of the last reemergence of the old-guard pro-Stalinist leaders in the Italian party; but their arguments regarding the ambitions and the diminished loyalty of the new generation left some mark in the Kremlin, where over the forthcoming years various degrees of mistrust continued to exist toward Amendola and even toward Togliatti. The document also showed how, among the Italian Communists, the subject of Yugoslav "revisionism" obscured the perception of growing tensions between the USSR and China.

The seriousness of the dispute became evident only in a closed meeting held in Bucharest in June 1960, at which Colombi was present.[55] More or less simultaneously, during a trip to the Soviet Union, Togliatti drew up a note in which he summarized the main points of disagreement between Moscow and Beijing, which had now surfaced regarding détente with the

United States and around Mao's choice of launching the "Great Leap Forward." This latter policy had exhumed the teleologism and mass violence that had characterized Stalin's "revolution from above" thirty years before with catastrophic results. Referring to declarations by Chinese leaders, in particular Liu Shaoqui and Deng Xiaoping, the note mentioned the contraposition between "peaceful coexistence" and the anticolonial struggles, the thesis of the inevitability—or not—of war, and the roads of peaceful or violent transition to socialism.[56] The preparation of the second world conference was not of use in finding a compromise. In a meeting with the Soviets in September 1960, Berlinguer noted that the divergences with the Chinese on the "peaceful road" had been born "right at the start," and that therefore it was only with great difficulty that they could be "negotiable."[57] Thus the world conference that brought together eighty-one parties in Moscow in November and December 1960 represented the high point reached by the spread of communist parties throughout the world, bound up as it was with the birth of new postcolonial states; but it also exposed a fracture in the movement destined to show itself as fatal.

The Italian delegation, led by Longo, worked to avoid the formation of two opposed deployments of parties and declared its opposition to attempts to transform political or ideological disagreement into a conflict "regarding state relations between a number of the socialist countries." The message to both sides of the conflict was that there could no longer be "a single world leadership of the entire communist movement." This choice of method was linked, once again, to a position adopted on the subject of war and peace. Following the anticatastrophist inspiration of Togliatti, underlined some months earlier in Moscow, Longo asserted that a nuclear war would have "destroyed the very bases of modern civilization," and that the revolution had no need to open its road "by using thermonuclear bombs, with countless deaths and ruins."[58] Difficulties immediately came to the fore. The Italian Communists' efforts at mediation in the name of unity were immediately thwarted by disagreements that had emerged between Khrushchev and Deng Xiaoping revealing the competition between two alternative leaderships. The Italian delegates adopted a position against the Chinese leader and insisted on the "peaceful road" to socialism.[59] The conference ended with a generic reaffirmation of "peaceful coexistence," and the PCI leading group was satisfied with this element, passing in silence over the fact that the conflict between the Soviets and the Chinese was paralyzing the adoption of any more precise position.[60]

For about a year, the crisis of détente in Europe and the relaunch of de-Stalinization in the Soviet Union constituted a serious diversion to the Chinese question. In August 1961 the Italian Communists unreservedly supported the decision to build the Berlin Wall, doing so in the name, among other things, of the antifascist image that assigned special emphasis to the GDR as compared to the other "people's democracies." Togliatti defended the wall as an unavoidable measure taken to counter Western policies.[61] At the same time, he drew a clear distinction between the confirmation of "peaceful coexistence" and the relaunch of the denunciation of Stalin made by Khrushchev at the Twenty-Second Congress of the CPSU. Togliatti's reaction to Khrushchev's denunciation of Stalin, this time a public one, was one of extreme irritation, as is documented in Barca's diary. He went to the lengths of asking explanations of Suslov, expressing his amazement at what seemed to him a "judicial trial."[62] In his report to the Central Committee of 10 November 1961, Togliatti limited himself to observing that the renewed denunciation of Stalin added little to the "secret speech," recalling the limits he had commented on in the interview he gave to *Nuovi argomenti*.[63] At a distance of five years from the shock of 1956, he had not changed his ideas. His vision of Central and Eastern Europe was still anchored to the conviction that the risks involved in de-Stalinization of the Khrushchev type were too high, and that it did not represent a vector of positive change. This conservative idea had led him to underwrite the worst acts of normalization in Hungary, beginning with the death sentence passed on Imre Nagy, and to avoid any reply to the dramatic letter that the leader of the Hungarian reforms had addressed to him and to other leaders such as Tito and Gomułka.[64]

Togliatti had, however, underestimated the consequences of his attitude on the younger generation. Several of its representatives expressed their perplexity and criticism. Once again, as in 1956, Amendola was the main spokesperson. He asserted the "liberatory value" of Khrushchev's denunciation, the risk of paying too high a price to the ritual of "fictitious unity" as established in the two conferences of 1957 and 1960, and the need to give birth to an internationalism that was not merely "for show," that would free itself from the "straitjacket" constituted by the system of relations that existed in the communist world. In Amendola's view, the main questions posed by the PCI in 1956 had been abandoned or put into cold storage: "They have remained in the refrigerator," to use his words. He was referring in particular to the subject of polycentrism, "the national roads to socialism," including those in countries where "there is no communist party," and an analysis of the transformations that the capitalist world had undergone. The most sensitive nerve Amendola touched was that of self-censorship, in the international debates as much as within the individual parties. In the case of the PCI, he singled out the fracture between national language, "a heritage of political culture," and internationalist language, which was difficult "to translate into Italian terms."[65] Expressed in other words, the most important figure of "national communism" was invoking a redefinition of the international conduct of the party, criticizing Togliatti for not having developed the premises of his own vision and arguing that the implications of de-Stalinization regarded Italian communism, too, and its capacity to modify itself over time. Analogous considerations came from Alicata and, in more moderate terms, from Pajetta and Giorgio Napolitano.

Togliatti was harsh in his censorship of critical voices. He had recourse to the arm of memory in asserting his authority and, with that, the sense of an era that he maintained was not yet exhausted. He re-evoked the "reserves" he himself had advanced on the Cominternist conception of obedience, in particular in 1929, in order to call everyone to order, to the "substance of the matters,"—that is to say "to what the socialist society was, which was then being constructed in the world." This was, in his view, a priority that had lost none of its validity and which remained at the basis of the identity of all communists. In this way he underscored a narrative that removed the crimes of Stalin and limited the critical reflection on his legacy which was long destined to weigh on the common sense of Italian communists, hindering the acquisition of an awareness of the role played by violence in the experience of the Soviet Union. Instead, Togliatti recognized as legitimate the "discontent" expressed for the situation of the international movement, especially in Western Europe, but limited himself to contraposing the "backwardness" of the communist movement in the capitalist world with the growth of the movement outside Europe. He professed confidence in the future, and claimed that it was an "exaggeration" to see the Chinese polemic against the Soviets and the European communists as a "fracture." In essence, he was not letting himself be shut up in a corner, and he recalled to everyone the need for international belonging, putting his listeners on guard against the risk of attributing a vain, excessive role to the Italian experience.[66]

Both Amendola and Togliatti placed themselves within the tradition of Italian communism as an active and thinking component of international communism, but they showed a serious divergence regarding the credibility and future of the movement. Amendola's rebuttal touched, indeed, on a fundamental aspect of political culture. The breakdown of unanimism between the communist parties, and within the parties themselves, implied that old mentalities had to be sloughed off and a new critical vision adopted, capable of orienting the internationalism of the communists—to the extent that this was possible—toward the left in the West. Togliatti skirted round the reasons underlying the division within the leading group. His reaction confirmed his conservative view of de-Stalinization, based on the idea that the systems of a Soviet type would with time be able to turn the page on the Stalinist setups of the past, seen as simple "degenerations" of a mythical Leninist "golden age." He remained fixed in his view that the "unity" of the communist movement and the international relations of the Italian Communists were factors that could not be relinquished. It made sense for them to insist on their own vision as long as it was accepted in Moscow and elsewhere, and much less so if it led only to isolating the leading group and weakening it without a practicable alternative at hand. However, the appeal for unity also represented a way of ignoring the twilight of the raison d'être of the internationalist tradition. Younger leaders were precisely realizing such a problem. This second dilemma was neither taken on board nor elaborated upon. The problem of "languages" that Amendola had indicated in the light of the fracture between national and international discourses pointed to a dimension that was not only Italian, and even at that time revealed the start of a disintegration of the connective tissues of the communist movement.[67]

Longo had the thankless task of informing the Soviets of the first discussion, in which they had been subject to criticism in a leading organ of the PCI since the 1920s. He did not speak solely of the interrogatives raised by Alicata and Amendola regarding the denunciations of Stalin, but presented the two leaders as defenders of "polycentrism," mistrustful of Moscow's attitude to the "national roads." Longo affirmed his support for the positions expressed by Togliatti, especially with regard to the positive judgment on the world conferences of 1957 and 1960. In other words, he understood Togliatti's conclusions as the reassertion of a principle of "unity in diversity" distinct from the ideas that lay behind "polycentrism." His approach appeased the Soviets, but also signaled a veritable aporia in the leading group in Italy about the meaning of the two terms. This did not save him from the crossfire of Suslov and Ponomarev, who regarded the criticisms of the Soviet Union as crimes of lèse-majesté. Alluding to the Chinese, Kozlov claimed that "polycentrism" would have favored those who in 1960 had defended "fractional activity in the communist movement."[68] In his report back to the Italian Party Directorate, Longo spoke of Moscow's disappointment at the "anti-Soviet" positions of some the leaders of the PCI, and of Soviet support for Togliatti despite the dissent over the thesis of "bureaucratic degeneration." Togliatti commented that the debate had damaged the prestige of the party in the international movement, a prestige based on "the method of not wounding the sensitivities of brother parties," and in particular he mentioned the susceptibilities of the Soviets, who were having to face "the great problem of the Chinese."[69]

Togliatti immediately made use of the Soviets' support to try to exert his influence on the Chinese question. On 12 January 1962 he wrote a letter to the CPSU expressing his doubts about the wisdom of calling Beijing to order by means of a document signed by the communist parties that had approved the 1960 resolution, since the Chinese would then have interpreted it as "the beginning of a struggle against them." He also rejected the proposal to convene a new conference of world communism, which would have led to an effect contrary to that of recomposing the disagreements.[70] However, the problem of what sense to give to the notion of communist "unity" remained open. A few months later, Amendola underlined to the Soviet ambassador his criticism of "democratic centralism," and stated that it was mistaken to use "the methods of diplomacy" in interparty relationships, not least between those that were not in power. Only in this way could they hope to increase the role of the communist and workers' movement in Western Europe, which had no influence on the reality of the Common Market. Among the Western communists there was not even a dialogue, according to him because of the PCF. While declaring himself a "disciple of Thorez" and recalling the close links between the Italian and French communists, he maintained that the latters' choice to avoid contact with the PCI was incomprehensible.[71] The imperative of unity, the controversial relation with the notion of polycentrism, and Western communism's weakness as a political actor would occupy a central place in Togliatti's activity in the last two years of his life.

"PEACEFUL COEXISTENCE," NATIONAL INTEREST, AND DECOLONIZATION

In 1956 the PCI had shown two faces in national politics. On the one hand, it was the party of "peaceful coexistence," which reflected Soviet foreign policy—as it had always done in the past—but also supported a change in the post-Stalin bipolar world favorable to the creation of "national roads" for the Western communists. On the other hand, it was the party of the Cold War, which, after the fall of the myth of Stalin and the Soviet invasion of Hungary, aimed at reinforcing its own social and political trench in the perspective of the reciprocal siege between the two blocs in Italy. The loss of the monopoly on Marxism among left intellectuals was compensated for by the monopoly on the front of opposition to the government after the rupture with the socialists. Under the conditions of antagonistic bipolarism, this ensured the defense of the party's popular base. Togliatti had recourse to the symbolic resource of antifascism, without ever presenting the PCI as a force in opposition to the system. The language he used was much more turned to the nation than to the "imagined community" of the communists, drawing only indirectly on the Soviet myth. The discourse on antifascism as political culture was placed before the myth of socialist economic modernity, thereby avoiding being engulfed in Khrushchev's promise of communism already within reach, which at the end of the decade, together with the technological challenge and the conquest of space, had become the hallmark of Soviet propaganda.[72] Togliatti's thesis that "antifascist democracy" had been a project under construction since the 1930s served to draw a veil over the authoritarian reality of the "people's democracies," but also presented the communists as the essential nucleus of a ruling class for the republic waiting in the wings.[73] Its foundation was a national narration (the historical "necessity" of the workers' movement), seen in the Gramscian perspective of a "movement that emerges from the depths of the current setup of society," that was inserted into a global vector: the unstoppable progress of socialism and the socialist camp of forces on a world scale.[74] The Gramscian canon thus continued to be intertwined with the Marxist-Leninist vision of the triumph of socialism. The affirmation of the international links of Italian communism was based on the fact that in the contemporary world, every political movement presented "a tendency to establish contacts outside its own country."[75]

"Peaceful coexistence" defined the vision of internationalism and the notion of national interest for the Italian Communists. Togliatti bet on the ability of international détente to balance the isolation of the PCI in national politics, which was accentuated after the Hungarian tragedy. The foreign policy of Stalin's successors stabilized bipolarism, smoothing over the most conflictual characteristics, and presenting the Communists with the chance to emancipate themselves from the role of a mere advance guard in the enemy camp. The international links themselves, which had made a strong contribution to creating the domestic Cold War and the split in Italian society into two blocs, now seemed to be a political resource. The PCI came out against the Treaties of Rome, holding firm to its negative judgment of the Common Market as the dominion of monopoly capitalism and sharing Moscow's evaluation of European integration as an appendix of the Atlantic Alliance.[76] It did, however, invoke concrete steps inspired as much by "peaceful coexistence" as by the "Mediterranean vocation" of Italy, which offered its flank to an allegation of neutralism, but nevertheless did touch a political subject after a decade of sterile propaganda against Atlanticism. Indeed, even in the political legacy of De Gasperi was the idea that Italy should function as the link between

Europe and the Mediterranean, supporting the end of imperial power in the region, but the coordinates and methods lying behind such an inspiration remained vague.[77]

The paternity of the attention paid toward decolonization was a matter of contention in the domestic scene. In the first postwar years, the Communists had prioritized national legitimation and had ambiguously avoided asserting the independence of former Italian colonies. After Stalin's death things started changing. The challenge came from both Catholic and socialist personalities and intellectuals, and in particular from people such as Giorgio La Pira and Lelio Basso.[78] Pietro Nenni and the Socialist Party instead toned down their own anti-imperialist positions in moving closer to the sphere of government.[79] The Italian Communists developed the idea of building a bridge between the two Europes and at the same time between Southern Europe and North Africa, thereby participating in the new relations established between the "socialist camp" and the Arab world. They counted on the hegemonic ambitions of Moscow toward the postcolonial world after the Suez crisis, and on the Soviet myth of an alternative model of development to Western capitalism.[80] This international linkage distinguished the Italian Communists from the nascent Third-Worldist tendencies in left opinion, and gave them a powerful influence over a number of choices in national politics.

From 1956 onward, Togliatti exerted pressure on the Italian governmental forces on the dual terrain of détente and decolonization. He outlined perspectives that were lacking in the ruling political circles. In prevalence these were hostile to détente, despite vague professions of dialogue between the two international blocs, and they were ambiguous on crucial questions such as the Suez crisis, which in their relations with Washington they opportunistically attempted to exploit against France and Britain. The Christian Democrats upheld the priority of the internal cold war and limited themselves to establishing a marginal role for Italy in Western policies, aimed at maintaining bilateral economic agreements and at backing the initiatives undertaken by the ruling economic classes, above all the personal diplomacy of Enrico Mattei.[81] Togliatti linked the idea of "peaceful coexistence" to the evolution of the world order, not merely in a bipolar dimension. In his view, the emergence of "a system of new states" at Bandung configured not just new powers but "new civilizations," characterized by the "defense of their independence against imperialism" and by the search for their own social paths. In an implicit claim for the cosmopolitan traits of his own biography, which very few people in the Italian parliament could vaunt, he mentioned the Indian leader Nehru as a figure who was emblematic of the epochal change underway, recalling that he had met him in Barcelona in 1938 in the midst of the Spanish Civil War. He thus alluded to intersections that linked communist internationalism and European antifascism with the trajectories of the anticolonial struggles, citing Nehru's recollection in his autobiography of having visited a place where one saw "the light of bravery," the determination "to do something that was worthwhile."[82]

Togliatti formulated a line based on two elements: the thesis that the conceptions bound with the "contraposition of the blocs" no longer corresponded "to today's reality of affairs," and the aim of making the Mediterranean "a zone of peace."[83] He was establishing a link between national interests, the possibilities of a new relationship between East and West, and postcolonial scenarios. In particular, he called for "a radical and clear change of direction" in Italian politics regarding what he defined as a French "war of extermination" in Algeria.[84] His public speech effectively struck at the limits of the traditional anticommunist vision faced with the import of the changes taking place in Asia and Africa. Such changes were registering the birth of protagonists who could hardly be reduced to the opposition between the "free world" and "totalitarianism." This allowed doubt to be shed on the directions of Italian foreign policy. *Rinascita* commented on the participation of the socialist countries at the Afro-Asian conference held in Cairo at the end of 1957, and stigmatized the "curtain of silence" that had fallen on Italian policy in the Mediterranean.[85] Togliatti's view was that the solidarity of the socialist world with the anticolonial independence movements represented "a convergence of the aims" of freedom.[86]

The Eisenhower administration showed its obsession with the Soviet presence in the Middle East, and oscillated between the legacy of bipolar militarization and the challenges posed by national independence and the development of the Third World. This provided renewed reasons for communist anti-Americanism, combined with the denunciation of racism and the negation of civil rights in the United States.[87] In European politics, it was difficult for a clear anticolonial vision and a reflection of postcolonial scenarios to come to the fore, not only among the Christian Democrats but also among the Socialists. The latter, most of all in the ranks of the Labor Party, had developed projects of "colonial development" with the aim of reducing poverty and inequality, but rejected the idea that national independence was the priority everywhere. The determination of the French socialists to keep the national and colonial link with Algeria constituted a problem in the Socialist International that was incapable of solution despite the growing discontent against the policies of Guy Mollet.[88] For the PCI, the collapse of the Fourth Republic in France and the advent of General Charles de Gaulle provided the occasion for reproposing on a European scale the subject of the "twilight of colonialism" and the idea of the convergence between socialism and decolonization.[89]

In underlining the reasons for détente and its intertwining with decolonization, especially in North Africa and the Middle East, Togliatti had the right cards in his hand as compared with the opportunisms of the Italian ruling classes and the deaf ear turned by the Vatican, which was trying to create for itself the role of mediator in colonial conflicts.[90] A similar approach laid bare the contradictions of Amintore Fanfani's "Neo-Atanticism," which aimed to claim a vague Italian role of mediation in the Mediterranean, cut out with Washington's approval, but at the same time created divisions within the Christian Democracy Party itself.[91] Togliatti invited the Italian rulers to understand better the "multiform and complex process" of the formation of new states in Asia and Africa, and defined "détente" to be a "new world structure."[92] He thus played on the contradiction of the Catholic ruling class's tendency to think of Italy's role in international politics as being autonomous, and its subordination to the constraints of the Cold War.[93] At the same time, Italy occupied a privileged position in the optics of détente between East and West, among other things because Moscow was attentive to the role of the Vatican and its importance for a number of countries of the Soviet bloc, in particular Poland and, within the Soviet Union, countries such as Lithuania.[94]

The visit to Moscow in 1960 by President Giovanni Gronchi—decided upon in the midst of the bitter polemics concerning the role of Italy in détente, and then resolved in what was a contradictory manner, to say the least—brought grist to the mill of the PCI. In a note in his diary at the beginning of January, the Italian ambassador to the USSR, Luca Pietromarchi, wrote, "There is no doubt that Togliatti has known how to ably exploit the government's mistakes," which, instead of launching a policy of "rapprochement" with the Soviet Union, showed signs of subjection to this prospect, leaving the Communists to "boast of having imposed it on a reluctant government."[95] Indeed, in his speech to the Ninth Congress of the PCI, Togliatti emphasized the novelties that had been generated by détente within bilateral relations, expressed satisfaction with Gronchi's announced visit, and stated that the Communists had the duty to contribute to the formation of a new policy for Italy, different from that of Adenauer in Europe and from "French militarism" in the Mediterranean.[96] While remaining within the rhetoric of the "superiority" of the socialist system and maintaining the harsh judgment on de Gaulle, Togliatti's line of argument brought up national political questions and corresponded to concrete developments in the transnational activities and practices of the PCI. As against this, Gronchi's Russian trip in February 1960 showed all the incongruencies of Rome's orientations; the Italian president received a very lukewarm reception in Moscow, where his attempt to define the presence of communist parties in Europe as a hindrance to détente revealed its maladroitness.[97] Fanfani, too, held to the same line in his meetings with the Soviets in July 1961, proposing an exchange between the development of diplomatic relations and the cessation of Soviet help to the PCI, which was clearly unacceptable to Moscow.[98] Notwithstanding this, in private Togliatti was positive in his assessment of Fanfani's trip. In his view, the PCI was interested not in propaganda but in making sure that "if a minimal amount is obtained for saving peace, then that modicum must not be dispersed, and not destroyed by the mobilization of the baying pack of Atlantic-American bloodhounds."[99] The opening shown by the Kennedy administration, the birth of the center-left, and the universalistic appeals expressed in the latter stages of Pope John XXIII's pontificate were not, however, to induce a clear revision of Italian foreign policy.

Togliatti constructed his line toward the center-left above all on the international terrain, in the attempt to guide the PCI away from the role of a mere frontal opposition.[100] This approach was linked to the watchword of "structural reforms" of capitalism, whose function was to match itself against the projects of the socialists without conceding any of the party's identity. The promise of "structural reforms" conveniently kept the level of political culture, inserted as it was in the revolutionary and anti–social-democratic tradition, separate from local reform practices that were widespread and effective in the "red regions" of the country. Togliatti posed the question in a way that also served to limit cultural divisions in the party between the different readings of the processes of modernization in the country and their linkups with Western interdependencies. The reading of the Italian "economic miracle" created serious divisions between those who, like Amendola, argued that it did not alter the traditional category of the backwardness of Italian capitalism and those, such as Bruno Trentin and Lucio Magri, who put forward the notion of "neocapitalism" and the scenario of the consumer society.[101] Such interrogatives brought into play the greater or lesser capacities to understand the transformations of the European West under the influence of Americanization, which involved the popular bases of the party, and the exercise of US hegemony, ever more incomprehensible through the lens of the catastrophic categories that characterized the ideological background formed in the Stalin era.[102] In the material then current, openings toward the Kennedy administration were not lacking. In particular, Gianfranco Corsini's articles from New York presented an analysis that was free enough from ideological conditioning, above all in the attention paid to the innovations introduced by "New Frontier" intellectuals such as Arthur Schlesinger. There was, for example, acceptance of the comparison with Roosevelt's New Deal.[103] However, it is not clear clear to what extent similar attitudes were shared in the leading group.

Italian communism survived modernization, despite American prophecies based on theories of development and their positivistic equation between prosperity and liberal democracy as a sure antidote to a consensus held to be founded on poverty.[104] But its update to the era of the economic boom required difficult cultural revisions, which subjected the ideas of an "alternative modernity," formed in the interwar years, to a hard test. There were obvious traits of a schematic nature inherent in Togliatti's vision of a "war of position." This was based especially on the conviction that socialism was the main vector of progressive world unification, and would have made the Cold War senseless as a Western project, by acquiring new forms and meanings through decolonization and the reaction this would produce on the postimperial West. The road would thus be opened to structural change, allowing new ways of combining the notions of socialism and democracy and claiming a role for Western communism that was quite distinct from social-democratic reformism. In this optic, reformed welfare capitalism was reduced to a subordinate and secondary aspect of global postwar capitalism. Togliatti's scheme did not foresee that the hegemony of the United States over the capitalist West could generate a "revolution without revolution," with its action in transforming the policies of productivity and, to a growing extent, in promoting widespread consumption.

And yet the international visions of the PCI did not reduce to a mere variant of anti-Americanism and to the organization of the peace campaigns periodically promoted by Moscow or by East Germany through the World Peace Council, activities that were quite markedly scaled down after 1956. The Italian Communists remained bound to the "cultural Cold War" and to its Manichaean canons, while at the same time drawing near to the visions of the end of the Cold War coming, above all, from actors outside the bipolar scheme.[105] They favored Soviet interests but were able to stabilize influence and credibility most of all in a country like Italy. This repercussion of communist visions on the national scene should not be underestimated. The Italian left had undergone the choices of Christian Democracy on how—with the nexus of transatlanticism—the country was to be constituted internationally after World War II. Ten years later, it was the Communists who provided the primary political impetus to indicate and influence Italy's national interest jointly with East-West détente and the reality of the postcolonial Mediterranean and Middle East. This impetus contributed to their forming an essential part of Italian identity in international politics by forging a vision and a presence in the Mediterranean and Middle East purged of the legacy of nationalism. Such a vision, with high and low points, would long remain a constant reference point for the country's ruling classes and public opinion.

THE "REDISCOVERY" OF THE THIRD WORLD

After Stalin's death, the Soviet and European communists "rediscovered" the world outside Europe, reacquiring and reformulating visions, in light of the processes of decolonization, that went back to the 1920s and seemed now to offer formidable perspectives for the expansion of socialism in the world.[106] The alliance between the Soviet Union and China appeared as a vector of forces of change generated by the encounter between socialist experiences and the birth of new subjects and anti-imperialist sovereignties. The communists established the vision of a necessary convergence between social progress, the expansion of the socialist camp, and the anticolonial liberation struggles, all of which would have put the capitalist West on the ropes. In the scenarios opened by the interaction between the "socialist camp," the liberation movements, and the postcolonial states, the Western communists were in most cases considered to be on the margins. However, they faced up to the repercussions of the phenomenon and redirected much of their energy and transnational linkages to it, while not seeking to basically update their conceptual tools. The notion of polycentrism coined by Togliatti revealed a partial rethinking of the strictly Eurocentric vision that had characterized the Italian Communists since the 1920s, and which had been accentuated in the Stalin era. The Cominformist thesis of the "two camps" had placed the Old Continent at the center of the new bipolar challenge of forging the world order. Togliatti, too, adopted a hierarchical view, characterizing the colonial liberation movements as a force auxiliary to the "socialist camp," and the great countries of the Third World as new subjects on the path to socialism. The polycentric vision seemed, however, to imply a less rigid version of the Eurocentric tradition and to reflect a growing awareness of the global import of decolonization. While belonging to a country that was marginal to the European colonialist tradition and even more secondary in postwar postcolonial dynamics, the Italian Communists felt themselves involved in a role in the Mediterranean that was contained in the archetype of the *svolta di Salerno*, the Salerno turn. In line with their mentality, they turned to the Soviets to coordinate orientations after the Suez Crisis, but provided their own responses by putting themselves forward as a link between the "socialist camp" and the movements of nationalist, socialist and antiimperialist inspiration, above all in North Africa.

Central to the Italian Communists was the perception of a situation of relative movement which, while not shedding doubt on the European bipolar order, opened up new possibilities in relations and strategies. The Soviet Union's openings to the world, symbolized by its leaders' various trips abroad, especially to the newly independent countries, allowed a broadening of internationalist practices and the possibility of thinking of them in a scenario of multiple interactions. In this aspect, post-Stalin internationalism could be configured as a complex of ideas and political practices aimed at mutual integration and competition on a global scale, much more than had been the case in the Stalinist Cold War.[107] The tenuous but growing permeability of the "Iron Curtain," which became manifest in the second half of the decade, also involved the practices of the Western communists, to a great extent reemerging from the underground of the Cominformist era. The relations between the parties remained on a strictly bilateral basis, except for the meetings having the scope of preparing regional or world conferences. Cadre formation continued to maintain a privileged nature.[108] A multilevel system of relations then began to take shape, especially of a cultural, youth, and trade-union nature. A similar multiplicity of exchanges became evident not only in the relations with the Soviet Union, but also, for example, in the case of the GDR, which at the same time still played the role of a guardian of orthodoxy aimed at keeping the PCI's influence from going beyond its national dimension.[109] The most visible transnational meeting point was the review *Problems of Peace and Socialism*, created in Prague in 1958 after the dissolution of the Cominform and after the first World Conference of Communist Parties. Its editorial apparatus amounted to a network connecting Prague with various countries of Europe and the Third World. It was an example of the incongruencies of the communist movement: the strictly centralized modus operandi, in the hands of the Soviet leadership, and the adoption of Russian as the lingua franca along Cominformist lines did not hinder a certain circulation of people and ideas, even though censorship remained invasive.[110] In Prague and Warsaw, particular connections were established between the ideas of reform of the planned economies and the perspectives of state-led development in the Third World, which configured a strategic agenda aimed at postcolonial subjects and set aside rigid definitions of the socialist model.[111]

What hits the eye, however, is not the interaction between the European communists around internationalist themes and practices aroused by decolonization but, on the contrary, the absence of any authentic political coordination. The economic interventions agreed to in the Comecon by states of the Soviet bloc expressed an ideological discourse on noncapitalist development, but were only very slightly integrated into forms of political synergy.[112] The European communists acted in shattered ways on the decolonization scene, even if all spoke the modernizing and progressive language of the "state of national democracy" to connote postcolonial sovereignty, a formulation adopted by the Soviets at the 1960 World Conference, and disliked by the Chinese since it alluded to a nonviolent path of transformation.[113] Among the Western communists and the party-states of Eastern Europe, the "rediscovery" of the Third World opened up processes of learning and intervention that operated in parallel and communicated only sporadically.

The decolonization scenarios offered the possibility of a change in the marginalized position the communists had experienced in Europe after the continent's geopolitical division, after the high tide of mobilization for peace had subsided, and after the Chinese Revolution had shifted the movement's axis toward Asia. At the February 1957 meeting referred to above, Longo and Spano had raised with Khrushchev the question of the role of the Italian Communists in the decolonization process. Longo declared that "for our party an important meaning is attached to the situation in the Arab world and North Africa," and that the communists of those countries, the Egyptians in particular, were turning to the PCI for advice. "What should we do?" Longo asked. "Who should deal with them, us or the French? Is it possible to meet and discuss their questions in agreement with the French comrades?" Longo also mentioned the Moroccan and

Tunisian communists, but avoided any direct reference to Algeria, probably because the subject was far too delicate in relations with the French. In essence, the Italian delegates posed concrete problems that had emerged from decolonization in the Mediterranean and which involved the role of the European communists. They also made reference to Latin America, albeit generically. Their interrogatives remained, however, in suspension. Khrushchev limited himself to observing that in the year that had passed since the Twentieth Congress, nothing had been done despite the agreement reached between the PCI and the PCF.[114] In spite of this, the PCI's Foreign Department established a working agenda for the Mediterranean and Africa under the impetus coming from leaders such as Spano, Giuliano Pajetta, and Maurizio Valenzi. Attention was focused mostly on Egypt and the figure of Gamal Abdel Nasser, who had acquired notable prestige in the Suez crisis and was a privileged interlocutor with the Soviets.[115] The main question was, however, represented by the war of liberation in Algeria. The Algerian National Liberation Front occupied a central position in the constellation of anti-imperialist and postcolonial subjects, with the goal of forming the notion of the Third World as a political project. At the World Conference at Moscow in November 1957, the voices of the Third World were above all those of the Asian delegates, the Indians and Indonesians in particular; but the question of Algeria also emerged and revealed itself as problematic. The French Communists, represented by Duclos, defended the link between Algeria and France, albeit from a socialist perspective, thereby arousing the dissent of the Moroccan leader Ali Yata, who invoked a greater international solidarity with the Algerian anti-imperialist struggle, alluding to the scant involvement of the PCF.[116] Togliatti proposed avoiding a head-on collision with the French Communists on the Algerian subject, but alluding to the Popular Front era, he brought up their inability to carry forward "the great policy of 1934." The nationalist ambiguities of the PCF were indefensible, especially from the viewpoint of a new wave of decolonization on the African continent.[117]

At the end of the decade, the Cuban Revolution confirmed to all communists that a revolutionary and anti-imperialist season was occurring on a world scale, with the ability to influence the entire Latin American subcontinent and weaken the global power of the United States. The Italian

Communists constructed their own role without any real coordination of initiative with the "socialist camp," though they had requested it. In January 1960, Longo informed Suslov that the PCI had direct links with the communists in Egypt and with the "left democrats" in Somalia, Cameroon, Ghana, Nigeria, and other African countries. He posed the question of the role to be played in terms of help and assistance. Suslov's reply was very generic; he was "positive" in his opinion that the PCI should cultivate those relations, and he offered Moscow's assistance for cadre formation.[118] In other words, the internationalist relation between Moscow and Rome on such a crucial question as African decolonization appeared very vague, at the time when the PCI was weaving its own transnational connections. And this is without taking account of the fact, which emerges from Longo's words, that the Italian Communists' outlook and links were directed not solely to North Africa but also to other colonial and postcolonial realities of the African continent. Attention to western sub-Saharan Africa had been developing for about a year, after the independence of Guinea had given an impetus to the decolonization of the continent. So it was even more surprising that Suslov gave an evasive reply. It may be asked whether this depended on Moscow's diffidence regarding the theses of the Italian Communists on the relation between democracy, nation, and socialism, considered too inclusive and unorthodox. In any case, the episode is eloquent in demonstrating how labile the coordination of international communism had become since the first phase of decolonization.

The PCI founded its transnational connections with North Africa and other postcolonial realities of the African continent on a syncretic pedagogy and a paternalistic approach aimed at reconciling nationalism, socialism, and mass democracy, and on the pattern of European antifascism and the "nationalization" that went back to World War II. This was the approach of Sékou Touré and the Republic of Guinea, seen by some as Africa's revolutionary equivalent to Cuba, with the difference that it was following a "peaceful path" and thus represented an example in line with the Italian model.[119] In the case of Egypt, the PCI expressed a judgment on the Nasser regime in terms of social progress despite its harsh repression of local communists. At the same time, the PCI sought to help a weak and fragmented communist movement to develop its own "national" profile.

The possibility of its exercising an influence in that country was limited. Egypt did, however, constitute a crossroad of passages and connections that were useful in the anti-imperialist movements in North Africa, and even deep into the continent.[120] Between 1960 and 1961 the Congo tragedy and the murder of Patrice Lumumba were interpreted as signs of the aggression of the West, but also as demonstrations of its vulnerability and a confirmation of the necessity of consolidating the autonomous development of the new nation-states.[121]

The Italian Communists were aware that the most influential models of state building in Africa—such as a Nasserist socialist type of authoritarianism, or the "mass democracy" of Touré—presented serious problems of coherence with their political discourse, which focused on the idea of socialist democracy. The contradiction could have repercussions, above all, on the Communists' credibility as a national force.[122] Considered in this light, the encounter with decolonization sharpened a constitutive and introjected aporia—namely, the identification with a single-party system in Europe, which had shown its oppressive face even after the death of Stalin. The main counterargument was that the convergences of various postcolonial state models with the socialist model revalued the socialist model's function of modernization and could characterize a stage of transition. The incongruency between the idea of a "democratic path" to socialism and the reality of authoritarian regimes in many postcolonial countries was set aside in the name of internationalism. Even more than in the past, the interpretation of this notion began to assume particular connotations.

The position of the Italian Communists emerged with clarity as they appreciated the first Conference of Non-Aligned Countries, held in Belgrade in September 1961. Togliatti's vision remained centered on bipolar détente and the idea of a socialist path for the emerging countries, but he recognized the legitimacy of Tito's politics and his choice to stay outside the blocs.[123] Above all, it was from this moment on that the notions of the Third World and of Western "neocolonialism," understood as economic domination maintained after the end of the empires, entered the lexis of the Italian Communists in a stable way. The vision of the Third World as an anti-imperialist subject was adopted sparingly, however, and was subordinated to the language of gradual modernization, centered on agrarian reforms, state-led industrialization, and mass democracy. It was in this optic that the Italian Communists looked favorably on initiatives such as the Cairo Conference of July 1962, which brought the nonaligned countries into contact with the more radical African leaders and also registered the presence of Latin America, thereby promoting the theme of alternatives to dependence on the capitalist markets and contesting the European Economic Community.[124] The Communists did not present themselves as ambassadors of the Soviet model of development, even if they believed in its potential, and they showed greater understanding than others of the hybrid solutions adopted by the postcolonial ruling classes, which combined statist approaches and access to world markets.

At the same time, the Italian Communists drew advantage from their national identity. They represented a country that since World War II had obliterated its colonist past and was going headlong through a vigorous modernization process, thus displaying opportunities and resources that were unavailable or lacking in other countries of Southern Europe, Yugoslavia included. They could rightly claim lasting coherence in their anticolonial struggles, going back to the time of the denunciation of Mussolini's imperialism in Ethiopia. The struggle against Fascist colonialism and the analysis of it as an essential trait of the regime was part and parcel of Italian antifascism itself. This legacy was recognized internationally, most of all in Africa, and was helped by the "decolonization without decolonization" that came about in Italy after World War II—the end of colonial domination without the traumas and conflicts that characterized the French and British empires.[125] To some extent, the Italian Communists may have contributed to spreading a deceptive narrative of Italy and Italians as extraneous to colonialism. Still, their vision diverged from those of other Western European communist parties. The French communists' inability to assume consistent positions on Algeria created a void that the Italians filled, establishing a relation with the National Liberation Front and with the Algerian communists which reconnected European antifascism with anticolonialism.[126] The Italian Communists knew that the national identity of the French Communists was producing an ambiguous position on Algerian independence: recognized as a principle, but put off to a vague future at the political level. They maintained that the French were having a negative influence on the Algerian communists, pushing them into preferring the fragile urban proletariat in their social alliances, according to a narrowly Eurocentric schema that dated back to the Stalin era.[127] At the moment of Algerian independence, the Italian Communists were perceived in FLN circles as an important and autonomous interlocutor, the protagonist of an authentic "national road," as compared to the constrictions imposed by the Cold War.[128] All this gave their transnational role substantial importance, even in the competition between the Soviets and the Chinese, since to a certain extent it balanced the tendency of the Algerian revolutionaries to look to Beijing rather than Moscow as a reference point in light of the problems of backwardness and national construction.[129] Togliatti hailed the end of the war in Algeria, claiming to represent one of the most consistent forces in the defense of the cause of independence from French colonialism, which had touched the sensitivities of vast sectors of public opinion and culture in Europe.[130]

The coincidence between the Cuban Missile Crisis and the birth of independent Algeria created the preconditions for a qualitative leap. In both cases, the Cold War was intertwined with decolonization even more closely than before. In the missile crisis, the Italian Communists were aligned with the Soviet positions, with particular emphasis on the need for détente, and at odds with the anti-imperialist internationalism of the Cubans. The relaunch of revolutionary vanguards represented by figures such as Fidel Castro and Che Guevara, but also by Ben Bella, exerted its symbolic attraction and coincided with the European peace movement's loss of momentum, already evident at the start of the decade. The prevalent approach in the PCI was to defend the link between the new subjects of the Third World and the scenarios of "peaceful coexistence," and to take onboard its symbolic impact without yielding to the temptation of contraposing the "peaceful road" against the more militant variants of anti-imperialism. The PCI, however, found itself competing with the first intellectual and political expressions of a "new left," the bearer of a clear Third-Worldist and anti-Eurocentric critique which launched a challenge on the new global space opening up after the conference of Bandung.[131] The communist vision, founded on the European political nation, was contested as a form of cultural conservatism, by using arguments of a cosmopolitan origin that were not familiar to the communists and were included in the mythology of the Resistance, rejecting the narration of a "second Risorgimento" in order to lay stress on that of the incomplete revolution.[132] This Third Worldism again proposed the legitimacy of violence against colonial oppression, openly invoked by Frantz Fanon's celebrated *The Wretched of the Earth*, which redefined discourses and practices of decolonization in light of the war of Algeria, and found ample intellectual consensus even in the West. The languages used by the Western left became pluralized, and expressed different meanings with the birth of a "new left" critique of the Soviet Union.[133]

Under this pressure, the propaganda and strategies of the leading group in the PCI demonstrated a double register. *Rinascita* hosted authoritative voices of Marxist Third Worldism, such as Jean-Paul Sartre, who invited his audience to see the overriding impact made by the Third World as a subject.[134] The journal broadened its readers' views on many anti-imperialist subjects, from the birth of the new postcolonial state in Algeria to the liberation struggles in Africa, linked to figures such as Kwame Nkrumah and Nelson Mandela.[135] At the level of strategies and practices, it paid more evident attention to development and geopolitical pacification, which meant an approach different from Third-Worldist thinking. The PCI aimed at putting the question of the Mediterranean and Africa on the political agenda of Italy and of Europe, and it supported the "Casablanca group" of countries making clear breaks with the colonial past.[136] It was not a question of diversified approaches between public and reserved spaces. The impact of the revolutionary Third World also defined a divergence in the party, and the vision of "peaceful coexistence" enjoyed far less consensus than it had a few years earlier. At the Directorate of October 1962, immediately after the end of the Cuban missile crisis, Togliatti spelled this out explicitly: "Among comrades, there are two conflicting and paralyzing positions: nothing will be done, the USSR will not risk a war. Against this, the USSR will make the Americans see what they do not expect to see. It is not understood that we shall arrive at peaceful coexistence through struggles that are even bitter ones on single concrete objectives."[137] The leading group was divided between a predominantly moderate faction represented by Amendola and Pajetta, who had the party's national function and consonance with the Soviet Union in mind, and a radical tendency represented by Ingrao, more sensitive to the revival of anti-imperialism and its apparent cultural dynamism. The implications of this split, operating along national as much as international lines, may have led Togliatti to promote a new generation of leaders, Berlinguer and Alessandro Natta in particular, who modified the equilibriums in the Secretariat and the Directorate.[138]

Togliatti did not assign to himself the role of mediator, but he relaunched his own vision of "peaceful coexistence," the authentic center of gravity of his politics after the death of Stalin. In his speech to the Tenth Party Congress on 2 December 1962, he asserted that "peaceful coexistence" was not one option among others, but a necessity for everyone, and not exclusively for the "socialist camp." He declared, "This is the alternative: either peaceful coexistence or atomic destruction and therefore the end of our civilization or the greater part of it." He foresaw a new détente stage in international relations after the Cuban crisis and after the end of border hostilities between China and India.[139] The position adopted by the PCI on the missile crisis provoked a public attack by the Chinese communists, who took the occasion to denounce the line of "peaceful coexistence" as a betrayal of the anti-imperialist struggles exemplified by the Cuban revolutionaries. The Chinese were now putting themselves forward as an alternative leadership in world communism, opposed to any compromise with Western "neocolonialism" and ever more inclined to exclude the Soviet Union from the forces of world revolution. In January 1963, Beijing attacked Togliatti, accusing him of "revisionism" for having substituted "class collaboration" on a world scale for the class struggle. Togliatti's response was calm, but firm in its essence, indicating the aim of "avoiding war by creating a regime of peaceful coexistence" as a condition, among other things, of effecting socialist nonviolent transformations.[140] In the new conjuncture of international détente following on the missile crisis, Togliatti saw the possibility for a strategic relaunch that would fulfill the role of containing Chinese criticisms but was not limited to that goal.

The most intense signal of such a vision was Togliatti's speech on the "destiny of humankind," in March 1963. In it he included the problems afflicting international communism within a much broader optic. And, still more than in the past, he underlined the multifaceted nature of developments in the world, soberly defined as "a new articulation and differentiation of the system of states," which registered the legitimate place of the socialist countries despite the "problems" and the "errors" that had been committed, and which made the Cold War obsolete. This analysis was inserted into a particularly explicit version of his anticatastrophism, re-elaborated in light of the nuclear era. Taking up again the threads of the discourse begun about a decade earlier, Togliatti argued that in the contemporary world, "war becomes something different from what it has ever been" in the past—that is to say " the possible suicide of everyone"— and that peace had become a "necessity, if man does not wish to annihilate himself."[141] Similar words, in an appeal directed to the Catholic world in light of the Second Vatican Council and the opening shown by John XXIII toward détente between the power blocs, demonstrated a profoundly matured conviction that relegated the doctrine of the inevitability of war to the past.

Togliatti knew well that this conviction did not enjoy a consensus within the communist world. Mao had radicalized his opposition to "peaceful coexistence," but the Soviets too held a rigid vision of the "two camps," ignoring the subject of interdependencies throughout the world, and maintaining marked ambiguities on the very concept of the unity of humankind. That notwithstanding, Togliatti seemed convinced that, through the end of the acute phase of the Cold War, new perspectives on the expansion of the "socialist camp" and of communism on a world scale would be offered once the controversy between Moscow and Peking had calmed down. The PCI approved the nonproliferation treaty agreed upon by the great powers in July 1963, which brought to an end the international crisis and was read by many outside Europe, beginning with the Chinese and Vietnamese, as Moscow's renunciation of support for the anti-imperialist front.[142] Togliatti criticized the Chinese publicly for their opposition to the treaty, and commented on the revelation that the Soviets had refused to provide Beijing with the nuclear bomb in 1959, asserting that through this action Moscow had wisely "served the cause of peace, of international détente and disarmament."[143]

The polemic between Moscow and Beijing underwent an escalation that left little space for mediation. The growing divergence between the Soviets and the Chinese laid bare many aporias in the structure and government of the "socialist camp," in the visions of anti-imperialism, and in Cold War strategies. But most of all, it showed how the encounter between communism and decolonization could provide as much a vector of world politics as a space for new conflicts and antinomies, which could not be resolved in the socialism/capitalism dichotomy. At the Party Directorate, Togliatti confirmed the line followed up to then: that a world communist conference would end up only "deepening the rupture," with serious consequences for everyone. He said he had "little enthusiasm" for the conduct of the Soviets, who had been too cautious on Cuba, only to then show their "exasperation." The PCI was one of the "strongest" parties, but if the conflict was to go on, it would have its difficulties.[144] Togliatti's forecast turned out to be right. The precondition for the PCI to exercise a role of mediation was that it should to a certain extent be accepted by the other communist parties. But only the Poles and the Romanians were near to the Italian positions. In particular, the supinely pro-Soviet positon of the French communists aggravated affairs. The PCF turned down the initiative of a conference of the communist parties of Western Europe which, in the Italian plan, would have provided an alternative to the world conference. Togliatti's worry was that the head-on policy conflict fueled by both sides of the Sino-Soviet dispute would compromise the bases of international communism. In his view, the polemic in favor of or against détente did not really go to the heart of the political problem, which was: "How must we develop the policy of détente?"[145]

Togliatti then defined the contours of a vision that linked more precisely the role of communists in the West to the postcolonial world. His idea was that the postimperial era registered the crisis of all the European ruling classes, most of all the social-democratic ones, and that this could open the road to a socialist and anti-Atlanticist way forward. The influence of the communists seemed practicable to him, as long as they did not limit themselves to the "simple and not always fruitful wait for a different future." Togliatti sought to outline a political perspective, as he had at other crucial moments in the past. His vision contained several approximations and was schematic, above all in its placing of de Gaulle's "authoritarian power" and Adenauer's Westpolitik on a par with Franco's Spain, without even mentioning the subject of European integration. The mentality of the Cold War had thrown a veil over the differentiated analysis of capitalist Europe, which Togliatti had frequently invoked in years past, and which he now practiced in his approach to the Third World. The strong point of his vision was the nexus implied between the role of the Western communists and the diversities of the postcolonial world, which were likely to modify the very notion of socialism. Perhaps it was not by chance that the same number of *Rinascita* that published his editorial on "socialism in the West" also contained a report on the colonial question dating from the Sixth Congress of the Comintern in 1928.[146] Togliatti was seemingly taking up the threads of a discourse that in its essence had been plunged into oblivion during the Stalin era.

It was difficult for such a vision to be acceptable in Moscow or even in Paris. The main specter haunting the Soviets in that moment was the Chinese attempt to gain influence and control over the communist parties in Asia and Africa. The no-holds-barred competition between the Soviets and the Chinese in the Third World was by now a definite fact, and was compromising the unity of the communist movement. At a Central Committee meeting in October 1963, Berlinguer drew attention to the expansion of Chinese influence among communist parties and groups in Asia and Africa. His preoccupation was not just with the containment of Chinese influence, but with the fact that the conflict between Moscow and Beijing would be an obstacle to confronting "in their real importance" the problems of the Third World. He praised "peaceful coexistence," rejecting its contraposition to anti-imperialist struggles, but he used words of uncustomary criticism for the "wholly inadequate" Soviet responses to these problems, which were not made public.[147] In other words, the Italian Communists were not limiting themselves to dissent against the option of an excommunication of the Chinese, but were making objections of a political nature to Moscow regarding the very conception of internationalism and the South of the world. It is not clear whether the whole of the leading group was in agreement with Berlinguer's positions. It was, however, within this optic that the Italian Communists intensified their initiatives in the Mediterranean and in Latin America, in parallel with Zhou Enlai's long diplomatic trip at the end of 1963 and the beginning of 1964, which confirmed China's entry into competition for the Third World not only in ideological terms but at the level of developmental aid.[148]

Through his meeting with Tito in January 1964, Togliatti consolidated the role of the PCI as a protagonist able to act, more so and better than the other European communist parties and even the Soviets, as interlocutor with other subjects and movements, most of all the nonaligned ones. He came over not only as a leader of world communism but as a mediator between revolutionary experiences and worlds that, despite their global presence, were to a great extent disconnected and did not communicate among themselves. His talks with Tito on 16 and 17 January were based on the common conviction that the "physiognomy of today's world" had to a large part been modified, and that a policy of "active peaceful coexistence" was by now a necessity. In this context, socialism represented a "a unitary social and economic process," albeit one destined to develop "in quite varied forms."[149] The two leaders converged on the view that Asia and Latin America represented the two epicenters of an acceleration of global change which saw a plurality of subjects as protagonists. The common aim was to encourage the socialist leanings of the local elites and to avoid the end of colonialism fueling regional and national conflicts. Tito, who had just returned from a journey to the Americas, outlined in detail the situation of the various countries of Latin America, passing silently over the role of Cuba, perhaps since it was too sensitive a subject given the difficulties in the relation between Belgrade and Havana, rivals for the leadership of the postcolonial world. The terrain for the main understanding between the two leaders was, however, the Arab countries of North Africa. They shared the opening toward Ben Bella and Nasser, including their vague socialist ideas.

They also found common cause in their highly critical assessment of China's policies, albeit with different nuances. Tito was of the opinion that the conflict between Moscow and Beijing was "in essence one between states," and he foresaw that the Chinese would not turn back. The conflict with Yugoslavia had risen, in his estimation, from the Chinese reaction to Belgrade's successes in its alliances with the countries of the Third

World. The Yugoslavs saw no short-term solutions, and said that the only way forward was to involve China in the policies of development of the Third World, since integration into the "socialist camp" was not enough to ensure the growth of the Chinese economy. This latter point threw considerable doubt on the Soviet Union's capacity to maintain a global challenge and found its hegemony on concrete policies of development. Togliatti made the point, in a comment more consonant with the political culture of the Italians, that Chinese pressure was making "the process of democratization more difficult" in the socialist countries. He foresaw the scenario of an understanding "between the communist parties of the West and the liberation movements of Africa, Asia and Latin America," and imagined a meeting of the progressive parties and movements of the Mediterranean as a way of challenging Chinese positions at the political level. These words reflected his idea of creating a sphere of intermediate relations between the Soviet Union and the nonalignment represented by Yugoslavia, by opening a perspective to the communists of the "capitalist West."[150]

The commonality of views between Tito and Togliatti outlined a non-indifferent change in the system of relations of the Italian Communists, even though they remained loyal to the "socialist camp." The convergence on the notion of "active coexistence" in particular allowed a detachment of this topic from mere identification with Soviet policy, and transferred it to the international level of the United Nations. Of no less importance was the opening of the possibility for the Italian Communists to acquire judgments and information on international politics through the leading group of an influential state, which represented an outlook different from that of Moscow or the other socialist countries. Among other things, the Yugoslavs shared with Togliatti their ideas of a change in "global economic relations" elaborated by the nonaligned states, and their criticisms of the Comecon, inadequate as it was for confronting these kinds of problems, or even for integrating the socialist countries. In addition, Tito provided Togliatti with an account of his own meeting with John F. Kennedy shortly before his assassination. On his side, Togliatti appeared to outline an inclusive and not solely bilateral strategy whose aim was to formulate an idea of a community of socialists and of the "socialist world" that much more nuanced and enlarged than that of the Soviets. The PCI's action therefore appeared not as a support for the policies of containment of China then in operation in the "socialist camp" loyal to Moscow, but as an attempt to construct political alliances. Even more than in the past, Togliatti was formulating a view of internationalism open to convergence with different political cultures.

The parallel visit of Longo to Algiers was closely connected to Togliatti's strategy, which saw the search for political convergences as the only sensible way, though not understood by the Soviets, of containing the Chinese. Revolutionary Algeria was then at the apex of its international profile, flanking Yugoslavia and Cuba in the nonaligned world. The definition, coined some years later by the Guinean leader Amilcar Cabral, of the "Mecca of revolution" fitted Algeria well. Algiers had numbered among its visitors figures such as Che Guevara, Yasser Arafat, and Nelson Mandela, and had justly acquired the reputation of being a crossroads of anti-imperialist leaders and militants from all over the world. The declared ambition of the Algerian leaders was not the foundation of an Arab nationalist socialism, but the project of an African revolution.[151] The PCI had expressed its full support for Ben Bella's regime after promulgation of the Algerian constitution in September 1963, which seemed to foreshadow reforms of a socialist nature and the creation of a single revolutionary party that would include the communists.[152] Ben Bella recognized the Italian Communists as a privileged interlocutor, which could not be seen in the PCF. The twofold reason for the standing accorded to the Italians consisted in the construction of an internationalist and anti-imperialist network in the Mediterranean, and the national interest in relaunching economic relations with Italy, which had been interrupted after the death of Enrico Mattei.[153] The Italian Communists' mission preceded that of Ben Bella to Moscow in May 1964, which established meaningful relations between Algeria and the Soviet Union.[154]

Ingrao's mission to Cuba completed the picture of the intense international activity of the Italian Communists at the start of 1964. The attention paid to the Cuban Revolution and its relations with Latin America had been slow in getting off the ground until the Americans' Bay of Pigs invasion. The presence of the PCI had been entrusted to old figures of Cominternist internationalism such as Vidali, and to the despatch of cadres resident in Czechoslovakia, but with little success. The missile crisis heralded a sharp change.

At the end of July 1963, after the breach in relations between Moscow and Havana had been healed by Castro's visit to Moscow in April, the PCI took an important step by sending a delegation headed by a member of the Directorate, Ugo Pecchioli. He took note of the fact that Castro had stepped back from accepting the alliance with the Soviet Union, the basic assumptions of "peaceful coexistence," and even the inapplicability of a single revolutionary model to national specificities on the Latin American continent. But Pecchioli could not avoid observing that the subject of a "democratic road" to socialism still sounded like "an extraneous political idea to the Cuban leaders."[155] Ingrao's trip, during which he met with Che Guevara, confirmed first of all the symbolic meanings attributed to the Cuban experience and the function of a contrast to Chinese influence. Ingrao insisted on the importance of anti-imperialism outside as well as within the communist movement.[156] Cuba, however, remained a reality distant from Italian communism, and represented a different tendency in the international communist movement. The PCI's most incisive relationships in Latin America regarded other realities, especially that of Chile, as clearly emerges from the missions of Alfredo Reichlin in 1962 and Renato Sandri, one of the main officials of the Foreign Department, in June and July 1964. The latter's report mentioned criticisms by many Latin American communists not only of the Chinese but of the Cubans for their "adventures," which were bound to increase repression under the aegis of the United States. It also underlined the prestige enjoyed in various places by the Italian Communists.[157] At the start of 1964, the PCI's influence therefore emerged in a network of world connections that no other Western communist party could boast. The new relationship between the PCI and Yugoslavia also represented a link between the "socialist camp" and the nonaligned countries, which allowed Italian communism to consolidate its networks and intermediations from the Mediterranean to Africa and Latin America.

THE YALTA MEMORANDUM

In the public account of his trip to Yugoslavia, Togliatti declared, "One cannot reduce the whole socialist world to one sole bloc, military or political as it might be." He took on board Tito's argument that the Chinese polemic against the Yugoslavs had intensified when the latter had won "sympathy and support among the newly liberated countries."[158] In other words, Togliatti maintained that socialism was too diversified and pluralized a reality to be contained within the conception of a hierarchical community. In February 1964, however, the CPSU sent a letter to all parties which spoke a different language and denounced the Chinese attempt to create a "fractional bloc" in the international communist movement.[159] On his return from the talks with Khrushchev, Suslov, and Ponomarev in Moscow, Longo reported that the Soviets were not attempting to hide their irritation with the arguments that distinguished the notion of socialism in the world from the reality of the "socialist camp," seeing the thesis of polycentrism coming to the fore again at the most inopportune moment. Longo seemed to share this viewpoint, and stated that "there is a conflict of hegemony between the CPSU and the CPC. The Chinese want the 'leadership' even at the cost of flatly rejecting the guiding role of the CPSU. We cannot remain indifferent and save our souls." Togliatti did not, however, intend to be held in the grip of the Soviets, and in his intervention he emphasized that there could be socialist experiences without entering into the "socialist camp." He observed that this was how the Yugoslavs had built their own experience, and that they were not equidistant between two "camps" but, rather, sought to expand "coexistence" into the Third World.[160] Once again the multiple meanings of polycentrism were presented as an unresolved question, a source of controversy in international communism.

In April 1964 the public stance of the French Communists in favor of a world conference of communism induced Togliatti and Longo to write to the Soviets, in an attempt to block a formal invitation that would be impossible to refuse.[161] Their main argument was that such an initiative would confirm the "schism" in the movement and create "two organizational centers" struggling against each other, thereby compromising the autonomy of the other parties. The two Italian leaders made it clear that they would not sign any formula that shed doubt on the "national roads."[162] However, the positon adopted by the PCF caused the failure of the PCI's diplomatic work. Togliatti confided to Kozyrev there was probably no alternative to the convening of the conference, even though he continued to doubt its usefulness.[163] The leading group concluded that it should maintain its reservations while presenting them as a better way of combating the Chinese positions, and it accepted the invitation to participate in the preparation of a conference.[164] The report that Togliatti presented immediately afterward to the Central Committee constituted a sobering and grievous appeal for unity. He underlined the condemnation of the "method of solemn excommunication" that would present the "danger of a resurgence of authoritarian and sectarian systems," and he did not give up the vision of diverse anti-imperialist subjects and possible forms of socialism. In this context he refused to locate "the peasant masses of the underdeveloped countries ... in the vanguard" of the world movement, as the Chinese were doing, but also lamented the fact that the Western workers' movement was not up to the task of putting together "the different sectors of the great front against imperialism."[165]

After a delegation composed of Ingrao, Berlinguer, and Colombi had ascertained in Moscow the Soviets' determination, Togliatti recalled the leading group to a sense of collective responsibility and loyalty. His guiding principle remained the idea that the international role of the Italian Communists should be conceived within its interaction with the "socialist camp," despite the acknowledgment that this was too narrow a confine for defining the global profile of socialism. "In the world there is the camp of the communist parties, only this," he declared, to avoid any misunderstanding. "We cannot imagine our party not being part of it."[166] Togliatti and Longo wrote to the Soviets recognizing the dangers of Chinese influence but also fearing that a break with the Chinese would have negative consequences for the Southeast Asian liberation movements.[167] On June 20, Togliatti communicated to Kozyrev that he no longer saw barriers to the convening of the conference, limiting himself to asking for significant preparatory work, and minimizing the divergences with the French Communists, while pointing out that Thorez had refused to meet him.[168] The moment of decision was reached at the beginning of July. Togliatti turned to his leading group, inviting them "not to give the impression that we do not understand the general needs of the movement. There is a centrifugal process at work that has to be brought under control. It is not in our interests that the prestige of the Soviet leadership should be shaken in the international movement...." Among other things, his insistence on this viewpoint arose from the presence of less lenient positions toward Moscow's demands, held especially by Ingrao and Berlinguer.[169] The PCI kept to its line that the conference was inopportune, and repeated its positions in a letter to the CPSU on 7 July, but consented to take part in its preparation.[170] On 30 July 1964 the Soviets began moves toward the conference, to be convened in Moscow at the end of the year.[171] The tensions between the Soviets and the Italians were not assuaged by this. According to an opinion expressed to the Soviet ambassador to France by the Spanish communist leader Santiago Carrillo, it would be important to depend on Togliatti while he was still alive, in order to avoid a shift by a PCI represented by Amendola and Berlinguer, who looked no longer to the existence of an international communist movement, but to a form of "national communism."[172]

In August 1964, Togliatti decided to go to the Soviet Union. The reasons for his visit have been open to very different speculations, since he met not with Khrushchev but with Ponomarev and Leonid Brezhnev. The hints of participation by Togliatti in a plot against Khrushchev, leading a few months later to Khrushchev's removal from power, appear to be without substance.[173] The urgency of Togliatti's mission is explained by the fact that the Chinese question had now come to a head and the PCI could no longer limit itself to posting a veto. Togliatti proposed lessening the tensions that had emerged with Moscow over the previous months by accepting the compromise of taking part in the preparatory work of the conference and giving weight to the role of the PCI in the discussion on how to combat the Maoist positions. It may be imagined that Khrushchev was less inclined than the other Soviet leaders to reach a mediation on the Chinese question, and that for this reason he avoided a meeting with Togliatti. In any case, the personal prestige of the Italian leader and the influence of the PCI in international communism and outside its boundaries lead one to exclude the possibility that the Soviets had given up easily on finding an agreement, or even that they intended to put the Italians under their scrutiny. The wide-ranging criticisms that Togliatti formulated in a memorandum he drew up in Yalta while awaiting a new meeting demonstrate that he felt himself in a position to make his voice heard as an international leader of the movement.

Togliatti's "memorandum" opened with the clarification that the Italian Communists would respond positively to the convening in Moscow of preparatory work, while at the same time maintaining their perplexity regarding an initiative that would register the absence of numerous communist parties from Asia. But his document ranged immediately over the analysis of "a whole series of problems" of international communism.[174] He criticized the Soviets for maintaining a "ideological and propagandistic polemic," which placed them on the same level as the Chinese, instead of developing a political action, as he himself suggested, which would aim at defining tasks and roles "in the different sectors of our movement," thereby isolating the Maoist positions. His appeal to safeguard the unity of the socialist world and avoid a "general and consolidated schism" was not only a question of principle. Togliatti located the heart of the challenge in Europe and in the West, where it was vital to oppose "capitalist planning" and its "antidemocratic and authoritarian tendencies" by developing the ideas of a "peaceful road for the transition to socialism." He had by now left behind the era of the "peace movement," which he did not mention, and instead posed the question of a "general plan of economic development" and a "progressive transformation" of the "nature" of the state in the capitalist West. In this perspective he expressed an unyielding criticism of many of the Western communist parties at the level of mass politics, by now a recurrent theme. An essential condition for political action seemed to him to be the recognition of diversity within the communist movement and in its global relationships, and this alluded to the subject of polycentrism. The document contained few, but important, references to the relations between the Western communist parties and the anticolonial liberation movements. Togliatti wrote that it would have been preferable to have a conference convened by the Western parties with a "broad area of representation from the democratic countries of the 'Third World' and their progressive movements," devoted "exclusively" to the problem of the "ways of development of the ex-colonial countries" in order to understand "what the aim of socialism means for them." In this way the Chinese would be fought "with facts, not just with words." His reference to the fight against the Chinese was a persuasive argument when put to the Soviets, but his questions were more general and involved the very meaning of socialism throughout the world. We have to ask ourselves whether this passage in the "memorandum" also implied an ebbing of the wave of revolution, rightly or wrongly associated with decolonization.

The questions also involved the socialist world and the Soviet Union. Togliatti indicated the need for "superseding the regime of the limitation and suppression of democratic and personal liberties that was installed by Stalin," regretting the "slowness and resistance to a return to Leninist norms," which for him were equal to democratic freedoms. He continued: "We find this slowness and resistance difficult to explain, especially [. . .] when capitalist encirclement no longer exists and economic construction has brought impressive successes." He was arguing that de-Stalinization was a process that still had to be developed in order to free up the potentialities of socialist societies. His exhortation to the Soviets showed an awareness of the problem different from what he had expressed three years earlier, when he had liquidated it with some disdain, provoking a reaction from Amendola. It is likely that Soviet ideological intolerance in managing the conflict with the Chinese had induced Togliatti to consider the limits of de-Stalinization. He accepted a neo-Leninist narrative and the idea that there was a contradiction to be resolved between the social and productive expansion of Soviet socialism, on the one hand, and its political and institutional setup on the other.

To capitalism Togliatti instead applied a simplified language, evoking a "crisis of the bourgeois economic world." He did not devote a word to the dynamic nature that postwar capitalism had been demonstrating for about a decade, or to its tangible consequences in terms of industrial development, prosperity, and consumption, which he had recognized all the same in Italy's most recent past. His negative assessment of the Italian situation, often expressed before his departure for Moscow, weighed heavily in the balance. Consequently, the conservative involution of the center-left stood out, and he was led to doubt the possibility of a "bourgeois reformism." The basic problem was, however, the contradiction between the idea of "structural reforms," which presupposed an anticatastrophist vision, and the refusal to admit the possibility of a "progressive" capitalism in light of the persistence of imperialism.[175] The Italian peculiarity, interpreted by Togliatti as the product of a dense agglomeration of inertial forces and cultural and structural resistances to change, thus led back to the international context.

Togliatti argued that the West was at the mercy of "reactionary groupings" after the assassination of Kennedy. His judgment that the European Common Market was a weather vane signaling the monopolistic concentration of capital downgraded the realistic positions, held by the PCI from the end of the Fifties, that recognized certain benefits accruing from economic interdependencies and made a distinction between the European Community and NATO, and which had been proposed in vain to the other Western European communists.[176] In other words, Togliatti did not think of the European Community as a possible articulation of a polycentric world order, not even from the viewpoint of a better exploitation of the margins of maneuver for its separation from the United States. The US attack on North Vietnam a few days earlier perhaps accentuated his pessimism. Probably he was purposefully using a schematic vocabulary appropriate for communication with the Soviets. But the hard evidence is that his memorandum revealed a vision almost unaltered after 1956, which bore the sign of the Great Depression and the obstinacy of not recognizing the dynamism of capitalism in spite of its postwar transformations. Togliatti did not give any credit to the modernizing challenge of liberal capitalism represented by the Kennedy legacy. All this restored the idea of a saving grace of socialist modernity, according to the vision of a unilinear historical finalism that he had never abandoned. Just such a similar idea dramatized the scenario of the rupture, but also threw a veil over the understanding of the profound causes of the conflict between the Soviet Union and China, such as the size of the deficit of Soviet hegemony, the difference between the two revolutions, and the contradictions that had emerged in communist political culture at the moment of the expansion in the Global South.

It was Togliatti's intuition that the conflict had to do with the subject of socialist sovereignty, not resolved by an "external forced unanimity," and with a form of "renascent nationalism" on the part of the Chinese, which would not have been too surprising in that it was a "constant fact in the working-class and socialist movement for a long period even after the winning of power." He did, however, recognize that "we cannot manage fully to explain" the appearance in the socialist countries of a "centrifugal tendency," and he invited the Soviet leaders to take on board this "obvious and grave danger." Even though the "authority and prestige" of the Soviet Union remained "enormous," the conflict between the two socialist powers, to his way of thinking, gave rise to worry among the masses insofar as it shed doubt on "the very principles of socialism." The conflict would have required "a great effort to explain what the historical, political, party, and personal conditions are that have contributed to creating today's contrast and conflict."[177] In other terms, the breakup of the "socialist camp" was compromising the vision of an irresistible growth of socialism as a vector of the unification of the world. In this way, Togliatti took on the task of expressing a critical conscience that was lacking in the Soviet and Chinese leaders. He was not only ringing alarm bells regarding the unity of the "socialist camp," but indicating that the end of unity could compromise the outcome of the movement. The "memorandum" thus took on the aspect of a prophecy destined to remain unheard.

Togliatti did not even mention the theory of "two camps," and actually reproposed the vision of polycentrism, which had become unwelcome and controversial in light of the conflict between Moscow and Beijing. The formula of "unity in diversity" presented a decidedly less pronounced profile, since it constituted a political imperative much more than an analytical and strategic concept. It is not without irony that Togliatti's dramatic appeal for unity re-echoed the one made by Gramsci almost forty years earlier in his letter of October 1926, published for the first time in the communist press in May 1964.[178] In Gramsci's letter, that principle had pertained to the Bolshevik leading group; now it involved the leaderships of the two great powers of the "socialist camp." Once again, what was at stake was the very notion of internationalism, its mass legitimation on a global scale, and the future of the communist project. Togliatti had previously rejected Gramsci's appeal to the ethic of responsibility in the name of political realism, convinced that a new unity would be rebuilt around Stalin, though with coercive methods. Now he himself was raising in dramatic fashion a problem of responsibility of the Soviet leadership. The conduct and mentality of the Soviets and Chinese showed no authentic inclination to recognize political and cultural differences capable of reconstituting connective tissues and communicative channels that had been torn and interrupted right at the apex of the global communist project. Deprived of a feasible political perspective, Togliatti's last message expressed a basically pessimistic outlook for the future of international communism.

By Longo's decision, the "Yalta memorandum" was published in September 1964 despite the Soviet request to keep it reserved, even though it had not been written to be made public.[179] Longo explained to the Soviet ambassador that it had been so decided since "indiscretions" had been leaked to the press, but he also aimed to avoid the opposition of "many party members" to participation in the preparation of the world conference.[180] In reality, such arguments only partially reflected the thought of the PCI leaders, who saw in the publication of the document a certification of the party's own autonomy. From that moment on the "memorandum" was considered to be Togliatti's political testament. His partners in Moscow saw it with ill-concealed perplexity.[181] His Marxist-Leninist adversaries, such as Enver Hoxha, considered it a "revisionist" document using the notion of polycentrism.[182] Togliatti's heirs interpreted it as a compendium of the main coordinates of the Party, announcing the end of the "iron link" with the Soviet Union.[183] In this sense, the "memorandum" acquired a sacrality in the political culture of the Italian Communists.

With the benefit of hindsight, it is not difficult to see how the "testament" of Togliatti could be anything more or different from how it was interpreted. The moment when he wrote it represented in many aspects the end of an era, which Togliatti to a certain extent seemed to foresee. Togliatti's political nous left his successors with a political vision based on polycentrism instead of monolithism, on mass democracy instead of a party-state, and on the inclusion of diversity instead of ideological exclusion. But this vision did not promise to become the common heritage of global communism. Togliatti's world was undergoing a rapid change of face. The conflict between Moscow and Beijing was showing a fracture between the socialist North and anti-imperialist South of the world. The authority and legitimation of the Soviet Union seemed challengeable in this light, other than in the wake of 1956 in Europe. It was difficult for relations between the "socialist camp" and the Third World to offer the meaning of a vector that was plural and convergent toward socialism. The real or imaginary links between a structural reform of capitalism in Europe, post-Stalinist modernization in Central and Eastern Europe, and postcolonial subjects did not get off the ground. The neo-Leninist narration was unable to explain the authoritarian nature of the socialist states and their link with the Cold War. In reality, Togliatti's political testament closed an entire era of communism, recognizing the crisis of the interdependences that had up to then been established between the great power of the Soviet Union, the "superiority" of its social system, the expansion of the "socialist camp," and the emergence of the postcolonial world.

PART THREE **TRANSFORMATIONS**

The Twilight of Internationalism, 1964–84

5
HUMANISTIC SOCIALISM AND THE "LONG 1968"

AFTER TOGLIATTI

The death of Togliatti coincided with an international conjuncture that would spoil the scenario set out in the Yalta "memorandum." In a short space of time, the hopes of avoiding a split between Moscow and Beijing, the socialist orientations among the new Third World States, and the prospects for a more credible and incisive de-Stalinization were lost or significantly diluted. Khrushchev's removal was an unexpected and disconcerting event that did not remedy the dispute with Beijing, and which reversed the course of political liberalization in favor of technocratic reforms of the planned economy. A coup d'état deposed Ben Bella in June 1965, thus scaling back the project for a revolutionary Algeria in the Mediterranean. A few months later Sukarno, a highly symbolic figure in the Third World, was deposed, while the Indonesian Communist Party was destroyed by ferocious military repression. At the beginning of 1966, Nkrumah fell from power in Ghana. Cuba's Third World internationalism maintained its vitality but also challenged Yugoslavian nonalignment and the "peaceful road" of the Italians. The global mobilization provoked by the American intervention in Vietnam took place in a context of profound fractures in the "anti-imperialist front," and of the Third World as an imagined subject.[1] The loss of Togliatti's authority and political mind gave rise to an inevitable sense of bewilderment, which the end of communist unity could only exacerbate.[2] Khrushchev's fall was one more reason for claiming Togliatti's "memorandum" as a badge of identity. Sent to Moscow at the end of October 1964 together with Bufalini and Sereni, Berlinguer manifested reservations and questions regarding the respect of "Leninist norms," using Togliatti's lexis and standing up to Ponomarev's complaints about the decision to make the "memorandum" public.[3] A little later, Berlinguer won a posthumous victory for Togliatti's line on the world conference, which the parties gathered in Moscow in March 1965 decided to postpone until times were ripe, perhaps in the hope that repairing the break with Beijing would be made possible by their shared aid to North Vietnam after the beginning of American bombing. The Italian Communists read the American war and the fracture in the "socialist camp" as two complementary aspects of a very real crisis of "peaceful coexistence." Berlinguer argued that trust should not be placed in "the illusion that détente could only be obtained via Moscow and Washington," an intuition which at that time did not present any concrete developments.[4] The Italian Communists' commitment was no less than that of others to relaunching the anti-imperialist theme centered on the war in Vietnam. In actual fact, it provided a point of aggregation more on the propaganda than on the political level. This was the terrain and the main point of the reestablishment of relations with the French Communists, at the meeting between Longo and Waldeck Rochet in Geneva in May 1965, which also set the tone for the conference of Western communist parties held in Brussels.[5] The same emphasis characterized the contemporary missions to Vietnam and Cuba, led respectively by Pajetta and Alicata. Internationalist solidarity and the anti-imperialist discourse constituted important symbolic elements, but did not, however, always present concrete political implications.[6] Indeed, in the case of the Cubans, they concealed serious divergences. The Cubans' pro-Soviet alignment in the conflict with the Chinese, recently reaffirmed by Fidel Castro, did not in reality imply better relations with Tito, who for the PCI instead remained a point of reference. Alicata was also negatively impressed by the "authoritarian and coercive tendencies" of the Cuban regime.[7]

The results of and prospects for the first international contacts to be undertaken without Togliatti left the leaders of the PCI unsatisfied, to say the least. The first to openly express unease was Ingrao, who in June 1965 reported that "everyone thinks in his own way and there is no longer any exchange of opinions about the real situation [. . .]. This is also true regarding the Third World [. . .]. The serious thing is not only that the USSR remains silent, but that it also does not stimulate." Pajetta responded that among the young there were tendencies for a "revision" of the policy of coexistence.[8] And he was right. The left of the party, with Ingrao as its reference point, and especially figures such as Rossandra, Magri, and Reichlin, but also Achille Occhetto at the head of the youth organization, had already for some time expressed impatience about the adequacy of "peaceful coexistence" for supporting the anti-imperialist forces in the world, thus substantially embracing elements of criticism that stemmed from Maoism. In October 1965, Longo confided his worries to Barca about Ingrao's positions on "peaceful coexistence," which he thought would imply an overall modification of strategy and a division within the party. Immediately thereafter, the secretary persuaded Ingrao to forgo raising the question in Congress, reminding him of Togliatti's legacy.[9]

However, the problem was not just that of the political line. Longo himself acknowledged the disorientation of the leading group at the end of the year, when in the Directorate he spoke of a "vacuum" in the PCI's international relations; and, referring to the other Italian parties, he even claimed that they all had international connections, but "we no longer do." This claim might have appeared paradoxical, given the influence the PCI had had in the internationalization of the Republic and its long-lasting ideological and practical ties with the Soviet Union and the "socialist camp," but it revealed a lucid despondency linked to the Chinese split. Berlinguer went even further, wondering whether the "presuppositions" of the Yalta "memorandum" still existed.[10] These words provoke the thought that some leaders were wondering about the "memorandum" in light of the significant changes that had affected the scenario in little under a year. A similar reflection did not take place, however. Clearly, Longo and Berlinguer were referring not so much to the web of transnational relations woven in previous years as to the crisis of meaning of the internationalist tradition after the end of communist unity. The unitary appeal of the "memorandum" and the exhortation to the Soviet leadership to take an initiative that could adequately deal with global questions had fallen on deaf ears. In contrast with the traditional anticommunist vision, the PCI's problem, already evident for some time, was not the control exerted by Moscow but the absence of any real exchange, and the consequent inefficacy of the partnership. The very rituality of the encounters between communist parties, especially bilateral ones, was experienced as too tight a jacket, but extending relations to other progressive forces in and beyond Europe could not come into being only via unilateral initiatives. The debate in the leading group ended, in the absence of other prospects, with a decision to improve relations with Moscow.

Longo feared a negative reflection on national politics, too. The relative advantage secured by the PCI after 1956 from a combination of "peaceful coexistence," influences in the Mediterranean, and national interests was running low. There loomed a disconnect between international ties and the domestic context. Togliatti's opposition to the center-left had yielded as its main success the party's strong position, demonstrated by electoral gains in May 1963, which were particularly significant in the "red regions." But there was another side to the coin. The PCI remained marginalized in the political system, while the reformist season that the country had experienced, with all its limits, had created divisions among its leaders too. The hold of Soviet myths seemed for the first time to be in decline among the new generations, who were more fascinated by Third Worldism. During the previous twenty years, the link with the "socialist camp" had produced positive or negative effects from the Italian Communists' point of view, but always in a close relation between the national and the international dimensions. Now that circuit seemed to be faltering. For the Italian leading group, which had devised its role by postulating a dynamic relationship between the two dimensions, this was a source of serious uncertainties. The mobilization for Vietnam acquired centrality for this reason. It associated the PCI with the variegated front of opposition to the war, which presented transnational connotations in Europe, the United States, and elsewhere. The symbolic space represented by Vietnam and by the promotion of "global anti-Americanism" concealed, but was no remedy for, the sense of decline in communist internationalism. It was a resource for aggregation in national politics, with the aims of defending the mass party's role as an antagonistic pole and finding points of contact with influential sectors of the Catholic world that opposed an escalation of the war.[11]

The conflict among the main components of the party, represented by Amendola and Ingrao, was at once a reflection of both national and international tensions. Amendola concentrated his vision on choices in national policy, such as the unitary relation with the PSI and the first openings toward the European Community, while Ingrao engaged mainly with social mobilization and the new popular and working-class impulse that emerged at the beginning of the decade. The "model of development" was a central question, together with the interpretation of the economic boom, which had already for some years fueled debates about the persistent backwardness of Italian capitalism or its "neocapitalistic" transformation.[12] The division between the two leaders, no longer mediated by Togliatti, reflected tension between the party "of government" and the party "of struggle," which mirrored the physiological dynamic of an opposition force, accentuated by the situation of a "blocked democracy." However, the figures of Amendola and Ingrao also represented different and tendentially irreconcilable international visions. Amendola believed that the Western communist movement was at a dead end, and that what was therefore necessary was a project for a new party of the workers' movement in the European mold. He had learned Togliatti's lesson regarding the risk of overestimating the Italian experience, however, and he stood by the link with the Soviet Union, limiting himself to reconfirming his judgment about the end of its universal model.[13] Ingrao and the left manifested greater discontinuity from Togliatti, in actual fact breaking away from the "peaceful coexistence" imperative and its moderate implications, despite the compromises of the Congress. The consequence was to intensify criticism of Stalin and of the social democracies, to focus on revolution in the countries of advanced capitalism, and to conceive of Italy as a political laboratory.[14]

The real question that surfaced within the principal mass party of the West was not so much the split between Soviet orthodoxy and the Maoist heresy, which had not given rise to any serious threat of a pro-Chinese split, as much as the divergence between visions and languages that gravitated in different ways around the notions of "peaceful coexistence" and anti-imperialism. Both notions could be interpreted in myriad ways. The realistic acknowledgment of the economic growth favored by the European community and its impact on Italy was linked to the prospect of bipolar détente. Readings of international affairs via the filter of "neocolonialism" and the legacy of anti-Americanism not only reproduced themselves but mutated. Global reactions to the war in Vietnam, and their cultural multiplicity, including mass protest in the United States, would for many years constitute the major catalyst.[15] In other words, the political culture of the Italian Communists presented a plurality of visions and forms of mutual interaction which could not be fitted into the dichotomous schema induced by the two communist powers. The traditional internationalist nexuses had been diluted, and revealed their lack of genuinely operational aspects, even though they belonged to the "socialist camp." Seen from an Italian perspective, the break between Moscow and Beijing appeared as part of a multiform phenomenon, the molecular and generational mutation of visions, culture, and identity which was achieving a mass dimension before the "global 1968" exploded on the scene.

The disorientation caused by the eclipse of communist internationalism gave rise to a growth of initiatives and contacts not always clearly regulated by a political compass. Longo followed the main coordinates set out by Togliatti and developed the PCI's networks of relations, but it is difficult to perceive in his action elements of a project inspired by polycentrism, which in any case had never been congenial to him even in previous years. The immediate effect, as appears from the memoirs of Carlo Galluzzi, Giuliano Pajetta's successor as the person responsible for the foreign section, was a rapprochement with the Soviets, which tended to reduce the distance created by Togliatti's "memorandum." With this aim, Longo met Brezhnev in March 1966 at the twenty-third Congress of the CPSU, while relations with the PCF remained at a very generic level.[16] The most important initiative taken by the PCI, however, concerned possible negotiation over the Vietnam War. The issue had at this point gained importance in the diplomatic arena, and linked domestic policy directly to internationalism. The position of the Italian government led by Aldo Moro, which expressed "understanding" of the massive military intervention decided by the Johnson administration, opened a space for the Communists, who supported a voluntary mission by La Pira, in contrast with the official line of the government. The mission was a failure and indeed provoked a negative reaction from Washington, but the Communists had managed to intervene in the political game and the contradictions of the center-left governments, finding an accord with Fanfani in his position as foreign minister, and encountering a receptive response from Nenni.[17] After a series of contacts with the Soviets and the Poles, the Italian leading group prepared a mission to Hanoi. The meeting between Longo and Brezhnev in August 1966 was dedicated to this objective and to mobilization for Vietnam. The Italian delegation also asked for and obtained financial support for its press.[18] Three months later, Berlinguer traveled to Vietnam, first stopping off in Moscow, where the Italian delegates realized the gravity of the conflict with Beijing and the growing tension between the two communist powers' attempts to exert influence over Hanoi. Conversations with Vietnamese leaders confirmed their pragmatism, and their refusal to choose between Moscow and Beijing.[19]

The PCI's initiative was accompanied by the so-called Operation Marigold, organized by Italy and Poland with the aim of exploring the conditions for a peaceful solution in Vietnam within a combination of parallel diplomacies and also involving the Vatican.[20] In reality, the Vietnamese leaders proved little inclined to commencing negotiations, and were determined to follow as far as possible their objective of unifying the country. The PCI's diplomatic attempts continued without success in the following months.[21] This Vietnam initiative reaped more success in the domestic arena, where the PCI managed to put pressure on the center-left government by connecting with conspicuous sectors of the nascent Catholic dissent and the Socialists. The mobilization for peace was reinforced by the positions of exponents of the Catholic Church, though they were only a minority. The significance of Vietnam was that it inscribed the Communists within a symbolic front, and this supported the idea of a gradual exit from the binary schemes of the Cold War.[22]

At the same time, the anti-imperialist mobilization had the effect of bringing the PCI toward positions that were closer to Moscow. By then a precise line had emerged from Khrushchev's successors. The new Soviet leaders maintained the idea of bipolar détente but put aside ideological and modernizing competition with the West, and even scaled back their alliances with national elites in the Third World. Their aim was to legitimize their European sphere of influence, to increase their geopolitical presence in the Mediterranean, and to maintain the loyalty of the main communist parties in an anti-Chinese perspective, especially in the Third World. This caused a chill in relations with Tito, which reflected on the PCI and damaged one of the most important connections established by Togliatti. In January 1967, Longo attempted unsuccessfully to convince Tito to take part in a conference of European communists, invoked by Moscow as the first step toward an international conference on the theme of "European security." The Yugoslavs disagreed with the idea of a conference with exclusively communist parties, and criticized the failure to invite progressive movements, in the belief that a world conference would encounter the same problems.[23] In short, the prospects that had been evoked during the meeting between Togliatti and Tito three years earlier now seemed to fade. The Italian leading group was aware of this, but what was really important was the standing inherited from Togliatti and the reestablished closeness to Moscow and Paris. Berlinguer stated that Moscow's worries about the "centrifugal forces" generated by China should be shared, while the PCI's positions had nothing in common with the autonomist positions of the Romanians and were also distant from those of the Yugoslavs. In his opinion, the PCI would have to take part in the conferences anyway, without "being in too much of a hurry, given the importance of our position." "Our international prestige is very much linked to such a position," he asserted, "though it is a little awkward and we mustn't push our luck."[24] Longo distanced himself from the Yugoslav positions in a conversation with Nikolai Podgorny, who together with Brezhnev and Aleksei Kosygin made up the troika of Khrushchev's successors, though he acknowledged that those positions had "some foundation."[25] He obtained from Brezhnev a postponement of the world conference, but not its enlargement outside the limits of the communist movement.[26]

On the public level, Berlinguer emphasized once more the mobilization for Vietnam in the perspective of involving liberation movements in the Third World, while the idea of recovering the Chinese was at this point dead and buried.[27] The Conference of the European communist parties of the East and the West which took place at Karlovy Vary, Czechoslovakia, in April 1967 revealed the centrifugal forces generated in Europe by the anti-imperialist mobilization and the rejection of the Chinese cultural revolution. The PCI ended up going one step further in its rapprochement with the "socialist camp" and acceptance of the pan-European framework, which hindered any eventual openness toward the integration of Western Europe.[28] The idea of including socialist, Catholic, and variously inspired "progressive forces" in communist conferences in Europe and the Third World remained a dead letter, thanks also to French opposition. According to Galluzzi, the only result of the conference was a cautious opening toward West Germany, requested by Italy.[29]

This opening allowed the Italian Communists to present themselves as mediators between the SPD and SED. Their go-between was Leo Bauer, an ex-communist and combatant in Spain, who had a direct relationship with Willy Brandt, secretary of the SPD and foreign minister in the Bonn coalition government. On 29 and 30 November 1967 an informal meeting took place in Rome between delegations led by Egon Franke and Berlinguer.[30] The common ground was represented by détente. A second meeting in Munich in January 1968 between Galluzzi, Sergio Segre, Leo Bauer, and Egon Bahr, an important figure in the SPD, consolidated the reciprocal exchange, and this time the Italian Communists achieved an opening from the East German Socialist Unity Party (SED).[31] The encounters between the PCI and the SPD were not without political significance, because they showed that in Western Europe the Italian Communists were the only interlocutor appreciated by the social democracies. However, they remained relegated to a contingency. The SPD's interest in the PCI was limited by questions of internal politics, but was also instrumental for the objective of establishing relations with the SED, later made redundant by the formation of a social-democratic government and the launch of Ostpolitik at the end of 1969. The Italian Communists harbored unrealistic optimism about the possibility of establishing relations with the social democracies for internal political reasons, and even of considering the experience of the Grosse Koalition in West Germany as a possible precedent for Italy. Thus, any mediation between the SED and the SPD was to remain but an episode in their intense international activity, and did not open the way to new relations with the social democracies. However, it was precisely the launch of Ostpolitik that was to set in motion a dynamic destined to influence their choices.

The PCI could in any case boast an enviable network of relations for a nongoverning party. It extended beyond the limits of the world it belonged to, and prevalently beyond the European continent. Apart from Tito, the Italian leaders had engaged in dialogue with, among others, personalities such as Nasser, Le Duan, and Fidel Castro; they had established relations with the government of Houari Boumedienne in Algeria and the Baath party inspired by nationalist socialism in Syria; they had met with delegates of the Palestinian liberation movements; and they had broadened their connections in Ethiopia and Somalia, in Portuguese colonial Africa, and in Francophone Africa while maintaining relations in Latin America. The problem, however, was a sense that decolonization in Africa and the Mediterranean was in crisis, as were the hopes held out for new "roads to socialism" in the first half of the decade. Romano Ledda posed the question also in relation to the expectations of the European communists, observing that national independence alone had not solved the problems linked to state-building and economic emancipation from former empires, with the result that the entire continent was undergoing a process of "Balkanization." There seemed to emerge, then, an awareness of the limits of the Soviet "model of development" proposed for the continent, in particular regarding the imbalance between industrialization and agriculture.[32] The position of the Italian Communists, however, was not clear regarding the strategic changes wrought by Khrushchev's successors in their relations with the Third World, which tended toward a growing militarization of the Soviet presence.

The scenarios imagined for the Mediterranean changed radically with the military coup d'état in Greece, and above all with the outbreak of the Six-Day War in the Middle East in June 1967. The presence of Soviet power in opposition to American "neocolonialism" and Israeli "Zionism" was superimposed on the "progressive" situations in Egypt, Syria, and Algeria, but in actual fact it marked the end of the Mediterranean being seen as a "sea of peace." The Italian Communists took pro-Arab and anti-Israeli positions while confirming their recognition of the State of Israel's existence. Napolitano criticized with moderation the positions taken by Moro at the United Nations for inadequate attention to the Palestinian question.[33] However, a vision of Zionism denouncing its character of "aggressive nationalism" came to the fore.[34] The PCI continued to favor relations with Algeria, and also with Egypt and Syria, which made up the United Arab Republic, oscillating between supporting the Soviet presence in the Mediterranean, viewed as a counterweight to American imperialism, and attempting to maintain the thread of dialogue with the nonaligned countries.[35] In this context, the party acted as a transnational agent contributing to the circulation of ideas that were against "neocolonialism" and aimed to challenge the ideology of development as a universal process, and to promote redistribution of resources in favor of the postcolonial States within the global economy.[36] A significant moment was the Conference on the Mediterranean, held in Rome in April 1968 with the participation of communist and socialist parties, the Algerian FLN, and the Syrian Baath party; it consolidated the PCI's international authority and its diplomacy, which in parallel to Italy's foreign policy in the Mediterranean aimed to put pressure on government forces for a greater commitment regarding the problem of development.[37]

However, the sense of an overall plan had clearly weakened since the beginning of the decade. The representation of the "three fronts" in the anti-imperialist struggle, as embraced by Longo (Middle East, Vietnam, and Latin America) was an admission that the idea of a subjectivity emerging from the Third World was being lost.[38] The equilibrium imagined in the polycentrist paradigm between the great cultural, economic, and geopolitical diversities of the postcolonial universe and the common denominator of political anti-imperialism seemed increasingly hard to find. The Third-Worldist ideas of unity split up into a Guevarist version which denied any important role for Western communism, and a search for a unifying platform on the theme of underdevelopment which belonged to the nonaligned rather than the communists.[39] Détente had lost its significance as a challenge to Western leading classes, and was being contested even among Italian leaders. The potential for a "rediscovery" of the Third World was exhausted, while the influence of Soviet geopolitical interests was becoming much more perceptible in the Mediterranean and the Middle East. As Togliatti had predicted, the end of the unity of international communism reduced the space of politics and fueled forms of ideological intransigence. The Maoist attack on Soviet communism turned out to be ineffective as a project for an alternative movement, but was very incisive as the critical language of the "New Left" movements inspired by the notion of a conflict between the North and South of the world. In Europe, the role of communism as an alternative to social democracy had yet to be created. The anti-imperialist mobilization ended up becoming a factor of internal politics, rather than acting as a bridge between the two Europes and the Mediterranean. The construction of transnational networks represented a relational resource and a parallel diplomacy influencing national dynamics rather than the outline for a political project. The "global 1968" would lay bare the PCI's conspicuous difficulties in reorganizing its own strategic vision after Togliatti's death, but it was also an opportunity for a response that was destined to modify the very terms of the problem significantly.

THE "PRAGUE SPRING"

For the Italian Communists, the epicenter of the "global 1968" was in Central and Eastern Europe. Between March and May 1968, the reforms enacted by the new Czechoslovak leadership under the guidance of Alexander Dubček attracted international attention and started an experience destined to mark the hopes and disenchantment of communists in Europe and in Russia. The leading group that took office at the end of 1967 brought back to Prague the notion of political reform that had been eliminated after the repression in Budapest twelve years earlier. The "top-down" reforms burst the banks of the technocratic and economic innovations and solicited a social reawakening, with demands for freedom which had seemed to be lost without a trace. There were significant differences from 1956. The "Prague Spring" took place in a peaceful context on the initiative of the communists, bringing to the surface subterranean currents that had remained imperceptible. Protagonists such as Zdeněk Mlynář, the main spokesperson for the idea of a socialist democracy based on a reequilibration of the relation between society and the state, represented the generation that had matured during the years of de-Stalinization. It was immediately evident that the ambitions of the Czechoslovak reformers were not limited to adding a variant of "national communism" to those of Hungary or Poland. Their "socialism with a human face" was not limited to the geopolitical context of the "external empire" of the Soviets. It marked the apex of de-Stalinization in the East, but also presented a transnational dimension characterized by the increasing permeability of the "Iron Curtain" and by an intersection with the spontaneous mobilization of 1968 movements.

The "Prague Spring" gave back to Italian Communists the sense of a mission, which had been overshadowed in the early years after Togliatti's death. Their judgment on Dubček's program of reforms, starting with measures to abolish state censorship and to pave the way for a liberalization, tended to establish a consonance of visions and expectations. Longo publicly stated his support for the creation of a "progressive socialist democracy" and inserted among the constitutive traits of this objective not only freedom and democracy but also "humanity."[40] He was the first Western communist leader to visit Prague after the start of the reforms. His meeting with Dubček took place under the sign of socialist democracy; he declared that his party was not looking for models, but he recognized the significance of the Czechoslovak experience for world socialism, expressing "very great appreciation."[41] The following day, in a closed-door meeting of the "Five" of the Warsaw pact, without the Czechoslovaks, Brezhnev expressed the fear that Longo's declarations might be exploited by "unhealthy forces" in Czechoslovakia, given their emphasis on "liberalization" and a "new model."[42] The French, Romanian, and Yugoslav communists also supported Dubček, but the Italian leaders distinguished themselves by their empathy, which brought together various tendencies in the party, from moderates to movimentists.[43]

The approval of several important actors in the communist world was, however, not enough to protect the Prague reformers. The Soviets and the main leaders of Eastern Europe read the reforms as a loss of control and a danger of contagion. Between the end of June and the end of July, when the Italian leaders met exponents of the CPSU more than once, the feeling became certainty that threats would become actions. The Soviets, fearing a convergence with the Yugoslavs' critical positions, rejected or ignored Longo's argument that the experience of the Prague reformers would reinforce socialism. The Italians were prudent but firm in rejecting the use of force. Pajetta acknowledged the legitimacy of Moscow's worries, declaring, however, that the PCI would not accept a military intervention.[44]

The invasion of Czechoslovakia by the Warsaw Pact during the night of 21–22 August did not take the Italians by surprise, though they had hoped for the compromise that had seemed to take shape at the beginning of the month in Bratislava. The decision by Longo, who was in Moscow, to express "dissent" after frantic phone calls with Rome was immediate, and it marked the first open dissociation of the Italian Communists from the Soviet Union.[45] In Longo's presence, the Directorate held on 23 August identified a raft of positions destined to remain over time, starting with the idea that military intervention had struck a hard blow to the credibility of the entire communist movement. In particular, Bufalini stated the need for "a hegemony of the Western European parties that would also be inclusive of the realm of ideas," implying distrust toward any future positive impulse coming from the "socialist camp" because "in those countries socialism has been realized under certain—authoritarian—conditions."[46] The Italian Communists were not isolated, given that the French, British, and Norwegians also distanced themselves from the invasion of Czechoslovakia. But they were more consistent in defending their positions.

What united the Italian leaders was that they criticized Moscow's choice not only in terms of autonomy and national sovereignty, but also regarding the notion of internationalism, severely put to the test by the use of imperial force in Central and Eastern Europe. At the Central Committee meeting held at the end of August while Dubček and his collaborators were detained in Moscow, Longo reaffirmed the closeness of the Italian Communists' ideas to those of the Prague reformers, which brought them together in a universalist vision that aimed to "enrich the entire socialist experience with new values and freedoms" in order to "create a modern, open, and profoundly human socialism."[47] Thus Longo, the old combatant of the Spanish Civil War, adopted in the name of his comrades a word that had characterized the "Prague Spring." The implication was that the Soviet variant of socialism did not correspond at all to the image of "human socialism," and that the tanks in Prague bore sad witness to a different logic and reality. The fact was that, up to this point, the Communist leading group had never embraced such an implication. The cadres and militants had absorbed the conviction that the logic of the blocs had been imposed by the West, but that they also represented a compass to be followed for reasons of international and class solidarity, as had happened at the time of the Hungarian tragedy. The idea that the bipolar order was less adequate to reflect global change, as had been claimed by the Yalta "memorandum," had not profoundly changed this vision. For the first time since the birth of the "new party," the leading group found itself facing choices that constituted a logical evolution but implied a possible fracture of its own political and social body, then still under the influence of the orthodox pedagogies and old-style narratives of internationalism.[48]

The Italian leaders set themselves the task of restoring meaning to the notion of internationalism. They had to avoid giving the impression that the positions taken against repression in Czechoslovakia should seem a repudiation of Togliatti's positions in 1956. Rejection of the "leading state," however, was no longer enough. It was necessary to find a point of equilibrium that, as Longo wished, allowed the expression of dissent without having to break with Moscow. It is indicative that the Italian Communists did not limit themselves to standing firmly by their positions during the fierce polemics aroused in national public opinion by the invasion of Czechoslovakia, in their handling of criticism both from the traditional anticommunist front and from the "New Left." They promoted a diplomatic initiative among the European communist parties. Pajetta, Galluzzi, Berlinguer, and Pecchioli held consultations in Paris, London, Budapest, Belgrade, Bucharest, Warsaw, and Berlin, weaving a web of consensus with the French, British, Romanian, and Yugoslav communists. The latter invited the Italians to acknowledge that the Soviet Union was returning to "Great Power" politics to reinforce the "socialist camp," with the objective of dividing the world into Soviet and US spheres of influence, and they stated their concern about a possible military invasion by the Warsaw Pact. Armando Cossutta, the coordinator of the secretariat and the person in charge of financial relations, was sent to Moscow. He reported back that Suslov considered the PCI's position "unjustified" at the international level; that he had inquired about Pajetta's mission to Bucharest, since the Romanian leader Nicolae Ceaușescu had abstained on the intervention in

Prague; and that Suslov had dramatized the risk of a profound laceration should there be any aggregation of a European communist pole.[49] The strongest reaction to the Soviet intransigence, which as always equated dissent with insubordination, was that of Berlinguer. He said he was not "completely" convinced by the Yugoslav analysis, but spoke of a "new phase" which also involved "our place in the communist movement" and did not exclude the possibility of a "political struggle with the Soviet comrades." Such a struggle evidently implied the possibility of building a Western communist pole.[50]

Public interventions by leaders such as Amendola and Ingrao showed, however, how the theme of internationalism could divide Italian communism too, and not simply along the lines of orthodoxy and autonomy. The various, differently calibrated statements traced the perimeter of the possibilities, but also the scenario of a rupture. Amendola reaffirmed the Togliattian concept of differences within socialism around the world, with strong emphasis on the "general crisis of capitalism" as evidenced by Vietnam. His political proposal centered on the theme of "peaceful coexistence," not as "division of the world into spheres of influence," but as a form of internationalism based on nonintervention."[51] Ingrao ignored the notion of "peaceful coexistence," however, and centered his contribution on relaunching the nexus between "mass democracy" and the development "of the whole anti-imperialist front" beyond the confines of the "socialist camp."[52] These two positions revealed not only an already consolidated divergence, but different visions of the "global 1968," which showed up in conflicting judgments on the student movement: respectively, of diffidence and of an opening. The handling of the crisis after the invasion of Czechoslovakia therefore called for a readjustment of the diverging trajectories.

At the end of September, the official enunciation of the doctrine of limited sovereignty in the "socialist community," known since as the "Brezhnev doctrine," consolidated in its turn the dissent of the Italian Communists. Between October and November the tension between the two sides reached unprecedented heights, despite a reciprocal will to avoid a break. The pressures from Moscow had an effect opposite to that obtained with the French Communists, who reconsidered their position. After a meeting in Budapest, Berlinguer informed the Directorate that the Soviets were presenting the PCI as the "most dangerous" actor, and as tending toward "an abstract model of socialism." He suggested intensifying the PCI's international activity in Western Europe, including "other left-wing forces," but also in Africa and the Middle East, with a conference on Vietnam in mind.[53] A second mission to Moscow by Cossutta did not change the state of affairs. Only Pajetta invoked "a nonbelligerence pact." Ingrao objected, saying that "the path toward a compromise has turned out to be impassable, the way things have gone." Bufalini invited the rejection of "any form of extortion" and the consideration of a radical change in relations with Moscow, including an end to financial support. Berlinguer warned that "our relationship with the CPSU can no longer be the same as before," and worried about the "psychological preparation of the comrades," acknowledging that "from this point of view we have been slow to act."[54]

With these premises, and with Longo stricken by a serious illness, Berlinguer went to Moscow between 11 and 13 November 1968. He adhered to the mandate of the leading group, which was to acknowledge the respective positions and divergences. He reaffirmed their "dissent," criticized the Warsaw Pact's "interference," and called into question the "normalization" in Czechoslovakia, remaining unimpressed by the Soviets' paternalistic tirades about internationalist solidarity. Their vision was that communist parties that were critical of the intervention were subject to "nationalist tendencies," as in Romania and in Yugoslavia, and that the "counterrevolutionary" activities in Czechoslovakia were to be seen in relation to the American war in Vietnam. Moscow was mechanically applying to Prague and Vietnam the nexus established in 1956 between Budapest and Suez. However, this argument was not sufficient to beguile Italian Communists and persuade them to change their minds.[55] Back in Rome, Berlinguer reported that he had faced strong pressures, but not to the point of a break, and also that "privately, some comrades of the [Soviet Party] Foreign Section invited us to hold out"—an anything-but-negligible detail from the perspective of exerting pressure without giving in on questions of principle.[56] The meeting between Berlinguer and Suslov in January 1969 did not shift the terms of the question by an inch. Indeed, Moscow's number-one ideologist threatened to desert the upcoming Twelfth Congress of the

PCI, an explosive act within communist liturgies. Berlinguer reported to Rome that the meeting had only illustrated Soviet incomprehension of the Italian position.[57]

Longo's choice to designate Berlinguer to handle relations with Moscow after August 1968 could be seen as an investiture for the succession. Generational change, which excluded Amendola and Ingrao from the leadership, was the solution adopted to prevent the crystallization of a dualism that had for some time been emerging and which was further boosted by the events of 1968. However, Berlinguer could also boast more solid internationalist experience than Amendola, who had never really handled that terrain, and more recent and intense experience than Ingrao, who had been in time to become familiar with the Cominform environment but had reduced his participation after the Moscow conference of 1957. Leader of the World Communist Youth between 1950 and 1953, Berlinguer had participated in the 1960 Conference and performed a conspicuous number of missions to Moscow, Eastern Europe, and elsewhere. In other words, the emergence of his authority in 1968 was closely linked to the internationalist legacy of Italian communism.[58]

During the Congress, Longo and Berlinguer confirmed the PCI's critical position regarding Prague. Longo responded to the invitation from Socialist Party Secretary Francesco De Martino, calling for the definition of a political line adequate for "the configuration of a socialism with a human face," and declaring that this was precisely "our endeavor and our objective."[59] This strengthened the Italian Communists in the national arena, where their adversaries could denounce the excessive caution of their critical lexicon toward Moscow, but could not ignore what was novel compared with 1956. However, the international isolation of the Italian Communists was evident. "Socialism with a human face" had not made inroads within the communist world, where its repression was accepted as justified by the global Cold War. In Western Europe, dissident communists were few and insignificant, while the French had thrown in the towel.[60] Outside Europe, no communist party had spoken against Moscow, apart from the Chinese, for reasons purely instrumental to denouncing Soviet imperialism. The only strong interlocutors, the Yugoslavs, were a partner that remained obstinately extraneous to the "socialist camp." The intention to launch an international initiative conflicted with this situation, which, despite the diplomatic efforts and the connections that had been created, had not progressed substantially since Togliatti's death.

Nonetheless, the Italian Communists held fast, persuaded that their dissent constituted a way to modify and reform relations in the communist world. Thus they carved out a special function for themselves, which enhanced their role as a critical conscience. They were forced to take note that Moscow identified socialism in the world with the "socialist camp," and that the Italians' attempts to differentiate the two notions had so far failed. But this did not make them give up. The "Prague Spring" had provided a glimpse of a range of possibilities that had immediately closed again, but which could be understood as a phenomenon destined to happen again. Their mission became to keep that possibility open. This now implied making a clear distinction between recognizing the anti-imperialist function of the Soviet Union within the context of global postcolonial movements, and abandoning the old hierarchies of meaning regarding the "superiority" of Soviet socialism, which were unacceptable in the West but also in the Global South. On this basis, the Italian Communists aimed to exert influence in the international movement and prevent their own marginalization. The use of this strategy was by definition subject to permanent negotiations, and risked becoming a dialogue of the deaf. But it constituted a form of political realism that was recognized even by exponents of the European social-democratic left. In the spring of 1969 there was a meeting at the highest level between the PCI and the SPD, which confirmed the parties' mutual interest in détente despite the Soviet repression in Czechoslovakia, and Brandt's acknowledgment that the Italians were carrying forward a "reform communism."[61]

This position, however, meant there was a price to pay. In the name of the principle of "unity in diversity," the PCI had to accept the authoritarian "normalization" in Czechoslovakia, which removed Dubček definitively after having humiliated him, and transformed many reform leaders and innumerable militants into persecuted dissidents. The decision to take part in the World Communist Conference, which met in Moscow in June 1969—after having been postponed many times over about seven years, partly because of the Italian Communists' opposition,—was a precise choice. The most decisive supporter of the need to avoid breaks was Amendola, who among the Italian leaders was the least involved in internationalist practices, but for this reason also little inclined to cultivate ambitious plans for transnational influence.[62] But it was precisely his criticism of unanimism a few years earlier that now served as a compass for behavior. Berlinguer came to the conference with the objective of defending the criterion that different conceptions could cohabit within the communist movement. In his contribution, he spoke of "a crisis of internationalism," criticized the Chinese, upheld international détente, and mentioned the sensitive subject of Czechoslovakia, reaffirming "serious dissent" against the invasion.[63]

The Italian delegation refused to sign all parts of the common final declaration, thus breaching the unwritten rules of the organization. The dissociation of the Italians was formalized despite the unanimism typical of communist ritual. On this point Berlinguer was inflexible, thus appearing stubborn as a mule to the highest Soviet leaders, and an awkward personality to Moscow's leadership.[64] Reporting to the PCI Directorate, he declared that the manifestation of divergences had been "a shock," though he had given Brezhnev prior warning and had specified that the PCI would not raise the issue of a Red Army withdrawal. According to information in his possession, the Soviet leading group had discussed the Italian positions and had split between negative opinions from Brezhnev, Suslov, and Ponomarev, on the one hand, and more open opinions from Kosygin, Podgorny, and Andrei Kirilenko on the other. To Berlinguer's eyes this was an important result, though it did not for a moment induce any optimism. "It is difficult to think," he stated, "that suddenly, today, the CPSU leadership might shift to admitting the legitimacy of dissent and accepting the principle of unity in diversity." He added that he did not believe "that this passage could take place in tranquility," because "the problem then also arises of internal dissent, if it is allowed on an international level."[65]

In other words, the Italian leaders were aware of the irreconcilability between the open recognition of diversities on the international level and the authoritarian stability of communist regimes, which made their path particularly impervious. The Italians chose to be deliberately ambivalent, confirming the continuity of traditionally cultivated relations, and at the same time a link to the legacy of the "Prague Spring." Amendola's irony hit the mark when he pointed to the risk of developing "the complex of being at the top of the class." It was not the first time that the Italian Communists were candidates for this role. Contrary to how it would be presented in posthumous self-narratives, the Prague 1968 movement was not the beginning of a slide toward the dissolution of relations with Moscow. The Italian Communists made a different choice. They picked up the banner of "socialism with a human face" in order to place themselves in a strategic position regarding the dynamics of reform and conservation open at that point in the communist world. They were the only leading group to connote themselves as reformers when that vision was banned in the "socialist camp," and to a great extent opposed in the Third World.

The position expressed on Czechoslovakia presented a precise linkage with the national scene. At the Directorate of 31 October 1968, Berlinguer declared that without the dissociation from Moscow there would have been a "total change in the political framework expressed by the elections of 19 May," when the PCI obtained the best results in its history, close to 27 percent of the votes.[66] Berlinguer's words expressed a widely shared attitude in the leading group—the awareness that the strength of the Italian Communists was at that point linked not only to their ability to defend their sphere of autonomy, but also to their distancing of themselves from the Soviet model of socialism. A little later at the Congress, he specified that the Communists would not make the same choice as the Socialists in 1956 and would not sacrifice their political, ideological and identitarian link with the "socialist camp" on the altar of the government of the country. "The question is very different," he declared, "and is that of confirming and relaunching internationalism [. . .] in new forms and with new content," in order to fill the gap between the potentials of a variegated movement with a "universal dimension," and its "effective weight," which was still inadequate in world politics.[67] In his opinion, on the national level it was not a question of the government that had to be posed, but that of a different quality of Italian democracy, of a "democratization of the political regime." Berlinguer relaunched the classic challenge of the reciprocal siege that characterized the two political and social blocs of Italian national life, banking on the push for change produced by the 1968 movement.

Thus a tension was recreated between an international belonging and the national dimension, in terms that were, however, very different from the past. In fact, the force of communism did not reside only in the polarization imposed by the Eurocentric Cold War, which had at the same time contained its social consensus and consolidated its hegemony in the left. It resided in its difference from other communisms, which was convincing to a growing portion of the Italian democratic electorate, and in its ability to live and prosper within the country's great transformation. This was a refutation of the thesis upon which the center-left project was to a great extent based: that modernization would have excised the roots of communism. In actual fact, the PCI showed a capacity for adapting to the initial impact of the consumer society, a formidable social and territorial rootedness in central Italy, and reform-based practice in local government.[68] The mass party and its ability to integrate into Italian society provided confirmation of Togliatti's decisive legacy, which at this point had taken on the character of a pillar of the political system, while the traditional leading class was starting to show signs of difficulty and a lack of prospects. The secularization of Italian society did not clip the wings of Italian communism. It was plain for all to see that the "political religion" constructed after the war had converted rapidly into a more secular force. It was capable of responding more effectively than political Catholicism, and in competition with the Socialists, to the demand for modern rights emerging from Italian society, and from positions of advantage after the end of the center-left season of reforms. That force therefore promised more of an expansion inasmuch as the 1968 movement had left a significant trace in Italian society, even though the contestation had laid bare contradictory and conservative elements present in the identity and innermost body of the party.

However, the Italian Communists could only partially perceive the crisis of the bipolar conceptual and existential horizon that was destined to characterize the "global 1968."[69] In actual fact, it revealed the decline of the mythologies linked to the Soviet Union's presence in the world. Even the return of Marxism among the young presented among its characteristic elements protests against the nature of systems of the Soviet type, or plain indifference to their significance. The Soviet myth had forever lost its function as a promise for the future and a revolutionary hope. Even anti-Americanism fed much more on the symbols and languages of American countercultures than on the stereotypes of traditional communist propaganda. The "imagined community" of international communism, endowed with an ethos, a language, and its own cultural code, in many aspects already belonged to the past.[70] But all this could not just be shrugged off without threatening the existence of the communist identity, even for a force like the PCI. Hence the need for the narrative of existing socialism—and of socialism yet to be realized, with the aim of salvaging what could be saved from its past—to feed the need for markers of identity, and also to deal with the challenge of the "New Left." The idea of Soviet power as a peaceful counterweight to Western imperialism, trust in the progressive mission of a society of the Soviet type, persuasion that a demand for socialism was intrinsic in the high points of capitalistic modernity, and expectations still placed in the anti-imperialist forces of the Third World—all this corresponded to such needs. Humanist socialism thus became an "invention of tradition," destined to live with the postmythological narratives of Soviet socialism, with removal of its inhumane face and with a search for new forms of internationalism.

This evolution created a precise dynamic between international and internal policy. While the leading group saw itself as a candidate to inherit the "Prague Spring," it enacted an intolerant turn of the screw by expelling the "Manifesto" group, to applause from the Soviets.[71] These two choices were mutually coherent. Defense of the Prague "Spring" did not in fact imply a split from the "socialist camp," such as was invoked by Rossanda, Magri, Pintor, and the other exponents of the radical left in their denunciation of the hypocrisies of "normalization" under the threat of tanks. At the Congress, Rossanda renewed criticism of "peaceful coexistence" as a practice centered on the interests of the Soviet Union and the Soviet bloc, invoking the subordination of these interests to liberation and revolutionary movements.[72] These arguments found a consensus among the politicized youth of the 1968 movement and laid bare the anachronisms of the old internationalism. The "Manifesto" group gathered together some of the most libertarian demands from countercultures, questioned the socialist nature of the Soviet Union, and in the meantime cultivated new mythologies on the left, of Maoist or Castroist inspiration. The leading group decided to close the ranks of "democratic centralism" as a way to shield the party from the influences of the "New Left" and from their possible disintegrative consequences. Natta's indictment of the "Manifesto" group in October 1969 presented two aspects: the rejection of a position which, on the international level, would have isolated the PCI from the "socialist camp" and from its interlocutors among the nonaligned, and a harsh reaction to the risk of the loss of cohesion of the communist political and social bloc at the very moment of its maximum consolidation, when social insubordination was extending from universities to factories during the "hot autumn" of 1969. Defense of the Soviet Union's anti-imperialist role was explicit; implicit was the fear that abandoning hope for self-reform by the socialist countries would deal a fatal blow to the communist identity.[73] In the following years, the Italian Communists would more than once reaffirm their dissent regarding the 1968 invasion and the doctrine of "limited sovereignty," maintaining intact in many aspects their relations with Eastern Europe, with the exception of Czechoslovakia. From this point of view, they were not authentic dissidents but the illuminated and minority wing of a post-internationalist communist universe, composite and fragmented between orthodoxies, heresies, nationalisms, and anti-imperialisms.

AFTER 1968: REDEFINING EUROPE

After the two movementist years of 1968–69, Italian communism underwent the conflicting influences and tensions of the new national, European, and global scenarios. National prospects appeared uncertain and fragile after the terrorist attack at Piazza Fontana in December 1969, which brutally triggered a drift toward political violence in the country. The idea gained strength that Italy—exceptional in being the sole democracy in Mediterranean Europe, surrounded by right-wing regimes in Spain, Portugal, and Greece—was under attack from subversive forces reacting to the 1968 movement. Such forces, with their accomplices on the international level, were characterized by destabilizing projects aimed at installing an authoritarian regime. This perception was not at all unfounded, and it presented a real danger. There was a return of a significant influence of a Cold

War imagery that had never really gone away. The Nixon administration interpreted the consequences of the 1968 movement in Italy solely as a risk of the Communists entering government, and retrospectively judged openness toward the center-left to have been a mistake.[74] Communist and leftist perceptions also contained the ideas of a conspiratorial threat embedded within the apparatus of the state and of NATO, resulting in dark pessimism about the destiny of democracy. The most immediate consequence of the perception of Italian fragility was its tendency to limit, if not invert, the PCI's distancing from the "socialist camp," seen as the only possible safety net. The Soviets were quick to notice this vulnerability of the Italian Communists, and they attempted to take advantage of it as an instrument of persuasion and extortion to put an end to the dissent to which the 1968 movement had given rise. For example, Moscow attacked exponents of the PCI's foreign policy like Galluzzi. In October 1970 he was replaced in full political continuity by Sergio Segre, known for his privileged relations with the German social democrats.[75] Soviet pressure turned out to be counterproductive, however, in that it stimulated a form of pride in the party and persuaded its leaders to reconfirm the full acquisition of democratic legality as a line of defense of Italian sovereignty.

Italy's pessimistic vision was to some extent counterbalanced by the evolution of the European scenario. The consolidation of European détente after the launch of Ostpolitik by Willy Brandt's government at the end of 1969 favored the project of acceptance of communists in the Western European context, which meant modifying their role as a bridge between the two halves of Europe while not renouncing that role. For some time it had been clear how the national legitimization of Italian communism implied the modification of positions that were hostile to European integration, though any visions of a supranational dimension amounted either to a generic hope for a pan-European agreement between the two divided parts of the continent, or were contradicted by the reaffirmation of national sovereignty as a bastion against control by international capital. After the "Prague Spring," the European question acquired new meanings. At the end of 1968, the PCI sent the CPSU a note outlining its Europeanist policy. This document only reiterated the already known positions: broadest possible enlargement of the EEC, overcoming of the blocs, and a distinction between European and Atlanticist policy. In this way too, however, the trajectory differed from that of Moscow because of the positive vision of the European Community and, implicitly, an open door for insidious questions about the future of Comecon and the Soviet influence in Eastern Europe.[76] Immediately thereafter, in March 1969, a representative group of Italian Communists entered the European Parliament at Strasbourg, the sole case in Western Europe. The trajectory was re-equilibrated by relaunching intransigent positions on NATO—a defensive reaction to the crisis of rejection provoked in the West by the invasion of Czechoslovakia, and at the same time, a reflexive reaction to the American war in Vietnam, intensified by competition with forces of the extreme left.[77]

The Italian Communists interpreted Ostpolitik as a new opportunity for political change on the European continent. In April 1970, Berlinguer claimed in the Directorate that the "crisis of internationalism" that had emerged some time earlier had never before reached "such a low point," and that in order to go beyond it, it was necessary to give center stage to "the questions of Western Europe."[78] A code was outlined that was destined to persist, and was adopted for the time being without modification of the structures of belonging. Amendola explained it in his way, in polemic with Terracini because of the latter's criticisms of Soviet socialism, and he placed before his comrades the logical alternatives that challenged them after 1968: maintain the historic link with the "socialist camp," to some extent accepting its constraints, or break it and join the political family of Western Europe, giving up, among other things, the financial resources provided by Moscow.[79] This was a rhetorical either/or question, because the Italian leading group had already made its choice and excluded a priori the second option. Amendola's intervention was also a warning to pay close attention to the limits of the party's transformation—that is, to the specter of "social democratization," which would expose the PCI to the criticism of all those who were against its specificities in Moscow, in East Berlin, in Prague, or among the rank and file of the extraparliamentary "New Left."

At the same time, the Italian Communists were convinced that only a connection between the workers' movement in Europe and the extra-European liberation movements could supply a horizon of meaning to the notion of internationalism. Their networks of relations, woven in the

Third World, displayed a fragmented picture, which did not always justify the ongoing substantial political and organizational investment. They had to confront growing competition from the neo-Marxist languages and the Third-Worldist positions which had spread on their left but also in the Catholic world, dividing the domestic "anti-imperialist front."[80] However, relations with the postcolonial world remained their most important international projection outside the "socialist camp," in various cases of greater importance than the diplomatized or half-frozen relations with Central and Eastern Europe.

The main effort fell to the Middle East and Palestine. The centrality of the relation with the Palestinian Al Fatah movement was established at Pajetta's meetings with Yasser Arafat, which started with the communist leader's visit to Amman in December 1969.[81] The basis of the accord was the idea that the link between the socialist world, including the Western communists, and the Palestinian cause, excluding the extremist and antisemitic components, might provide new incentives to the anti-imperialist movement. The Italian Communists supported the prospect of a multiethnic state—which, however, presupposed incompatibility with the State of Israel in its present form and was therefore not conducive to a political solution. But the problem was not only the question of Israel. The PCI's relations with various actors in the Arab world demonstrated the difficulty of promoting the Palestinian cause as a catalyst for an anti-imperialist relaunch on the Algerian or Vietnamese model. Even the Algerians, the main interlocutors of the Italian Communists and prominent Third-Worldist actors, revealed an impasse in this regard, maintaining their distance from the policies of the "socialist camp."[82] The contacts initiated in Algiers, Cairo, and Beirut for a new conference of the "progressive and anti-imperialist" forces in the Mediterranean yielded no results.[83] Nasser's death and the Sadat regime in Egypt removed any residual illusion about the "progressive" prospects of relations that had long been cultivated.[84]

The most significant fallout from the Italian Communists' transnational activity concerned their tendency to integrate and surrogate the foreign policy of their country, albeit from anti-Atlanticist positions. From 1969 to 1972, for the first time in the history of the Republic, an authentic mirroring took place between a number of the Communists' fundamental options and the strategies of the government, which, under the guidance of Moro as the minister for foreign affairs, produced significant innovations after a decade of substantial conservatism. The points of contact were détente, seen as a process of mutation and breakdown of the blocs, the enhancement of Europe as a pole of world politics, and the creation of more extensive relations with the Third World than were traditional for Italian policy.[85] Generally speaking, these perspectives were seen as Moro's personal evolution; but they were, rather, the result of competition and interaction with the Communists, more than the protagonists themselves were willing to admit. The vision of the Middle East question as a part of the national interest led the main Italian political forces at this point toward empathetic positions vis-à-vis the Arab countries of the Mediterranean.

Despite the impasse regarding the prospects of the prosocialist Arab countries, the strength of anti-imperialist forces in the world was confirmed, in the eyes of the Communists, not only by the Vietnam War but by the victory of Unidad Popular in Chile and the election of president Salvador Allende in 1970. The Chilean experience represented the realization of a peaceful "national road" in the Latin American context, albeit in an ambiguous relation with Cuba, which was, however, justified in light of the United States' undifferentiated hostility. The PCI had supported the policy of alliances of the Chilean communist leader Luis Corvalán, seen as the only Latin American experience that was consonant with the Italian inspiration. Even the Chilean political situation was suited to being interpreted as similar to the Italian one, given the presence of a strong Christian Democrat government party.[86] At the same time, Unidad Popular offered a link to developing countries, which could consolidate the path to autonomous management of a nation's resources, contributing to the growth of tendencies toward emancipation from American "neocolonialism." The Italian Communists valued both of these aspects, and offered themselves as diplomatic intermediaries between Chile, Italy, and Europe, offering a much more pronounced internationalist solidarity than the Soviets' shrewd conduct.[87] The identification between the Chilean and Italian experiences developed over the years of the Allende presidency, but also reached its limit because of problems linked to Frontism. A perception gradually emerged of the left-wing Chilean government's difficulty in realizing its program of nationalizations in a society riddled with strong divisions and at risk of a radicalization of the middle classes. At the beginning of 1972, Secchia met Corvalán and sent an anxious note to the party secretariat.[88]

The developments in Chile were a reminder of the world's division into spheres of influence, but in the meantime the postwar order was deteriorating in ways that would have been unpredictable only a few years earlier. In September 1971 the Directorate of the PCI met to discuss the end of the Bretton Woods system, announced by President Nixon a month earlier. Amendola's report underlined the political consequences of the American decision, which in his opinion brought to a head the "growing contrast" between the United States and the European Community. American unilateralism implied a search for a different world order, and was not to be read through the catastrophist lens of a terminal crisis. Amendola lamented the lack of discourse on this matter from the socialist countries, which was particularly negative because "by now there are not only two economic areas."[89] This observation increased the representation of a decline of the bipolar world in the vision of the Italian Communists. It was Berlinguer who drew the main lesson from this. He claimed that the "two camps" thesis was no longer adequate for interpreting the contemporary world.[90] The category of imperialism was still valid, but was no longer founded on a dichotomic conception of world politics. In reality, that conception had already been liquidated de facto by Togliatti in the final years of his life; but Berlinguer was now proposing an explicit rejection, in light of the end of an entire phase of American supremacy. The Communist leading group now saw the European Community as an aggregating factor even while criticizing its Atlanticist nexus. They used, in a different way than in the past, the language of sovereignty, seen as the protection of national interests within the new economic interdependences on the horizon, which would create a need to liquidate the model based on low-technology products and wage compression. In a conference in Rome in November 1971, Amendola presented the PCI positions in favor of enlarging the Community and democratically redefining its political profile.[91]

In this connection, it is hard to underestimate Amendola's decisive influence in Italian communism's Europeanist choice, destined to become a crucial element of its strategy. When Berlinguer became general secretary of the PCI in March 1972, he developed this choice as a priority in the new world setup marked by the end of Bretton Woods, international détente, and the long wave of the 1968 movement, which in Italy and other countries was also giving rise to conservative repercussions. In January 1973 he accentuated the vision of "an international phase of a new type," indicating détente as no longer just a project for containing imperialism, but a sign of decline of the "conception of world domination by two"—a loss of control over global processes by the military blocs, which was destined to hollow out their significance. Thus he set as joint and interdependent objectives "the struggle against neocolonialism" and the "problems of Europe," coining the formula of Europe as "neither anti-Soviet nor anti-American," immediately thereafter made public at a meeting of the Central Committee. His vision of Europe was thus characterized no longer as an acknowledgement of its integration, but as a project destined to play a role in global relations and in the Global South. Berlinguer was criticized in the leading group from realist positions. In particular, Napolitano asked "not to repropose the discussion of ten years ago" on coexistence as "going beyond the blocs." Bufalini criticized the wishful thinking of the invocation "Italy out of NATO, USSR out of Prague," taking a position closer to the conception of Brandt and Bahr about the need to recognize the blocs in order to allow détente to progress. In this way a dilemma, rather than a divergence, was delineated regarding how to view détente and its more or less dynamic character.[92]

In any case, Berlinguer proposed seeing Europe as a new actor in world politics, in a panorama already made more plural by the emergence of the postcolonial world. His Europe did not coincide with the European Community, but the latter was recognized as an autonomous entity and an arena for the possible relaunch of progressive and socialist objectives. He envisaged not integration between the Western communist forces and European social democracy, but rather a new competition based on the recognition of their respective identities, as appeared to have been enshrined in the common program of the French left-wing parties in 1972. From this point of view, the cards that the communists could play were above all criticism of reformism, legitimized by the wave of the 1968 movement, the languages of humanistic socialism, and the persistent linkage with anti-imperialist liberation movements.

Once the coordinates of his vision and strategy had been established, Berlinguer engaged in personal diplomacy largely toward the European communist world. During 1973 he traveled to Moscow, Paris, Sofia, and East Berlin to meet Brezhnev, Georges Marchais, Todor Zhivkov, and Erich Honecker. It is not too paradoxical that European and global scenarios were rather limited in the talks Berlinguer had with Brezhnev in Moscow on 12 and 13 March 1973. Berlinguer characterized the formula of Europe as "neither anti-Soviet nor anti-American," but the Soviets saw the idea of Europe as an actor in world politics as a threat to their own sphere of influence. The coldness between the two leaders was aggravated by the tenacious dissent of the Italian Communists regarding the invasion of Czechoslovakia. Berlinguer was very clear on that point, declaring that the act of violence had damaged the image of socialism and the ideological influence of the communist movement in Europe. Brezhnev claimed that the democratic reforms in Czechoslovakia had been an obstacle to agreements between the USSR and West Germany and had compromised détente.[93]

The divergence between the two visions was difficult to bridge. Berlinguer refused to accept the argument that the repression of the "Prague Spring" had been a necessary condition for the launch of détente. In his opinion, the prospects of the communist movement depended instead on the opposite nexus—that is, the idea that European détente was a process that aimed to modify the Cold War system, not to guarantee the status quo, and that humanistic socialism constituted the main resource of political culture for the realization of that change. For four years the Italian Communists had followed a line with the aim of diplomatizing their dissent, with the result that the Soviets remained irremovable and impermeable to their arguments. At this point, the linkage between Europeanism and humanistic socialism, as delineated by the leading group of the largest Western communist party, seemed more difficult to circumscribe within a bilateral relation and took on more general meanings. Clearly, the vision of the Italian Communists diverged from the rigid Soviet bipolarism. The point of agreement between Berlinguer and Brezhnev was that détente represented a success for the Soviet Union in containing the Western Cold

War. But they drew opposite lessons in Europe and the Mediterranean. Berlinguer envisaged scenarios of change which in reality challenged Moscow's response to the Six-Day War and the "Prague Spring"—power politics in the Mediterranean, and the stabilization by force of the European sphere of influence.[94]

The meetings between Berlinguer and Marchais in May and September 1973 seemed to announce a success for communist Europeanism. With the entry of the PCF into the European Parliament, for the first time a pole of Western communism took shape. This created an unprecedented division between pro- and anti-European communists. Moscow, in fact, inspired a front of resistance against the Italo-French initiatives among the small Western communist parties. At the Brussels Conference in January 1974, Berlinguer and Amendola invited Western communists for the first time to unite around the project of a Europe that was "neither anti-Soviet nor anti-American," capable of standing as an actor on the world stage. But only the French, the Belgians, and the Spanish followed them.[95] The new Europeanist watchword encountered the comprehension of Honecker, who was interested in détente with the Federal Republic of Germany but was hindered by Moscow's refusal, together with that of the majority of the Eastern European regimes, which feared the threat, however remote, of destabilization caused by the emergence of Western Europe as a political actor.[96] The Italian leading group knew it had a narrow path to follow, and indeed had already chosen it as its way of exerting influence both in the West and in the East. Its action gave rise to a tension that was destined to last over time, and to fuel one crucial transversal divergence in the communist world.

In September 1973 the military coup d'état in Chile and the death of Allende had a very strong impact on the definition of the nexus between national and international politics. In three celebrated articles, Berlinguer formulated the strategy of a "historic compromise" with the Christian Democrats, which drew from the Chilean events the lesson that any frontist split in the political system and in society had to be avoided. With this in mind, he was induced to put forward a political proposal that could be inscribed in the Italian communist tradition, harking back to the precedent of "national unity" at the end of World War II. The myth of antifascist unity as a foundational pillar of the Republic remained alive to the point of configuring the basis for a strategy that was still functioning after the parenthesis of the Western Cold War. From the first comments on the coup d'état in Chile, this vision was shared by the leading group. Pajetta mentioned a recent conversation of his with Corvalán to criticize the tendency of the Chilean socialists to force change, and Allende's underestimation of the subversive threat.[97] Now the intertwining imagined between the Italian and Chilean experiences changed its character. Chile fueled a perception of Italian fragility—more precisely, the idea that the democratic exception the country represented in the Mediterranean might vanish. Pinochet's dictatorship interacted symbolically with the scenario of a "broad front of a clerico-fascist type" evoked by Berlinguer as the "central political problem" of Italian history. Hence Berlinguer's thesis that even a left-wing government based on an absolute majority of votes and seats in Parliament would not easily survive, and that instead a policy of much wider alliances was absolutely indispensable.[98] In his vision, faith in Italy's resources to overcome the crisis coexisted with a basic pessimistic undercurrent which believed that the Italian nation was subjected by anticommunist ideology to "an imminent threat of a split." Berlinguer's conceptions, in other terms, oscillated between, on the one hand, the idea of Italy as a trailblazer of progressive transformations in Europe and as a laboratory for ending the Cold War and, on the other, the perception of a country exposed to the collapse of institutions and democratic structures that had never been truly consolidated.

Communist mobilization against Pinochet's dictatorship was extremely significant, and it also had the objective of dividing the DC and forcing its leaders to take a critical position on the support for subversion by a part of the Chilean Christian Democrats, which suggested a suspicion of similar grey areas in Italy. The campaign was highly successful and contributed to making Italy, even at a governmental level, the nation most committed to solidarity with the dictatorship's victims. The PCI's public discourse constituted the foundation of a true political myth counterposed to the Guevarist and Maoist mythologies of the extreme left.[99] The events in Chile and their myth also suggested considerations of an international character. Berlinguer dedicated the first of his three articles to the theme of "imperialism and coexistence." In it he called for a "dynamic and open" conception of détente in Europe counterposed to that, attributed to "imperialism," of an instrument for maintaining the status quo.[100] However, he avoided making an analogy between Chile and Czechoslovakia. In both cases the great powers had reacted within their respective spheres of influence, limiting national sovereignty and suffocating potentially transnational forces of change. Détente expressed not only the decline of the Cold War but an ambiguous sense of uncertainty that could give rise to opportunities for change, endemic disorder, or simply the maintenance of order.[101] The question was whether and how forces of change might find their moment on the European and global scene. The Communists were not equidistant in formulating this question. They indeed considered American interference in Chile and all of Latin America to be illegitimate, while they did not discuss the legitimacy of the Soviet presence in Eastern Europe, seen as a legacy of antifascism per the official discourse of the communist regimes. Within these limits, as was their tradition, they elaborated visions that went beyond the perimeter of a "national road" and confronted global scenarios using a lens and a language that did not always coincide with the rest of the communist world.

AFTER THE OIL SHOCK: REDEFINING THE WORLD ORDER

Between the end of 1973 and the beginning of 1974, the oil shock caused by the Yom Kippur War spread throughout the West predictions of a crisis that brought to mind the Great Depression of the Thirties.[102] The consequences for Italy were ambivalent. The crisis of the ruling class and the push for change accelerated, putting the "communist question" on the agenda. At the same time, intervention by West Germany and the United States to avoid the country's financial collapse configured a new "external constraint" that combined economic and political conditions inscribed within a conservative conception of international détente.[103] As seen from Washington and the main West European capitals, there was agreement that Italy was the "sick man of Europe," made worse by the deficit of legitimacy of its traditional ruling class; but no solutions for a political turnover existed. Indeed, its recovery implied the maintenance of anticommunist prejudice, though the ways in which this was interpreted showed diverse nuances and scenarios. The implications of the "communist question" split the Italian ruling class, but also European leaderships, into hawks and doves. An analogous division seemed to loom also in the Soviet bloc. In particular, it was legitimate to doubt that Henry Kissinger's policy might sacrifice democracy on the altar of anticommunist containment not only in Latin America but also in Southern Europe. No less legitimate was the suspicion that Brezhnev preferred a PCI that was more oriented toward social mobilization than to prospects of government, in the bipolar context of the European spheres of influence.

The Italian Communists experienced the Chilean coup d'état and the Yom Kippur War as two events that created a geopolitical short circuit. Chile cast a long shadow for at least a year, intensified by the tragic resurgence of subversion with bombings at Brescia and on the Italicus train, and by the threat of a right-wing coup d'état. The new Arab-Israeli conflict involved Italy, as tragically shown by the terrorist attack at the Rome Fiumicino airport on 17 December 1973. Similar events intensified already existing perceptions of a dramatic spiral between world instability, the economic shock putting Italy at the risk of being marginalized, and an end to its being a democratic exception in the Mediterranean. At the same time, the siren calls of the "crisis of capitalism," understood as confirmation of Marxist-Leninist axioms immediately invoked in the analyses by Soviet and East European elites, could exert their attraction and subtract space from PCI's peculiarities. The vision of the Italian Communists was shaped by Amendola, as it had been two years earlier. In his opinion, the crisis provoked by the war in the Middle East should not be read solely through the lens of economic power mechanisms, since this highlighted the attrition of American hegemony and of the axis between the United States and Europe. But Europe was largely unprepared for the challenge.[104]

The Communist leading group held fast to its already adopted coordinates and positionings—that is to say, a nondeterminist interpretation of the world economic crisis, its inspiration as a "party for order" that aimed to defend the Republican institutions, and the project of putting an end to Cold War legacies thanks to international détente. The ability to focus on the ambivalences of the events of 1974 came more slowly, as alongside profiles of crisis they revealed accelerations and transformations in Italy and in Europe. The "long wave" of the 1968 movement and its contribution to the secularization of Italian society determined the first real political defeat of the Christian Democrats and the Catholic Church, in the referendum on divorce in May 1974 and with it the exit of the clerico-reactionary anticommunist option from the scene. The Italian political scene experienced an evolution by the end of the year with a return to government for Moro, who made no secret of his adherence to the prospect of national solidarity and displayed attention toward the communists' democratic function. Moro's tortuous language cautiously showed that he was now, much more than in the past, in accord with a series of themes beloved by Italian Communists—in the first place, an idea of détente unlike that of a "crystallization of the already existing." This placed him in direct contrast with Kissinger.[105] The fall of the dictatorships in Portugal and Greece, in April and July 1974 respectively, suddenly started democratic transitions in Southern Europe, opened up further possibilities for enlarging the European community, and dissolved many specters of the encirclement of a democratic Italy in the Mediterranean. The Portuguese Carnation Revolution had repercussions for all the principal forces of the European left. At the same time, the consequences of the oil shock delineated on a world level a transformation of agendas and public discourse, which emerged in the UN General Assembly in April 1974. The resolution on the "new international economic order" retraced the language of the nonaligned countries, indicated the priority of the sovereignty of developing countries, and challenged the power of the United States within the international economy.[106]

The project of the "new international economic order," which now forced itself onto the global agenda, seemed to announce a passage from the revolutionary phase of the Third World, which had come to an end in the previous decade, to a reforming phase that aimed to envisage an alternative to Western supremacy. A variegated alignment of anti-imperialist national actors shared the prospect of gradually modifying economic relations between North and South. Their shared vocabulary could, however, take on different meanings, starting with the notions of sovereignty and internationalism, self-determination, and interdependence.[107] The

Communists shared in the good wishes presented at the UN by the Italian representative Giolitti, underlining how the objective of postcolonial sovereignty had turned out to be insufficient without a new architecture of world economic interdependencies, which brought the role of Europe into play. They believed that the Soviet Union represented an indispensable force to make such developments practicable, and favorably interpreted the commitment to détente presented by Soviet Minister of Foreign Affairs Andrej Gromyko, in polemic with the Chinese.[108] The nexus between détente and the end of the Cold War was, however, not at all evident outside Europe, where the stabilization of the Old Continent could instead mean new violence and wars.

In this rapid national and international evolution, the friction between the Italian Communists and the "socialist camp" remained contained within the diplomatic modality. During a series of meetings with the ideologist Ponomarev in July 1974, Segre presented Italian foreign policy as an "essential part of our struggle for a democratic turn," insisted on the commitment of the PCI within the ambit of the European Community, and declared that if in the past the positions of the Italian Communists were seen as "exoteric," interest was now growing not only among Western communists but also among socialists and social democrats. These were all questions that displeased the Soviets but were not discussed face-to-face.[109] Even the crucial Middle East scenario, which in the recent past had prevalently shown convergence between the two sides, now seemed to increase the elements of friction. Just after the Yom Kippur War, Moscow was losing ground in the region and tended to support extremist subjects and demands. The PCI instead assigned an important role to the European Community and reaffirmed its own convergence with the foreign policy of the Italian government, taking a pro-Arab position, but on the basis of recognition of the State of Israel.[110]

Ponomarev attempted above all to play on the drama of the Italian internal context, which was marked by a new upsurge in subversive violence, and renewed pressure on the Italian leading group to realign to a classist vision of politics and prepare to confront returning "fascism" by putting itself under the protective wing of the "socialist camp." Among Moscow's worries was evidently the possibility that the PCI might take advantage of the new law concerning the public financing of political parties to increase its autonomy. This was in fact the intention of Berlinguer, who a little later would instruct Gianni Cervetti to put an end to the financial flow from Moscow. Berlinguer rejected Ponomarev's reminder about the "class struggle," confirming that the Italian Communists would work for a "democratic revolution."[111] This, as far as we know, was the last Soviet attempt to put an end to the Italian semi-heresy by invoking the spectre of reactionary involution in Italy. Changes in international scenarios in mid-decade would produce new discursive and conflictual political circuits, eroding further the link between the two partners.

In December 1974, Berlinguer made an important speech to the Central Committee, in which he rejected the idea of a "collapse" of capitalism but outlined a scenario of world ungovernability, open to threats and opportunities. His analysis was in reality very prudent and traditional. The category constituted by world "relations of force" favorable to socialism and anti-imperialist forces remained intact. The notion of crisis applied to the capitalist world, while the socialist world was immune to crisis. What changed was the idea of the "need" for socialism in the world, which no longer flowed from the self-evident force of Soviet socialism and its encounter with the postcolonial world. In Berlinguer's opinion, in 1968 a mass rebellion had emerged against an organization of society that sacrificed "essential human values" by subordinating them to profit. He saw a new social awareness coming to the surface "outside the logic of capitalism," which linked to anti-imperialist struggles and needed to be expressed in language more suited to humanistic socialism and less to the "class struggle." In this panorama, the center of gravity remained the nexus between the Second and Third Worlds. Berlinguer recognized that the latter could not be seen as "a homogeneous and autonomous entirety," but he evoked its "mold-breaking, explosive character" as an element that was "external" to the power system of Western capitalism. He claimed for the communist movement the irreplaceable role of interlocutor and revolutionary actor which had shifted "multiple real forces and currents of ideas" in an anti-imperialist direction.[112]

Berlinguer's speech is usually cited on account of its revision of the anti-Atlanticist prejudice. In reality, he did nothing more than adhere entirely to the Ostpolitik philosophy and the idea of recognizing realistically the existence of the blocs in order to set the long-term objective of overcoming them. The decision to drop the demand for Italy to leave NATO was already implicit in the Europeanist revision of the PCI, which thus became more effective and coherent. The principal novel element in Berlinguer's speech was, however, something else, and it arose from the distinction between praise for détente and the decline of the bipolar order. Détente between the great powers represented a condition that was necessary but not sufficient. In this way, the role of Western Europe and its nexus with the Third World occupied a crucial position which could open up prospects for international cooperation "as a revolutionary objective on the world level." In other words, Berlinguer not only adopted as his own the vision of the "new international economic order" envisaged by the UN General Assembly, but assigned to the European Community a key role in this context. The revision of the Italian Communists' policy toward Europe was linked to a new globalist vision. This vision was not a figment of the imagination, but was based on the plurality of postimperial orientations of the European leading classes and of the socialists in particular. The Yom Kippur War and the oil crisis had delineated a new Mediterranean identity for Europe and greater autonomy within the transatlantic context.[113]

With this mixture of transformative visions and geopolitical realism, Berlinguer intended to legitimize the PCI, seek an agreement with Moro, and safeguard Communist identity.[114] His synthesis prevented a division between moderates and intransigents within the leading group. Among the former were Bufalini and Napolitano, and among the latter were Pajetta and Ingrao, who gave expression to the anti-Atlanticism of the cadres, militants, and intellectuals. However, this division was not the same as the one that had arisen around the figures of Amendola and Ingrao in the previous decade. Berlinguer's leadership established a strong equilibrium and created consent. The exclusion from the secretariat of Cossutta, who according to Barca had become too powerful and was linked to Moscow, completed the picture.[115] Berlinguer adopted for domestic policy the same realist and project-based approach as for international policy. He relaunched the "historic compromise," understood as "something more than a new government formula," but also floated the idea that the Italian crisis was the opportunity to introduce "elements of socialism." Such a concept echoed Togliatti's "structural reforms" but alluded to forms of public control over the economy and the restructuring of consumption, which in the conjuncture of the oil shock could appear as a more general orientation in Europe. The narrative of Italian history after the war was positioned entirely in the Togliattian tradition, based on the paradigm of the responsibility of the working class, on the theme of national sovereignty, and on the argument that the Cold War had interrupted an authentic democratic transformation of the country. Berlinguer added the idea that renewing the season of antifascist unity and liquidating anticommunism would not simply repair damage and unblock the democratic system, but would turn Italy into a political and social laboratory in Europe.[116] His emphasis on the action to be performed in West Europe thus presented a dual implication: the combined prospect of a European global role and of a national transformation destined to exert international influence.[117]

Berlinguer shifted the center of gravity of the Italian Communists in West Europe, recognizing de facto the need to re-equilibrate a system of relations that were historically directed toward East Europe and the Third World. Relations with the Western European left, however, were to a great extent yet to be built. The self-complacency regarding the interest aroused by Italian communism was in many ways excessive. Various European socialist leaders showed attention for and curiosity toward the PCI's evolution, seen above all as a force that could contribute to stabilizing the Italian situation. Two of these were the Swedish socialist Olof Palme and, famously, Brandt, who however in July 1974 yielded the leadership of the SPD to Helmut Schmidt, who represented the more moderate and anticommunist components. The French Socialist leader François Mitterrand, too, had opened toward the Italian Communists, with the aim of proposing his model of "union of the left" in the South of Europe—a model disliked by the Northern European social democrats. However, none of the main European socialist leaders was inclined to establish a public and committed relation, and even less to cede anything in terms of identity.[118] This was true of both sides. The creation of a Western communist pole implied competition, as in France, much more than integration between the two major political cultures of the European left. The split between Europeanists and anti-Europeanists, highlighted by the Brussels Conference, prevented communism from becoming a magnet for electors, militants, and trade unionists on the left in the West. The ideas professed by the Italians could exert greater influence among the East European communists, a side effect certainly not extraneous to the intentions of the leading group. In synthesis, the Italian Communists did not really launch their own Westpolitik, although such a prospect was openly called for by Segre.[119]

The interlocutors who were most consonant with their positions turned out to be the Yugoslavs, an influential and authoritative force, but more outside than inside Europe. In his encounter with Tito on 29 March 1975, Berlinguer declared, in the knowledge that he was speaking a shared language, that he considered "ever less adequate for the times the concept and the very notion of the international communist movement," because it responded to "a restricted vision of the possibilities."[120] These words appear at the same time as innovative and contradictory, since the Italian leading group continued to act to a great extent within the perimeter of the movement. Certainly, no other communist leader apart from Tito would have subscribed to or even understood such a thesis. Berlinguer's vision signaled a profound change of mind destined to have significant consequences, but for the moment it remained confidential.

In the representations of the Italian Communists, the sense of a self-reliant force was not based exclusively on elements of a national character, although those elements leaped to the forefront with the Communists' conquest of a third of the votes in the June 1975 municipal elections. The electoral growth of the PCI, which maintained substantial mass bases from the 1968 period and had renewed its electorate by about a quarter, found itself in a particularly favorable conjuncture both in Europe and on a global level. The Carnation Revolution in Portugal and its international consequences, the final victory of the communists in Vietnam, the conclusion of the Conference on cooperation and security in Europe, the end of Franco's regime in Spain were all promising scenarios that, in different ways, also impacted on Italian communism. The institutional crisis produced by the Watergate scandal provoked the resignation of Nixon in August 1974, integrated these scenarios, and created a connection between the world economic shock and the apparent weakening of American primacy. On a public level, leaders like Bufalini and Segre claimed, in light of the Middle East and Indochina, that bipolarism represented a survival from the past, that the role of the great powers at this point was to respond to local and national actors instead of imposing their own models, and that Europe had to come to terms with this new reality.[121] A similar perception of world politics in the mid-Seventies united many political actors, though with often opposite views. In the running to govern an important Western country, the Italian Communists could with good reason feel that they had become protagonists, capable of participating in the dynamics of global change and occupying the role of a driving force among Western communists.

The Carnation Revolution had repercussions throughout the European political context, concentrating the attention of the great powers and the Western governments. Different ideas emerged on both sides of the Atlantic on the eve of the first political elections, in April 1975. Washington considered the possibility of applying the same illiberal version of containment used in Chile in order to prevent the axis of government from shifting drastically leftward, given the active presence of a strong communist party under Moscow's influence. Bonn, London, and Paris excluded such an option, and bet on the political actors who were capable of ensuring a democratic transition, starting with the socialists.[122] All shared the vision of Southern Europe as the theater of a unitary and interdependent crisis, but the main European governments opposed any doctrine of "limited sovereignty" in the West, and influenced American conduct.[123] The fallout on the European left was significant because the Portuguese question involved governing social-democratic parties, and represented a critical moment for the Western communist parties. The opinions of the only two mass parties—the PCI and the PCF—on Álvaro Cunhal, the leader of the Portuguese Communist Party, diverged totally. Berlinguer understood that the credibility of the Italian Communists depended to a great extent on this opinion. Unlike Marchais, he distanced himself from the attempt by the Portuguese Communists to prevent the Christian Democrats from taking part in the elections, and defended the principle of political pluralism. The Italian leading group's worry was aggravated by the language of the Portuguese about "bourgeois democracy." For example, Segre reported that, in a confidential encounter, the government exponent Mário Ruivo, who was close to the PCP and would shortly be nominated foreign minister, had confided that he was considering "a Cuban model with a little more pluralism and freedom."[124]

Once more the Italians found themselves almost isolated within European communism and in contrast with Moscow. Apart from Tito, only the secretary of the Spanish Communist Party, Santiago Carrillo, expressed the same opinion as Berlinguer. In a confidential meeting a few months later, the two leaders agreed that Cunhal's position would have damaged their Europeanist and democratic project.[125] In the entire matter, the Italian Communists were much closer to the positions of the European socialists that to those of the other main communist parties. This did not, however, indicate a substantial change in the reciprocal relations, though contacts had intensified at the level of foreign sections. Returning from a trip to the United States in September 1975, the exponent of the SPD, Horst Ehmke, framed the dilemma that Western communism represented for social democrats: How could a break from Moscow be favored without increasing the communists' influence in their respective countries?[126] From this point of view, the Italian question was even more controversial than the Portuguese one.

The Carnation Revolution presented a further aspect: the end of the last European empire on the African continent. The Italian Communists distinguished themselves by their attention to and connections with the liberation movements in Angola, Mozambique, and Guinea-Bissau, which were in various cases mediated by Algeria. Since the mid-Sixties, the PCI had established relations with the leader of the Liberation Front of Mozambique (Frelimo), Marcelino dos Santos, and with Amilcar Cabral in Guinea-Bissau, which had taken the place of Guinea as the "revolutionary vanguard" in sub-Saharan Africa. The centrality of a "national" character was a terrain for agreement, and it solicited the pedagogical vein of the Italian Communists while it remained hard to digest for the French Communists and was shelved by the Soviets in the name of ideological loyalties.[127] The Italian Communists therefore saw the Carnation Revolution and the new postcolonial independence in Portuguese-speaking Africa as entwined events in which they took part not only for solidarity but as actors with a certain amount of influence. Their language, which differed from the classist and pro-Soviet vision of the Portuguese Communists in Europe, linked up with the effort to profess "national roads" in Africa even after their involvement with the initial independence experiences. This marked a clear distancing from the Cuban and Soviet Marxist-Leninist approach, which had emerged some time earlier and had increased after Havana's military intervention in the Angolan civil war. Even the inevitable nexus with the triumph of the communists in Indochina highlighted different languages. Berlinguer presented the end of the war in Vietnam as the beginning of a "new democratic international setup" within which Europe would contribute its share.[128] Thus the relaunch of anti-imperialism, from a "national" and not a Marxist-Leninist perspective, superimposed itself on the antifascist motif on the Italian and European scene. The terms and the meanings of such a combination had changed decisively with respect to the Sixties, as the coordinates established at that time between the Western left, the "socialist camp," and the postcolonial world were redefined in the light of détente, cooperation, and the diversification of Third World actors.

By the mid-1970s, the "rediscovery" of the Third World had lost its original meaning for Italian Communists. Most past hierarchical and paternalistic views had yielded to the idea of backing a new agenda of relations between Europe and the Global South, as a crucial passage to ending the Cold War order. Not least, the Italian Communists could now hardly set aside in the name of internationalism the incongruities between their idea to combine democracy with socialism and the resilience of authoritarian one-party regimes in most of the postcolonial countries—as they had done in the years of de-Stalinization and decolonization. Berlinguer's November 1975 trip to Guinea, Guinea-Bissau, and Algeria took place under the sign of "new internationalism," which was imagined as going beyond the confines of the communist movement and as tying closer bonds between European progressive forces and the strategic countries of the postcolonial world. The coincidence with Angola's declaration of independence conferred a particular symbolic significance to the journey.[129]

The ambition of the Italian Communists was to contribute to designing a new role for Europe on the North-South axis of the world. For the most part, they adhered to the vision of Claude Cheysson, the European commissioner for development, who was the socialist promoter of the Convention of Lomé, signed in February 1975 by the European Community and forty-six developing countries in Africa, the Caribbean, and the Pacific, which introduced a new policy of cooperation and a revision of community aid. The project could be seen as a strategic convergence of the EC toward developing countries and the idea of the "new international economic order" which aimed to make a post-bipolar world emerge.[130] The problem was to convincingly reconcile the Euro-African perspective with East-West détente, which aroused the mistrust of many actors in the Global South—for example, the Algerians. While the Soviet Union and the socialist bloc were critical of the EC, which they labeled a form of "neocolonialism," they feared above all the favorable implications for the nonaligned movement. Comecon explicitly rejected the partition between the North and South of the world, which it considered a Maoist formula.[131]

For the PCI this global context increased the significance of the alliance among the Western communists, but it also amplified its political disagreements with the PCF, evident both in the two parties' respective judgments of the Portuguese revolution and of Europe's role in Africa. The PCI's Directorate dedicated significant energy to relations with the French and to preparing a new pan-European conference of communist parties, which was stuck in an impasse owing to disagreement between the supporters of an ideological relaunching of the movement, invoked above all by the SED but also by the PCF, and by those who supported détente and international cooperation—that is, the Italians and the Yugoslavs.[132] Most of the leaders, starting with Amendola, came to the conclusion that the French were maintaining positions that were hard to reconcile with the European policy of the PCI.[133] In the meeting between Berlinguer and Marchais in Paris on 29 September 1975, it was acknowledged that the sole common ground was a generic interest in "certain common traits" of the relation between democracy and socialism in Western Europe.[134] This situation was not modified by subsequent meetings between Berlinguer and Marchais in Rome, in November of the same year.[135] Nonetheless, the generic message had an impact on the general public even outside the respective national borders. The agreement proclaimed by the two principal Western communist parties fed a perception that a left with a new face, neither pro-Soviet nor social-democratic, was the protagonist in Southern Europe, including in Spain after the death of Franco.

The changing panorama in Southern Europe highlighted even more the strategic character of the Italian crisis, capable of shifting leftward the trajectories of the democratic transitions, and threatening instability precisely at the historic moment of the equilibrium between the blocs sanctioned by the Conference of Helsinki. For the great powers and for the principal European governments, Italy constituted a reason for alarm, and its "communism of prosperity" was an enigma. Kissinger feared the prospect of Italy transformed into a second Yugoslavia, which would have threatened the cohesion of the Atlantic alliance. In his vision, destined to remain the same in the following years, communists in power in Western Europe would "totally redefine the map of the postwar world."[136] Under such premises, the results of the administrative elections in Italy could only increase the tension. In summer 1975, US President Gerald Ford and Kissinger harshly rejected Moro's arguments about the political evolution of the Italian Communists and the democratic nature of their electoral consensus.[137] In a meeting with representatives of France, West Germany, and Great Britain in December 1975, Kissinger declared emphatically that the Atlantic Alliance would not survive "domination" by the communist parties in the West. The European leaders substantially shared his conviction that the PCI still believed in the "dictatorship of the proletariat," and that its relative independence from Moscow did not mean a great deal. The shared conviction was, therefore, that participation of the Communists in the Italian government would destabilize NATO.[138] Parallel to this, Moscow more than once expressed serious reservations and distrust for the PCI's European choice and the hypothesis of a Western communist pole, which configured an idea of détente that was inconsistent with the bipolar framework, a challenge to Soviet hegemony within the movement, and a threat to the stability and future of the Warsaw Pact.[139]

In public discourse, directed toward Western international opinion, Berlinguer took pains above all to underline that the Italian Communists had no intention of altering the equilibria between the blocs.[140] He was aware that a conservative policy prevailed in Washington and Moscow, but he continued to believe that détente could have multiple implications. In particular, he detected "an anti-European element" in Kissinger's policy, as he had stated in his meeting with Tito, which could increase the differentiation between Europe and the United States.[141] On the other hand, the Final Act of Helsinki in August 1975 had acknowledged the division of Europe that dated back to thirty years earlier, but it had also softened the borders of the "Iron Curtain" and could therefore be understood as a point of departure instead of a destination. Precisely for this reason, however, as Natta noted, the Soviets saw in the conferences of the communist parties an "ideological counterweight" to Helsinki—that is, a way to reconfirm the compactness of the "socialist community" and of European communism.[142] The question revealed a range of opinions among Italian Communists. Berlinguer and Bufalini were in favor of the prospect of dynamic détente, subordinating to it the requests from Amendola and Napolitano to intensify relations with the social democracies in Europe.[143]

This choice reflected the PCI's convergence with the Moro government, which identified Helsinki with national interests, and with the visions of the Catholic Church, which by its very presence had legitimized the interpretations that imagined an end to the Cold War.[144] At the same time, it is probable that Berlinguer's orientation should also be understood in the light of the world conjuncture marked by the dissolution of the Portuguese empire in Africa, by the end of the war in Indochina, and by the relevance of the Palestinian question in the Middle East. The nonaligned movement presented itself as an alliance that was not only negative, as in its rejection of the logic of the blocs, but a sufficiently proactive actor that had imposed the theme of the "new international economic order" on the world agenda. The recognition obtained at Helsinki of the geopolitical status quo that dated from the end of World War II represented the definitive entry of Europe into the postimperial era, and the possibility of progress toward the end of the security syndrome that was still entrenched in Moscow. This was also why the Italian Communists developed their own dual vision of détente: on the one hand, acknowledgement of international compatibilities and a search for legitimacy based on their belonging to the West; on the other, the idea that global change might contribute to breaking down the compatibilities of the bipolar system, induce changes in the "socialist camp," and pave the way for the birth of a new international system.

This dual vision was the most evident expression of different, superimposed responses to the challenges of the past decade. In the first place, the impulse of the 1968 movement had given rise to a relation between "socialism with a human face" and the Western European dimension, a new genealogy with an internationalist vocation, albeit motivated primarily by the lexis of national legacy and Togliattian polycentrism. This implied a transnational function both toward the Western left, with the objective of giving answers to the "demand for socialism," and toward the communist establishments, with the aim of influencing reforms. Secondly, the impulse of the world economic shock induced a reading of the evolution of the West using the category of crisis, while the image was accepted of a socialist world that was undamaged, though not as dynamic as before. Even though its effects needed deciphering, the global shock seemed able to create consensus for strengthening the role of the state in the capitalist economy, tipping the scales in favor of new forms of mixed economy. But above all, the world conjuncture included the active presence of postcolonial actors and an attempt to stabilize a post-bipolar agenda. In this context, the nexus between Europe and the Third World acquired centrality, while the Soviet Union maintained the function of anti-imperialist bastion, though its reluctance to engage with the themes of cooperation and development constituted a sore point. The Italian Communists based their motivations and ambitions on the representations and perspectives of humanistic socialism, of reforms in the socialist world, and of the global role of Europe.

6
EUROPEANISMS AND GLOBALISMS

THE LAUNCH OF EUROCOMMUNISM

The aspirations of the Italian Communists introduced themselves into the political and cultural transformations in the mid-1970s in different ways. In the national context, the Communists expressed the drive to modify Italy's "blocked democracy," a position that won consensus especially in the more modernized regions of the country. They shared with a number of prominent figures of the government parties a deep-seated anxiety about the social and political impact of the crisis, and put themselves forward as a responsible force in the nation. Having muted their militant anti-Atlanticism, they integrated Italian foreign policy in Europe and the Mediterranean, or competed with it, without the neutralist leanings of the past. In many ways they exercised a greater influence than that of a political opposition party, and acted as an intermediary for the country in global relations. Thus they were perceived in Washington, as in other parts of the world, in opposite ways: as a threat, or as a resource for Italy.[1]

In the European context, they aimed at becoming part of the forces of change by giving voice to the more dynamic interpretations of détente and the attempts to introduce a distinction between Atlantic loyalty and belonging to Europe. The Communists represented a minority subject in the institutions of the European Community, but with other progressive forces they shared in the discourse regarding its global role; this they systematized in the version of a new relationship between the North and

South of the world, in light of the idea of a "new international economic order." The idea that the economic shock would open a season of rethinking welfare policies, in the sense of a more intense inclination toward public and state intervention, brought them near the sectors of social democracy. Their proposal of a Western communist alliance founded on the marriage between socialism and democracy had gained credibility and contested the logic of the blocs. This, however, glossed over a number of important differences regarding, above all, European integration itself and the principles that underlay it, irreconcilable with the regimes of a Soviet type. The Italian Communists' ideas of reform did not interact with the leadership of the parties in power in the "socialist camp," but they found a hearing among some members of the establishment, as well as among the dissidents.[2]

In the global context the PCI came over as a force that was autonomous from the Socialist bloc, and which possessed a solid network of relations going well beyond the confines of the communist movement. The links with the Third World, most of all in the Mediterranean and in Africa, no longer intersected with the revolutionary charge of the anticolonial struggles. They contributed instead to the idea of a reformed new world order, different from the unequal and "neocolonial" one, whose ambition was to modify the global agenda thanks to the eclipse of American hegemony after Vietnam. Reform communism did not extend outside Europe, but it made use of the conspicuous networks of transnational political relations that had been established over a twenty-year period.[3] In different intellectual circles, in Anglo-American academia as much as in Latin America, the prestige of Italian communism was linked to the new international diffusion of the thought of Gramsci, who by now was freed of the national image established in the postwar years and was authoritatively presented by Eric Hobsbawm as the sole "theoretician of politics" in the history of Marxism. The nexus established between Gramsci's thought and the reality of Italian communism was in many ways superficial, but it was on target regarding the specific intellectual qualities of its tradition.[4]

It was in Moscow that Berlinguer launched internationally the project of a pluralist socialism centered on Europe, when he spoke at the Twenty-Fifth Congress of the CPSU in February 1976.[5] The choice had a highly symbolic value, and showed the extent to which the project could not be separated from the idea of a reform in the Soviet-type states. As was to be expected, the Soviet response was icy. Berlinguer was insistent in vain with Brezhnev regarding the opportunities opened on a world scale by the American "decline," on the need for the Soviets to free themselves of their "besieged fortress" complex, and on "international cooperation" and the role of Europe. On the most controversial questions, he defended freedom of expression regarding Andrei Sakharov, while saying that he did not share his ideas, and made reference to the Helsinki principles. For the first time, a communist leader extended to the socialist world the notion of human rights, which until then it had applied almost exclusively to the Third World as a way of condemning Western colonialism, and which was now legitimized as one of the tesserae in international détente.[6] By diplomatic choice, the conflict over intellectual dissent was limited to private talks, but was not destined to lessen. In any case, Berlinguer's public pronouncement had left its mark, and behind the scenes it was not found displeasing in less conformist circles in Moscow and Eastern Europe.

Berlinguer confirmed the interaction of realism and universalism in his vision of affairs, the search for Western legitimation, and the prospect of relaunching internationalism on a new basis. The operation of this reforming and anticapitalist political culture comes across clearly in the note sent him a few days later by Antonio Tatò, his personal secretary, referring to a talk between the two of them on the subject of a "qualitative difference" of the social and economic bases of Soviet society as compared with Western capitalist societies. Unlike in the past, the rejection of social-democratic culture was dictated not by support for the Soviet Union or lack of it, but by the scenario of a "socialist transformation" in the West, which would have provided an impetus to the reform of regimes and society within "actually existing socialism." This perspective would have given Italian communism a role "of international importance."[7] Tatò's writing conveyed concepts shared with Berlinguer, but he seemed to be trying to exert pressure on him by placing extreme emphasis on the mission of the Italian Communists, a position which recalled the Marxist and Catholic thought of Franco Rodano. In firm opposition to moderate tendencies within the leading group, this vision insisted on the specificity of Italy in light of

Catholic and communist universalism, up to the point of outlining a form of "exceptionalism." Berlinguer was not insensitive to such an inspiration, but was careful to avoid a point of rupture. With a general election in the offing, which the crisis in Italy had made inevitable, he gave space to realism and Westpolitik. In this juncture, Giorgio Napolitano became the reference point for the moderates, replacing Amendola, who, after having given the decisive impetus to the Europeanist option, had retreated from the strategy of Eurocommunism due to its detachment from the "socialist camp." It was precisely on this point that two personalities as different from each other as Berlinguer and Napolitano established even an intellectual relationship in turning to an Italian and international audience.[8]

The Italian leading group began an unprecedented diplomatic overture toward social democracies. This above all was the meaning of Napolitano's trip to Great Britain in March 1976, where interest was shown fin Berlinguer's Moscow speech. In parallel with this, Sergio Segre went to West Germany, while two delegations, headed respectively by Alfredo Reichlin and Aldo Tortorella, visited Sweden, Norway, Denmark, and Holland, Belgium, and Luxembourg. The work agenda was aimed at the "demand for socialism" emerging from the changes in world politics, which would have set into motion—if not actually shifted—social democratic traditions, would have endowed with new value the Communists' reasons for a radical reform of capitalism, and would have justified a rapprochement between themselves and the social democrats.[9] Such an approach responded to the idea that the Italian Communists were the authentic vanguard, even in the context of the European left and not only as compared with other communist parties, a conviction that was not always suitable for building relations in Europe. In any case, for the first time in their history, the Italian Communists became involved in establishing relations with social democracies. A limit was seen in the political and symbolic absence of top-level meetings, which both sides avoided for reasons of internal consensus and international opportunity.

To integrate the search for insertion into the Western context, Berlinguer argued in a famous interview in the *Corriere della sera* on 15 June 1976, just a few days before the general election, that full recognition of Italy's international alliances was not a reluctant or opportunistic choice for the Italian Communists to make, since it also guaranteed their political strategy. Replying to the question of whether the North Atlantic Treaty might provide a protective shield for constructing "socialism in freedom," he replied: "I also do not want Italy to leave the Atlantic Treaty for this reason."[10] In saying this, Berlinguer, appealing to public opinion in Italy, defended himself from charges of incompatibility with the Western system, and distanced himself from the "Brezhnev doctrine" in the Soviet bloc. On 20 June the PCI received an all-time high of nearly 35 percent of the vote, even if it remained the second party in the country. The juxtaposition between the two political and social blocs of Republican Italy went past an equilibrium point beyond which it was impossible to govern without finding some form of collaboration, which the size of the economic crisis made it urgent to negotiate.

The main Western actors by and large showed themselves insensitive to the Italian dilemma. With all its specific nature, Italian communism remained different from the social democracies in its political culture. While it had an agenda in national politics that was ever more similar to that of the social democracies, and a wide consensus built on programs and functions that could be associated with them, the PCI did not possess strong international connections in Western Europe. Seen from the most important Western capitals, the main difference between Italy and Portugal or Spain was the longtime continuity of communist hegemony over the left. This had created a paradox in which Italy, the only country having a democratic experience in Southern Europe, had undergone less flexible treatment than had the other countries of the region. Even though social-democratic leaders' opposition to Kissinger's idea of a "Brezhnev doctrine" in the West implied an important change in the Western political modus operandi, they all respected the limits imposed by the division of Europe. The Italian question seemed to make Western governments more united under the sign of anticommunism. The Puerto Rico summit of the major Western powers, held at the end of June 1976, established an intertwining between political and economic conditionalities. This meant that it would be possible for Italy to accede to a loan from the International Monetary Fund in order to avoid a precipitous fall in its financial situation, but on the condition that the Communists not enter the government. This condition was made public in a statement attributed to German Chancellor Helmut Schmidt on 15 July, before the formation of the new government in Italy. Such a statement avoided invoking Kissinger's domino theory, and aimed at a democratic stabilization in the framework of Western economic interdependencies. But it also represented an interference that reflected the unwritten rules of the bipolar order.[11]

Berlinguer's participation at the Berlin Conference of the European Communist Parties at the end of June sent an ambiguous signal that could be read either as a further demonstration of difference or as confirmation that the Italians still belonged to the communist family, notwithstanding those differences. Berlinguer had decided to go to Berlin after long negotiation, on the basis of a conviction that to interrupt the understanding, however vague, between the PCI and the CPSU would have been a strategic error. In the catalog of questions presented by Berlinguer there were no omissions, beginning with the subject of Europe's role in the "new international economic order" and ending with a demand for the recognition of dissent regarding the invasion of Czechoslovakia. Berlinguer took the opportunity to publicly adopt the term "Eurocommunism," whose circulation, in his view, demonstrated the breadth of the aspiration for a socialist transformation "of a new type" in Europe. He defined three planes of action: all-European détente, convergence with other progressive European forces, and the prospect of "democratizing" the European community.[12] The main objective was to position the discourse of the Italian Communists in what amounted to a pluralist panorama of the communist movement, thanks also to the participation of Tito. Berlinguer won apparent toleration from the Soviets, who had chosen a conciliatory line while demonstrating their capacity to gather the European communist parties around the banner of "proletarian internationalism."[13]

The formation of the Andreotti government, based on the abstention of the PCI in Parliament, offered a precarious but sufficient solution for obtaining the international financing necessary for the country, on the basis of a harsh program of sacrifices. The PCI found itself in the awkward position of supporting that program without, for the benefit of its militants and electors, being able to put its entry into government on the other side of the scale. Right from the start, the Christian Democrat strategy had an ambiguous nature: there was the need for an understanding, but the Christian Democrats also tried to gnaw away at the consensus around the PCI, even if Andreotti and Moro had different ideas about the more or less appropriate and inclusive strategies to obtain this result. Berlinguer had no options available other than working toward a future participation in government, at the same time as also engaging the PCI in a hard-fought battle to overcome internal and international vetoes. The formula of "national solidarity" did not therefore constitute a return to the "national unity" of the immediate postwar period invoked by the Communists. It represented instead an opening toward collaboration between the two blocs and, with that, the apex of the reciprocal siege going back to the origins of the Cold War. Much less than in the past, Italian bipolarism possessed the aspect of diametrically opposed international loyalties, but the constraint of the great powers was active no less than the intransigent components in the two social and political blocs.

The advent of the Carter administration and Kissinger's exit from the scene seemed to introduce substantial changes in the panorama. The new US national security advisor, Zbigniew Brzezinski, distanced himself from his predecessor by liquidating the priorities of the balance of power. This meant not that Washington had shifted to a dynamic perspective of détente, but rather that it had adopted an approach aimed at tying together détente in Europe, imperial rivalries in the Third World, and global strategies.[14] In a contest of the like, Eurocommunism could be seen as an opportunity and not only as a problem, since it shed doubt on the influence of Moscow and contributed to increasing Soviet vulnerability in Eastern and Central Europe. On the eve of elections in the United States, an unusual and significant passage took place. Segre was invited to a meeting of the Trilateral Commission, the informal group created three years earlier by David Rockefeller and animated by Brzezinski, and he brought back to Berlinguer the impression that an opening existed.[15]

The PCI's expectations were encouraged by the empathy toward Eurocommunism in American liberal intellectual circles, especially among the academics who after 1968 had liquidated the theories aimed at establishing a link between the ideology of development and the social establishment of the communist parties. This was the case of Joseph La Palombara, Sidney

Tarrow, Donald Blackmer, and Peter Lange. The refusal of a US visa for Giorgio Napolitano, whom Stanley Hoffmann had invited in 1975, had not prevented a growing positive attention toward the PCI, in contrast with the orientation of Kissinger and aimed at suggesting a more realistic line by the American administration toward Italy.[16] The beginning of the term of office of the new US ambassador to Italy, Richard Gardner, a member of the Trilateral Commission, was marked by extreme caution and fueled the conception of a new American policy in Italy which might, according to one's point of view, give rise to hopes or apprehensions. However, Eurocommunism remained a critical point, above all in the eyes of Gardner and Brzezinski.[17] The Italian Communists developed contacts with the US Embassy, set in motion two years earlier by Segre and carried on by Barca, but not to an extent equal to those of the other political forces.[18] Put succinctly, the expectation that the Carter administration's watchword "neither interference nor indifference" signified a clear distancing from Kissinger's geopolitical thinking was misleading. In July 1977, during a conversation with Communist Senator Franco Calamandrei, the *Washington Post* journalist Leo Wollemborg criticized the Italian Communists' simplistic view of the Carter administration.[19]

The perception of a new US policy made itself felt even in Moscow. One of the leaders of the International Department of the CPSU, Anatoly Chernyaev, thought that Brzezinski had begun "to play with Eurocommunism," and that for an "ideological power" like the Soviet Union the game could turn out to be "more dangerous than the nuclear potential of the United States."[20] The destabilizing potential singled out in Eurocommunism by an empathetic analyst such as Chernyaev was equally well noted by the conservative leaderships in Moscow and Eastern Europe. Once the PCI had begun to participate in "national solidarity" without being able to count on any concrete opening in the West, it had to face the reaction from Moscow. Berlinguer's speech at the Berlin Conference had given rise to repercussions in Eastern Europe, which Segre mentioned publicly.[21] The tolerance of the Soviet leaders, backed by the East Germans, evaporated. At the start of 1977, Berlinguer was told by Ceaușescu that Brezhnev had explicitly invited the leaders of Eastern Europe to adopt an intransigent and aggressive orientation, once again leveling a finger at the Europeanism of the Italian Communists.[22] With the Italian Communists involved in a governmental pact and the unforeseeable repercussions of the end of the Kissinger era, the Soviet leadership feared the risk of instability in its own sphere of influence, especially in Poland after the workers' protests of summer 1976. The aggravating circumstance was that the Eurocommunists were among the voices critical of the repression of freedom of expression in the socialist countries. The question of human rights had become a particularly burning issue since the Carter administration had made it its main subject of attack, while the Charter 77 dissidents in Czechoslovakia had indicated a legal path of self-defense in their appeal to the Helsinki Accords. The symbolic figure Mlynář turned in January 1977 to the leaders of Eurocommunism and the Western left to denounce repression of the signatories of Charter 77, recalling the communist and antifascist past of many of them.[23] His message linked the legacy of the "Prague Spring" to criticism of the Soviet type of society, and was founded on the language of human rights and liberties, without dispensing with socialist ideals. It was received in this way by a number of intellectuals close to the PCI.[24]

The three Eurocommunist parties organized a meeting in Madrid at the end of February 1977, which was to be the final act of the alliance. The event covered up significant tensions, and the protagonists were not in agreement among themselves on the notion of Europeanism. Amendola observed at a meeting of the Party Directorate that "socialists, social democrats, Christian Democrats, and liberals have constituted parties at the European level" while "we will not be able to create a European CP" since "on the concept of Europe, the communists are the most divided."[25] At the same time, Moscow attempted to prevent the meeting from taking place, sending a message that warned anyone against taking irreparable steps toward a "scission."[26] Europeanism and dynamic détente now implied a collision path with Moscow.[27] In Madrid, Berlinguer, Carrillo, and Marchais generically once again asserted the idea of exploiting the space of détente to bring about changes in their respective countries. At this point Eurocommunism had become an international factor of the first rank, able to combine consensus and the national role of the three parties with an apparently uniform profile. It was challenging the bipolar order through putting itself forward as a candidate for entry into the sphere of governments of important countries in the Western world. It also fueled the ambition to found a perspective of socialist and democratic transformation, the critique of the Soviet model and the language of human rights, the vision of détente as change, participation in the European community, and the linkup with the demands of nonaligned countries for a restructuring of world economic relations.

Each of these aspects and aims could alter delicate strategic equilibriums. In reality, none of them formed a fabric that the Eurocommunists shared in common. Their criticisms of Soviet socialism were a mainly instrumental demonstration for use in domestic politics, and much less a common transnational code. The notions of pluralism and Europeanism constituted a controversial and imprecise table of principles. Their respective visions of the crisis of the bipolar order and of the "new international economic order" did not fit together. In any case, the influence of Eurocommunism appeared limited, and something that could be contained. In Europe, the social democracies and party-states of the East provided barriers from all points of view, on the ideological plane and as regarding the rejection of any option that could destabilize détente. Outside Europe, the global relations that the French and Italians had long been cultivating did not necessarily find sustenance in the Eurocommunist alliance, which instead could have been seen as a strategic hypothesis active along the East-West axis.

And yet it is a fact that the Western and the communist establishments considered Eurocommunism to be a threat, despite the evidence of such fragilities and incongruences. In this sense, the phenomenon shows how deeply their viewpoints centered on the Cold War. In Washington the nightmare of the "domino effect" had not been dispersed. It was, however, Moscow that raised the level of containment, defining Eurocommunism as a form of "revisionism." Over the next few months, covert KGB operations began, aimed at discrediting Berlinguer and sowing discord among the Western communists.[28] The perception of Eurocommunism as an ideological threat defined other communist establishments, particularly that of East Germany.[29] At the beginning of July, when Moscow had opened its public polemic by attacking Carrillo, Suslov met an Italian delegation composed of Bufalini, Pajetta, and Macaluso. The Soviet leader accused the PCI of having renounced "proletarian internationalism," and of offering support to accusations of violations of human rights that the West had directed against the Soviet Union. He took as a target Napolitano, who had expressed himself publicly in confirming the line of realistic recognition of Italy's international alliances. But the aim of his frontal attack also included Berlinguer. The PCI leaders had chosen in advance to adopt the maximum of diplomacy, and they avoided heightening the tension.[30]

Berlinguer held firm to his chosen path, despite the difficulties in relations with the PCF, which were worsened by the crisis of the Union de la Gauche in France. He presented Eurocommunism as a table of principles and not merely as a political alliance. In doing this, he chose not to follow the advice of two of his main interlocutors: Tito and the Hungarian leader, János Kádár. Both Tito and Kádár showed solidarity but also skepticism in advising caution regarding Berlinguer's positions of principle, which in the East risked provoking rigidity and prevent change instead of encouraging it.[31] Berlinguer's speech in Moscow on the sixtieth anniversary of the October Revolution was a challenge in terms of values, with its definition of democracy as a "historically universal value." Such a definition indeed posed the problem of the relation between socialism and democracy, right in the heart of "actually existing socialism." The meeting between Berlinguer and Brezhnev took place in a reciprocally frosty atmosphere and without any authentic exchange of opinions[32]—while Berlinguer's universalist language attracted international media attention.[33]

"NATIONAL SOLIDARITY" AND THE "EXTERNAL CONSTRAINT"

In the experience of "national solidarity," Berlinguer combined his own realist side with a vision of Italy's transformation. He presented the sacrifices asked of the working people as a form of "austerity" that contained a U-turn from the trajectory of the consumer society, and an idea of a society aware of the problems bound up with development and the environment.[34] The subject of anticonsumerism was in harmony with the feelings and aspirations present among those Catholics who, after the referendum on divorce, stopped regarding the Christian Democrats as their reference point.[35] The austerity argument also formed a reason for accord with social-democratic trends trying to rethink the welfare experience, so much so that Olof Palme praised Berlinguer in a private talk with Segre.[36] The Italian Communists played an important role in the policies of rights and the construction of a national health service, which provided the country with an essential welfare service. Their participation in the government thus closed a reforming cycle that had been set in motion over a decade earlier.[37] The choice of Europeanism and the abandonment of intransigent anti-Atlanticism consolidated the government pact and was a vehicle of legitimation in the light of the solemn declaration in Parliament at the end of 1977 on the country's international alliances.[38] In terms of ideals, this agreement demolished a wall in the domestic Cold War and sanctioned a long process of convergence which saw the Communists overcome their handicap regarding European integration and contribute to the formation of a broad national European consensus. Along with this, the accent placed on the politicization of the European space put them in an active positon—and not only as converts, since it constituted part and parcel of their discourse on détente as the end of the Cold War.

"National solidarity," however, could not contain various manifestations of disagreement, opposition, and protest in Italian society, but rather in many ways fueled them. The sense of responsibility and necessary sacrifice that was the central aspect of the discourse of the Communists and the Christian Democrats was not recognized as sufficient to counterbalance the fears of the intransigent anticommunist circles, to reassure the forces alarmed by a preponderant political consociation, or even to justify moderate policies among the more politicized sectors of the younger generations. Social tensions were seriously worsened by the spread of political violence. The decision taken in December 1977 by the Communist leading group to open a government crisis was in many ways inevitable, bound up as it was with the growing perception of a loss of consensus, even among workers and in the Communist electorate, and with the need to open up a prospect of government.[39] This represented a logical sequence after the conclusion of the programmatic agreement shared in Parliament on domestic policy and on foreign policy, which had its significance on the national scene, but much less on the international scene.

In the context of the government crisis, the range of the Communists' international links was developing noticeably, albeit without any protective network. The time of the PCI's Westpolitik did not coincide with its political acceleration in Italy. The first private meeting between Berlinguer and Brandt took place in June 1977.[40] Brandt was a prestigious figure, recently elected president of the Socialist International, but in a minority in the SPD. The contacts with other social-democratic parties, especially with the UK Labour Party and the Swedish Socialists, took place in an atmosphere of lukewarm interest on both sides and did not give rise to any concrete initiatives, with various personalities and sectors of the socialist parties remaining firm in their anticommunism. At the end of 1977, the relations between the Italian Communists and the European socialists began to take a negative turn due to the repercussions of the rupture in the left alliance in France, which clearly weakened the Eurocommunist prospect.[41] The limits of the Western relations of the PCI emerged from the account given to Berlinguer by Segre immediately before his trip to Moscow, regarding a meeting of the Trilateral Commission in Bonn. At the meeting there had been an attack by Kissinger, with the support of Gardner, on the social democrat Richard Löwenthal, with the aim of rejecting any credit for Eurocommunism, while Brzezinski's positions apparently remained more cautious. The attitude of the social democrats was different from that of the Americans, given that the former were interested in integrating Eurocommunism into a dimension of stability in West Europe, while the latter wanted to use it as an instrument of destabilization in Eastern and Central Europe. No one, however, contemplated the short-term prospect of an entry into government by the Italian Communists. Segre's source suggested that the real point was not to arrive at a break with Moscow, but to obtain West German assent to the principle and practice of "noninterference."[42] It was unclear how this passage could happen. Certainly, the conflict with Moscow was taking place largely behind the scenes, and contributed toward demonstrating the autonomy of the Italian Communists less than might have been possible. This conduct responded to the quest for influence that for some time had become a inalienable feature of the PCI's strategy, and which was now tracing out a vicious circle. The Europeanist evolution and the Italian Communists' quest for legitimation multiplied the reasons for conflict with Soviet socialism. However, the eventuality of a break would have compromised the possibility of urging reforms of the socialist systems and, in the last analysis, put at risk the PCI's own identity, as different from that of social democracy. As a result, an extreme tension developed between the aim of Western legitimation and the identity of reform communism.

The weakness of the PCI's international alliances made the task of Ambassador Gardner easier, decided as he was to stop the Communists from becoming part of the Italian government. Between the end of 1977 and the start of 1978, Gardner urged the Carter administration to adopt a position to prevent any steps that might favor communist influence.[43] On 12 January, the US State Department released a statement that reasserted the American veto on communist participation in government in any of the member countries of the North Atlantic Alliance. The crisis in bipolar relations, the reluctance of the European governments to risk compromising détente, and Italian contradictions and tensions on the home front all contributed to keeping the Kissinger paradigm alive.[44] The Italian Communists reacted strongly to the American statement, arguing—by no means mistakenly—that this was a blatant violation of the principle of "noninterference." However, their bargaining strength was less than in summer 1976, while relations in Western Europe remained substantially unaltered. The cards they could play depended, even more than before, on the gradualist strategy of Moro, who proposed introducing the PCI into the parliamentary majority. Berlinguer had no other option but to follow this path, as was evident in the last meeting the two leaders had on 16 February, even if they considered it a "necessary passage" to going "beyond current times" in order to realize governing jointly for a limited period, with the aim of mutual recognition.[45]

Attention has often been drawn to the convergences on politics and purpose between Moro and Berlinguer. Both attempted to provide responses to the crisis of an entire postwar set-up, even if Moro aimed at containing the long wave of 1968 and Berlinguer at developing it. They were aware of having inherited an essential task from the founding fathers of the Republic, that of governing Italian bipolarity by bringing its most conflictual and destabilizing aspects under control. From this point of view they shared the idea that the self-containment of the two poles in Italy in the Cold War was not enough to guarantee the democratic setup of the Republic and to get out of the crisis. They were also close in the idea that European détente, inserted within a wider and more stable Economic Community, could allow the negotiation of a renewed "external constraint" and modify the "material constitution" of Italian politics without actually dismantling the bipolar structure. Moro's figure symbolized many things altogether: Christian Democratic power and the attempt to reconstitute its hegemony on new bases, the cooptation of a big communist party into the sphere of a Western government, and a strategy of national change which left Cold War schemes behind. All this made him many enemies—a fate that he had in common with Berlinguer.[46] The two leaders, however, expressed different perspectives regarding the very notion of "national solidarity." Moro became the referent for a line aiming at gradual mutual recognition with the objective of including the Communists in an institutional responsibility, more than involving them in real government decision-making. Berlinguer instead invoked the defense of national sovereignty as a shield for the "historic compromise," with the aim of forming a government coalition that found its inspiration in the previous antifascist unity. This difference was not only contingent; in actual fact, a common front took shape not with the intention of redesigning the connection between international order and national politics in Italy, but rather involving a quest for the collaboration necessary to face the crisis.

The kidnapping of Moro by the Red Brigades on 16 March 1978 broke asunder a precarious equilibrium. The tragedy of Moro's imprisonment, which concluded with his murder on 9 May, lay bare the entire political fragility of "national solidarity." The firm line adopted by the leading groups of the DC and the PCI reflected a unity brought about by emergency. Moro's assassination was a shock for the whole ruling class and for Italian public opinion, but it did not produce the effect of real political solidarity. The "Moro affair" did not cause a recomposition of the national community, whereas it did lay a foundation for the decline of terrorism and political violence in the country. The Red Brigades centered their accusations against Moro on the stereotype of the Christian Democrat "regime" as a mere emanation of global capitalism. The very idea that to subject the prisoner to interrogation was the way to unveil the hidden face of power manifested a subculture and a mythology of conspiracy. In actual fact, the terrorists of the Red Brigades did not disseminate the texts created in the interrogations—Moro's so-called "memorial"—perhaps because his political and autobiographical reflections did not lend themselves to a propagandistic use such as they wanted.[47] At the same time, their schematic Marxist vocabulary was enough to reveal a lineage that was difficult for the Communists to accept, and which was even lacerating and embarrassing for them. Areas of consensus existed for red terrorism especially in workplaces and universities. There was evidence of shared roots and languages in the Italian left—a "family album," to use Rossana Rossanda's famous description—even if Marxism was not the Brigades' only ideological matrix.[48] Among the symbolic effects of the "Moro affair," it is difficult to overestimate the media amplification of the Marxist language appropriated by the Brigades, and the repercussions it had in the political body of a nation which, more than any other in Europe, numbered among its fractures the antinomy between communism and anticommunism.

The Communists' reaction was to place full emphasis on the defense of state institutions, but the prospects of "national solidarity" were shattered. They felt that a connection could be established between the persistence of the Cold War cleavage in Europe and the terrorist attack in Italy. Two years earlier, in the celebrated interview with the *Corriere della sera*, Berlinguer had recognized that there was a "certain danger" in following a road that would be found pleasing "neither here nor there" in the two international poles of the Cold War. Two years later, a balance sheet in line with such a prophecy could be drawn up of "national solidarity." The constraints of the Cold War had been made amply manifest before the "Moro affair." After the kidnapping, Washington used its weight to support the orientation of firmness prevalent in the Andreotti government—without making any concession to the Communists, since it feared the danger of a destabilization of Italy. In his letters from the Red Brigade imprisonment, Moro more than once alluded to the role the Americans were playing in hindering the possibility of negotiations.[49] Traces of connections, identified by the Italian Communists, between the Red Brigades and the secret services of Eastern Europe provided further evidence of Soviet hostility toward Berlinguer.[50]

The fact of the matter was that the PCI formed part of the government majority, but with Moro's death it had lost its only major interlocutor in the Christian Democrats' leading group, which was otherwise opposed to the Communists' full participation. The local government elections of May 1978 showed the first signs of a serious loss of political consensus. The PCI's priority became that of defending an identity that had lost its shine, both in the party's promise to the electorate to bring the "blocked democracy" to an end, and in the one made to its militants to introduce "elements of socialism" into Italian society. The Moro tragedy took on the sense of implying a path not followed, and such it was destined to remain in many narratives after the event. These narratives, however, represented a simplification of still open problems that involved the Communists as much as they did the whole of Italian society. The paradox of "national solidarity" was that it had laid the basis for saving the country from a serious economic and social crisis without having created a stable and legitimate political solution. This was the combined consequence of rigid external compatibilities and impassable boundaries between the national political blocs themselves.[51]

The "historic compromise" and Eurocommunism underwent a simultaneous crisis. Amendola, ever lukewarm toward both strategies, wrote to Berlinguer to criticize what he maintained was "acritical support" for Italian foreign policy and subordination to the Christian Democrats.[52] Berlinguer's reaction was not without ambiguity, as he was torn between the appeal to the PCI's identity and the safeguarding of the results achieved. This was the double register adopted publicly on 24 July 1978 at the Central Committee. While asserting the line of austerity and the position of firmness in the "Moro affair," he stated explicitly that it was necessary to correct the impression that there had been a weak defense of the Communist identity when it was faced by the other national political forces. He also, after a period of silence, touched on the theme of internationalism. His main point consisted of the "double refusal" to put forward "the models until now realized in the East, as they did not provide "guarantees of freedom," and those of the social democrats, because the capitalist system no longer had "a perspective ensuring an indefinite development of productive forces and of democracy." It was according to such evidence that Western communist identity really had to be forged. Berlinguer defined it as the project of a "European socialist renaissance," the aim of which was not only to restore health and innovation to Italian society, but to have a global significance.[53] At the moment of greatest difficulty, he was relaunching the ambition of his own political vision, which pictured Italian communism as a vanguard force in Europe.

Berlinguer's speech followed the lines of a note sent to him a few days earlier by Antonio Tatò, who was fiercely opposed to Bettino Craxi, the main adversary of the "historic compromise" and of Eurocommunism. The subtext of the note was a vision not equidistant between Soviet socialism and social democracy. The former remained "superior, however" to the latter, and to deny this would have meant breaking ranks and admitting an original "error."[54] Tatò's words took to the extreme a logic shared by a political and intellectual circle broader than that of the PCI's leading group. It expressed the idea that the Soviet types of society had as yet unexpressed "potentiales" that could be realized if they were reformed and freed from the leaden hood of the authoritarian regimes. The position of the Italian Communists on Eastern dissent, which demanded freedom of expression but also tended to discriminate between socialist and nonsocialist dissidents, depended on this vision.[55] The judgment of social democracy as a failed exercise was not new, and neither was the idea that the Italian Communists would have benefited from the end of the thirty-year period of the welfare state. Berlinguer seemed, however, to be shifting his sights to the priority of asserting an identity stemming from the Leninist tradition, which he brought to the fore in his public pronouncements in summer 1978.[56]

The Westpolitik of the Italian Communists thus reached its limit. Napolitano's visit to the United States in May 1978 could be seen only from the standpoint of making a long-term investment, since it had taken on the nature of a tour in intellectual and liberal circles without any contact with significant personalities at the political and institutional level.[57] Berlinguer's meeting with Brandt in July 1978 was limited in the reciprocal contributions that could be made from different positions to safeguard European détente.[58] In the second half of the year, Berlinguer met the PCI's main interlocutors of the previous few years, with a view to knowing their respective opinions on the comatose state of détente, but his attitude was more disenchanted and less purposeful than before. He saw Marchais, Brezhnev, and Tito, in that order. As had happened previously, his meeting with Marchais was inconclusive and this meeting with Brezhnev was bitter, while he and Tito found themselves on the same wavelength.

Berlinguer was in conflict with Suslov, Ponomarev, and Brezhnev in a way that was without precedent in the history of postwar relations between the Italian Communists and Moscow. The divergence between the two sides had by now reached tones that, had they become public, would have been impossible to express diplomatically. Berlinguer established a direct link between the "Prague Spring" and the subject of human rights, dissent, and pluralism, receiving in reply the accusation of defending "spies" and supporting Carter's campaign. He transformed his previous exhortations into a reproof, maintaining that while the crisis of capitalism was getting worse and the "need for socialism" was increasing, there lacked "a great force of attraction of the socialist ideal," clearly letting it be known that this was above all a consequence of the Soviet Union's image and conduct. The Soviets warned him again that theirs was the only "real socialism" while Eurocommunism would be only an abstract ideal, and that what made it worse was that it was dividing the communist movement. Brezhnev made his accusation of a "new Munich" represented by the appeasement between the United States and China, and criticized the Italian policy of "national solidarity," which in his view had bound Italy too closely to NATO at such a serious time. Berlinguer's consultations led to a pessimism he shared with Tito, although both agreed that that it was in the interest of the Soviets to preserve détente.[59] On his return to Rome, Berlinguer appeared to Barca to be particularly discouraged.[60] The Italian leaders felt the risk of isolation, which in their eyes increased the value of a peaceful mass political mobilization, given the international tension represented by the problem of ballistic missiles in Europe.

Berlinguer decided to bring "national solidarity" to a close at the end of 1978. The Communists voted in Parliament against Italy joining the European Monetary System, which they considered rigid and irreconcilable with social policy perspectives. This choice was above all their way of getting out of the constraints of the majority and did not diminish their Europeanist vocation, which was instead consolidated in view of the first European elections by universal suffrage. In line with his own views, Amendola advocated an acceleration toward European integration and the creation of a "strong plurinational force."[61] However, the crisis in détente cast a shadow over the possibility of distinguishing between Europeanism and Atlanticism, the essential political space that had allowed the Italian Communists to end their understanding on foreign policy with the government forces a year earlier. That understanding now proved the point of arrival of a long national convergence, rather than the programmatic charter for a new policy in Italy. On the national scene, Berlinguer continued to assert the line of austerity and firmness against terrorism, reproposing the question of the Communists' role in government as the keystone for exercising a political leadership role; otherwise Italy would have plunged toward decadence and nongovernability. But the profile of institutional responsibility had largely overshadowed the expectations of reform that had been the basis of consensus for the PCI. The Communists had not presented a clear plan to reform the "blocked democracy," but only the prospect of being associated with the government in order to face the national emergency by involving the world of labor; at the same time, they fueled ambitions for transformation that were hardly realistic. The end of the emergency and the crisis of détente made the "communist question" in Italy less actual.

Berlinguer concentrated most of all on the defense of identity and political culture. After the beginning of the government crisis in January 1979, he made explicit his previously outlined vision of the "third way" between social democracy and Soviet socialism. In his speech at the PCI's Fifteenth Congress on 30 March, he inserted this notion into a historicist vision that assigned to the Western European workers' movement the task of opening a new era after those of the Second International and the October Revolution. He was therefore using a historical grammar distinctive of the Italian communist tradition, and a code for asserting, but also setting aside in ideals, the connection with Soviet communism. As already noted, this posing of the question left the experience of social-democratic welfare state policies completely in the shadows.[62] Thus, Berlinguer seemed to aim toward renewing the Italian Communists' identity card but also reasserting their roots at the moment of their opening to other progressive subjects and audiences. The attempt to bring about the "historic compromise" was now behind, but the prospect of a revolutionary Western movement was not. This vision allowed Berlinguer to make manifest a thought he had been incubating for years. He declared that it "did not correspond to the times" to speak "in a strict sense of an international communist movement."[63] Expressed otherwise, he was enunciating a principle of the self-sufficiency of the PCI, which sought to turn its political isolation into a point of force—that is, in the condition of the free affirmation of a universalist vision. In this way, Berlinguer seemed to be looking beyond the elections of June 1979, which were in many ways taken for granted, and sharpening his weapons for a new phase of a "war of position." In effect, the elections marked a defeat for the Communists, and rewarded the Christian Democrats' strategy of wearing down the adversary. The mass force of the PCI remained more or less integral, but the perspectives and motivations for keeping it together needed revision. Berlinguer held high the peculiarity of Italian communism and its nonreducibility to social democracy: "Social democracy is one thing, we are another, and so we must remain."[64]

THE MEANING OF THE GLOBAL CRISIS

Italy faithfully reflected the "return of geopolitics" that emerged in the West at the end of the decade.[65] The Cold War was beginning to implode as a global order, but it continued to define elements of sovereignty and political space in Europe. Even within the growing multilateral character of Western governance, Italian national politics provided ample evidence of this persistence. The lasting importance of the country in Cold War strategies, underlined by the Euromissiles, in appearance counterbalanced the loss of its international profile and its exposure to the new gospel of deregulation, monetary discipline, and competition, which assigned new meanings to Western interdependencies.[66] The Italian Communists faced up to this scenario by adapting their language to the "second Cold War" without turning back on their tracks regarding international choices, and held tightly to the Europeanist connection as a safeguard against the logic of the blocs. There revolved around such connection the main coordinates of the cultural transformation of Italian communism.

The "national solidarity" pact had been based on a solemn affirmation of faithfulness to European and Atlantic commitments, but it was also motivated by the ideas and practices of international cooperation. The Communists' vision was strongly articulated around the Lomé Convention, which came into force in April 1976. They hoped that the transition from the issue of "developmental aid," going back to the previous decade, to the practices of economic and political cooperation, with the aim of intervening in the international division of labor, could create a new prospect of interaction between the European Community, the socialist countries, and the Third World. Their guidelines, expressed in particular by Renato Sandri in the European parliamentary group, followed the more radical interpretations of the convention: to go beyond regionalist aspirations and make it into a global model, with its center of gravity in the Mediterranean and ramifications in the whole of the Third World and Latin America. Sandri established a dialogue on this with the European commissioner, Claude Cheysson.[67] The priorities of national politics relegated similar questions to those of a second order, but it was in this context that for the first time there came to be a clear change of idiom with implications for political culture. In April 1978 Sandri defended the Lomé Convention, judging it to be "qualitatively the most eminent realization of the EEC [. . .], the most advanced on the terrain of reforms." It appeared to him, if anything, unsatisfactory that apart from generic statements it was silent on the "question of the rights of man." He was of the opinion that one should not yield on the tendency of many African countries to defend "their own infamous regimes" using the argument of Western interference. The question of human rights was not new, but it took on a different weight because it did not spare the pro-Soviet African regimes and linked up with an important correction of the stance adopted in international politics. Sandri thought, in fact, that invoking the principles of the United Nations would be an antidote to the interfering influence "of the capitalist superpower or the socialist superpower."[68] He indicated the need for a European Community policy toward southern Africa, which was at risk of being merely a theater of conflict between the superpowers. He was thereby putting on the same level the conduct of both the United States and the Soviet Union in Africa, without absolving the latter by using internationalist arguments, and was also employing human rights language in opposition to power politics.[69] The osmosis between the condemnation of power politics and the adoption of an ethical more than a political perspective would then become accentuated in the overall discourse of the Italian Communists.

To their way of thinking, the new politics of the European Community toward the Third World offered a concrete terrain for the attempts to update the Communist agenda. But on this terrain, too, they ran up against difficulty and disillusion. In the socialist world, the tensions between the Cubans and the Yugoslavs regarding the vocation of nonalignment and the question of equidistance between the two blocs were combined with Soviet indifference on the subject of the "new international economic order," which seemed to become accentuated as Moscow became more entwined in the African Cold War. The absence of a communist discourse on the question was more problematic insofar as the Socialist International, under the leadership of Brandt and Leopold Senghor, was launching an initiative in Africa that proposed overcoming traditional Eurocentrism. In the view of the Yugoslavs, this initiative promised to enter into serious competition even with the nonaligned countries, as well as with the pro-Soviet forces.[70] In essence, at the end of the decade, what had historically been a strategic card of the European communists against the social democrats—the view toward and meeting with the world outside Europe—risked being weakened.

The Italian Communists did not expect much from the Cuban and Soviet intervention in Africa. They had urged greater Soviet dynamism in the Global South, without taking account of Moscow's ever more obvious slippage from the alliance with anti-imperialist nationalism toward movements and regimes characterized by declared ideological faith.[71] Soviet support for the Marxist-Leninist regime of Mengistu Hailé Mariam in Ethiopia, in its war against Somalia that had broken out in the summer of 1977, created serious dilemmas. For a number of years the Italian Communists had seen the regime of Mohammad Siad Barre in Somalia as the realization of an "African road" to socialism, and they were also cultivating relations with the liberation movement in Eritrea, which had gone on a collision course with the revolutionary power in Addis Ababa. They kept a safe distance from the repressive regime of Mengistu and were sceptical of the idea, cultivated by Castro, that the revolution in Ethiopia would inflict a mortal blow on Western influence in the continent of Africa. The PCI put itself forward as mediator in the conflict, playing on the fact that its role was recognized by the local actors, as was shown by Pajetta's meetings in 1977 and 1978 with Mengistu, Barre, and the representatives of Eritrea. An attempt was made to coordinate the party's attempts with the Italian foreign minister, Arnaldo Forlani, in order to safeguard Italian interests in Ethiopia.[72] The PCI proposed to Moscow the opening in Rome of negotiations between Ethiopia and Somalia.[73] When this proposal failed, Pajetta engaged in a polemic with the Cubans, relaying the opinion of the Italian leading group that their interventionism in Africa was damaging for nonalignment.[74] Berlinguer later met with Barre, and then informed Moscow on the substance of that meeting during his visit there in October 1978, insisting on the socialist orientation of the Somalis and on the importance of "winning them back"; but he clashed with the Soviets on their alignment behind Mengistu. Brezhnev rejected Berlinguer's objections regarding the negative effect on détente of Soviet policy in Africa.[75] In this way, the result of the PCI's diplomatic activity in the context of the Horn of Africa was prevalently to deepen the fracture in international communism produced by Eurocommunism. It was these events that gave rise to serious questions about the politics of Soviet power in the South of the world. Such questioning now entered into the arsenal of reform communism.

The political crisis in Italy combined with a chain of changes that radically altered the international context as perceived by the Communists, but not only by them, around the middle of the decade. The conjuncture that had marked the high point of détente in Europe, the triumph of the communists in Indochina, and Western "malaise" evaporated like morning dew. The most visible change was the eclipse of bipolar détente, which had begun around the question of human rights and Soviet expansionism in Africa. At the end of 1978, Deng Xiaoping's announced visit to the United States brought substance to the Soviet nightmare of an alliance that would modify the Cold War chessboard to the Soviet Union's disadvantage. Immediately following this, and after various border conflicts,

Vietnam invaded Cambodia, provoking a military reaction from China. In parallel with this, the Islamic Revolution in Iran opened a scenario alien to the categories and understandings of Third World progressivism, even if those went on being used. As if this were not enough, the Iranian Revolution generated a second crude oil shock wave, with consequences for inflation and recession that caused restrictive monetary policies in the West. In Europe, NATO opened a harsh dispute that had been in the air for some time regarding Soviet ballistic missiles, putting an end to the times of bipolar understandings. In March 1979, Tatò wrote to Berlinguer that in the "passing of an era" then underway, détente was no longer a sufficient condition, above all because the Soviets considered it a "static guarantee," a "dual hegemony" in world affairs. According to Tatò, the Soviet Union had reacted with realism to the American "unipolar" line, first followed in a "conservative Metternichian" form by Kissinger and then in an "aggressive and adventurist" one by Brzezinski. The Soviet reaction had been, in his opinion, understandable but inadequate. The note went on to consider the war hot spots at the world level, most of all as the consequence of a deficit of government on the part of the two superpowers, but dividing the responsibilities asymmetrically, and indicating catastrophic outcomes if Western Europe were not to occupy a different role.[76]

In his speech at his party's Fifteenth Congress. Berlinguer used a hierarchy of meaning centered on the crisis of capitalism and on the dark side of "consumer civilization," while at the same time developing the question of the "global crisis." He saw the ambiguity of interdependences in the world, a source of mass anxiety no less than one of economic and scientific progress, and a theater of war which underlined a more general "crisis of institutional setups." His tone became pained when he spoke of the war between communist countries in Indochina. He even made an appeal to Beijing and Hanoi, paraphrasing Gramsci and presenting the Italian Communists as the "expression of a people that had drawn profound international inspiration from its own history." He relaunched the idea of a "new internationalism," able to face up to the problems of cooperation and development, and therefore not limited to the communist movement. The Europeanist choice, he made clear, was an essential part of this perspective, since European integration was a factor in the project of a new world order, as well as a "condition for the real independence of the countries that make up part of the Community."[77]

At this point, Europeanism quite noticeably formed the central element in the international vision of the Italian Communists. The European vote of June 1979 was its symbolic moment, with the election of Berlinguer together with Altiero Spinelli, the key figure of Europeanism, who was put forward as an independent candidate in the Communist list. For Berlinguer, Europe did not represent a "choice of civilization," but the years of "national solidarity" had contributed to the adoption of a solid Europeanist paradigm. The convergence on European integration, albeit with very different sensitivities, represented the point of firmest juncture of the national community. At the same time, the fact of having undergone the Atlanticist "external constraint" amounted to a lesson that drove the Communists to envisage the future European Community as a safety net and a guarantee of sovereignty. The main point was that, faced with the decline of communist internationalism, Europe should become a horizon of meaning for the universalist ideas of the Italian Communists.

However the completion of the passage from the realistic recognition of the European Community for the national interest to the identification of integration as the main focus of a political project presented various problems. The Euromissile crisis quashed the distinction between Europeanism and Atlanticism, which for the Communists still remained a strategic one. The judgment regarding the greater or lesser responsibility of the Soviet Union for the end of détente was an element of division with the other forces of the left in Europe. For the Italian Communists, the Soviet Union was no longer the center of gravity of socialism in the world, but its role as a counterweight to imperialism remained essential. In the leading group, a tendency showed itself to defend détente without many distinctions being made between its interpretation as change and as the status quo. After all, dynamic détente was exhausted or negated precisely in the outcome of "national solidarity."

Berlinguer advocated avoiding a "choice of camp" if the intention was to speak "to the Italians and to the other Western European forces."[78] Among other things, he announced at the Congress the adoption of a stance analogous to that of the Brandt Report on the North-South axis of the world.

But for him it was difficult to see the socialist world as part of the "global crisis." He met the Soviet leaders in August and September 1979 with the intention of sounding out their assessment of international politics. They were obviously pleased by the PCI having gone into opposition, and by the eclipse of the Eurocommunist alliance. Brezhnev and Suslov confided that the mobilization for peace and the diplomatic work of the Italian Communists could lead to a rapprochement with them.[79] The PCI leading group was divided on negotiations over the Euromissiles, on whether to come together with the SPD or, in effect, line up with Moscow. Bufalini and Napolitano were the firmest in opposition to the latter option, put forward above all by Pecchioli and Pajetta, which would have also signified liquidating the common declaration with other political forces of the Republic dating back to 1977. Berlinguer declared to the Directorate that the PCI could not be the "spokesperson" for Soviet foreign policy, and criticized Moscow's position as lacking credibility and even of being "suspect" in various parts of the world.[80] His choice halted a slide that would have risked canceling an essential part of the peculiar nature of Italian communism, but it could not avoid domestic and international isolation. Italy approved the NATO decision regarding the installation of Western missiles, albeit leaving a margin for future manuever. The PCI's vote against this decision distinguished it from the choices of the SPD despite diplomatic contacts between the two parties. The French and Polish communists launched an anti-American mobilization orchestrated by Moscow without even consulting the Italians.

For the Italian Communists the Soviet invasion in Afghanistan at the end of December 1979 had a much stronger impact than did the Euromissiles. The Italians had vainly hoped that the Politburo would avoid such a fatal decision to defend the "Marxist-Leninist" government in Kabul, with its factions torn by internecine feuds under the fire of guerillas inspired by Iran. Their harsh condemnation was however immediate and not reconcilable with the reactions of other European communists, including the French, who closed ranks around Moscow in a parody of the internationalism of other eras. Afghanistan thus put a tombstone over the Eurocommunist alliance. In reality, the experience had by and large come to an end, its time period coinciding with "national solidarity" in Italy. Soviet disciplining reaction had played a role in successfully calling the

French—though not the Italians—to order, but numerous motives of dissent had been present from the start and had accumulated rather than being dissipated. The problem had never been confined to national diversities. The Eurocommunists had been divided on central points, such as the role of Europe as a subject in the crisis of bipolarism and the way of dealing with the North-South axis of the world, which only the Italians had connected together, criticizing the power politics employed by Moscow. Until very recently the literature has often assumed Eurocommunism to have been a unitary and coherent phenomenon, and has thus missed focusing on its basic disunion.[81] The point is that not all Eurocommunists were reform communists. It was only the Italian leading group that cultivated the prospect of liquidating the old internationalism and transforming political culture so as to acquire new languages and paradigms in relation to the forces of the change that had emerged globally outside the binary schemes of the Cold War.

The leading group of the PCI rejected the logic of the blocs and explicitly repudiated the principle of loyalty to the Soviet Union in matters of world politics. Bufalini confided to Calamandrei that in his view the invasion of Afghanistan was the "inevitable end of the line along a mistaken track."[82] The opposition of Amendola, who like the Soviets regarded a world war as imminent and justified the choices made in this light, had no important influence. Berlinguer turned down the "choice of camp," which would have been the sequel, as a political and cultural regression.[83] He then publicly condemned the invasion in a speech in the European Parliament, a step that was also symbolic in its separation of the destiny of Italian communism from the orthodoxy of the other communist parties.[84] The global vision of the Italian Communists had been constructed over time through the real and imagined combinations between the socialist world, the Western workers' movement, and the postcolonial world, according to modalities and variable contingencies. A consequence of the invasion of Afghanistan was the collapse of the architecture of that project, which for some time had been in decay and uncertain in its underpinning. The myth of the "peaceful power" and its asserted mission in the Third World was undergoing a fatal blow, and the Soviet Union now found itself on the front lines in the global Cold War. In a meeting with Pietro Ingrao, the top-ranking official of the International Department of the CPSU, Vadim Zagladin, presented Moscow's conduct as an aid to autonomous revolutions otherwise destined to failure, which had consistently gone on from the era of Cuba—for example, in Yemen or in Ethiopia—right up in fact to Afghanistan. Zagladin foresaw that this strategy would be accentuated in the future, a thought not shared by other Soviet international experts such as Chernyaev or Karen Brutents, but which reflected the opinion prevalent in the Politburo.[85] The Soviets identified the Cold War with the development of anti-imperialist revolutions, or such revolutions as were assumed to be anti-imperialist. For the Italian Communists, on the other hand, a similar way of thinking established a line of division between the socialist states and the nonaligned countries, and could therefore only cause damage. Socialism in the postcolonial world appeared as a constellation of authoritarian and militarized pro-Soviet regimes, while the galaxy of the Third World was exploding in multiple trajectories that the anti-imperialist imagination was no longer able to unify.

This point of divergence greatly widened the spectrum of the differences between the Italian Communists and other communists in the world. The experience of Eurocommunism was over, with a harsh downscaling of the ambition to increase the role of revolutionary forces in the capitalist West. At the end of the decade, the European political panorama even underwent a weakening of the socialist left to the advantage of conservative and neoliberal forces. A change in the spirit of the times was being heralded, unfavorable to all projects that in whatever way were bound up with socialism. The Italian Communists cultivated their "third way" and their Europeanism, awaiting better times and combining the two notions with a de-ideologized and cooperative approach to the subject of North-South world relations. They were no less oriented then before toward influencing the political elites in the Soviet Union and East Europe, even if they could not boast any authentic result in that matter. However, the ways of exercising such an influence came to be modified. The PCI's leading group decided not to participate in the communist conference convened in Paris to support the Soviet Union. This was the first time that the PCI had not taken part in a conference of the European communist parties. Berlinguer bet on the self-sufficiency and "international importance," as he defined it, of Italian communism in the face of the nexus of problems represented by the "second Cold War," Afghanistan, and the future of nonalignment.[86]

The PCI's diplomacy was turned toward the Yugoslav communists and the European social democracies. The Yugoslavs stated that they felt themselves to be in the front line together with the Italians in resisting the Soviet ideological offensive, as well as playing a counterweight role to Cuba, as had been seen in the Summit Conference of the Non-Aligned Countries in Havana in the summer of 1979.[87] In March 1980, for the first time officially, Berlinguer met with both Brandt and François Mitterrand at Strasbourg—a signpost of a significant change after a long period of informal relations subjected to the restraints of national politics and conditioned by mutual reserve. The European setting thus became the institutional key for establishing a new relationship, notwithstanding the insistence of the Italian Communists on their difference from social democracies.[88]

The newest and in certain ways striking fact in the Italian Communists' international policy was, however, their retrieval of relations with the Chinese Communist Party. After preparatory work that began at the start of 1979 thanks to the mediation of the Yugoslavs, Berlinguer, Bufalini, Pajetta, and Antonio Rubbi, who had replaced Segre in the Secretariat as head of the Foreign Department, visited Beijing in April 1980. The implications of this visit were numerous. First, in the context of the war in Afghanistan, it was an initiative considered inconceivable the Soviets, who among other things were justifying their invasion by citing the need to put an end to "counterrevolutionary" interference in that country by the United States and China. And, judged more widely, the meetings with Deng Xiaoping, Hua Guofeng, and Hu Yaobang symbolized the end of a fracture in communist history, which had lost its meaning since the communist movement was no longer an indispensable reference agency. From this point of view, the event signaled an encounter between subjects of the communist tradition that in Europe and in Asia had experienced significant metamorphoses and were now providing their own responses to the ending of the bipolar world. This symbolism relegated to a secondary position even the asymmetry between the giant represented by the Chinese party-state and a nongoverning party such as the PCI, whose international profile was recognized by the Chinese leaders. In his memoirs,

Rubbi recalls the particularly open tones used by Deng in his talks with Berlinguer.[89] The latter knew he was treading on the toes of the Chinese when he declared that "the old internationalism" was over forever, even though he upheld the legacy of Togliatti's "Yalta memorandum." The recognition of the respective differences of the Italians and the Chinese was taken for granted from the start, and did not impede the exercise of that diplomacy which in different ways constituted threads in the national heritage of both sides. Berlinguer held Moscow and Washington equally responsible for the "global crisis," and underlined the necessary role of the European Community and of the nonaligned countries in avoiding a catastrophe. The two sides shared a condemnation of the war in Afghanistan. Their obvious point of disagreement was the Chinese leaders' assessment of Soviet "hegemonism" as the main danger. They continued to maintain that war, albeit in the long term, was inevitable, thereby showing that they had not relegated the doctrine of Stalin and Mao to the attic.[90] On his return to Rome, Berlinguer presented the relation established with the Chinese communists in a well-tried ecumenical key, which had, however, the sense of constructing networks of deterrence against an incontrollable spiral in the deterioration of relations between the superpowers. He recognized that Beijing had not been completely wrong in its perception of a Soviet encirclement from Afghanistan to Vietnam.[91]

Berlinguer's vision was different from the apocalyptic reading present in the peace movement of that time. He saw clearly how the crisis of détente was hiding a more general phenomenon, the gradual implosion of the bipolar order, while the superpowers' agenda remained centered on the Cold War. The lucidity of this vision was dimmed, however, at the point of defining the place occupied by the Soviet Union in the "global crisis" and, in connection with this, of confronting the immobility of socialism of the Soviet type when faced with the transformations underway in the societies of the West. The expectations placed on the ethical potential of state socialism did not seem to take due account of the signals of crisis in Eastern Europe. But above all, the visions of modernity implicit in such expectations risked sounding obsolete and ineffectual as responses to the individualistic drives and postindustrial transformations in the Western world, which were overturning perceptions dating back to the first oil shock. The audience inclined to credit communism and its revolutionary legacy as a vector for global processes was visibly shrinking in the West, but not only there. The Italian Communists were aware of the problem, but maintained the view that it was bound up with a reversible contingency and did not present features of a deeper and longer-lasting nature.

COMMUNISM ENTERS THE "GLOBAL CRISIS"

The strikes in Gdańsk in the summer of 1980 shifted the focus of the "global crisis" in Europe. Their consequences posed serious questions about the import of the problems that had opened up in "actually existing socialism" and in the Soviet bloc, since the worker protests gave rise to an independent trade union, Solidarność (Solidarity), after a decade of periodic social rebellions against the Polish regime. Right from the first assessments, evidence of an opposition "from below" militated against the hopes of a reform "from above" along the lines of the Prague Spring. Berlinguer invited the PCI's leading group not to put the seal of Eurocommunism on Stanisław Kania, who had replaced Edward Gierek as the leader of the Polish Communist Party. Berlinguer knew that the structures of power were at risk of disintegration, and feared a bloodletting analogous to the situation in Hungary in 1956.[92] The PCI worked for a compromise that would foresee the recognition of the free trade union, rejecting the term "counterrevolution," which had immediately been adopted by Moscow and the other European communists. This diplomatic initiative was not unimportant, above all because it took place in correspondence with the Catholic Church. It was not the first time that a parallelism and a contact had been established between the Italian Communists and the Vatican, since such contacts had been operative for some time in various scenarios in the Third World. The conditions for developing relations along the lines of Ostpolitik had seemed compromised by the initiative of John Paul II, who had relaunched the political role of the Vatican with an anticommunist bent by making a triumphal journey through Poland in 1979. This did not, however, prevent interaction between the two diplomacies. Rather, the PCI's links with the Polish establishment and the Vatican's links with the Solidarność movement represented an international role of the first rank. The diplomatic mediation of the PCI and the Vatican, thanks most of all to Bufalini and Pajetta and to Cardinal Casaroli, was perhaps the most important buffer for mitigating the impact of the Polish crisis in the heart of Europe. The Italian Communists were obstinate in refusing the nationalistic tendencies of Catholicism in Poland, but were able to share aspects of the universalist inspiration of John Paul II and spoke not dissimilar languages of peace, harshly opposed by Moscow.[93] In a certain sense, this dynamic compensated for the PCI's trajectory diverging from the Atlanticist foreign policy of the new center-left, created by the Euromissile question. The Polish crisis represented a chance for the PCI's function of bridging the two Europes to be recognized.

The Italian Communists played a similar role in stubbornly opposing the repetition of an armed intervention by Moscow along the lines of 1956 and 1968. For a long time, they hoped to open a breach among those Soviet and Eastern European exponents more disposed to possible compromises and to a recognition of the reality of the Polish popular movement. This was the case with Chernyaev, who had become deputy head of the International Department of the CPSU. He maintained that it was necessary to avoid "internationalizing" the Polish question, and to recognize the "mass discontent" that had generated the crisis. However, his views did not reflect the orientation within the Politburo.[94] The pro-reform forces within the Polish establishment provided a main reference point for the Italian Communists and contributed to their reading of the crisis, but their weakness weighed in the balance.[95] In a harsh verbal exchange at the end of December, Zagladin confirmed to Berlinguer that the space for avoiding any type of repressive Soviet action, externally or internally, was almost nonexistent. The Moscow spokesman recalled that the interests of the Soviet state were at risk, implying that the PCI had not taken this sufficiently into consideration.[96] The Polish crisis thus subjected the hopes of the reform communists to a hard test. The absence of a meeting between the Italian Communist leaders and Lech Wałęsa during his visit to Italy in January 1981 provided an insight into the difficulty of reconciling the PCI's relations with the Polish Communist establishment with an opening toward an actor representing an opposition and a counter-power. It was the leaders of the Italian General Confederation of Labor (CGIL) who acknowledged the independent Polish trade union as a protagonist of the necessary changes in the East European countries, and who urged a recognition that the crisis of the socialist systems was political and not merely economic.[97]

The Polish crisis coincided with the most unfavorable political conjuncture in Italy and the West that the PCI had had to face in years. The relaunch of the Cold War and of Atlanticism announced by the Reagan administration, together with its neoliberal economic policies, interacted with a conflictual qualitative leap in Italian domestic policy, generated by the explicit exclusion of the PCI from the sphere of government, by the Euromissile question, and by the duel with Craxi and his Mitterrand-type strategy for establishing socialist hegemony on the left. Each of these factors was clearly bound to be of long duration. For this reason, Mitterrand's victory in the French presidential elections of 1981 could provide no relief, but instead exposed the socialist alignment with the choices being made by NATO and the minority position of the communists in the left coalition. The link between international and national politics had undergone a comprehensive positive-to-negative change in a relatively brief period of time. The scenario that had combined international détente, Europeanism, and space for progressive projects was inverted into one dominated by the Cold War, Atlanticist orthodoxy, and new neoliberal or neoconservative projects, while at the same time the bipolar division of the national political system remained intact.

Berlinguer attempted to initiate a barrage against Craxi, whom he saw as the key figure in the "second Cold War" in Italy. To his eyes, the aggravating factor was the illusion that social democracies could play an important role in Europe, as had happened in the classic Cold War era, while the political climate threatened a return to "reactionary" states of affairs, to the point of endangering democracy itself. Thus there reemerged the recurrent apprehension of the risk to democracy in Italy, which had lain behind the proposal of a "historic compromise" in a completely different national and international context. Now it could appear as a syndrome that was more difficult to justify. Some of the PCI leaders saw in Berlinguer's choice a negative entrenchment without a clear political way out. In private, as early as the beginning of 1981, Nilde Iotti and Napolitano drew strong attention to the risk of the PCI becoming isolated.[98] Berlinguer made his position even more radical by shifting the focus of his discourse from the political conflict to a moral criticism of the parties in power. His celebrated denunciation that there was a "moral question" in Italy, made in the course of an interview in July 1981 given to Eugenio Scalfari, founding editor of the newspaper *La Repubblica*, touched a serious, real, and deep-rooted problem in the life of the nation. But it also came across as an incentive to political polarization. Berlinguer was using a new vocabulary to highlight a permanent factor—namely, the reciprocal siege between the two political and social blocs of the Republic. The "moral question" regarded the government parties, while the Communists could claim their "diversity," which was no longer related to class but had an "ethical" connotation. Napolitano criticized Berlinguer publicly for having derailed Togliatti's teaching regarding "political engagement." A ferocious political polemic ensued that brought into the open splits in the leading group that were destined never to be healed.[99]

The positioning of the "moral question" as a "national question" ran the risk that the subject of the nation might be considered separate from international connections. The project of a "third way" implied a unique identity for Italian communism, not to be reduced to one like that of the social democracies. It was an argument that the body of the party understood, deep down, better than detachment from the communist movement. The polemic against the "degeneration" of the party system in Italy was thus bound up with a clear demarcation line drawn against the European social-democratic forces, traced out precisely at the moment of the greatest possible closeness to the "left" components of German social democracy. Tatò wrote for Berlinguer a note emphasizing the PCI's distinctive "innovative synthesis" as the "main force for change and innovation in Italy and the West."[100] The risk of such a self-referential vision was noteworthy. It could encourage the idea of an Italian "exceptionalism," strengthened by the presence of a force that put itself forward as a vanguard as compared with both the communist and the social-democratic worlds, as well as one entering into dialogue with the Catholic world. Such exceptionalist thinking was a risk that Togliatti had stigmatized, defending the Soviet Union as a necessary anchor for avoiding it, and one that

Berlinguer had sought to avoid in the past through the combination of the "historic compromise" and Eurocommunism. To draw a boundary against the hegemonic forces of the Western left also meant consenting to stay on the margins of the choices and alliances within the European Community, despite the convinced Europeanism of the PCI.

Berlinguer developed analyses and visions of the "global crisis" without turning back on his tracks. For the first time, he recognized that a "crisis" existed in Soviet socialism, a notion that still remained vague and which alluded to the loss of universality and influence of the states and societies of the Soviet type, and to the danger of their ungovernability.[101] A similar vision implied even greater emphasis on the reform of Soviet socialism, which no longer constituted a demand for socialist democracy but was an urgent measure to ward off any tendency to move backward. The idea of the "reformability" of Soviet-type systems also represented a way of defending the identity of communist reformers while challenging the notion of totalitarianism that had returned to the limelight in the neoliberal discourse in the West. The question of reform in the Soviet Union and Eastern Europe was by now a fixed item on the agenda of the cultural "second Cold War," and for the Italian Communists it implied something like an act of faith rather than a realistic option based on an analysis developed over time. Berlinguer was aware, however, that his defense of identity made sense if it were expressed as the ability to change oneself.

The Charter for Peace and Development, presented in October 1981 at the PCI Central Committee after two years of discussion, which took into account the Brandt Commission Report to the UN the previous year, had precisely this function.[102] Romano Ledda linked it to the analysis that constituted the main ground of consensus in the PCI's leading group, focused on the "decline in the centrality of the great powers"; on the emergence of new state, national, and social subjects; on the persistence of inequalities in exchange relations and in the international division of labor; and on the "gap between the 'real world' and the 'legal world'" in global affairs. The criticism of Soviet policy was directed at the post-Helsinki situation in which Moscow had shown no inclination toward the construction of a "new world setup." Ledda developed the logic of this thesis to the point of presenting the coming to power of the Reagan administration as a reaction to the power politics of the Soviet Union. For the first time, in a public meeting destined to have its effect in the media, a member of the leading group of the PCI maintained the equivalence, to all intents and purposes, of the responsibility of the Soviets and the Americans. The stress Ledda placed on the "culture of peace" was directed at the European left and implied a renewed anti-Americanism, but this time without being aligned to a pro-Soviet stance.[103] The step forward taken by Ledda was not to the liking of all. Bufalini, Pajetta, and Cervetti expressed their reservations precisely on the point of the judgment passed on the equal responsibility of the Soviets and the Americans. Cossutta defended an entirely pro-Soviet point of view, showing himself to be, in effect, Moscow's reference point. Berlinguer, however, held fast to the idea that the choices made by Moscow after Helsinki in terms of power politics had been decisive at the domestic and international levels. In the Directorate he asked, in such a way as to leave no misunderstanding: "Was the policy of the USSR one of the causes of Reagan's victory, together with the events in Iran and the criticism of the domestic economic situation? I think this really was the case...."[104]

General Jaruzelski's coup d'état in Poland on 13 December 1981 did not take the Italian Communists by surprise, but their responses were also not a foregone conclusion. Berlinguer made a personal decision to face the PCI's leading group with a fait accompli, by giving a television interview in which he pronounced words destined to become famous: the "propulsive capacity" of the societies of East Europe, he said, had arrived at a point where it was "becoming exhausted."[105] These words caused a sensation in the party and in public opinion, even if they were not much more than a statement of the fairly obvious. For some time, "actually existing socialism" had been transmitting the message of an experience with no sense of a political project, far distant from the radical social transformations in the history of communism. The socialist states were clothed in what was merely a conservative ideological orthodoxy which presided over a social pact based on authoritarian stability, welfare, and timid forms of consumerism.[106] The social model inherited from Sovietization had never been attractive in Europe, and had made few recruits even outside Europe, where the principle and practice of the party-state had found its followers. A great part of the "post–long '68" generations was aware of this. To a certain extent, an important number of PCI cadres and even militants were no exception. The birth of Solidarność had swept aside the remaining mythologies of an identification between the working class and the socialist states. But more than proving the end of an impulse imagined in the past, the crisis in Poland gave rise, if anything, to questions regarding the strength of the authoritarian social pact, and therefore the legitimation of the regimes. Berlinguer's public stance was aimed above all at consolidating the historicist view of the "third way," which was intended to put the Soviet experience to the test without reneging on it. This schema had been known and reiterated over the previous few days in Tatò's private notes, with the usual stress laid on the exceptionality of the Italian Communist experience and its hegemonic ambition.[107] And yet the fact that Berlinguer preferred to act without consulting even with Tatò says much about the existential and political resistance rooted at the most varied levels among the Italian Communists. They were largely in the dark about the most serious tensions that had arisen in the previous years with Moscow, and they often remained tied to uncritical narratives of the Soviet experience even after 1968. Although Berlinguer's words expressed meanings not entirely new in his political discourse, they had the effect of removing a veil, and were amplified by use of the medium of television.

The coup d'état in Poland brought to the fore the contradictions of Italian communism regarding the Soviet crisis and its connections with the "global crisis." More than being divided along precise lines, the PCI's leading group found itself fragmented into accents and nuances that were very different from one another, but which revolved around the central question of whether they were faced with a rupture in the relations between the PCI and the socialist world. Some in the group, like Napolitano and Emanuele Macaluso, dated back to the repression of the "Prague Spring" the loss of credibility of the communists in power, and argued that the narrative of the peaceful role of the Soviet Union could no longer be sustained. Others, such as Bufalini and Pajetta, insisted on Moscow's function as a brake for imperialism. On this question Berlinguer did not come down clearly on one side or the other. He showed a disenchanted attitude toward the Soviet Union, in which he implicitly suggested that there should not be too many illusions about the near future, while underlining the possibilities of reform. In his view, the critical front opened up on Poland could have the effect of exalting the Italian Communists' sui generis role ("without yielding to impulse and without illusions") while providing "a point of contact" between the different versions of socialism in the world. He was thereby relaunching the universalist aspect of his own vision, circumventing the versions of political realism represented by Napolitano and Bufalini, and relegating Cossutta's pro-Soviet positions to the sidelines.[108] At this most critical moment of the communist world, even as compared with the previous one of 1968, Berlinguer's leadership was founded on the internationalist mission of the Italian Communists, which could not be reduced to old and new political families, and was bound to a "peaceful" idea of the national tradition.

The PCI's public statement of 30 December 1981 avoided the most critical concerns, such as the power politics of the Soviet Union and the need for reform, limiting itself instead to defining as "outdated" the conception of a communist movement separate from the forces of progress.[109] This notwithstanding, Moscow's reaction brought the two sides to the edge of a breakdown, and for the first time led to a public exchange of accusations. In a turbulent Central Committee meeting, Berlinguer publicly criticized the Soviets for not having recognized the "depth and nature of the Polish crisis," and held up the distinctiveness of the PCI as a "communist force rooted in the West."[110] No one, however, wanted to reach a point of no return. Berlinguer declared in the Party Directorate that the defense of the PCI could be construed as a "national and patriotic fact," but excluded the possibility of conceiving a pole opposed to Moscow, which would have compromised the strategy of influence that had long been pursued. His idea was that the "break" could have its consequences above all in domestic politics—in other words, the end of anticommunist discrimination, as the other parties would no longer have an "alibi" for excluding the Communists from government. He knew that a public conflict with the Soviets would strengthen his popularity in the party, and that any attempt at a breakaway would have to come to terms with this. He firmly warned the leading group that the trial of strength with Moscow was not destined to end, and that the reasons for the heterodox line pursued by the Italian Communists had to be reasserted in order to maintain the unity of their setup.[111]

The tone used by the Soviets, especially by Suslov, was akin to that of an excommunication. However, Brezhnev and Yuri Andropov—the strongman of the regime and head of the KGB—were of the opinion that to break relations with the only mass communist party of the West would be a self-inflicted wound.[112] Behind the scenes, Chernyaev noted in his diary that the Italian Communists saw their internationalist task as that of speaking of the "crisis" in the East in order to forestall "something worse." The scenario of "disorder" in the Soviet bloc could have taken on such proportions as to make the crisis in Poland seem "like a kindergarten." The voice of the Italian Communists had shown that "the emperor has no clothes" and that "the international communist movement no longer exists."[113] These notes show how the strategy of influence of the Italian Communists was by no means deprived of sense. Their critical consciousness could give rise to reasons for reflection and common agreement between the enlightened spokespersons of the communist establishments. However, the PCI's effective influence was uncertain and difficult to estimate. The conjuncture of the Polish crisis added an element of distance even from the more moderate components of Central and Eastern Europe, such as the Hungarians. They converged on the Soviet and Polish narrative that Jaruzelski had avoided a civil war that could have involved Europe, while the Italian Communists saw the installation of a military dictatorship as causing a damage to socialism in the world that would be difficult to repair. For a number of years, the Italian Communists had failed to fully realize that the end of right-wing dictatorships in Southern Europe around the middle of the previous decade had exposed the regimes of Central and Eastern Europe to a serious democratic delegitimation as the sole remaining continental dictatorships. Now that realization was inevitable.

BERLINGUER'S LAST BATTLE

Berlinguer was by now the bête noire for the majority of the communist leaders in Europe. The Soviets oscillated between threats of severing relations and the usefulness of maintaining them in the hope of bringing the PCI back into the fold of orthodoxy. Zagladin foresaw a growing difficulty for Berlinguer's leadership which would have brought about a change at the top of the PCI, and he collected harshly critical opinions about him even from among the Western communists, Marchais in particular. But solitude in the communist world did not frighten Berlinguer, who knew he had "many enemies" even among the leaders of his own party, as he would say to Zagladin in a tense meeting at the moment of Brezhnev's funeral in November 1982.[114] This did not seem really to affect the choices made by Berlinguer, who used the real or assumed threat of a severance of relations to strengthen his own authority in the party and weaken the moderate alternative represented by Napolitano.

The mass dimension reached by the peace movement in Western Europe led Berlinguer to relaunch his visionary vein. In one of the darkest and tensest moments of the postwar era for international politics, he re-proposed the prospect of an end to the Cold War. In his view, the subject of "overcoming the blocs," which had been set aside in the previous decade in the name of realism, had become "a concrete political objective." His argument was that the blocs were now a "factor of instability," instead of one for the governance of the world.[115] In saying this, he was speaking in terms that were suitable for the new European peace movement, in many ways dissociated from the old binary logics. To be anti-American and in favor of peace no longer meant being pro-Soviet. In this sense, through participation in the mass peace movements, the Italian Communists were able to acquire renewed resources of identity and connections in Europe that were denied to the French and to other communists.[116] Making use of the credit gained through the polemic with Moscow, Berlinguer intensified his exchanges with the European socialists, at that moment in power in West Germany and France. As was predictable, the meetings with Mitterrand and with the French Socialist Party secretary, Lionel Jospin, in Paris in March 1982 registered positions that were in line on some topics, such as the relation between the North and South of the world, and much less so on others, such as the Euromissiles. This was true, however, even in the relations between the various socialist parties, especially between the Germans and the French. For the PCI it seemed important above all to become part of the dialectic that characterized the European left. The main stumbling block was the Italian vision of a "third way," equidistant between Soviet socialism and social democracy, which could not provide a meeting ground.[117] The fall of Helmut Schmidt's government in October 1982 and the defeat of the SPD at the elections of March 1983 increased the possibility of the PCI entering the ever more tense arena of the European socialists and giving rise to a left turned toward constructing Brandt's idea of a Europe more autonomous from the superpowers.[118] This perspective was the hallmark of Berlinguer's report at the PCI's Sixteenth Congress in March 1983. Berlinguer's analysis of the "global crisis" included the socialist countries and their inadequacy for overcoming the destructive logics of the East-West conflict and for supporting a reform of the unequal relations between the North and South of the world. It was precisely the notion of a "global crisis" that at the same time led him to read Reaganism in a very traditional optic. He denounced the combination of neoliberalism and militarization as demonstrating the incapacity of capitalism to resolve its own "contradictions." Berlinguer now assigned to the peace movement a moral and political primacy in regard to both anti-imperislism and the class struggle. He painted the PCI as a force of the European left involved with others in seeking a way out of the crisis of the welfare state.[119]

The Italian Communists followed inspirations that converged with those of the social democrats, but which differed from them with respect to the networks and relations that had been constructed over time with the Global South. The political initiatives undertaken by Berlinguer in the early 1980s in China, the Mediterranean, the Middle East, and Latin America constituted a unitary picture. Perhaps the contact with China was born of considerations limited to ecumenicalism and the desire to heal old fractures, but its results formed part of a broader strategy. Implicit was the idea of a reform of the traditional anti-imperialist vision, and an attempt to respond to the fragmentation of the Third World with cultural instruments that were different from those of the past. This also involved a response to the Soviet invasion of Afghanistan, by aiming at the construction of networks of relations that had in common the critique of the logic of the blocs and the subject of North-South relations. The PCI thereby added another tessera to its vocation of transnational mediator. Its more traditional interlocutors, the Yugoslavs, indeed passed a negative judgment on the role of the Socialist International in the Third World, maintaining that in Africa it no longer represented a progressive force and that its presence fueled the logics of the blocs in opposition to the "socialist camp."[120] The Italian Communists did not share such a drastic judgment, but thought they could play a role of their own in modifying those dynamics.

The Charter for Peace and Development, therefore, presented various implications. It was intended as a manifesto convergent but also in competition with the Socialist International, a development of the relations with the nonaligned countries, and a point of reference for the practices of the PCI as compared with those of the "socialist camp." In October 1981, Berlinguer used the framework of the charter in his journeys to Latin America and Algeria, and presented it at the UN Conference in Cancún. This was his first time in Latin America, but the trip meant more than solidarity with the Cuban and Sandinista revolutions. Castro, who had become the key figure in the nonaligned movement after the death of Tito in May 1980, represented a radicalization that denied the reform-oriented premises of a re-equilibrium between the North and South of the world and reflected the increasing splintering of the political subjects of the Global South. This was a strategic change that the Italian Communists saw as a mortal risk and intended to limit. The talks between Berlinguer and Castro confirmed all the limits to an authentic political understanding, and above all to the connection between the anti-imperialist struggle, democracy, and development. Berlinguer expressed his reservations regarding Cuban intervention in Africa, underlining in particular the growing political and civil degeneration of Ethiopia. He argued that the forced installation of "Marxist-Leninist" regimes in Africa and Yemen had no authentic progressive significance, but his words were to no avail. Castro showed generic interest, but also his scepticism regarding the thesis of the "new international economic order."[121]

In addition, Berlinguer's meeting with Daniel Ortega and the Sandinista leadership in Nicaragua, who at that moment were in the midst of a campaign of forced modernization and were also in conflict with the United States, had above all the result of bringing to the fore the distance between the sensitivities of their respective political cultures.[122] The equivalence made between the two superpowers in the crisis of the bipolar order and the "peace-oriented framework of the charter was a divisive thesis in the communist world, and was difficult to accept in Latin America. The Italian

Communists offered the Cubans and the Sandinistas the alternative of avoiding relations too close to Moscow and instead establishing them in Europe. But Berlinguer's trip to Latin America was a disappointment in the light of the substantial failure of the Cancún conference, which marked the definitive burial of the "new international economic order."[123] The absence of the Soviet Union was a desolating signal of immobility and a lost chance, as Berlinguer stated in his meeting with the Mexican president, José López Portillo.[124]

Algeria, on the other hand, was a different interlocutor, consonant with the visions of the Italian Communists even after the death of Houari Boumedienne. At the end of 1980, Boumedienne's successors decided to form a triangular pact of informal consultation between the Algerian FLN, the PCI, and the Yugoslav League of Communists. Their idea was that the socialist world had "set itself apart" on the questions of the North-South relationship, while Brandt's approach had not taken into consideration a "global negotiation" inclusive of the South-South dimension. This had to be the objective to pursue in the Mediterranean.[125] Berlinguer presented the charter to the Algerian leader, Chadli Bendjedid, in October 1981 and confirmed his willingness to inaugurate a new cycle of Mediterranean conferences, aimed at involving all the political forces and movements of the region without the exclusions of the past. But in actual fact, the divisions among the countries on the Mediterranean's southern shore once again hindered the full implementation of the intiative.[126]

The difficulties encountered in building a transnational front in the Mediterranean were no novelty, and constituted a recurrent reason for frustration. The sense of the end of an era was, however, on the increase. The radicalization of a good number of the protagonists on the southern shore, who were ever more unwilling to countenance political mediations on the questions of "imperialism" in the Mediterranean and the Middle East, was apparent. At the same time, the marked presence in the area of European governmental, nongovernmental, and community actors induced Remo Salati, a member of the PCI Foreign Department, to express a certain pessimism regarding the possibility of maintaining the influence of the Italian Communists, who were perceived as "social democrats not in power" and therefore less "powerful" and interesting.[127] This led back to the difficulty of an interaction and co-penetration between European reform communism and the extra-European anti-imperialist traditions that had emerged as long ago as the "Prague Spring." It was obvious, however, that the PCI was losing credibility as a bridge between different worlds, since various institutional or transnational protagonists had appeared on the scene, bringing new points of union or fracture. The expectations placed on the European Community for an extension of the Lomé Convention were, by and large, cut down to size. And what became strident was the contrast between the projects aiming at a re-equilibrium along the North-South axis, and the concrete choices made by the European Community and national governments.[128]

However, the action of the Italian Communists in the Middle East after the Israeli invasion of Lebanon in June 1982 demonstrated their considerable influence on Italy's orientation. They aimed at integrating and conditioning Italian foreign policy, with the objective of obtaining recognition of the Palestine Liberation Organization (PLO). At the same time, they proposed influencing Soviet positions and reducing support for intransigent forces in the Arab world, especially in Syria, Iraq, and Libya, whose radical anti-Zionism was hindering any negotiation for the Palestinian cause. The PCI rejected the Soviet position on the Israeli intervention in Lebanon, which Moscow denounced as imperialism, and shared the decision of the government headed by Giovanni Spadolini to take part in a multinational force that would have allowed a truce in the siege of Beirut and a retreat by the Palestinian forces.[129] Bufalini moved to invite Arafat to the Italian Parliament, while Rubbi met him in Algiers to prepare the contents of the visit. In September 1982 Arafat met President Sandro Pertini and Pope John Paul II, thereby emphasizing the political profile of the Palestinian organization. His meeting with Berlinguer was limited to a few minutes, since the visit was interrupted by news of the massacre of civilians by Lebanese Christians in the refugee camps of Sabra and Shatila. This stopped Berlinguer from urging Arafat toward recognition of Israel and negotiations on the subject of "peace for land."[130]

The event in any case was a success for the diplomacy of the Communists, who had put the reluctant head of government on the spot. Symbolically, Arafat's visit represented the destination point of a long construction of relations that had begun after the 1967 Six-Day War, which the greater part of Italian political forces now regarded as important as an aspect of the national interest. But the sensitivities of the Italian Communists had also been subject to a serious change from that time. Alfredo Reichlin invited his readers to avoid generic and ambiguous condemnations of "Zionism" and to criticize the Israeli premier, Menachem Begin, on exclusively political grounds.[131] The disputes around the Israeli-Palestine question remained open, since they registered possible dissent between the PCI's leading group and a significant number of the militants who were bound to anti-imperialist mythologies.

It was not clear whether the action undertaken by the PCI in the Mediterranean opened up further possibilities of influence. At the start of 1983, the meetings with the traditional interlocutors in the Mediterranean, in Algiers and in Belgrade, were not encouraging. In a talk with Alessandro Natta, the Algerians turned down the prospect of an incisive action by the European Community in the Mediterranean, which they considered marginal in the power games taking place in the region, even as compared with the renewed presence of China.[132] The Yugoslavs pointed out to Pajetta that the Soviet Union's position on Middle Eastern affairs had not changed.[133] Belgrade remained an essential reference point. In a note written to Berlinguer in February 1983, the party member Gerardo Chiaromonte reported what he had shared in a meeting with Tito's successors: the idea that the "crisis of the welfare state" in the West showed analogies and intertwinings with the crisis of statism of the Soviet type; and the proposal for a "new Bretton Woods" and a world negotiation on financial relations that had met with deaf ears in Moscow.[134]

In August 1983, Berlinguer made a second visit to Beijing, and in his meeting with Hu Yaobang he received appreciation for the international positions of the PCI, judged by the Chinese to be pragmatic and not far from their own opposition to the "expansionism" of the great powers. Nevertheless, mutual understanding had its limits. Hu Yaobang did not rule out normalization of Chinese relations with Moscow, but said it was improbable in the short term, thus disappointing Berlinguer's hopes for a de-escalation between the two socialist powers. The Chinese were also insensitive to the urging to include in their projects for modernization the subject of political democracy, and did not share in the PCI's condemnation of the coup d'état in Poland.[135] Berlinguer's feverish activity had led the global involvement of a peculiar political actor such as the PCI to the highest possible level. After the failure of the Eurocommunist project, the PCI had probably reached the limits of the possibility to construct networks without being in government or belonging to an international family. The prestige of Italian communism was still recognized, but the political and symbolic resources at its disposal were showing themselves to be on the wane.

Berlinguer's last year was marked by the search for a new diplomatic channel to Eastern Europe. Andropov, Brezhnev's successor, was certainly not the most suitable interlocutor for melting the ice with the PCI, even though he had secretly agreed with Cossutta on the inappropriateness of working toward a split of the PCI.[136] Berlinguer proposed exploring realistic solutions to the Euromissile problem, among other things, on the urging of Brandt and Palme. But the negotiation did not really begin, and this stall gave rise to a further reason for conflict in Italian domestic politics after the Craxi government took office in August 1983. Berlinguer strenuously opposed Craxi's decision to proceed with the installation of American missiles following the timing and methods of what NATO had resolved four years earlier. He employed the notion of interdependent security in Europe, and accused both superpowers of adopting a vision centered on military rather than political instruments, a critical argument that was current in the European social-democratic left.[137] The PCI's relationship with the European social democracies remained unresolved, however, as Napolitano commented in a note on the Congress of the French Socialist Party in October 1983, where he had observed "a lesser interest as compared with other periods in the Italian situation and in our policies."[138] The divisions among the European socialists on the subject of the Euromissiles and security—which saw the parties in government in France and the countries of Southern Europe holding pro-Atlanticist positions, and the German social democrats, then in opposition, against the immediate installation of the missiles—allowed the PCI to enter the arena of the European left forces. But that did not presuppose political alliances. The duel between Berlinguer and Craxi in domestic politics was the most visible obstacle to this sort of evolution, but not the only one. The risk of "social democratization" represented, more than ever, the worst specter before Berlinguer's leading group.

Berlinguer trusted most of all in the role of the "third" forces. His accent now fell much more on the peace movement, on the churches, and on the nonaligned countries, rather than on the European Community.[139] The Europeanism of the Italian Communists was not in doubt, but he maintained that the sensitivity toward questions of peace and development was a reason more for divergence than for convergence in the European Parliament.[140] In his view, the prospect of deeper European integration was meeting with a barrier in the inadequate consciousness of vital European Community interests; Europe should have overturned the "structural" fact of geopolitical East-West priorities by rethinking the economic nexuses and models of development in the relationship between the North and South of the world.[141] The question of the Euromissiles seemed to him only one aspect of strategies followed by the two superpowers, basically aimed toward expanding their areas of global interest and containing the political role of the postcolonial countries. Berlinguer recognized the roles of individual personalities such as Brandt, Palme, Mitterrand, and Austrian Chancellor Bruno Kreisky, but he maintained that there was a lack of a progressive strategy that could bind the subject of European integration with that of an autonomous role for Europe. Such a criticism was not limited to the PCI. These same personalities did not hesitate to put forward critical points regarding the international profile of the European Community, but consonance among the leaders did not add up to the emergence of common strategies.

In a talk with the Yugoslav leaders Ante Marković and Dobrivoje Vidić, Berlinguer complained of the lasting absence of strong ties between the "Western workers' movement" and "progressive forces" in the Third World, and proposed a new initiative between the PCI, the Algerian FLN, and the Yugoslav League of Communists. It was Marković who noted the possibility of extending this proposal to Brandt and the SPD. Berlinguer agreed, but his proposal confirmed a lack of confidence in effective collaboration with the social democracies regarding North-South relations in the world after the marked convergence of previous years.[142] It is possible that this step backward on his part was also a defensive reply to the Craxi government's competition with the Communists not only on the subject of dissent and repression in Eastern Europe, but on the topic of foreign policy and international cooperation.[143] The problem, however, was that the network of relations constructed by the Italian Communists between Italy, Europe, and the Third World was showing signs of fraying. The fact of being the sole mass communist party in the West was no longer viewed by many interlocutors as being as important as it had been in the past, except by the pro-reform factions in the Soviet Union and in Central and Eastern Europe.

The most important international card in the hands of the PCI remained the role it could undertake in its relations with Moscow and Eastern Europe, with the aim of negotiating over the missiles, even after their installation in the West. Berlinguer obstinately followed this path to the end. With this goal in mind he met with Ceauşescu, Honecker, and Greek Prime Minister Andreas Papandreou around the end of 1983 and the start of 1984. The meeting with the head of East Germany was not a banal circumstance, given that the precedents dated back to ten years earlier and to the Berlin conference of 1976. Honecker confirmed the GDR's interest in maintaining détente with the Federal Republic despite its change in government, but did not provide any material support for the mediation that Berlinguer was promoting, and referred him to the Soviets about the effective possibilities of a negotiation.[144] Berlinguer reported back to Pertini and to Craxi, while he noted in the Directorate that the analysis of the reasons for the crisis between the superpowers divided the PCI from the SPD. He commented in particular that it was "strange" that it should have been the Soviets who proposed bringing the missile level back to that of 1976, when it was Moscow who had altered the balance which had existed in that year.[145] Berlinguer could not meet Andropov, whose funeral he attended in Moscow in February 1984. There he re-proposed that the PCI act as mediator in the context of a now somewhat disenchanted vision of the Soviet world.[146] Berlinguer's public speeches before his untimely death in June 1984 centered on the truce in the deployment of missiles no less than on domestic policy, especially inflation and the compensatory "sliding scale" for salaries, which led to a head-on confrontation with the Craxi government.[147] Over his last few months, Berlinguer's tone had at times become apocalyptic regarding the possibility of thermonuclear war, with the consequence that stress was laid on the "concrete utopia" aspect of the peace movement. However, he did not become a prophet of misadventures. In one of his last interviews he singled out the peace movement as the main cultural factor of Europeanism, once more anticipating a vision that would last after his death.[148] He made a very clear division between, on the one hand, the idea of politics as the regulation of conflicts and a sphere of real possibilities, and on the other, the idea of it as a definition of identity and long-term thought. At the time of his death, the tension between these two dimensions had reached its highest point.

Berlinguer left a strong legacy, on which a good part of the PCI's leading group converged, and which marked the formation of a younger generation. In Italian communism his figure represented the rereading of the Marxist vision of the world in an ethical key. His language was a mixture of realism and universalism, hybridization and self-sufficiency, tradition and postmodernity. His coordinates were anchored on the "invention of tradition" of post-1968 humanistic socialism, as much as on the acquisition of new syntaxes and spaces—above all, Europeanism in its various realist and visionary declensions. Both sets of coordinates could be symbolically written into the original sources of antifascism, but they implied a cultural setup that had been transformed.

The connection between class and nation was transmuted into the moral judgment of the Communists on the social and civil costs of the Cold War and of the "blocked democracy." In this sense, the Cold War remained at the center of their vision. Despite its profound social and economic transformations, Italy still bore the signs of a fracture along the communism/anticommunism axis born at the end of World War II, and it remained the Western European country most conditioned by an antagonistic bipolarism that, as an architecture, overlay politics. Much more than the Christian Democrat ruling classes, the Communists had sought to modify the "external constraint" without being able to imagine a decomposition of Italy's fundamental political and social blocs. Once the experience of "national solidarity" was over, the Italian political system reorganized following the binary logics of the Cold War. The

Communists could count on the advantage stemming from the division of the Republic into two blocs, confirmed by their winning first position in the European elections held immediately after Berlinguer's death. However, unlike in the past, they thought of the Italian nation as being in a relationship of close interdependence with European integration, while their "new internationalism" implied a choice to depart from the communist movement. In this optic, the idea of Europe as a subject of world politics acquired a privileged position while the struggle against the inequality of North-South relations was intertwined with the language of human rights.

The basic aim of this transformation was to provide a reply to the decline of communism as a unitary political subject, which had emerged with the rupture between the Soviet Union and China, the "long 1968," and the global Cold War. By definition, such a response could not be national, but had to be aimed at a European and international resonance conferred upon the PCI by its uniqueness as the only mass communist force in the West. Berlinguer's PCI represented itself as a distinct entity among the progressive forces in both Europe and the extra-European world, which could not be understood as being limited either to social democracies or to the various anti-imperialist tendencies. The assertiveness of the party's identity was therefore particularly insistent. The project of contributing to a radical change in the capitalist model of development in the West, and influencing the reforms of Soviet communism, was an essential part of this identity, but it also created a zone of tensions that were difficult to reconcile. Its foundations were represented in a linear historical scheme that was not to be renounced. Such a scheme presented the communist experience begun in 1917 as a passage that had been necessary for human progress but now was no longer sufficient. The societies of the Soviet type still had a role to play on the global scene, on the condition that authentic reform would liberate their human potential and that a new anticapitalist consciousness would develop in the West, adopting the new languages of environmentalism and the "new international economic order." In this light, the experience of social democracy and the European welfare state amounted to a relatively marginal page lacking any anticapitalist drive or projection outside the Old Continent.

The political project of Berlinguer's latter phase presented a strong normative imprint that seemed to become more radical as its possibilities were less legitimized by the vectors and hegemonic relations in Europe and the world. All this revealed an aporia that had built up over time. Berlinguer's universalist vision lent itself to the charge of a hypertrophic assessment of the role of the PCI and Italy on the world scene. Moreover, the idealization of the cultural links between communists and Catholics was hardly realistic in the second Italian modernization in the 1980s. The patrimony of transnational relations constructed by the Italian Communists was capital that was ever more difficult to spend in light of the disintegration of the Third World and the inertia of the Second World. The integration of Italian communism into the European left risked the assumption of a subaltern rather than a vanguard position, precisely because of a peculiarity that could not be reduced to a culture of reformist inspiration.

The persuasion that capitalism had no future threw a veil over the decipherment of the dynamics of post-Fordist and post-Keynesian transformation that had already become evident in the early 1980s. But above all, it left in the shade the change of paradigm that had now emerged in the juxtaposition of communism and capitalism. The general perception in Europe, and increasingly in the Global South, was that Soviet socialism had lost the challenge of modernity, and that the antagonism between the West and the Soviet Union had been reduced to geopolitics and nuclear armaments. The ambition of designing alternative globalizations was a memory of the past, and its decline by and large compromised the visions of progress and emancipation that had been expressed in Marxist discourse for more than half a century.[149] This allowed neoliberalism to assert itself by constructing a canon that marked the end of the Keynesian compromise and delegitimized any statist or mixed economy model. The neoliberal season in the West thus posed problems common to all cultures of the European left, more than the Italian Communists were inclined to admit. If the defense of the welfare state was defensive and suffering terrain for social democracies faced with the wave of monetarism and financial globalization, that was even more true of the idea of going beyond the welfarist experience, which risked appearing an illusion and a form of self-reference.[150]

The cultural transformation of the Italian Communists still represented a vital resource, unique in the context of world communism, through its syncretic capacity to assume the visions, sensitivity, and late twentieth-century languages of modernity. But the influence in the West of the Italian Communists was extremely reduced after the end of Eurocommunism. The chances of their exerting an influence on the circulation of reform ideas in Eastern Europe and the Soviet Union were not yet exhausted, despite appearances to the contrary. Their ability to recognize in time the crisis of communist internationalism was a thorn in the side of their orthodox self-representation, and an attempt to fight marginalization. Europeanism represented an important nexus for the latent reform factions in the Soviet world, since it allowed a rethinking of internationalism and a chance to conceive visions of integration without violating the taboo of "social democratization." However, the problem was not represented simply by the Italian Communists' possible exercise of influence in the Soviet socialist world, though that influence was anything but negligible. Reform communism implied a search for new forms of legitimacy, as well as the imagining of a different post-bipolar world order, in a historical conjuncture that seemed to mark the end of the line for the century's main revolutionary tradition. Furthermore, the European global perspective on North-South relations—which had been so important to the Italian Communists' vision—was hardly a shared project that could open roads not taken previously. Their ideas of a new world order had been confronted by the harsh reaction of the United States and the indifference of the Soviet Union, but they were also undermined by divisions among the different actors of the Global South. In this light we should probably see the trajectory of the PCI as a piece, if a small one, of a wider, fractured puzzle that signaled the twilight of progressive political internationalism in the late twentieth century.

EPILOGUE
The Dream of a New World Order

THE ADVENT OF GORBACHEV

The aporias experienced by the Italian Communists in the mid-1980s were stronger than those that dated from Togliatti's "Yalta memorandum" of twenty years earlier. The Italians were the sole subjects in the communist world to have sought to provide answers to the global shock and the problems that had emerged in the socialist bloc, though their analytical tools in many ways were still influenced by rigid categories of crisis, or by long-lasting mythologies. Their strategy relied on a strong pride in their own identity, differentiated both from social democracy and from socialism of the Soviet type; but it also produced political isolation. The idea of the "third way" was more a manifestation of an expectation of better times ahead than a basic idea capable of winning people over. The reinvention of internationalism outside the logic of the blocs revealed itself to be a difficult task. The existential link with the destiny of the socialist world represented a much more visible connotation than was the devising of a political project in Italy and in the West. The tension between the PCI's legitimation as a governmental force in the West and the prospect of the reform of communism remained open. Berlinguer's successors confronted these contradictions by internal divisions, especially between generations.

The ascent to power of Mikhail Gorbachev, elected general secretary of the CPSU in March 1985, was the central factor for everyone in the PCI, notwithstanding the political and cultural distance that separated them from Soviet-style socialism, and their growing integration into the agenda of the European left. Just as Togliatti's successors had identified in the "Prague Spring" the sense of a renewed mission, so the successors of Berlinguer saw in the Soviet reformers the chance to relaunch a cosmopolitan vocation that in different ways had characterized Italian communism throughout its history. After an initial cautious phase, they maintained that their first prophecies and hopes had been justified. Albeit with different nuances, communist leaders, intellectuals, and militants of separate generations perceived Gorbachev as confirmation of their reasoning. After years of frustration, however, their vision was not limited to this conclusion. In their eyes, what counted was not only perestroika—the beginning of a new season of liberalization and reform of the Soviet system—but, more than anything else, the "new way of thinking," which meant a universalist vision that referred to the "invention of the tradition" of humanistic socialism. Such a vision indeed constituted a form of cultural hybridization inspired by the prospect of a post–Cold War era in which communism could converge with other political and religious cultures without reneging on the narratives aimed at vindicating communist identity.

The memoirs of the protagonists of that era, beginning with Gorbachev, have drawn attention to the key moment represented by the funeral of Berlinguer in June 1984. Gorbachev recalls how the popular national emotion he then perceived revealed a "mentality and a political culture greatly different from ours." For him, this experience possessed a meaning even superior to the reading of Gramsci.[1] Chernyaev, too, records in his memoirs the strong impression made on the Soviet delegates by the breadth and depth of the mass valediction by the people.[2] Rubbi observed that in those circumstances, Gorbachev recognized the influence Berlinguer had exerted on the younger generation of Soviet leaders.[3] On the occasion of the funeral of Andropov's successor, Konstantin Chernenko, on 14 March 1985, Gorbachev's decision to meet just one European communist leader, PCI Secretary Alessandro Natta, was in itself a sign of change.[4]

This notwithstanding, the Italian Communists, conditioned by experience, welcomed the new Soviet leader with great caution. In his conversation with Natta, Gorbachev did not go beyond rather traditional formulations, and generically reasserted the role of all communists in the "fight for peace."[5] A few days later, Natta said that one could expect "some change and a certain dynamism, but we know how complex the problems of the USSR and the CPSU are regarding the positions we are aware of. Confidence and caution together, then."[6] As Giuseppe Boffa recalls, "We placed some hopes, rather than certainties, on him."[7] The first Italian Communist to talk with Gorbachev on strategic topics such as Europeanism was Gianni Cervetti, in an informal conversation before the Soviet leader's meetings with Craxi and Andreotti in June 1985.[8] The initiative taken by Craxi, one of the first European heads of government to see Gorbachev, relaunched Italian Ostpolitik and was aimed at subtracting from the Communists the role they had previously played in the negotiations over the Euromissiles.[9] The question of foreign policy did not cease to be a factor in domestic policy, as had been the case in the first half of the decade.

It was only in January 1986 that an obvious consonance between the Italian Communists and the new Soviet leadership took shape. The attention that Gorbachev paid to the positions of the PCI was much more concrete, especially regarding their Europeanist orientations.[10] He put forward his own picture of an interdependent world, and made it clear that winning back a "dynamism" in the Soviet system had also to involve the political system and "socialist democracy." His idea of developing "the potentialities of socialism,"—which he considered to have been inhibited "for historical-objective reasons," such as conditioning by the Cold War, but also for "subjective reasons"—was in evident harmony with the positions of the Italian Communists. However, their respective ideas on international communism remained distant from each other. In Gorbachev's view, the communist movement, though "weakened," still represented an "enormous force at the world level," which could respond to "the economic-cultural-political counterattack of capitalism" by returning to its "inspirational aims." "We do not propose to exhume the Communist International," he clarified, "but to meet one another is necessary." Natta's reply marked the distance that still separated the two sides: "The PCI is not, and neither does it feel, part of an i[nternational] c[ommunist] m[ovement] which in the traditional meaning of the definition does not exist today and whose refoundation, as well as being impossible, would bring about serious harm." At this point Gorbachev had to recognize that "different ideas" were at stake, but he underlined his wish to establish closer relations with the PCI. Both leaders knew that their respective outlooks might diverge on the vision of the communist movement, but they had in common the idea that it was precisely the reform-oriented perspective that required them to distance themselves from social democracy. Gorbachev asserted that communists could not be reduced to a "variant" of social democracy: "If the communists pass over to the positions of the social democrats, where will the communist perspective end up? There would be no historical reason for its very existence."[11]

Natta reported to Rome that he had seen in Gorbachev an attempt to reestablish relations, basing them on "something of a Ptolemaic" vision of the links between Moscow and the communist parties. He maintained, however, that Gorbachev's characterization of the "lack of progression" in the Soviet system could be taken as synonymous with Berlinguer's "exhaustion" of its "propulsive capacity." The PCI leaders accepted these assessments, even if the accents they placed on them were different. The most sceptical was Napolitano, in whose view everything regarding Soviet intentions for a renewal was subject to "being verified," while the PCI could not think of "returning to identify with the old blocs and movements." On the basis of his own experience, Rubbi presented the scenario of a game yet to be played, noting that in Moscow there had been "a three-year struggle" regarding the possibility of bringing the PCI back to "orthodoxy" or to "understand our reasons and [. . .] coexist."[12] After the Chernobyl catastrophe, the Italians detected some signals of a more decisive change in Gorbachev's conduct.[13] During a meeting in June 1986 with a delegation from the PCI headed by Napolitano, Zagladin expressed "understanding" for the PCI's positions on the European left, and accented the Soviet "revision" of its assessment of the social-democratic parties. Napolitano gained the impression that things were in motion, as was demonstrated by the difference between one interlocutor, such as Ponomarev, and another, like the diplomat Anatoly Dobrynin.[14]

At the end of the year, despite the failure to obtain a concrete understanding, the Reykjavík summit between Gorbachev and Reagan signaled the possibility of a new bipolar détente based on disarmament, while the release of Andrei Sakharov heralded liberalization in the Soviet Union.[15] The personality of Gorbachev as a reformer was now starting to be acknowledged internationally. The Italian Communists could boast a privileged relationship, based on a common language that had again been found. The interview that Gorbachev gave to *L'unità* on 20 May 1987 constituted one of the vehicles for the resonance of his visions in Italian and European public opinion, first of all on the subject of the "common European home," which had been put forward in Prague a month earlier, and which alluded to the reunification of a divided continent.[16] The changes underway in Moscow interacted with the strategies of the Italians, encouraging, above all, renewed contacts in Central and Eastern Europe; but they did not induce any substantial modifications for a certain length of time.

Natta followed the international coordinates he had inherited from Berlinguer, continuing to construct relations with the left forces in Europe, and with the traditional interlocutors in the Mediterranean basin: Yugoslavia, Algeria, and Palestine.[17] In October 1985 he met Deng Xiaoping and Hu Yaobang in Beijing, noting the convergence of their respective positions against the logic of the blocs. Deng emphasized the importance of the autonomous role of Western Europe, which would promote something analogous in Central and Eastern Europe; and he stated that he had given up the view of the inevitability of war. Natta reported to his comrades the significance of this conceptual change in Chinese foreign policy, which consolidated China's opposition to the blocs and its solidarity with the Third World, based on its critique of the Soviet model in Africa and on the prospect of the end of the bipolar order.[18] Some months later, meeting Hu Yaobang in Rome in June 1986, Natta and Napolitano pressed him for his assessment of Gorbachev. The Chinese were of the opinion that military expenditure was the main problem that perestroika had to solve. The only way to save the Soviet Union was for it to give up its current "strategic position" in the world.[19] This was an argument linked to Mao's criticism, but one that was also fairly realist. The Italian Communists did not appear to fully realize the striking nature of the Chinese detachment from the Soviet model of an administered economy, and their delegitimizing influence on Soviet socialism in the Third World, which by the mid-Eighties was then visible.[20] For the Italians, what counted more was the idea that they could create convergent visions regarding the birth of a post–Cold War world, and that they were able for the first time to bring the PCI together with the Soviets and the Chinese.

The Italian Communists inserted a new relationship with Moscow into an already preexisting framework of international relations, without aiming at a preferential axis, and while limiting themselves to sounding out the first repercussions of perestroika in Eastern Europe. In the course of 1987, however, Gorbachev came to be recognized as the key figure in a change of the world order that involved Europe directly, and not only in the context of the superpowers. Gorbachev intensified his relations with Western Europe, conceived of as a central aspect of the "new way of thinking."[21] The initial aim of halting the Soviet decline and liberating resources by putting a brake on the arms race acquired more pronounced tones and horizons, inspired by the idea of creating new forms of political legitimation and relaunching a universalistic mission. This gave rise to a growing consensus among the Italian Communists , but also to different accents. Napolitano observed that the drive toward reform in the Soviet Union had to be better understood and not merely seconded uncritically, precisely because it posed questions that were "now strongly interwoven with those of the new system of international relations," which one could no longer limit to Western multilateralism. Looked at in this light, the most important problem, in Napolitano's view, was the role of Europe in international détente. One part of the PCI's leading group—including Reichlin, to use a representative name—argued that the scenarios opened by Gorbachev implied a "crisis" of neoliberalism, as had been shown by Wall Street's "Black Monday" on 19 October 1987.[22] The short circuit between the hopes that had been kindled by the Soviet reformers and the illusions of a crisis of Western neoliberal hegemony would remain influential in the visions of the leading group even after the fall of the American stock exchange showed itself to be a contingent phenomenon.

In his speech on the occasion of the seventieth anniversary of the October Revolution, Gorbachev declared that it was impossible to analyze "global developments" solely in the optic of the juxtaposition between "two opposed social systems" and without understanding world interdependences. He thereby sanctioned the end of a dichotomous vision of the world as forged by the communists well before the Cold War. A similar note could not but sound harmonious to the social-democratic delegates present in Moscow, and also to the Italian Communists and the reformers from Eastern Europe who had remained silent during the Brezhnev era. On the other hand, it was probably disquieting for the Eastern European establishments, which had cultivated their own power in the shadow of the Wall. Gorbachev complained in private that his reforms were arousing more interest among the social democrats than among many of the communist parties.[23] The Italian Communists were the main exception. Their press was now presenting the Soviet leader as a reformer who was following the footsteps of Berlinguer. On the seventieth anniversary of the October Revolution, Gorbachev was celebrated as a symbolic resource of Italian communism, while the other communist parties were lukewarm or even hostile.[24] His figure was, for many, equivalent to a demonstration that the Soviet system was capable of reform, thus resolving once and for all a question that had been fiercely debated in Western intellectual and political circles. The idea became prevalent that the "new way of thinking" had now hegemonized the international agenda. In the PCI's Directorate, the deputy secretary, Achille Occhetto, argued that the "world government of processes" was now a "truly concrete utopia".[25]

In March 1988, in a memorandum on his trip to Italy, Zagladin reported to Gorbachev the impression of a "radical and profound change" in the attitude of the Italian Communists toward Moscow. In his view, the conflicts of the past had now been overcome, including the Soviet failure to understand Eurocommunism and the PCI's initial mistrust of Gorbachev himself. The memorandum also contained some indiscretions about the situation inside the PCI, which showed conflictuality and a leadership crisis. According to the information gathered by Zagladin, the main point of fracture was born from the attempt, attributed to Napolitano, to bring the Italian Communists into line with social democracy and thus reach a "mutual understanding" with the United States. One of the men who most directly represented the link with the legacy left by Berlinguer, Antonio Tatò, confided to Zagladin that the noticeable weakening of the PCI's "links with the masses," which had emerged after the electoral defeat of 1987, and which was a reason for growing worry among the party leaders, should also be attributed to the activity of those who were pushing the party in the direction of a "social democratization." Tatò attacked Napolitano head-on, referring implicitly, among other things, to his claim, which had given rise to largely negative reactions within the PCI, that the Italian Communists had now "left the confines of the communist tradition."[26] With the aim of inverting this tendency, Berlinguer's former secretary opined that it was necessary to have a generational change in the leadership, and indicated Occhetto as the right person to bring about such a "perestroika in the PCI."[27] It cannot be dismissed that these statements were made to sound out the attitude of the Soviets, if not to obtain their favor, toward Occhetto's candidacy for the post of general secretary. In any case, the information reported in Zagladin's memorandum was reliable in its general lines. What divided the Italian Communists was not the judgment on Gorbachev, but the greater or lesser consistency of the demarcation line of identity separating them from the European social democracies, a nexus closely interrelated with the national political scene and the prospects of government.

The main leaders of the PCI met Gorbachev in Moscow on 29 and 30 March 1988.[28] The subject of Europe was at the center of the understanding between the two sides. Natta underlined the PCI's position regarding the role of Western Europe in détente and the fact that the European Community had not led to Europe being subaltern to the United States, in contrast to what was being argued by other communist parties. Gorbachev confirmed that the Soviet Union considered itself "most of all a European country," and did not judge the European Community "solely in negative terms." He put the significance of the notion of a "common European home" in this context, maintaining that "if interdependence is advancing in the world, that is even more true for Europe." To the Italian Communists he posed the dilemma that anguished them most, pointing out that it was a question not of recognizing integration as an "objective tendency," but of asking whether the European left had a "project for governing this integration, for refounding it to their own ends." In his opinion, the Italian Communists should have formed alliances with the Socialists in government "in order to modify orientations in which they were co-responsible." He maintained that the only alternative to perestroika was the decline of the presence of the Soviet Union "in world affairs," which put at risk "'the destiny of socialism itself." He reassured his interlocutors, however, about the gradual nature of the change "without destabilization" in Central and Eastern Europe.[29] After the meeting, Gorbachev reported back to the Politburo that together with the Italians, he had noted "the serious and dangerous backwardness in the conceptions of many communist parties [...] in the first place, the ones that are most faithful to us."[30]

The action of the Soviet reformers reached a climax in the spring and summer of 1988. Gorbachev harvested the fruit of his diplomatic offensive in the two summits held in Washington in December 1987 and in Moscow in May 1988, which finalized the agreements between the superpowers on the reduction of medium-range nuclear weapons. In his walk around Red Square on 31 May 1988, Reagan stated that he no longer considered the USSR to be an "evil empire," thereby withdrawing the celebrated appellation elevated to being the dominant sign of the "second Cold War." The Euromissile problem which had tormented European and world politics for a decade was thus liquidated.[31] On the crest of this success, Gorbachev launched the project of separating the party from the state, announced the proposal to introduce market reforms, and abandoned the idea of "peaceful coexistence" as a form of class struggle. In this context, Chernyaev, an old acquaintance of the Italians and now Gorbachev's right-hand man for international policy, took on the task of liquidating communist internationalism as an anachronism.[32] In a note to Gorbachev, he was incisive regarding the sense and very existence of the movement ("It is clear to everyone that the communist movement, which we traditionally are used to seeing as such, in reality does not exist"). According to Chernyaev, the time had come to bring the international communist movement to an end, insofar as it was a "political category" that could not offer solutions to "global problems." He cited the French communists as an example, and asked in what way and "for doing what" they could be considered "allies." What was needed instead was "a rebirth of ideological kinship," which would take time.[33]

The new party leadership of Occhetto, who had replaced Natta in June 1988, was immediately invested in the interaction with Gorbachev. A joint document from the PCI and the CPSU was planned on Europe as a space and a central notion for redefining an internationalist mission, envisaging the organization of an all-European "round table," at which political forces of different orientations were to take part, including ones not of the left.[34] In October, the PCI Directorate discussed a document on the "new political course" of the party, which indicated interdependence as the "new law" of the world order and projected a "new reforming front" in Europe against neoliberalism, whose aspiration would be the "political sovereignty of the European people." The language of the leading group under Occhetto was interwoven with that of Gorbachev, and only Napolitano criticized the "attractive definitions from which, however, we are unable to draw consequences."[35] On 27 December 1988, Gorbachev made a speech at the United Nations that was destined to represent his manifesto as it focused on world interdependences, the end of bipolar antagonism, and the "erosion of the bases of the Cold War."[36] On 24 January 1989 he posed a striking question to the Politburo: How would Moscow have reacted if Hungary had made a request to enter the European Community? This was a scenario that could not be excluded, given that the reform communists were asserting their own agenda after the retirement of Kádár, which had happened less than a year earlier. Gorbachev explained that he would not have opposed that choice, but would rather have accepted the challenge in creating a new system of international relations.[37] In February there took place in Poland, thanks also to pressure from Moscow, the "round table" between the Communist regime and Solidarność, with the aim of legalizing the opposition eight years after the military coup d'état.

The vision of the Italian Communists was now concentrated almost exclusively on Europe, following the priorities of the end of the Cold War, which appeared within reach thanks to the "new way of thinking." They abandoned the paradigm that Togliatti had created in connecting "peaceful coexistence" and decolonization. The connections in practice and in conceptual terms with the Third World represented a legacy within communist history that the Italian leading group had modeled and integrated according to its own lights at different times. Those connections also acted as an "identity card" that for a long time had been crucial to the PCI for claiming its difference from the social democracies. Berlinguer had conceived of the Europeanist choice in relation to the agenda of the "new international economic order" and the North-South axis in the world. The Europeanism of his successors seemed instead to foreshadow a renunciation of the task of once again establishing difficult and nonproductive bonds, a realization that fractures could not be mended, and, together with this, the start of a redefinition of identity that understood Europeanization as a sphere of self-sufficient values.

It was in this way that the PCI interacted with the Soviet Union's "withdrawal" from the Third World, a sign of the failures experienced by the communists in the Global South, especially regarding the model of development. The most symbolic aspect of this withdrawal was the decision taken by Gorbachev to withdraw the Soviet military from Afghanistan, which had been under consideration since 1985 and was announced in April 1988, in recognition of the fatal mistake made in the choice to invade. But the very same "way of thinking" implied the abandonment of interventionism in the Third World, taking on board criticisms by a number of Soviet analysts and Eurocommunists at the end of the 1970s against support for African socialist regimes.[38] The tendency of the countries of the Soviet bloc to abandon the developmental policies promoted in previous decades was also ever more evident, basically because they were too pressured by their own indebtedness to the West to be able to seek solutions to the growing indebtedness of the Third World.[39] The reform communists tried to provide meaning to the decline of their ideas and practices of an alternative globalization, recentering in Europe their visions of a world order and their political culture. The subject of North-South relations in the world remained essential, but it no longer had its former significance as a political agenda. A similar dynamic came to the fore in Europe through the growing importance of the subject and language of human rights in defining the very mission of European integration.[40] The twofold decline of the Cold War and the Third World seemed thus to imply a new form of transversal cultural Eurocentrism.

THE COLLAPSE OF COMMUNISM

At the beginning of 1989, the Italian Communists found themselves in a situation that was in many respects the reverse of the situation of five years earlier, at the time of Berlinguer's death. In national politics, erosion of the party's electoral consensus had become manifest, accompanied by a fear that its mass strength might decline, within the trend of a structural deterioration of the political organization of the Republic. The immobility of the political system, centered around the concept of a "blocked democracy," contrasted stridently with the dynamism of Italian society, but also with the radical change in international politics. The special relationship established with Gorbachev had removed the Italian Communists from their awkward position as preachers in the desert, offering them a role of a certain significance, with positive consequences for national politics, given the growing popularity of the Soviet leader in Europe and in Italy. Occhetto proposed investing the PCI's national policy with dynamism by acknowledging de facto that the marginalization of the last decade had also been a form of self-exclusion. The Soviet reformers encouraged the new PCI leadership. Chernyaev told Rubbi of his gratitude to the PCI for having expressed, ten years in advance, "ideas, judgments and criticisms that found total confirmation in the facts," and also for its support for reforms in the Soviet Union. On the other hand, he complained of the serious difficulties caused by the reform process, of resistance within the party establishment, and of a "hostile group among our allies," in which Cuba, East Germany, and Romania stood out. Chernyaev stressed his view that if Gorbachev were to fail, it would be a hard blow for all communists: "We do not wish to bind anyone to our experience, but how can anyone say that perestroika concerns only the Soviets [a reference to Marchais]? We all need to change—and quickly, if we are still to have a future."[41] The Soviet official embraced, so to speak, the international sense and mission of perestroika, a gesture destined to be well received by the Italian Communists. Indeed, the generational turnover represented by Occhetto's election would increase the intensity of the relations between Italian Communists and the Soviet reformers. At the same time, the isolation of both actors within the communist world was plain to see. Instead of giving rise to a reformist movement, perestroika had strengthened a transnational front of conservative opposition involving the principal establishments of Central and Eastern Europe, in particular the East Germans; most Western communists, especially the French and the Portuguese; and by far the majority of communists in Asia, Africa, and Latin America. In more or less dissimulated ways, Gorbachev was seen as a dangerous dreamer and a revisionist who betrayed the anti-imperialist struggle.[42] Reform communists eliminated the notion of international communism from their vocabulary, but the problem remained.

The Italian Communists turned to both Brandt and Gorbachev at the same time, but the relationship with the latter was more intense. Occhetto and Napolitano met with Brandt and other SPD leaders in January 1989. Reciprocal openings were noticeable, but went no further than the limits reached during the Berlinguer years. The establishment of formal relations still remained an impracticable option, while agreements in the European Parliament were restricted to a thematic approach. The Germans pointed out that Italy's Europeanist federalism did not favor the prospects for cooperation.[43] A month later, on 28 February, Occhetto went to Moscow to meet Gorbachev. The realism that had previously distinguished the Italian leaders' conduct had given way to pure identification. Occhetto declared that the Italian party now supported Gorbachev, and stressed the importance of the new relations established outside the old context of the communist movement, with the prospect of "recomposition of all progressive forces active on the terrain of Europeanism" in order to define "a new, less ingenuous conception of progress." Occhetto specified that "our problem is, however, not that of asking to join the Socialist International." The principal shared cipher remained a neo-Leninist narrative in which Stalinism was a "degeneration," and the stumbling blocks of communism's origins were overlooked, along with the idea of bringing about a political metamorphosis of the entire century-old socialist tradition. Gorbachev imagined it thus: "If I'm right, you are thinking about movement along a road that leads to more economic, social, and political democracy. Thus it will be a process, if I understand correctly. My question is this: Does the party dissolve, become social democracy? My impression is that it is not so." He revealed that he had suggested to Brandt a prospect of shared reconsideration ("After 1914, should we not start on a new road?"). The Soviet leader believed that "a general rethinking of what socialism is today" was taking place in the communist world, but he did not fail to point to "the risk of throwing explosive material into the fire of perestroika," that is to say, of destabilizing Central and Eastern Europe, which could give rise to "phenomena and decisions of the opposite sign."[44]

Chernyaev remembers the talk between Gorbachev and Occhetto as a particularly challenging exchange, given the increasingly acute state of uncertainty being experienced by the Soviet reform group.[45] Reporting back to the Directorate of the PCI, Occhetto spoke of an encounter "between two reform processes" which aimed to "go beyond schematics" in bilateral relations, and the definitive setting aside of the "communist movement." This claim provoked a marked divergence with part of the old generation. Natta and Ingrao, in particular, opposed breaking off relations with the other communist parties.[46] In reality, Occhetto was proposing emotional and political identification with Gorbachev, in the belief that he was acting as a bridge between perestroika and the European left. Others, however, put the European nexus before the relation with Gorbachev, also for domestic political reasons. Regarding the European elections, two leaders as differently positioned as Napolitano and D'Alema stressed how a progressive front in Europe might be able to help cure the Italian "anomaly."[47]

The encounter between the Italian Communists and the Soviet reformers concealed an unsolved question. Did they both intend to renew the communist tradition, in the conviction that it possessed sufficient resources within itself to carry out its own revitalization as a new progressive left? Or was there a will to go beyond that tradition, recognizing that reform communism would modify the very roots of its own identity? The answers to these two questions were clear neither in Rome nor in Moscow. Occhetto's new party was opening up to new relations with European socialism, but was leaning more toward the former option than toward the latter, taking inspiration from the later period of Berlinguer and his stress on the "diversity" of Italian communism. The choice of creating a new parliamentary group in the European Parliament, distinct from both the communist and the social-democratic ones, pointed to how special a case Italy was.[48]

Matters started coming to a head in June 1989. It was then that two different models of response to the Gorbachev challenge emerged. In Poland, the first semifree elections since 1945 marked a resounding victory for Solidarność, thus sidelining the Communist Party. It became immediately clear that the one-party democracy model had already run its course as a transitional form, and that this concerned not just Poland but also the other socialist states, including Hungary, then governed by a pro-reform leading group. In China, the Communist Party's reaction was to use violence against the student protests that had been inspired by perestroika and by Gorbachev's visit to Beijing in May. The Tienanmen Square massacre was a repressive practice frequently found in the history of communism: it was an order-based alternative to the liberalization proposed by Gorbachev, and it completed the model of market authoritarianism constructed by Deng. The decision to employ force in Tienanmen shattered the pro-reform convergence of Moscow and Beijing that had seemed possible. The PCI leading group condemned Beijing's repression, and greeted the birth in Poland of the government headed by Tadeusz Mazowiecki, the first noncommunist premier in Central and Eastern Europe since World War II. The positions of the PCI were aligned with those of Gorbachev also regarding the idea that the new Polish government and the democratic reforms in Hungary delineated gradual and controllable change that was destined to break the shackles of the Cold War and liquidate the old spheres of influence. That was not at all unimportant in Italy, where an anachronistic agreement to exclude the Communists from power still persisted.

The idea that a gradual change in Central and Eastern European socialism would take place under the impulse of perestroika evaporated rapidly. In September and October 1989 the gradualist scenario was eliminated by an extraordinary and unforeseen acceleration, marked by mass demonstrations in East Germany. All the main international players were surprised by the speed of the events that followed, and which led to the fall of the Berlin Wall. Gorbachev displayed his consistency by avoiding the use of force, a decisive choice for a peaceful outcome of the communist collapse in Europe.[49] However, his vision of "top-down" reforms suffered a mortal blow. The fact was that the reform communists had underestimated the crisis of legitimacy in the Central and Eastern European regimes. They were surprised not only by the speed of events but by their nature: that is to say, a pacific revolution combined with a collapse of the institutions' authority.[50] The Italian Communists were no exception: they supported the reasons for the nonviolent mass protests that were spreading across East Germany, but they had not considered the delegitimization of state power. The prospects for reform cultivated up to this point implied the idea of a renewal of the communist leading classes, not a generalized loss of significance. Twenty years on from the Prague Spring, the myth of socialism's self-reform provided authentic motivation, but was also illusory. The conviction that rebirth of the reform ideas at the heart of the "socialist camp" would prevent their repression and thus give rise to unstoppable change was not without foundation. But the change that took place was very different from what had been expected. The Italian Communists underestimated the scale of the existential crisis in the East, and the quagmire represented by reform projects that exacerbated the discrediting of establishments and triggered destructive dynamics.

The ideas, analyses, and perspectives of change linked to Gorbachev and followed by the PCI's leading group were no preparation for handling the radicality of the scenarios created by the fall of the Berlin Wall on 9 November 1989. Occhetto's decision to propose the dissolution of the PCI in order to found a new party of the left, which happened shortly thereafter, was a courageous move in the course of action followed up to that point, though it would not have been at all possible had it not been for an earlier change of register, especially after the Tienanmen massacre.[51] In any case, such a "turn" meant a realization that the residual bond with the century-old history of world communism had come to an end. The Directorate of the PCI that was held on 14 and 15 November inaugurated a lacerating transformation process that would not terminate until a year and a half later. Occhetto justified the discontinuity by closely linking the national and international dimensions of politics. In his opinion, the Yalta world order had come to an end, and the problem of "a new world governance" was on the agenda; but there was also the issue of "the loss of basic identity," and the reality of a "historical crisis" to come to terms with. Occhetto laid claim to the original identity of the Italian Communists, but admitted that there was no point in exalting it, and that their specificity "either re-situates itself or is destined to extinction," becoming nothing more than "a provincial function." He acknowledged that claiming to no longer be part of the communist movement was at that point "completely insufficient," and that instead, should the party wish to have an international function, the role of the Socialist International had to become "central." Only some in the PCI leading group adhered to this position. Napolitano called for an "organic relation" with the Socialist International, which implied a more precise commitment than that indicated by the party secretary, and a different direction for the new party's identity. More than others, D'Alema recognized the risk of isolation for Italian communism and remarked that safeguarding its international function was a "great Italian question."[52] Both questions would, however, remain decisively in the background in the debate—in many aspects self-referential—that took place over the following months.

A few days later, on 29 November, Gorbachev made his first visit to Italy. The Soviet leader's stature on the international stage was at its zenith: his liquidation of the "Brezhnev doctrine" and his decision to avoid any interference in the "velvet" revolutions constituted a decisive test for the "new way of thinking." According to Chernyaev's diary, the visit took place "in an atmosphere of astonishing mass euphoria wherever Gorbachev made an appearance."[53] Gorbachev met with Andreotti and Pope John Paul II, both of whom expressed their total approval of perestroika. As head of the Italian government, Andreotti was a point of reference for the idea of a postbipolar European order, which would be reconstructed in the spirit of the Helsinki Accords, and which was also desired by the Italian communists.[54] They had contributed to the preparations for the visit, and Rubbi had met Gorbachev himself in Moscow at the end of October.[55] Gorbachev's November visit to Italy took on particular significance as a legitimization of the Italian Communists' "turn." Occhetto discussed with Gorbachev his opinion that it would be opportune to accelerate the move toward the Socialist International, a step about which the Soviet leader could only express his agreement.[56] A few days later, Occhetto wrote the Soviet leader a letter requesting a meeting in Moscow before the decisive Congress of the PCI regarding the "turn," which was planned for March 1990.[57] However, this meeting never took place.

The Italian Communists were completing their transformation while perestroika was entering its terminal phase. The decision of the Soviet reformers to accept the reunification of Germany within NATO in the summer of 1990 completed the plan to bring to an end the structures of the Cold War, but it was also a clear sign of weakness. The idea that the Soviet Union would maintain its capacity for influence in Central and

Eastern Europe even after the fall of the communist regimes was shown to be illusory, as was confirmed by the disintegration of the Warsaw Pact.[58] Many observers, including Boffa, sensed a retreat from the reform project in Moscow.[59] At the same time, the "turn" of the Italian Communists revealed contrasts and fractures in the political culture. In July 1990, Occhetto appealed for the discussion to be not about a "metaphysical identity," but about the role the new political formation would have to play, inviting all involved to be aware of the ongoing international political transformations, starting with the reunification of Germany and its implications for Europe. He invoked "the world of interdependence," criticizing the perspectives of a unipolar world, pointing to the limits of visions centered on the "victory of the West," and to the risk of underestimating conflicts and inequalities in the Eurasian space and the Global South. Fundamentally, his speech aimed to sketch the dimensions of the challenge for "world governance" that 1989 had presented. Occhetto was persuaded that "democratic socialism with a human face" still had cards to play and was indeed "an idea and a force with a strong presence, well-rooted in Europe and the world," capable of giving rise to post–Cold War internationalism. This passage is precise evidence of a strong component of wishful thinking, given that it was difficult to discern the real consistency of the alliances and the imagined shared values, especially in the European left. In other words, an enormous gap had opened up between awareness of the global or supranational challenges and the possible responses—such as, for example "people's diplomacy," "Europe of the peoples," or the appeal for a "constituent phase" in domestic politics.[60]

On 15 November 1990, Occhetto presented Gorbachev with the political outcome of the PCI's transformation into a "democratic party of the left," declaring his intention to "go beyond the communist and social-democratic traditions," and not to "go from one to the other." The sense of the request to join the Socialist International was, therefore, not to "accept everything," but to "introduce the reforming traditions of the Italian communists." Gorbachev's support was unconditional, and was based on his conviction that "we and you are taking similar roads, though each in total autonomy and each under their own responsibility." His references to the past had become much more essential and disillusioned after the decision to liquidate the one-party system. The reform-oriented Soviet leader said he was convinced that "it is not true that the last seventy-three years have been a waste of time," yet he defined the Soviet model of socialism as "a system that stifled individuals, a totalitarian regime, a state monopoly on everything." Gorbachev's hope was that "perhaps for the first time we will manage to avoid what has always happened in this country—that is, that attempts at reform end up leading to regimes that are even harder and more severe."[61] His stubborn conviction, however, was that perestroika was of universal significance, and that the world was "on the threshold of an era of great and effective common civilization."[62]

Retrospectively, Occhetto claimed that the Italian Communists and Gorbachev had already shared the visions of a "new world order" before the Wall fell, but that because of the fall of the Soviet leader, the "new world order" remained a road not taken.[63] That road would have been built upon an extension of the Helsinki Accords, aimed at increasing Europe's role and including a reformed Soviet Union in a cooperative economic and political order. Gorbachev's vision of a "common European home" favored recognition of the model of prosperity and democracy represented by the European Community, and at the same time, the adoption of a view of Europe as a civilization and a cultural space that was not restricted to the Western experience of integration, and which aimed to become more inclusive. It may have been an ingenuous vision, even one that owed a debt to the pan-Europeanism of the Soviet tradition, but it performed the task of disactivating the material and mental structures of the Cold War. Without the effects of deterrence produced by Gorbachev's reforms on establishments that were potentially aggressive but which at that point lacked self-confidence, the Cold War might have ended in a nonpeaceful manner. From this perspective, reform communism was a decisive force in a field of contrasting tensions between the persistence of the Cold War, the siren calls of European integration, and the winds of economic globalization.[64]

However, the interdependent "new world order" imagined by reform communists also reflected their limits and contradictions. The language of humanistic socialism and the vision of internationalism based on a hybridization of political cultures lacked consensus not only among communist establishments, including that of China, but also in the postcolonial world. The visions of a "common European home" clashed with the severe responses of geopolitics and the persistence of the Cold War mentality. The Soviet reformers, and also the Italian Communists, vainly hoped for support from the West and for a Marshall Plan for the Soviet Union—an idea supported in Italy by Andreotti but opposed by Craxi. The reunification of Germany in NATO, the demise of the Warsaw Pact, and the first Gulf War, between the end of 1990 and the beginning of 1991, delineated the principal components of a European and world order that could either exclude Russia or include it in a minority position. In this context, the effectiveness of Gorbachev's strong main idea was inexorably ground down. Reform communism ended up expressing more of a metamorphosis and final destination of the century's main revolutionary tradition, than a new beginning.

In his memoirs, Napolitano sees Gorbachev as an obstacle, rather than a stimulus, for the evolution of the PCI toward European socialism.[65] Indeed, the Italian Communists completed the exit from their own tradition a little before the demise of the Soviet Union, and only thereafter did they join the Socialist International. Occhetto and the younger leaders rejected the option represented by Napolitano and the moderates—the reunification of socialism in Italy as in Europe—in order to abandon century-old traditions and seek a new identity. Rather than acting as a brake, Gorbachev was the mirror of a political culture that was reinventing itself while holding on to its moral and political "diversity." The tormented transition to the new party ended up as a clash between ideal passions and existential tensions, which revealed the removal of communism's historical failures and concentrated almost exclusively on national specificities. The self-representations that aimed to exalt the continuity and uniqueness of the Italian experience without fully coming to terms with its contradictions, or with the tragic and oppressive extremes of communism in power, presented their consequences. Although the "turn" did imply a negation of the exceptionality narrative, the latter remained below the surface and emerged in public debate, integrated by the superficial assimilation of two crises: that of communism and that of social democracy. In this way, the premises were laid for privileging a search for an identity that was distinct from the socialist tradition, and which needed to be reflected in the name chosen for the new party: Democratic Party of the Left.

The postcommunist formation was paradoxically, at one and the same time, a factor of Italian society's withdrawal to a peripheral standpoint, and the inheritor of a political culture which, while maintaining the sense of the international order as a superordinating element, interacted with the national dimension. The main legacy of the culture of Italian communism was probably the vision of Europeanism as a political bond that was needed by the Italian nation. The Communists' idea of Europe never coincided completely with that of the European Community, because as their compass they maintained their opposition to the logic of blocs, to the prospect of a progressive supranational construct, and to the idea of creating bridges to the socialist world and the Third World. This was not particularly unusual, given the historical multiplicity of European projects and their many interconnections with the reality of nation-states.[66] The European dimension had shown itself to be a source of legitimation, a clearinghouse for the communists' marginalization on the national scene, and a vector for resituating the internationalist tradition. In the end, the idea of Europe as a "community of values" prevailed, and was destined to strengthen after the dissolution of the Soviet Union and the birth of the European Union. The dream of a new world order transformed itself into a vision of Europe as a "civil power" and a political actor. With all the aporias that arose, the consolidation of the European nexus as the fundamental national interest would represent the decisive contribution from the ex-communists after the collapse of the other mass parties. The Italian Communists had long pursued the objective of putting an end to the Cold War in Europe and in Italy, imagining their country in diverse transnational and global contexts. The price they paid to make this happen was the end of their story and of their identity.

Notes

Introduction

1. *Documents and Conspiratorial Addresses from the Archives of the Communist Party of Italy (PCI)*, Nara (National Archives Records Administration), Crest (CIA Records Search Tool), April 1951.

2. B. Studer, *The Transnational World of the Cominternians* (London: Palgrave Macmillan, 2015); S. Dullin and B. Studer, "Communism+Transnational: The Rediscovered Equation of Internationalism in the Comintern Years," *Twentieth Century Communism* 2017, no. 14, pp. 66–95; J. Friedman, *Shadow Cold War: The Sino-Soviet Competition for the Third World* (Chapel Hill: University of North Carolina Press, 2015); T. Rupprecht, *Soviet Internationalism after Stalin: Interaction and Exchange between the USSR and Latin America during the Cold War* (Cambridge, UK: Cambridge University Press, 2015).

3. For recent examples of the new approaches to the history of communism from a global perspective, see S. Pons, general ed., *The Cambridge History of Communism*, 3 vols. (Cambridge, UK: Cambridge University Press, 2017).

4. S. Pons, *The Global Revolution: A History of International Communism 1917–1991* (Oxford and New York: Oxford University Press, 2014).

5. R. Doucoulombier and J. Vigreux, eds., *Le PCF, un parti global (1919–1989): Approches transnationales et comparées* (Dijon, France: Éditions universitaires de Dijon, 2019).

6. E. J. Hobsbawm, *Anni interessanti: Autobiografia di uno storico* (Milan: Rizzoli, 2002), pp. 388–89; originally published as *Interesting Times* (London: Allen Lane, 2002), pp. 347–48.

7. A. Gramsci, *Quaderni del carcere*, ed. V. Gerratana (Turin: Einaudi, 1975), p. 1190.

8. M. Mazower, *Governing the World. The History of an Idea* (New York: Penguin, 2012); G. Sluga, *Internationalism in the Age of Nationalism* (Philadelphia: University of Pennsylvania Press, 2013); A. Iriye, *Cultural Internationalism and World Order* (Baltimore and London: Johns Hopkins University Press, 1997); S. Conrad and D. Sachsenmaier, eds., *Competing Visions of World Order: Global Moments and Movements 1880s-1930s* (London: Palgrave Macmillan, 2007); T. C. Imlay, *The Practice of Socialist Internationalism. European Socialists and International Politics, 1914-1960* (Oxford, UK, and New York: Oxford University Press, 2018).

9. A. Giardina, ed., *Storia mondiale dell'Italia* (Bari and Rome: Laterza, 2018); S. Patriarca and L. Ryall, eds., *The Risorgimento Revisited: Nationalism and Culture in Nineteenth Century Italy* (London: Palgrave Macmillan, 2012); R. Forlenza and B. Thomassen, *Italian Modernities: Competing Narratives of Nationhood* (New York: Palgrave Macmillan, 2016): F. Romero and A. Varsori, eds., *Nazione, interdipendenza, integrazione: Le relazioni internazionali dell'Italia (1917-1989)*, 2 vols. (Rome: Carocci, 2005); G. Formigoni, *Storia d'Italia nella guerra fredda (1943-1978)* (Bologna: Il Mulino, 2016).

Chapter 1

1. G. Eley, "Marxism and Socialist Revolution," in S. Pons and S. A. Smith, eds., *The Cambridge History of Communism: I. World Revolution and Socialism in One Country* (Cambridge, UK: Cambridge University Press, 2017), pp. 49-73.

2. G. Berti, "Appunti e ricordi 1919-1926," in *I primi dieci anni di vita del Partito Comunista Italiano: Documenti inedita dell'Archivio Angelo Tasca*, ed. G. Berti, Istituto Giangiacomo Feltrinelli, in *Annali* 8 (Milan: Feltrinelli, 1966), pp. 14-17. See also F. De Felice, *Serrati, Bordiga, Gramsci e il problema della rivoluzione in Italia 1919-1920* (Bari: De Donato, 1971).

3. For a reconstruction of Gramsci's thought in the final phase of World War I, see L. Rapone, *Cinque anni che paiono secoli: Antonio Gramsci dal socialismo al comunismo (1914-1919)* (Rome: Carocci, 2011). On the subject of the Russian Revolution, cf. also S. Pons, "Gramsci e la Rivoluzione russa: Una riconsiderazione (1917-1935)," *Studi Storici* 58. no. 4 (2017). On Bordiga, see B. Bongiovanni, *Il socialismo contro la nazione: Il caso di Amadeo Bordiga (1911-1918)*, in M. Cattaruzza, ed., *La nazione in rosso: Socialismo, comunismo e "questione nazionale" (1889-1953)* (Soveria Manelli, Italy: Rubbettino, 2005), pp. 83-106.

4. A. Gramsci, "La rivoluzione contro 'Il Capitale,'" *Il Grido del popolo*, 1 December 1917 (completely censored), and *Avanti*, Roman edition, 22 December 1917, now in Gramsci, *Scritti (1910-1926)*, vol. 2, 1917 (Rome: Instituto della Enciclopedia Italiana, 2015), pp. 617-20. For an English translation, see A. Gramsci, *Selections from Political Writings 1910-1920*, trans. J. Mathews and ed. Q. Hoare (London: Lawrence and Wishart, 1977), pp. 34 and 35.

5. A. Bordiga, "Gli insegnamenti della nuova storia," *Avanti*, Roman edition, 27 and 28 February 1918; now in A. Bordiga, *Scritti 1911-1926*, vol. 2, *La Guerra, la rivoluzione russa e la nuova Internazionale* (Genoa: Graphos, 1998), pp. 419 and 422.

6. A. Gramsci, "Utopia," *Avanti*, 25 July 1918; now in A. Gramsci, *Il nostro Marx 1918–1919*, ed. S. Caprioglio (Turin: Einaudi, 1984), pp. 204–11. In English, see "The Russian Utopia" in *Selections from Political Writings 1910–1920*, p. 53.

7. [A. Gramsci], "La fortuna di Robespierre," *Il Grido del popolo*, 2 March 1918, now in Gramsci, *La città futura 1917–1918*, ed. S. Caprioglio (Turin: Einaudi, 1982), pp. 703–5.

8. [A. Gramsci], "Le opere e i giorni," *Avanti*, 5 July 1918, now in Gramsci, *Il nostro Marx*, pp. 157–59.

9. B. Settis, *Tra Wilson e Lenin: America and americanismo nella formazione dei comunisti Italiani, 1917–1921*, in P. Capuzzo and S. Pons, eds., *Gramsci nel movimento comunista internazionale* (Rome: Carocci, 2019), pp. 35–38.

10. R. Gerwarth, *The Vanquished: Why the First World War Failed to End* (New York: Farrar, Straus and Giroux, 2016).

11. Rapone, *Cinque anni che paiono secoli*, pp. 121–22.

12. [A. Gramsci], "Wilson e i socialisti," *Il Grido del popolo*, 12 October 1918, now in Gramsci, *Il nostro Marx*, pp. 313–17.

13. [A. Bordiga], "Wilson?" *Il Soviet*, 1 January 1919, now in Bordiga, *Scritti 1911–1926*, vol. 3, *Lotte sociali e prospettive rivoluzionarie nel dopoguerra, 1918–1919* (Formia, Italy: Fondazione Amadeo Bordiga, 2010), pp. 37–39.

14. A. Tooze, *The Deluge: The Great War and the Remaking of Global Order, 1916–31* (New York: Penguin, 2014), pp. 20, 232–34.

15. E. Manela, *The Wilsonian Moment: Self-Determination and the International Origins of Anticolonial Nationalism* (Oxford, UK, and New York: Oxford University Press, 2007).

16. [A. Gramsci], "L'armistizio e la pace," *Avanti*, 11 February 1919, now in Gramsci, *Il nostro Marx*, pp. 538–41.

17. Mazower, *Governing the World*, p. 175.

18. [A. Gramsci], "Uno sfacelo e una genesi," *L'ordine nuovo*, 1 May 1919, now in Gramsci, *L'ordine nuovo 1919–1920*, ed. V. Gerratana and A. A. Santucci (Turin: Einaudi, 1987), pp. 3–6.

19. [A. Gramsci], "L'Italia, le alleanze e le colonie," *Avanti*, 10 May 1919, now in Gramsci, *L'ordine nuovo*, pp. 11–12.

20. [A. Gramsci], "L'unità nel mondo," *L'ordine nuovo*, 15 May 1919, now in Gramsci, *L'ordine nuovo*, pp. 19–20.

21. [A. Gramsci], "L'internazionale comunista," *L'ordine nuovo*, 15 May 1919, now in Gramsci, *L'ordine nuovo*, p. 35; and [A. Bordiga], "La farsa di Parigi" (1919) in Bordiga, *Scritti 1911–1926*, vol. 3, pp. 242–44.

22. A. Gramsci, "La marea rivoluzionaria," *L'ordine nuovo*, 7 June 1919, now in Gramsci, *L'ordine nuovo*, pp. 70–71.

23. [A. Gramsci], "La Germania e la pace," *L'ordine nuovo*, 21 June 1919, now in Gramsci, *L'ordine nuovo*, pp. 101–2.

24. [A. Gramsci], "Per l'Internazionale comunista," *L'ordine nuovo*, 26 July 1919, now in Gramsci, *L'ordine nuovo*, p. 152.

25. [A. Gramsci], "La Russia e l'Europa," *L'ordine nuovo*, 15 November 1919, now in Gramsci, *L'ordine nuovo*, pp. 267–71.

26. [A. Gramsci], "I rivoluzionari e le elezioni," *L'ordine nuovo*, 1 November 1919, now in Gramsci, *L'ordine nuovo*, pp. 315–17; and [A. Bordiga], *I partiti della Terza Internazionale e il metodo elezionista* (1919), in Bordiga, *Scritti 1911–1926*, vol. 3, pp. 376–78.

27. [A. Gramsci], "Cercando la verità," *L'ordine nuovo*, 4 October 1919.

28. Rapone, *Cinque anni che paiono secoli*, p. 409.

29. [A. Gramsci], "L'anno rivoluzionario," *Avanti*, 1 January 1919, now in Gramsci., *L'ordine nuovo*, pp. 373–75.

30. [A. Gramsci], "Primo: Rinnovare il partito," *L'ordine nuovo*, 24–31 January 1920, now in Gramsci, *L'ordine nuovo*, pp. 394–98.

31. [A. Gramsci], "La rivoluzione tedesca," *L'ordine nuovo*, 20 March 1920, now in Gramsci, *L'ordine nuovo*, pp. 469–71.

32. [A. Gramsci], "La relazione Tasca e il Congresso camerale di Torino," *L'ordine nuovo*, 5 June 1920, now in Gramsci, *L'ordine nuovo*, pp. 538–42; for the English translation, see *Selections from Political Writings 1910–1920*, pp. 255–59, here pp. 257–58.

33. [A. Gramsci], "Due rivoluzioni," *L'ordine nuovo*, 3 July 1920, now in Gramsci, *L'ordine nuovo*, pp. 569–74; for the English translation see *Selections from Political Writings 1910–1920*, pp. 305–9.

34. Pons, *The Global Revolution*, pp.19–21.

35. [A. Gramsci], "La Russia, potenza mondiale," *L'ordine nuovo*, 14 August 1920, now in Gramsci, *L'ordine nuovo*, pp. 616–18.

36. K. H. Jarausch, *Out of Ashes: A New History of Europe in the Twentieth Century* (Princeton, NJ, and Oxford, UK: Princeton University Press, 2015), p. 156 et seq.; S. Colarizi, *Novecento d'Europa: L'illusione, l'odio, la speranza, l'incertezza* (Rome and Bari: Laterza, 2015), pp. 127–31; and S. Lupo, *Il fascismo: La politica di un regime totalitario* (Rome: Donzelli, 2000), pp. 86–98.

37. A. Gramsci, "Contro il pessimismo," *L'ordine nuovo*, 15 March 1924, now in Gramsci, *La construzione del partito comunista* (Turin: Einaudi, 1971), pp. 16–20; English translation, "Against Pessimism," in *Selections from Political Writings 1921–1926*, ed. and trans. Q. Hoare (London: Lawrence and Wishart, 1978), pp. 213–17, esp. pp. 214–15; *Pre-Prison Writings*, ed. R. Bellamy and trans. V. Cox (Cambridge, UK: Cambridge University Press, 1994), pp. 255–59, esp. p. 257.

38. F. Andreucci, *Da Gramsci a Occhetto: Nobiltà e miseria del PCI, 1921–1991* (Pisa, Italy: Della Porta, 2014), pp. 58–61; and P. Spriano, *Storia del partito comunista italiano*, vol. 1, *Da Bordiga a Gramsci* (Turin: Einaudi, 1967), pp. 152–64.

39. M. Taber, ed., *The Communist Movement at a Crossroads: Plenums of the Communist International's Executive Committee, 1922–23* (Leiden, Netherlands: Brill, 2018).

40. On the activities of Russian emissaries in Italy before the Livorno Congress, see A. Venturi, *Rivoluzionari russi in Italia 1917–21* (Milan: Feltrinelli, 1979);

and V. Lomellini, *La grande paura rossa: L'Italia delle spie bolsceviche (1917–22)* (Milan: FrancoAngeli, 2015).

41. P. Togliatti, *La formazione del gruppo dirigente del partito comunista italiano nel 1923–24* (Rome: Editori Riuniti, 1962), p. 178; in English see *Selections from Political Writings 1921–1926*, p. 185.

42. Rossiiskii Gosudarstvennyi Arkhiv Sotsial'no-Politicheskoy Istorii (Russian State Archive of Social and Political History; hereafter RGASPI), f. 513, op. 1, d. 69, l. 20.

43. RGASPI, f. 513, op. 1, d. 155, ll. 43, 50–55.

44. RGASPI, f. 513, op. 1, d. 180, ll. 132–38. On tension between center and periphery as a constant trait of the Comintern, see S. Wolikow, *L'internationale communiste (1919–43): Le Komintern ou le rêve déchu du parti Mondial de la révolution* (Paris: Editions de l'Atelier, 2010).

45. G. Sas, *Der Faschismus in Italien* (Hamburg: C. Hoym, 1923); D. Renton, *Fascism: Theory and Practice* (London: Pluto Press, 1999), pp. 58–60. See C. Natoli, *La Terza Internazionale e il fascismo* (Rome: Editori Riuniti, 1982), p. 286 et seq.

46. P. Togliatti. *La politica nel pensiero e nell'azione: Scritti e discorsi 1917–1964*, ed. M. Ciliberto and G. Vacca (Milan: Bompiani, 2014), pp. 43–67.

47. RGASPI, f. 513, op. 1, d. 187, ll. 14–17; and RGASPI, f. 513, op. 1, d. 166, ll. 6–11.

48. Fondazione Gramsci (hereafter FG), Partito Comunista d'Italia (hereafter PCd'I), Riunione della Commissione Italiana, 21 June 1923, box Ic 1922–25.

49. Gramsci, *La costruzione del partito comunista 1923–1926*, pp. 456–57; and also Spriano, *Storia del partito comunista italiano*, vol. 1, *Da Bordiga a Gramsci*, pp. 293–95; in English, *Selections from Political Writings 1921–1926*, pp. 154–46, here p. 155.

50. A. Tasca, *I primi dieci anni del PCI* (Rome and Bari: Laterza, 1973), p. 115.

51. G. Vacca, *Modernità alternative: Il novecento di Antonio Gramsci* (Turin: Einaudi, 2017), pp, 63–66; in English, *Alternative Modernities: Antonio Gramsci's Twentieth Century*, trans. D. Boothman and C. Dennis (Cham, Switzerland: Palgrave Macmillan, 2021), pp. 44–48.

52. Togliatti, *La formazione del gruppo dirigente* pp. 187–90; in English, Gramsci, *A Great and Terrible World, The Pre-Prison Letters* (London: Lawrence and Wishart, 2014), here p. 221; and, with an alternative wording, in *Selections from Political Writings 1921–1926*, p. 194.

53. Togliatti, *La formazione del gruppo dirigente*, p. 197; in English, *A Great and Terrible World*, p. 227; or, alternatively, *Selections from Political Writings 1921–1926*, p. 199.

54. Togliatti, *La formazione del gruppo dirigente*, p. 263; in English, *A Great and Terrible World*, p. 264.

55. [A. Gramsci], "Capo," *L'ordine nuovo*, 1 March 1924, now in Gramsci, *La costruzione del partito comunista*, pp. 12–16; in English, *Selections from Political Writings 1921–1926*, pp. 209–16. The actual words quoted are those of Zinoviev in the introduction to his *Works* (cf. Vacca, *Alternative Modernities*, p. 15).

56. [A. Gramsci], *Lettere 1908–1926*, ed. A. A. Santucci (Turin: Einaudi, 1992), p. 204; in English, *A Great and Terrible World*, p. 250. (Translator's note: In both the Fondazione Gramsci [Rome] and the Moscow Comintern archives, with this handwritten fragment there is a typed date of "10.I.24"—obviously wrong, since Lenin died on 21 January 1924. We tentatively assign the date of 20 March 1924; cf. the explanatory note on p. 300 of *A Great and Terrible World*.)

57. V. Serge, *Mémoires d'un révolutionaire de 1903 à 1941* (Paris: Éditions du Seuil, 1951), pp. 204–5.

58. On Gramsci in Vienna, see G. Somai, *Gramsci a Vienna: Ricerche e documenti 1922–24* (Urbino: Argalia, 1979); and F. Giasi, *Gramsci a Vienna: Annotazioni su quattro lettere inedite*, in F. Giasi, R. Gualtieri, and S. Pons, eds., *Pensare la politica* (Rome: Carocci, 2009), pp. 185–208.

59. [A. Gramsci], "Contro il pessimismo," in *L'ordine nuovo*, 15 March 1924, now in Gramsci, *La costruzione del partito comunista*, pp. 16–20; in English, "Against Pessimism," in *Selections from Political Writings 1921–1926*, here p. 214; or, alternatively, *Pre-Prison Writings*, pp. 255–59, here p. 257.

60. [A. Gramsci], *La costruzione del partito comunista*, p. 33. In English, see "The Italian Crisis" in *Selections from Political Writings 1921–1926*, pp. 258–59.

61. RGASPI, f. 513, op. 1, d. 243, l. 96, Executive Committee (CE) of the PCd'I to Zinoviev, 15 July 1924.

62. FG, PCd'I, *Lettre ouverte au Parti communiste italien*, 23 July 1924, box Ic 1922–25; RGASPI, f. 513, op. 1, d. 244, ll. 6–14.

63. A. Gagliardi, *Di fronte al fascismo: Gramsci e il dibattito nel movimento comunista internazionale*, in Capuzzo and Pons, eds., *Gramsci nel movimento comunista internazionale*, pp. 109–13.

64. Arkhiv Vneshnei Politiki Rossiiskoy Federatsii (Archive of the Foreign Policy of the Russian Federation; hereafter AVPRF), f. 098, op. 7, p. 107, d. 8, l. 68.

65. *Moskva-Rim: Politika i diplomatiya Kremlya 1920–39* (Moscow: Nauka, 2002), doc. 86, pp. 216–18.

66. E. Dundovich, *Bandiera rossa trionferà? L'Italia, la rivoluzione d'Ottobre e i rapport con Mosca 1917–1927* (Milan: FrancoAngeli, 2017), pp. 83–92; and G. Petracchi, *La Russia rivoluzionaria nella politica italiana: Le relazioni italo-sovietiche 1917–25* (Rome and Bari: Laterza, 1982), pp. 254–57.

67. In a letter to Zinoviev dated 25 November 1924, Manuilsky recorded the great sensation caused by Trotsky's intervention among the German, French, and Italian communists; cf. RGASPI, f. 324, op. 1, d. 551, ll. 87–89.

68. H. Weber, *Die Wandlung des Deutschen Kommunismus: Die Stalinisierung der KPD in der Weimarer Republik* (Frankfurt: Europäische Verlagsanstalt cop., 1969); It. trans., *La trasformazione del comunismo tedesco: La Stalinizzazione della KPD nella Repubblica di Weimar* (Milan: Feltrinelli, 1979), p. 102.

69. Gramsci, report to the Central Committee of the PCd'I, 6 February 1925, now in *La costruzione del partito comunista*, pp. 473–74; in English, see *Selections from Political Writings 1921–1926*, p. 284.

70. A. Di Biagio, *Coesistenza e isolazionismo: Mosca, il Comintern e l'Europa di Versailles (1918-1928)* (Rome: Carocci, 2004), p. 201.

71. RGASPI, f. 513, op. 1, d. 285, ll. 31-35.

72. Gramsci, *La costruzione del partito comunista*, p. 63; in English, see *Selections from Political Writings 1921-1926*, pp. 293-94.

73. Gramsci, *La costruzione del partito comunista*, pp. 302-3.

74. F. Giasi, "La bolscevizzazione tradotta in 'linguaggio storico italiano,'" in Capuzzo and Pons, eds., *Gramsci nel movimento comunista internazionale*, pp. 157-84.

75. P. Capuzzo, *La questione agraria e contadina*, in Capuzzo and Pons, eds., *Gramsci nel movimento comunista internazionale*, pp. 81-102.

76. AVPRF, f. 098, op. 20, p. 159, d. 51329, ll. 31-32.

77. C. Daniele, ed., *Gramsci a Roma, Togliatti a Mosca* (Turin: Einaudi, 1999), doc. 1, pp. 165, 168-70.

78. RGASPI, f. 513, op. l, d. 372, l. 11, minutes of the meeting of the Italian delegation, 23 February 1926.

79. *Gramsci a Roma, Togliatti a Mosca*, doc. 18, pp. 296-97.

80. *Gramsci a Roma, Togliatti a Mosca*, doc. 24, pp. 317-18.

81. *Gramsci a Roma, Togliatti a Mosca*, doc. 25, pp. 326-27.

82. P. Togliatti, *Opere*, vol. 3, 1926-29, ed. E. Ragionieri (Rome: Editori Riuniti, 1972), pp. 47-54.

83. *Gramsci a Roma, Togliatti a Mosca*, doc. 32, pp. 357-65.

84. Gramsci, *La costruzione del partito comunista*, pp. 113-24; in English, see *Selections from Political Writings 1921-1926*, pp. 400-411, here pp. 408-10; alternatively, *Pre-Prison Writings*, pp. 288-300, here pp. 296-98.

85. *I primi dieci anni di vita del Partito Comunista Italiano*, pp. 296-99.

86. Pons, *The Global Revolution*, p. 56 et seq.

87. Di Biagio, *Coesistenza e isolazionismo*, pp. 209-12.

88. Tooze, *The Deluge*, pp. 472-76.

89. *Gramsci a Roma, Togliatti a Mosca*, doc. 35, p. 376.

90. *Gramsci a Roma, Togliatti a Mosca*, doc. 37, p. 380.

91. [A. Gramsci], "L'URSS verso il comunismo," *L'unità*, 7 September 1926, now in Gramsci, *La costruzione del partito comunista*, pp. 315-19; and L. Paggi, *Le strategie del potere in Gramsci* (Rome: Editori Riuniti, 1984), pp. 353-54.

92. For a detailed reconstruction, see S. Pons, "Gramsci e il 'testamento' di Lenin," in G. Francioni and F. Giasi, eds., *Un nuovo Gramsci: Biografia, temi, interpretazioni* (Rome: Viella, 2019), pp. 95-111.

93. M. Eastman, *Since Lenin Died* (London: Labour Publishing Company, 1925; and New York: Boni and Liveright, 1925).

94. RGASPI, f. 17, op. 2, d. 246; S. Kotkin *Stalin*, vol. 1, *Paradoxes of Power 1878-1928* (New York: Penguin, 2014), p. 607.

95. *Gramsci a Roma, Togliatti a Mosca*, doc. 35, p. 376.

96. M. Eastman, "Lenin's 'Testament' at Last Revealed," *New York Times*, 18 October 1926.

97. *Gramsci a Roma, Togliatti a Mosca*, doc. 42, p. 376; in English, see *A Great and Terrible World*, ll. 370-76 (emphasis in Gramsci's original); or, in alternative wording, *Selections from Political Writings 1921-1926*, pp. 426-32, or *Pre-Prison Writings*, pp. 306-12.

98. RGASPI, f. 513, op. 1, d. 187, ll. 14-17; RGASPI, f. 513, op. 1, d. 166, ll. 6-11.

99. *Gramsci a Roma, Togliatti a Mosca*, doc. 35, pp. 404-12.

100. *Gramsci a Roma, Togliatti a Mosca*, doc. 42, p. 40; in English, see *A Great and Terrible World*, pp. 375 (emphasis in Gramsci's original); alternatively, *Selections from Political Writings 1921-1926*, p. 430, or *Pre-Prison Writings*, p. 310.

101. *Gramsci a Roma, Togliatti a Mosca*, doc. 45, pp. 420-21, 425. Letter from Togliatti to Gramsci of 18 October 1926; in English see *A Great and Terrible World*, p. 385; or, in alternative wording, *Selections from Political Writings 1921-1926*, pp. 433.

102. *Corriere della sera*, 19 October 1926.

103. *Gramsci a Roma, Togliatti a Mosca*, doc. 46, pp. 426-27.

104. *Gramsci a Roma, Togliatti a Mosca*, doc. 47, pp. 428-33.

105. *Gramsci a Roma, Togliatti a Mosca*, doc. 49, pp. 435-39. This is from Gramsci's letter to Togliatti of 26 October 1926; in English see *A Great and Terrible World*, pp. 378-81; or, in alternative wording, *Selections from Political Writings 1921-1926*, pp. 437-40 (emphasis and abbreviated forms in Gramsci's original).

106. G. Vacca, "Introduzione," in *Gramsci a Roma, Togliatti a Mosca*, pp. 138-39.

107. Kotkin, *Stalin*, vol. 1, pp. 389-90.

Chapter 2

1. E. Ragionieri, *Palmiro Togliatti: Per una biografia politica e intellettuale* (Roma: Editori Riuniti, 1976), pp. 205-10.

2. P. Togliatti, "Le basi sociali del fascismo" (1926), in Togliatti, *Opere*, vol. 2, pp. 28-38.

3. P. Togliatti, *Opere*, vol. 2, pp. 102, 108-9.

4. P. Togliatti, *Direttiva per lo studio delle questioni russe* (1927), in Togliatti, *Opere*, vol. 2, pp. 187-89.

5. P. Togliatti, *L'Italia fascista, focolaio di guerra* (1927), in Togliatti, *Opere*, vol. 2, pp. 142-47.

6. A. Di Biagio, "Togliatti e la lotta per la pace," in R. Gualtieri, C. Spagnolo and E. Taviani, eds., *Togliatti nel suo tempo*, Fondazione Istituto Gramsci, *Annali* 15 (Rome: Carocci, 2007), p. 112.

7. Togliatti, *Opere*, vol. 2, pp. 155-65.

8. G. M. Adibekov et al., eds., *Politburo TsK RKP(B)—VKP(B) i Komintern 1919-1943: Dokumenty* (Moscow: Rosspen, 2004), doc. 253, pp. 417-22.

9. Pons, *The Global Revolution*, pp. 59-60.

10. RGASPI, f. 495, op. 166, d. 29, l. 12. *Togliatti negli anni del Komintern (1926–1943): Documenti inediti dagli archivi russi*, ed. A. Agosti, Fondazione Istituto Gramsci, *Annali* 10 (1998) (Rome: Carocci, 2000), doc. 5.

11. A. Di Biagio, *Moscow, the Comintern and the War Scare*, in S. Pons and A. Romano, eds., *Russia in the Age of Wars 1914–1945*, Fondazione Giangiacomo Feltrinelli, *Annali* 34 (1998) (Milan: Feltrinelli, 2000), pp. 94–97.

12. Imlay, *The Practice of Socialist Internationalism*, pp. 160–64.

13. Iriye, *Cultural Internationalism and World Order*, p. 88.

14. Di Biagio, *Coesistenza e isolazionaismo*, p. 233 et seq.

15. Togliatti, *Opere*, vol. 2, pp. 299–303, 322.

16. A. Gagliardi, "Fascismo, socialismo, capitalismo: Angelo Tasca tra analisi economica e cultura politica," in D. Bidussa and G. Vacca, eds., *Il fascismo in tempo reale: Studi e ricerche di Angelo Tasca sulla genesi e l'evoluzione del fascismo in Europa 1926–1938* (Milan: Feltrinelli, 2014), pp. 3–18.

17. Togliatti, *Opere*, vol. 2, pp. 427–29.

18. Kotkin, *Stalin*, vol. 2, pp. 550–51.

19. G. Vacca, "Introduzione," in P. Togliatti, *Sul fascismo* (Rome and Bari: Laterza, 2004), pp. XLII–LII.

20. Togliatti, *Opere*, vol. 2, pp. 551–54.

21. RGASPI, f. 495, op. 29, d. 23. Cf. *Rossiiskaya Revolyutsiya: Komintern i Latinskaya Amerika* (Moscow: Rosspen, 2019), pp. 329–30.

22. "Il Congresso antimperialista di Bruxelles," *Lo stato operaio* 1, no. 1 (1927).

23. RGASPI, f. 513, op. 1, d. 644.

24. Ragionieri, *Palmiro Togliatti*, 360.

25. Imlay, *The Practice of Socialist Internationalism*, pp. 202–3. See also M. Goebbel, *Anti-Imperialist Metropolis: Inter-War Paris and the Seeds of Third World Nationalism* (Cambridge, UK: Cambridge University Press, 2015).

26. Togliatti, *Opere*, vol. 2, pp. 472–505.

27. S. Datta Gupta, *Communism and the Crisis of the Colonial System*, in Pons and Smith, eds., *The Cambridge History of Communism: I. World Revolution*, pp. 220–21.

28. Tasca, *I primi dieci anni del PCI*, p. 162.

29. *I primi dieci anni di vita del Partito Comunista Italiano*, 1928, docs. 16, 21, and 22, esp. pp. 576 and 583.

30. *I primi dieci anni di vita del Partito Comunista Italiano*, doc. 23, pp. 588–93.

31. "Pravyi uklon" v KPG i stalinizatsiya Kominterna: Stenogramma zasedaniya Prezidiuma Ikki po germanskomu voprosu 9 dekabrya 1928g, ed. A. Yu. Vatlin and Yu. T. Tutochkin (Moscow: Airo-XX, 1996); and J. Humbert-Droz, *De Lénine à Staline: Dix ans au service de l'Internationale Communiste 1921–1931* (Neuchatel, Switzerland: Éditions de la Baconnière, 1971), p. 341.

32. *I primi dieci anni di vita del Partito Comunista Italiano*, 1928, document 29, p. 617.

33. RGASPI, f. 558, op. 11, d. 763, ll. 50–52 and 54–56.

34. (Translator's note: The phrase "lord and master" occurs in canto 33, stanza 28 of Dante's *Inferno*, found in this wording in Longfellow's translation; while "moving everything" is Tasca's paraphrase of the last line of the *Paradiso*.)
35. *I primi dieci anni di vita del Partito Comunista Italiano*, 1928, doc. 12, p. 670.
36. Togliatti, *Opere*, vol. 2, pp. 672–73.
37. *I primi dieci anni di vita del Partito Comunista Italiano*, 1928, doc. 23, p. 592.
38. Ragionieri, *Palmiro Togliatti*, p. 389.
39. RGASPI, f. 558, op. 1, d. 2886.
40. Togliatti, *Opere*, vol. 2, pp. 739, 742, 743.
41. Togliatti, *Opere*, vol. 2, pp. 796–97. Cf. Ragionieri, *Palmiro Togliatti*, pp. 393–404.
42. Fondazione Feltrinelli, Fondo Tasca, PCI-PSI, f. 1, 1929 I, 12 July 1929.
43. A. Agosti, *Palmiro Togliatti* (Turin: Utet, 1996), p. 128.
44. E. J. Hobsbawm, *Interesting Times* (London: Allen Lane, 2001), pp. 138–39. See also M. Neumann, "Communism, Youth and Generation," in Pons and Smith, eds., *The Cambridge History of Communism: I. World Revolution*, pp. 484–87.
45. A. Höbel, *Luigi Longo: Una vita partigiana (1900–1945)* (Rome: Carocci, 2013), pp, 132–47; and M. Albeltaro, *Pietro Secchia, Le rivoluzioni non cadono dal cielo: Una vita di parte* (Rome and Bari: Laterza, 2014), pp. 45–54.
46. P. Capuzzo, "Identità e storia: La lunga ombra di Togliatti," in P. Capuzzo, ed., *Il Pci davanti alla sua storia: Al massimo consenso all'inizio del declino, Bologna 1976* (Rome: Viella, 2019), pp. 122–28.
47. Andreucci, *Da Gramsci a Occhetto*, pp. 115–24.
48. U. Terracini, *Sulla svolta* (Milan: La Pietra, 1965), pp. 26–27, 38.
49. Cf. D. Boothman, "The New Edition of Gramsci's 'Lettere dal carcere,'" *International Gramsci Journal* 4, no. 2 (2021), pp. 177–93, here p. 188.
50. RGASPI, f. 495, op. 221, d. 1826/1, ll. 122–28.
51. G. Vacca, *Vita e pensieri di Gramsci* (Turin: Einaudi, 2012), pp. 115, 119–26.
52. RGASPI, f. 82, op. 2, d. 99 (15 May 1931).
53. E. H. Carr, *The Twilight of the Comintern* (London: Macmillan, 1982), pp. 42–43, 246–47; and P. Togliatti, "La politica del partito comunista tedesco" (1931) in P. Togliatti *Opere*, vol. 3 (1929–35) (Rome: Editori Riuniti, 1973), tome 1, pp. 404–9.
54. Togliatti, *Opere*, vol. 3, tome 1, pp. 104–28.
55. RGASPI, f. 495, op. 221, d. 1, ll. 322–26.
56. RGASPI, f. 495, op. 221, d. 33/1.
57. M. Boarelli, *La fabbrica del passato: Autobiografie di militanti comunisti (1945–1956)* (Milan: Feltrinelli, 2007), pp. 63–85; and B. Studer, "Communism as Existential Choice," in Pons and Smith, eds., *The Cambridge History of Communism: I. World Revolution*, pp. 503–25.
58. T. Noce, *Rivoluzionaria professionale* (Milan: La Pietra, 1974), pp. 122–23.
59. G. Amendola, *Una scelta di vita* (Milan: Rizzoli, 1976), pp. 255–57. Cf. G. Cerchia, *Giorgio Amendola, un comunista nazionale: Dall'infanzia alla guerra partigiana (1907–1945)* (Soveria Mannelli: Rubbettino, 2004).

60. S. Kotkin, *Stalin: Waiting for Hitler, 1929–1941* (New York: Penguin, 2017), pp. 352–54.

61. On political faith among the Soviet elites, see Yu. Slezkine, *The House of Government: A Saga of the Russian Revolution* (Princeton, NJ: Princeton University Press, 2017).

62. Pons, *Gramsci e la rivoluzione russa*.

63. Ragionieri, *Togliatti*, p. 444.

64. Carr, *The Twilight of the Comintern*, p. 389.

65. P. Togliatti, "Sulla situazione tedesca" (1933) in Togliatti, *Opere*, vol. 3, tome 2, p. 177.

66. P. Togliatti, "La marcia del fascismo in Francia (1934), in Togliatti, *Opere*, vol. 3, tome 2, pp. 370–71.

67. G. Dimitrov, *Diario: Gli anni di Mosca (1934–1945)*, ed. S. Pons (Turin: Einaudi, 2002), pp. 11–14; cf. in English, *The Diary of Georgi Dimitrov, 1933–1949*, ed. I. Banac (New Haven, CT: Yale University Press, 2003).

68. Dimitrov, *Diario*, p. 26; and *Politburo TsK RKP(B)—VKP(B) I Komintern 1919–1943: Dokumenty*, doc. 438, pp. 701–3.

69. *Togliatti negli anni del Comintern*, p. 108.

70. Agosti, *Palmiro Togliatti*, p. 180 et seq.; and Wolikow, *L'Internationale communiste*, pp. 89–91.

71. Studer, *The Transnational World of the Cominternians*, pp. 104–7.

72. Bidussa and Vacca, eds., *Il fascismo in tempo reale*, pp. 424–34, 435–39, 469–72.

73. Gagliardi, *Di fronte al fascismo*, p. 122 et seq.

74. Vacca, "Introduzione," in Togliatti, *Sul fascismo*, p. LXXXIX et seq.

75. P. Togliatti, *Corso sugli avversari: Le lezioni sul fascismo*, ed. F. M. Biscione (Turin: Einaudi, 2010), pp. 72–74; in English, see *Lectures on Fascism*, trans. D. Dichter (New York: International Publishers, 1976, and London: Lawrence and Wishart, 1976).

76. See Giuliano Procacci's assessment, cited by F. M. Biscione in Togliatti, *Corso sugli avversari: Le lezioni sul fascismo*, p. 323.

77. See the considerations on the "dynamic dictatorships" in I. Kershaw, *To Hell and Back: Europe 1914–1990* (London: Penguin, 2015). On the despotism of the Stalinist state and the regressive aspects of Soviet modernization in the early 1930s, see A. Graziosi, *L'URSS di Lenin e Stalin: Storia dell'Unione Sovietica 1914–1945* (Bologna: Il Mulino, 2007), p. 363 et seq.

78. Togliatti, *Corso sugli avversari*, pp. 179–84.

79. On the notion of "passive revolution" and its nexus with international politics in Gramsci's notebooks, see Vacca, *Modernità Alternative*, pp. 135–49; in English, *Alternative Modernities*, pp. 128–43.

80. Among the many examples that could be cited, see P. Spriano, *Il compagno Ercoli: Togliatti segretario dell'Internazionale* (Rome: Editori Riuniti, 1980).

81. U. Terracini, *Al bando del partito: Carteggio clandestino dall'Isola e dall'esilio 1938-45* (Milan: La Pietra, 1976), pp. 13-36.

82. "Positeli kremlevskogo kabineta I. V. Stalina," *Istoricheskii Arkhiv* 1998, no. 4, p. 199; and *Pis'ma I. V. Stalina V. M. Molotovu 1925-1936 gg. Sbornik dokumentov* (Moscow: Rossiya Molodaya, 1995), p. 252.

83. A. Dallin and F. I. Firsov, eds., *Dimitrov and Stalin, 1934-1943: Letters from the Soviet Archives* (New Haven, CT, and London: Yale University Press, 2006), doc. 1, pp. 13-14.

84. F. De Felice, *Fascismo, democrazia, fronte popolare: Il movimento comunista alla svolta del VII Congresso dell'Internazionale* (Bari: De Donato, 1973), p. 21.

85. P. Togliatti, *La preparazione di una nuova guerra mondiale da parte degli imperialisti e i compiti dell'Internazionale comunista* (1935) in Togliatti, *Opere*, vol. 3, tome 2, pp. 732-39; in English, see Togliatti's speech as published in the pamphlet *On the Tasks of the Communist International in Connection With the Preparation by the Imperialists for a New World War*, whose phrases cited in the text are found on pp. 86, 80 and 95 respectively. Cf. also G. Sapelli, *L'analisi economica dei comunisti italiani durante il fascismo* (Milan: Feltrinelli, 1978), pp. 71-72.

86. Togliatti, *Opere*, vol. 3, tome 2, pp. 799, 812-14. The English phrases used, with their page numbers, are those of the report by "M. Ercoli" in pamphlet form: *The Fight for Peace* (New York: Workers Library, 1935), accessed 4 May 2022 at https://stars.library.ucf.edu/prism/682/.

87. S. Pons, *Stalin and the Inevitable War (1936-1941)* (London: Routledge, 2014).

88. RGASPI, f. 558, op. 2, d. 89, l. 1.

89. G. Procacci, *Il socialismo internazionale e la guerra d'Etiopia* (Rome: Editori Riuniti, 1978).

90. R. Grieco, "I compiti del popolo italiano nella lotta contro la guerra," *Lo Stato operaio* 9, no. 10 (1935).

91. P. Togliatti, *Opere*, vol. 4 (1935-44), tome 1, F. Andreucci and P. Spriano, eds. (Rome: Editori Riuniti, 1979), pp. 23-28, 33-35.

92. G. Candreva, "Nazionalismo e comunismo di fronte alla guerra d'Etiopia," *História: Debates e tendências* 8, no. 1 (1913), pp. 150-66; A. Mattone, *Velio Spano: Vita di un rivoluzionario di professione* (Cagliari: Della Torre, 1978).

93. RGASPI, f. 527, op. 1, d. 14,. ll. 42, 44, 56-57.

94. G. Procacci, *Dalla parte dell'Etiopia* (Milan: Feltrinelli, 1984); and N. Srivastava, *Italian Colonialism and Resistance to Empire, 1930-1970* (London: Palgrave Macmillan, 2018).

95. L. P. D'Alessandro, "Per la salvezza d'Italia: I comunisti italiani, il problema del fronte popolare e l'appello ai 'fratelli in camicia nera,'" *Studi storici* 54, no. 4 (2013), pp. 951-88.

96. Studer, *The Transnational World of the Cominternists*, pp. 128-35.

97. Agosti, *Palmiro Togliatti*, pp. 197-98.

98. RGASPI f. 531, op. 1, d. 72, ll. 21-32.

99. RGASPI, f. 495, op. 73, d. 12, l. 72. For a reconstruction of the debate of March-April 1936 in the Comintern, see Pons, *Stalin and the Inevitable War*, ch. 1.

100. RGASPI, f. 495, op. 3, d. 222, ll. 20–24.

101. *Dimitrov and Stalin*, doc. 8.

102. Togliatti, "Sulle particolarità della rivoluzione spagnola" (1936), in Togliatti, *Opere*, vol. 4, tome 1, pp. 139–54.

103. E. J. Hobsbawm, "Gli intellettuali e l'antifascismo," in *Storia del marxismo*, vol. 3, *Il marxismo nell'età della Terza Internazionale*, tome 2, dalla crisi del '29 al XX Congresso (Turin: Einaudi, 1981), p. 485.

104. G. Procacci, "La 'lotta per la pace' nel socialismo internazionale," in *Storia del marxismo*, vol. 3, p. 578 et seq.; see also S. Wolikow, *L'Internationale Communiste*, pp. 193–95.

105. L. A. Kirschenbaum, *International Communism and the Spanish Civil War: Solidarity and Suspicion* (Cambridge, UK: Cambridge University Press, 2015), pp. 111–15.

106. L. P. D'Alessandro, *Guadalajara 1937: I volontari italiani fascisti e antifascisti nella guerra di Spagna* (Rome: Carocci, 2017).

107. Dimitrov, *Diario*, pp. 71–72.

108. F. I. Firsov, H. Klehr, and J. E. Haynes, *Secret Cables of the Comintern 1933–1943* (New Haven, CT, and London: Yale University Press, 2014), pp. 72–74.

109. P. Karlsen, *Vittorio Vidali: Vita di uno stalinista (1916–1956)* (Bologna: Il Mulino, 2019), pp. 173–98.

110. Höbel, *Luigi Longo, una vita partigiana*, p. 237 et seq.

111. FG, Archivio del partito comunista italiano (Archive of the Italian Communist Party, hereafter APCI), Togliatti's manuscripts relative to his stay in Spain, b. 2010/4. See also the assessment of G. Ranzato, *L'eclissi della democrazia: La guerra civile spagnola e le sue origini* (Turin: Bollati Boringhieri, 2004), p. 579.

112. R. Radosh, M. R. Habeck, and G. Sevastianov, eds., *Spain Betrayed: The Soviet Union in the Spanish Civil War* (New Haven, CT: Yale University Press, 2001).

113. Pons, *Stalin and the Inevitable War*, pp. 51–52.

114. W. J. Chase, *Enemies within the Gates? The Comintern and the Stalinist Repression, 1934–1939* (New Haven, CT: Yale University Press, 2001).

115. Karlsen, *Vittorio Vidali*, p. 199.

116. A. Elorza and M. Bizcarrondo, *Queridos camaradas: La Internacional comunista y España* (Barcelona: Planeta, 1999), p. 398 et seq.

117. Dimitrov, *Diario*, p. 87 (17 February 1938); also Firsov, Klehr, and Haynes, *Secret Cables*, pp. 78–79.

118. Dimitrov, *Diario*, p. 91 (27 August 1938).

119. RGASPI, f. 495, op. 74, d. 250.

120. RGASPI, f. 495, op. 10a, d. 182.

121. E. Dundovich, F. Gori, and E. Guercetti, "Italian Emigration in the USSR: History of a Repression" in *Reflections on the Gulag: With a Documentary Appendix on the Italian Victims of Repression in the USSR*, Fondazione Giangiacomo Feltrinelli,

Annali 37 (2001) (Milan: Feltrinelli, 2003), pp. 139–86; and E. Dundovich, *Tra Esilio e castigo: La repression degli italiani in URSS (1936–1938)* (Rome: Carocci, 1998). On the origins of the Italian community in the Soviet Union, see F. Lussana, *In Russia prima del Gulag: Emigrati italiani a scuola di comunismo* (Rome: Carocci, 2007).

122. RGASPI, f. 495, op. 10a, d. 182.

123. Togliatti, "Antonio Gramsci: Capo della classe operaia italiana (1937)," in Togliatti, *Opere*, vol. 4, pp. 199–231.

124. RGASPI, f. 495, op. 74, d. 250, ll. 130–40.

125. RGASPI, fond 513, op. 1, d. 1494, minutes of the Secretariat, 16 September 1938.

126. *Palmiro Togliatti: La politica nel pensiero e nell'azione*, p. 444.

127. RGASPI, f. 513, op. 1, d. 1494.

128. RGASPI., f. 495, op. 74, d. 254, l. 35.

129. Firsov, Klehr, and Haynes, *Secret Cables*, pp. 82–83; Togliatti, *Opere*, vol. 4, pp. 325–32. On the concluding events of the Spanish Civil War and Togliatti's role, see Ranzato, *L'eclissi della democrazia*, p. 647 et seq.

130. Dimitrov, *Diario*, pp. 166–67.

131. RGASPI, f. 495, op. 10, d. 409a, ll. 49–50.

132. See Dundovich, Gori, and Guercetti, eds., *Reflections on the Gulag*, pp. 528–52. Also P. Robotti, *Scelto dalla vita* (Rome: Napoleone, 1980).

133. S. Pons, "L'affare Gramsci-Togliatti' a Mosca (1938–1941)," *Studi storici* 45, no. 1 (2004), pp. 83–117.

134. Dimitrov, *Diario*, pp. 194–95.

135. C. Negarville, *Clandestino a Parigi: Diario di un comunista nella Francia in guerra (1940–1943)*, ed. with an introduction by A. Agosti (Rome: Donzelli, 2020), p. 123.

136. G. Amendola, *Intervista sull'antifascismo* (Rome and Bari: Laterza, 1976), p. 157.

137. Terracini, *Al bando del partito*, pp. 49–50.

138. U. Terracini, *Intervista sul comunismo difficile*, ed. A. Gismondi (Rome and Bari: Laterza, 1978), pp. 123–24, and C. Ravera, *Diario di trent'anni (1913-1943)* (Rome: Editori Riuniti, 1973), p. 637. Cf. S. Bertelli, *Il gruppo la formazione del gruppo dirigente del PCI 1936-1948* (Milan: Rizzoli, 1980), pp. 90–92; P. Spriano, *I comunisti europei e Stalin* (Turin: Einaudi, 1983), p. 103; Höbel, *Luigi Longo, una vita partigiana*, pp. 296–97.

139. Agosti, *Palmiro Togliatti*, p. 254.

140. RGASPI, f. 495, op. 221, d. 2, l. 73.

141. E. Fischer, *Erinnerungen und Reflexionen* (Hamburg: Rohwohlt, 1969), pp. 423–24; in Italian, *Ricordi e riflessioni* (Rome: Editori Riuniti, 1973), pp. 510–11.

142. Pons, *L'affare Gramsci-Togliatti' a Mosca*.

143. RGASPI, f. 495, op. 74, d. 253, l. 73.

144. P. Spriano, *Storia del partito comunista italiano*, vol. 4, *La fine del fascismo: Dalla riscossa operaia alla lotta armata* (Turin: Einaudi, 1973), p. 30.

145. Dimitrov, *Diario*, pp. 243 (16 November 1940) and 271 (11 February 1941).
146. Dimitrov, *Diario*, pp. 302–3 (20 and 21 April 1941).
147. M. Lazar, "The French Communist Party," in N. Naimark, S. Pons, and S. Quinn-Judge, eds., *The Cambridge History of Communism: II. The Socialist Camp and World Power 1941–1960s* (Cambridge, UK: Cambridge University Press, 2017), pp. 631–32.
148. Dimitrov, *Diario*, p. 321 (23 June 1941).
149. Dimitrov, *Diario*, p. 330 (12 July 1941), 333 (19 July 1941).
150. A. Roasio, *Figlio della classe operaia* (Milan: Vangelista, 1977), p. 173.
151. Negarville, *Clandestino a Parigi*.
152. RGASPI, f. 519, op. 1, d. 114, ll. 9–10.

Chapter 3

1. Pons, *The Global Revolution*, pp. 116–17. See Dimitrov, *Diario*, p. 618.
2. For a reconstruction of the events of Togliatti's life between 1941 and 1943, see G. Fiocco, *Togliatti, il realismo della politica* (Rome: Carocci, 2018), pp. 159–64. For detailed analysis of the question of prisoners of war, see M. T. Giusti, *I prigionieri italiani in Russia* (Bologna: Il Mulino, 2014).
3. C. Pavone, *Una guerra civile: Saggio storico sulla moralità della Resistenza* (Turin: Bollati Boringhieri, 1991), p. 26.
4. R. Forlenza, *On the Edge of Democracy: Italy, 1943–48* (Oxford, UK, and New York: Oxford University Press, 2019); E. Aga Rossi, *Una nazione allo sbando: L'armistizio italiano del settembre 1943 e le sue conseguenze* (Bologna: Il Mulino, 2003); and M. Fioravanti and C. Fumian, eds., *1943: Strategie militari, collaborazionismi, Resistenze* (Rome: Viella, 2015).
5. Gori and Pons, *Dagli archivi di Mosca: L'URSS, Il Cominform e il PCI*, Fondazione Istituto Gramsci, *Annali* 7 (1995) (Rome: Carocci, 1995), docs. 1 and 2, pp. 223–25.
6. Gori and Pons, *Dagli archivi di Mosca*, doc. 4, pp. 227–29.
7. AVPRF, f. 07. op. 4, p. 30, d. 37, ll. 12–16.
8. Gori and Pons, *Dagli archivi di Mosca*, doc. 6, p. 231.
9. RGASPI, f. 495, op. 221, d. 1, l. 256.
10. Terracini, *Intervista sul comunismo difficile*, p. 148; Bertelli, *Il gruppo*, p. 215.
11. RGASPI, f. 495, op. 221, d. 2, ll. 47–48ob.
12. Höbel, *Luigi Longo, una vita partigiana*, p. 148; and Albertaro, *Le rivoluzioni non cadono dal cielo*, pp. 93, 110–11.
13. P. Spriano, *Storia del Partito comunista italiano*, vol. 5, *La Resistenza, Togliatti e il partito nuovo* (Turin: Einaudi, 1975), p. 110 et seq.; G. Amendola, *Lettere a Milano 1939–45* (Rome: Editori Riuniti, 1974).
14. A. J. Rieber, *Anti-Fascist Resistance Movements in Europe and Asia*, in Naimark, Pons, and Quinn-Judge, eds., *The Cambridge History of Communism: II. The Socialist Camp*, pp. 38–46.
15. AVPRF, f. 07, op. 5, p. 53, d. 230a, ll. 1–2.

16. Gori and Pons, *Dagli archivi di Mosca*, doc. 8, p. 223, and Dimitrov, *Diario*, p. 681.

17. RGASPI, f. 495, op. 166, d. 29, l. 12.

18. Gori and Pons, *Dagli archivi di Mosca*, doc. 9, pp. 234-38; and Dimitrov, *Diario*, p. 689.

19. For the thesis regarding the influence exerted from December 1943 by Italian diplomacy on Vyshinsky in favor of the accord between the Soviet Union and Italy, concluded in March 1944, see E. Di Nolfo and M. Serra, *La gabbia infranta: Gli alleati e l'Italia dal 1943 al 1945* (Rome and Bari: Laterza, 2010); and M. Clementi, *L'alleato Stalin: L'ombra sovietica sull'Italia di Togliatti e De Gasperi* (Milan: Rizzoli, 2011).

20. RGASPI, f. 495, op. 74, d. 259, l. 7.

21. Dimitrov, *Diario*, p. 691-93; RGASPI, f. 495, op. 74, d. 259, l. 8.

22. For a reconstruction of the whole incident based on Soviet archives, see S. Pons, *L'impossibile egemonia: L'URSS, il PCI le origini della guerra fredda (1943-1948)* (Rome: Carocci, 1999), ch. 3. See also Pons, *Togliatti e Stalin*, in Gualtieri, Spagnolo, and Taviani, eds., *Togliatti nel suo tempo*, pp. 195-214.

23. On this interpretation, see E. Aga Rossi and V. Zaslavsky, *Togliatti e Stalin: Il PCI e la politica estera Stalinista negli archivi di Mosca* (Bologna: Il Mulino, 1997). See E. Aga Rossi, *L'Italia tra le grandi potenze: Dalla seconda guerra mondiale alla guerra fredda* (Bologna: Il Mulino, 1919), p. 325 et seq.

24. B. Croce, *Taccuini di guerra*, ed. C. Cassani (Milan: Adelphi, 2004), p. 109.

25. RGASPI, f. 495, op. 10a, d. 433b, ll. 143-46.

26. AVPRF, f. 098, op. 27, p. 159, d. 11, ll. 103-8.

27. E. Collotti, "Introduzione," in *Archivio Pietro Secchia 1945-1973*, ed. E. Collotti, Fondazione Giangiacomo Feltrinelli, *Annali* 19 (1978) (Milan: Feltrinelli, 2004), p. 74.

28. RGASPI, f. 558, op. 11, d. 283, ll. 12-13.

29. E. Kardelj, *Memorie degli anni di ferro* (Rome: Editori Riuniti, 1980), pp. 39, 40.

30. Pons, *L'impossibile egemonia*, pp. 73, 77-78.

31. FG, APCI, Directorate, minutes, 16-18 December 1944. See R. Gualtieri, *Togliatti e la politica estera italiana: Dalla Resistenza al Trattato di pace 1943-1947* (Rome: Editori Riuniti, 1995), pp. 50 ff.

32. Iriye, *Cultural Internationalism and World Order*, pp. 138-39; and G. Sluga, *Internationalism in the Age of Nationalism*, p. 81 et seq.

33. Dimitrov, *Diario*, p. 696.

34. Togliatti, *La politica nel pensiero e nell'azione*, pp. 567, 574-75, 578 (11 April 1944).

35. Dimitrov, *Diario*, pp. 725-26.

36. D. Forgacs and S. Gundal, *Mass Culture and Italian Society from Fascism to the Cold War* (Bloomington and Indianapolis: Indiana University Press, 2007), p. 260.

37. M. Tambor, *The Lost Wave: Women and Democracy in Postwar Italy* (Oxford, UK: Oxford University Press, 2014).
38. G. Pajetta, *Il ragazzo rosso* (Milan: Mondadori, 1983).
39. RGASPI, f. 17, op. 128, d. 799, l. 282.
40. AVPRF, f. 098, op. 27, p. 159, d. 9, l. 3.
41. AVPRF, f. 06, op. 7, p. 34, d. 480, l. 69.
42. On the Italian Communists and the question of Trieste, see the synthesis of Fiocco, *Togliatti, il realismo della politica*, pp. 195-201. In greater detail, L. Gibianskii, "Mosca, il PCI e la questione di Trieste," in Gori and Pons, *Dagli archivi di Mosca*, pp. 85-133.
43. AVPRF, f. 098, op. 26, p. 152, d. 8, ll. 266-67.
44. AVPRF, f. 098, op. 26, p. 152, d. 8, l. 370.
45. FG, APCI, Fondo Mosca, microfilm 272, p. 152, 13 May 1945.
46. Gori and Pons, *Dagli archivi di Mosca*, doc. 11, pp. 240-41.
47. Dimitrov, *Diario*, p. 838.
48. AVPRF, f. 098, op. 26, p. 152, d. 8, l. 403.
49. FG, APCI, Palmiro Togliatti, Carte Ferri Amadesi, 1945, *discorsi*, intervention at the Directorate, 5 August 1945, p. 22.
50. Gori and Pons, *Dagli archivi di Mosca*, doc. 12, 13 and 14, pp. 256, 260-61, 264.
51. Togliatti, *La politica nel pensiero e nell'azione*, p. 679.
52. A. Brogi, *Confronting America: The Cold War between the United States and the Communists in France and Italy* (Chapel Hill: University of North Carolina Press, 2011), pp. 38-39.
53. Formigoni, *Storia d'Italia nella guerra fredda (1943-1978)*, p. 59.
54. P. Togliatti, *La guerra di posizione in Italia: Epistolario 1944-1964*, ed. G. Fiocco and M. L. Righi (Turin: Einaudi, 2014), doc. 22, pp. 76-78.
55. Forlenza, *On the Edge of Democracy*, p. 59.
56. G. Cerchia, *Giorgio Amendola: Gli anni della Repubblica (1945-1980)* (Turin: Cerbona, 2009), pp. 86-90.
57. *La politica del Partito comunista italiano nel periodo costituente, I. Minutes of the Directorate between the Fifth and Sixth Congresses, 1946-1948*, ed. R. Martinelli and M. L. Righi, Fondazione Istituto Gramsci, *Annali 2* (1990) (Rome: Editori Riuniti, 1992), p. 573.
58. *Cold War International History Project Bulletin* 10 (1998), pp. 113-15, 127, 135; and A. Nevezhin, *Zastol'nye rechi Stalina* (Moscow and St Petersburg: Airo-XX, 2003), p. 484.
59. AVPRF, f. 098, op. 29, p. 165, d. 10, l. 126.
60. FG, APCI, Fondo Mosca, microfilm 222, pacco 2, 29 June 1946.
61. FG, Palmiro Togliatti, Carte della scrivania, 19 June 1946.
62. Pons, *L'impossibile egemonia*, pp. 173-74.
63. On the notion of "people's democracy" and its limits, see N. Naimark, "Stalin e la lotta degli europei per la sovranità," in S. Pons, ed., *Globalizzazioni rosse: Studi sul comunismo nel mondo del Novecento* (Rome: Carocci, 2020),

pp. 91–108. See also F. Bettanin, *Stalin e l'Europa: La formazione dell'impero esterno sovietico (1941–1953)* (Rome: Carocci, 2020), pp. 169–81.

64. FG, APCI, Central Committee, minutes, 18 September 1946.

65. Dimitrov, *Diario*, p. 802.

66. Pons, *L'impossibile egemonia*, p. 89.

67. D. Sassoon, *Togliatti e il partito di massa: Il PCI dal 1944 al 1964* (Rome: Castelvecchi, 2014).

68. G. Vacca, "Togliatti e la storia d'Italia," in Gualtieri, Spagnolo, and Taviani, eds., *Togliatti nel suo tempo*, pp. 3–21; and E. Gentile, *La grande Italia : Ascesa e declino del mito della nazione nel Ventesimo secolo* (Milan: Mondadori, 1997), pp. 328–35.

69. Pavone, *Una guerra civile*, pp. 179–80; R. Forlenza and B. Thomassen, *Italian Modernities: Competing Narratives of Nationhood* (New York: Palgrave, 2016), pp. 193–201; and R. Colozza, *Repubbliche comuniste: I simboli nazionali del Pci e del Pcf (1944–1953)* (Bologna: Clueb, 2009). On the more general implications in the history of the Italian Republic, see F. Focardi, *La guerra della memoria: La Resistenza nel dibattito politico italiano dal 1945 a oggi* (Rome and Bari: Laterza, 2005); and P. Craveri and G. Quagliarello, eds.) *La Seconda Guerra Mondiale e la sua memoria* (Soveria Mannelli, Italy: Rubbettino, 2006).

70. Andreucci, *Da Gramsci a Occhetto*, p. 254 et seq.; and M. Degl'Innocenti, *Il mito di Stalin: Comunisti e socialisti nell'Italia del dopoguerra* (Manduria, Italy: Lacaita, 2005).

71. G. Formigoni, *La Democrazia Cristiana e l'Alleanza occidentale (1943–1953)* (Bologna: Il Mulino, 1996), p. 48.

72. A. J. McAdams, *Vanguard of the Revolution: The Global Idea of the Communist Party* (Princeton, NJ: Princeton University Press, 2017), pp. 245–58.

73. F. Romero and A. Varsori, eds., *Nazione, interdipendenza, integrazione: Le relazioni internazionali dell'Italia (1917–1989)*, 2 vols. (Rome: Carocci, 2005).

74. See, for example, E. Galli Della Loggia, *Credere tradire vivere: Un viaggio negli anni della Repubblica* (Bologna: Il Mulino, 2016); and G. Crainz, *Autobiografia di una Repubblica: Le radici dell'Italia attuale* (Rome: Donzelli, 2009).

75. T. Judt, *Postwar: A History of Europe since 1945* (London: Penguin, 2005), pp. 63–67; Kershaw, *To Hell and Back*, pp. 488–89; and Jarausch, *Out of the Ashes*, pp. 411–12.

76. Gualtieri, *Togliatti e la politica estera italiana*, pp. 198–201.

77. *La politica del Partito comunista italiano nel periodo costituente*, p. 465.

78. RGASPI, f. 17, op. 128, d. 1101, l. 142.

79. FG, APCI, Central Committee, minutes, 1 July 1947.

80. RGASPI, f. 82, op. 2, d. 1231, ll. 26–27.

81. Brogi, *Confronting America*, pp. 82–83.

82. M. Gilas [i.e., Đilas], *Se la memoria non m'inganna* (Bologna: Il Mulino, 1987), p. 144.

83. FG, APCI, Central Committee, minutes, 1 July 1947.

84. P. Togliatti, *Discorsi parlamentari*, vol. 1, 1946–51 (Rome: Camera dei Deputati, 1984), p. 167.

85. G. Dimitrov, *Dnevnik*, 9 March 1933–6 February 1949 (Sofia: Universitetsko izdatelstvo "Sv. Kliment Okhridski," 1997), p. 556.

86. *Archivio Pietro Secchia*, p. 208.

87. E. Reale, *Nascita del Cominform* (Milan: Mondadori, 1958), p. 17.

88. G. Procacci, ed., *The Cominform: Minutes of the Three Conferences 1947/1948/1949*, Fondazione Giangiacomo Feltrinelli, *Annali* 30 (1994) (Milan: Feltrinelli, 1994), pp. 217–51.

89. RGASPI, f. 77, op. 3, d. 92, ll. 48–49.

90. *The Cominform*, pp. 299–301, 313–26.

91. Reale, *Nascita del Cominform*, p. 39.

92. *La politica del Partito comunista italiano nel periodo costituente*, pp. 498, 500.

93. *La politica del Partito comunista italiano nel periodo costituente*, pp. 499–500, 507, 520.

94. *La politica del Partito comunista italiano nel periodo costituente* pp. 525–26.

95. AVPRF, f. 098, op. 30, p. 170, d. 13, ll. 158–9.

96. A. Agosti, ed., *La coerenza della ragione: Per una biografia politica di Umberto Terracini* (Rome: Carocci, 1998).

97. See the brief note on the front page of *L'unità*, 23 October 1947; and *Terracini precisa e rettifica le sue affermazioni*, *L'unità*, 24 October 1947.

98. FG, APCI, Central Committee, minutes, 11 November 1947.

99. AVPRF, f. 098, op. 30, p. 170, d. 13, l. 187.

100. E. Bernardi, "La Democrazia Cristiana e la guerra fredda," in *Ventunesimo secolo* 5, no. 10 (2006), pp. 127–66; and Formigoni, *La Democrazia Cristiana e l'Alleanza occidentale*, p. 166 et seq.

101. RGASPI, f. 17, op. 128, d. 1101, l. 184; RGASPI., f. 77, op. 3, d. 90, ll. 86–90; and Gori and Pons, *Dagli archivi di Mosca*, docs. 18 and 19, pp. 276–88.

102. Gori and Pons, *Dagli archivi di Mosca*, doc. 20, pp. 289–93.

103. Collotti, *Introduzione*, p. 102.

104. RGASPI, f. 17, op. 128, d. 1101, l. 189; Gori and Pons, *Dagli archivi di Mosca*, doc. 22.

105. RGASPI, f. 17, op. 128, doc. 1074; Gori and Pons, *Dagli archivi di Mosca*, doc. 21, pp. 294–307; and *Archivio Pietro Secchia*, pp. 618–27.

106. Gori and Pons, *Dagli archivi di Mosca*, doc. 20, p. 292.

107. *Istoricheskii Arkhiv* 1996, no. 1, p. 11.

108. For a reconstruction of Secchia's mission to Moscow, see Pons, *L'impossibile egemonia*, ch. 4.

109. RGASPI, f. 17, op. 128, d. 1159, l. 54.

110. AVPRF, f. 098, op. 31, p. 179, d. 15, l. 124. Immediately after Tito's excommunication by the Cominform, on 30 June 1948, Matteo Secchia mentioned to Kostylev these words of Togliatti, pronounced in a confidential setting in January 1948 during the Sixth Congress of the PCI. Togliatti's collaborator also

acknowledged their error of having seen Yugoslavia "as our rear area in the case of a conflict with the Americans."

111. N. Naimark, *Stalin and the Fate of Europe: The Postwar Struggle for Sovereignty* (Cambridge, MA, and London: Harvard University Press, 2019), pp. 136-39; Brogi, *Confronting America*, pp. 101-10; and J. L. Gaddis, *George F. Kennan: An American Life* (New York: Penguin, 2011), p. 305.

112. AVPRF, f. 098, op. 31, p. 180, d. 17, ll. 24-25.

113. Aga Rossi and Zaslavsky, *Togliatti e Stalin*, pp. 232-33.

114. AVPRF, f. 098, op. 31, p. 179, d. 14, ll. 197-99.

115. AVPRF, f. 098, op. 31, p. 179, d. 14, l. 162.

116. Pons, *L'impossibile egemonia*, p. 233n157.

117. On De Gasperi's moderate conduct in 1948, see P. Craveri, *De Gasperi* (Bologna: Il Mulino, 2006), pp. 343-44, 365-66.

118. K. Mistry, *The United States, Italy, and the Origins of the Cold War: Waging Political Warfare, 1945-1950* (Cambridge, UK: Cambridge University Press, 2014).

119. AVPRF, f. 098, op. 31, p. 179, d. 15, l. 48.

120. M. Del Pero, *L'alleato scomodo: Gli USA e la DC negli anni del centrismo (1948-1955)* (Rome: Carocci, 2001), pp. 57-59.

121. RGASPI, f. 77, op. 3, d. 106, l. 18.

122. *The Cominform*, p. 585.

123. G. Gozzini, R. Martinelli, *Storia del Partito comunista italiano, vol. VII: Dal attentato a Togliatti all'VIII Congresso* (Turin: Einaudi, 1998), pp. 36-37; and E. Macaluso, *50 anni nel PCI* (Soveria Manelli, Italy: Rubbettino, 2003), pp. 58-59.

124. AVPRF, f. 098, op. 31, p. 180, d. 16, l. 7.

125. FG, APCI, Central Committee, minutes, 24-29 September 1948.

126. Naimark, *Stalin and the Fate of Europe*, p. 268.

127. Del Pero, *L'alleato scomodo*.

128. F. Romero, *Storia della guerra fredda: L'ultimo conflitto per l'Europa* (Turin, Einaudi, 2009), pp. 70-72; and M. Antonioli, M. Bergamaschi, and F. Romero, eds., *Le scissioni sindacali: Italia e Europa* (Pisa: Bfs Edizioni, 1999).

129. Aga Rossi and Zaslavsky, *Togliatti e Stalin*, pp. 217 ff.; V. Zaslavsky, *Lo Stalinismo e la sinistra italiana: Dal mito dell'Urss al fine del comunismo (1945-1991)* (Milan: Mondadori, 2004); M. Caprara, *Lavoro riservato: I cassetti segreti del PCI* (Milan: Feltrinelli, 1997); G. Pacini, *Le altre Gladio* (Turin: Einaudi, 2014).

130. P. Cooke, "Red Spring: Italian Political Emigration to Czechoslovakia," *Journal of Modern History* 84, no. 4 (2012), pp. 861-96.

131. M. Caprara, *Quando le botteghe erano oscure: Uomini e storie del comunismo italiano, 1944-1969* (Milan: Il Saggiatore, 1997), pp. 105-7; and Gozzini and Martinelli, *Storia del Partito comunista italiano*, vol. 7, p. 153.

132. V. Riva, *Oro da Mosca: I finanziamenti sovietici al PCI dalla Rivoluzione d'Ottobre al crollo dell'URSS* (Milan: Mondadori, 1999).

133. A. Tonelli, *A scuola di politica: Il modello comunista di Frattocchie (1944-1993)* (Rome and Bari: Laterza, 2017).

134. Brogi, *Confronting America*, pp. 162 ff.

135. N. Naimark, "The Sovietization of East Central Europe 1945–1989," in Naimark, Pons, and Quinn-Judge, eds., *Cambridge History of Communism*, vol. 2, *The Socialist Camp*, pp. 66–74.

136. A. Guiso, *La colomba e la spada: "Lotta per la pace" e antiamericanismo nella politica del Partito comunista italiano (1949–1954)* (Soveria Mannelli, Italy: Rubbettino, 2006).

137. Archives of the Hoover Institution, Dmitrii A. Volkogonov papers, box 27, reel 18, 6 January 1949.

138. Togliatti, *Discorsi Parlamentari*, vol. 1, 15 March 1949, p. 416.

139. FG, APCI, Directorate, minutes, 29 March 1949.

140. Formigoni, *Storia d'Italia nella guerra fredda*, pp. 142–52; and Craveri, *De Gasperi*, 368–84.

141. M. De Nicolò, *Emilio Sereni, la guerra fredda e la "pace partigiana": Movimenti sociali e ideologie politiche in Italia (1948–1955)* (Rome: Carocci, 2019), p. 54 ff.

142. Brogi, *Confronting America*, pp. 123–36.

143. F. Andreucci, *Falce e martello: Identità e linguaggi dei comunisti italiani fra stalinismo e guerra fredda* (Bologna: Bononia University Press, 2006).

144. Forlenza, *On the Edge of Democracy*, pp. 110–11. See M. Fincardi, *C'era una volta il mondo nuovo: La metafora sovietica nello sviluppo emiliano* (Rome: Carocci, 2007).

145. Boarelli, *La fabbrica del passato*. Communist memoirs to a great extent converge on this point. See in particular P. Ingrao, *Volevo la luna* (Turin: Einaudi, 2006); and G. Napolitano, *Dal Pci al socialismo europeo: Un'autobiografia politica* (Rome and Bari: Laterza, 2005).

146. P. P. D'Attorre, ed., *Nemici per la pelle: Sogno americano e mito sovietico nell'Italia contemporanea* (Milan: FrancoAngeli, 1991); Gozzini and Martinelli, *Storia del Partito comunista italiano*, vol. 7, pp. 456–68; and D. Saresella, *Catholics and Communists in Twentieth-Century Italy: Between Conflict and Dialogue* (London: Bloomsbury Academic, 2019).

147. Forgacs and Gundle, *Mass Culture and Italian Society from Fascism to the Cold War*, p. 262.

148. A. Vittoria, *Togliatti e gli intellettuali: La politica culturale dei comunisti italiani (1944–1964)* (Rome: Carocci, 2014).

149. A. Mariuzzo, *Communism and Anti-Communism in Early Cold War Italy: Language, Symbols and Myths* (Manchester, UK: Manchester University Press, 2018), pp. 113–19.

150. Guiso, *La colomba e la spada*, p. 445 et seq.

151. Togliatti, *La politica nel pensiero e nell'azione*, pp. 1565–1611.

152. Forlenza, *On the Edge of Democracy*, p.109.

153. K. Morgan, *International Communism and the Cult of the Individual: Leaders, Tribunes and Martyrs under Lenin and Stalin* (London: Palgrave Macmillan, 2017, p. 237.

154. *The Cominform*, pp. 783-803.

155. S. Bianchini, ed., *Valdo Magnani e l'antistalinismo comunista* (Bologna: Unicopli, 2013).

156. FG, APCI, Palmiro Togliatti, Carte della scrivania, 26 December 1949. See *Posetiteli kremlevskogo kabineta I. V. Stalina*, p. 173.

157. FG, APCI, Palmiro Togliatti, Carte della scrivania, 26 December 1949.

158. FG, APCI, Central Committee, minutes, 12-14 April 1950.

159. Gori and Pons, *Dagli archivi di Mosca*, doc. 34, pp. 378-87.

160. Guiso, *La colomba e la spada*, pp. 322-25.

161. Fiocco, *Togliatti, il realismo della politica*, pp. 238-39.

162. Formigoni, *Storia d'Italia nella guerra fredda*, pp. 167-71; and Del Pero, *L'alleato scomodo*, pp. 103-6.

163. Guiso, *La colomba e la spada*, pp. 328-30.

164. Gori and Pons, *Dagli archivi di Mosca*, docs. 36 and 37, pp. 394-414; and FG, APCI, Directorate, minutes, 6 December 1950.

165. The meetings recorded between Togliatti and Stalin took place on 13 and 18 January, and 12 February 1951. See *Posetiteli kremlevskogo kabineta I. V. Stalina*, p. 173. Two of the meetings took place with two successive PCI delegations; see Archivio Pietro Secchia, pp. 229-32. We have neither Soviet nor Italian minutes for the meetings.

166. Gori and Pons, *Dagli archivi di Mosca*, doc. 39, pp. 417-20.

167. Gori and Pons, *Dagli archivi di Mosca*, doc. 40, pp. 421-22.

168. *Archivio Pietro Secchia*, pp. 229-31, 445.

169. L. Barca, *Cronache dall'interno del vertice del PCI*, vol. 1, *Con Togliatti e Longo* (Soveria Mannelli: Rubbettino, 2005), pp. 270-72.

170. Fondazione Giangiacomo Feltrinelli, Archivio Pietro Secchia, serie documenti, contenitore 14, fascicolo 7.

171. Gozzini, Martinelli, *Storia del Partito comunista italiano*, vol. 7, pp. 193-99; and Albeltaro, *Le rivoluzioni non cadono dal cielo*, p. 145.

172. Brogi, *Confronting America*, pp. 136 ff.; and Del Pero, *L'Alleato scomodo*, pp. 130-34.

173. Gozzini, Martinelli, *Storia del Partito Comunista Italiano*, vol. 7, pp. 222 ff.

174. M. Del Pero, "Containing Containment: Rethinking Italy's Experience during the Cold War," *Journal of Modern Italian Studies* 8, no. 4 (2003), pp. 532-55.

175. Hobsbawm, *Interesting Times*, p. 203.

176. P. Togliatti, *Discorsi parlamentari*, vol. 2, 1952-64 (Rome: Camera dei Deputati, 1984), pp. 776-78.

177. G. Orsina and G. Panvini, eds., *La delegitimazione politica nell'età contemporanea: 1. Nemici e avversari politici nell'Italia repubblicana* (Rome: Viella, 2016); Orsina and Panvini, *Delegitimizing Political Opponents in Republican Italy*, in F. Cammarano, ed., *Praxis, Language, and Theory of Political Delegitimization in Contemporary Europe* (Rome: Viella, 2017), pp. 103-20; A. Ventrone, *Il nemico*

interno: Immagini, parole e simboli della lotta politica nell'Italia del Novecento (Rome: Donzelli, 2005); and Mariuzzo, *Communism and Anti-Communism in Early Cold War Italy.*

Chapter 4
1. P. Togliatti, *Opere*, vol. 5, ed. L. Gruppi (Rome: Editori Riuniti, 1984), pp. 832–46.
2. G. Amendola, *Il rinnovamento del PCI* (Rome: Editori Riuniti, 1978), p. 54.
3. Togliatti, *La guerra di posizione in Italia*, doc. 66, p. 204.
4. G. Vacca, *L'Italia contesa: Comunisti e democristiani nel lungo dopoguerra (1943–1978)* (Venice: Marsilio, 2018), pp. 170–78.
5. Fiocco, *Togliatti, il realismo della politica*, p. 264. On Amendola's role in 1954, see Cerchia, *Giorgio Amendola: Gli anni della Repubblica*, p. 192 et seq.
6. Barca, *Cronache dall'interno del vertice del PCI*, vol. 1, p. 124; Gozzini, Martinelli, *Storia del Partito comunista italiano*, vol. 6, p. 347 et seq.; Albeltaro, *Le rivoluzioni non cadono dal cielo*, ch. 7.
7. Del Pero, *L'alleato scomodo*, pp. 239–41.
8. *Prezidium TsK KPSS, 1954-64*, vol. 1 (Moscow: Rosspen, 2003), p. 205.
9. *Naslledniki Kominterna: Mezhdunarodnye soveshchaniya predstavitelei kommunisticheskikh i rabochikh partii v Moskve; Dokumenty (noyabr' 1957g.)* (Moscow: Rosspen, 2013), pp. 16–20.
10. *Quel terribile 1956: I verbali della direzione comunista tra il XX Congresso del PCUS e l'VIII Congresso del PCI*, ed. M. L. Righi (Rome: Editori Riuniti, 1996), 20 June 1956, p. 59.
11. Barca, *Cronache dall'interno del vertice del PCI*, vol. 1, p. 143.
12. Gozzini, Martinelli, *Storia del partito comunista italiano*, p. 521.
13. FG, APCI, Fondo Mosca, microfilm 124.
14. Togliatti, *La politica nel pensiero e nell'azione*, pp. 1612–40.
15. *Quel terribile 1956*, 20 June 1956, p. 60.
16. *Quel terribile 1956*, pp. 75 and 81.
17. FG, APCI, Fondo Mosca, microfilm 124. Cf. *Quel terribile 1956*, 18 July 1956, pp. 138–42, 149; G. C. Pajetta, *Le crisi che ho vissuto: Budapest Praga Varsavia* (Rome: Editori Riuniti, 1982), pp. 63–68.
18. *Quel terribile 1956*, 18 July 1956, p. 117 et seq.
19. Togliatti, *Discorsi parlamentari 2*, 13 June 1956, pp. 928–29.
20. O. A. Westad, *The Cold War: A World History* (London: Allen Lane, 2017), pp. 270–71; Mazower, *Governing the World*, p. 261.
21. *Quel terribile 1956*, 20 June 1956, p. 54.
22. FG, APCI, Fondo Mosca, microfilm 124.
23. Togliatti, *Opere*, vol. 6, ed. L. Gruppi (Rome: Editori Riuniti, 1984), p. 154.
24. *Sovetskii Soyuz i vengerskii krizis 1956 goda: Dokumenty* (Moscow: Rosspen, 1998), docs. 123 and 128. For the debate in the leading group of the PCI, see *Quel terribile 1956*.

25. *Quel terribile 1956*, 30 October 1956, pp. 221 and 239.
26. *Quel terribile 1956*, pp. 222–24.
27. Gozzini, Martinelli, *Storia del partito comunista italiano*, p. 588 et seq.
28. G. Scirocco, *Alla ricerca di un socialismo possibile: Antonio Giolitti dal PCI al PSI* (Rome: Carocci, 2012), pp. 116–20.
29. *Eugenio Reale, l'uomo che sfidò Togliatti*, ed. A. Carioti (Florence: Libri Liberal, 1998).
30. J. Haslam, "I dilemmi della destalinizzazione: Togliatti, il XX Congresso del PCUS e le sue conseguenze," in *Togliatti nel suo tempo*, pp. 215–38.
31. S. Radchenko, "Il 1956 globale: Gli effetti internazionali della destalinizzazione," in *Globalizzazioni rosse*, pp. 109–30.
32. Togliatti, *La politica nel pensiero e nell'azione*, p. 813.
33. Togliatti, *La politica nel pensiero e nell'azione*, p. 792.
34. "Attualità del pensiero e dell'azione di Gramsci," *Rinascita*, April 1957, now in Togliatti, *La politica nel pensiero e nell'azione*, pp. 1102–20; "Il leninismo nel pensiero e nell'azione di A. Gramsci (1958)," in Togliatti, *La politica nel pensiero e nell'azione*, pp. 1121–41: In English, "Leninism in the Theory and Practice of Gramsci," in D. Sassoon, ed., *On Gramsci and Other Writings* (London: Lawrence and Wishart, 1979), pp. 161–81.
35. Togliatti, *La politica nel pensiero e nell'azione*, p. 827.
36. FG, APCI, Fondo Mosca, microfilm 198.
37. A. Guiso, "'Il lungo '56'": I rapporti tra 'partito adulto' e gioventù comunista dalla destalinizzazione al Sessantotto: Modello organizzativo, generazioni, cultura politica," in *La politica dei giovani in Italia (1945–1968)*, ed. G. Quagliariello (Rome: Luiss University Press, 2005), pp. 69–118; G. Sorgonà, *La svolta incompiuta: Il gruppo dirigente del PCI tra l'VIII e l'XI Congresso (1956–1965)* (Rome: Aracne, 2011), pp. 62–71.
38. Archives of the Hoover Institution, Volkogonov papers, box 24, reel 16, pp. 42–57; Rossiiskii Gosudarstvennyi Arkhiv Noveishei Istorii (Russian State Archive of Contemporary History; hereafter RGANI), f. 81, op. 1, d. 306.
39. FG, APCI, Directorate, minutes, 30 January 1957.
40. Zhihua Shen and Yafeng Xia, "Zhou Enlai's Shuttle Diplomacy in 1957 and Its Effects," *Cold War History* 10, vol. 4 (2010), pp. 513–35; Radchenko, *Il 1956 globale*.
41. *Nasledniki Kominterna*, pp. 61–72; *Prezidium TsK KPSS*, vol. 1, docs. 138 and 139, pp. 280–81, 1022; *Prezidium TsK KPSS*, vol. 2, doc. 138, pp. 720–30; Zhihua Shen and Yafeng Xia, "Hidden Currents during the Honeymoon: Mao, Khrushchev, and the 1957 Moscow Conference," *Journal of Cold War Studies* 11, no. 4 (Fall 2009), pp. 74–117.
42. *Nasledniki Kominterna*, pp. 222–26.
43. FG, APCI, Fondo Mosca, microfilm 252, busta 99; *Nasledniki Kominterna*, pp. 325–41.
44. FG, APCI, Palmiro Togliatti, Carte Botteghe Oscure, PCI, fascicolo 27.

45. *Nasledniki Kominterna*, pp. 367–77, 566–74.

46. L. M. Lüthi, *The Sino-Soviet Split: Cold War in the Communist World* (Princeton, NJ, and Oxford, UK: Princeton University Press, 2008), pp. 74–79; Jian Chen, *Mao's China and the Cold War* (Chapel Hill, NC, and London: University of North Carolina Press, 2001).

47. Among other things, Togliatti made a note of the passages in Mao's speech on thermonuclear war in the following terms: "There are war maniacs / we must always allow for the worst / a third of humankind, even half and more may die as a consequence of an atomic war." He did not make a note of Mao's words on the fact that the world would be socialist on the morrow of a nuclear war. FG, APCI, Palmiro Togliatti, Carte Botteghe Oscure, PCI, fascicolo 26, p. 6.

48. Ingrao, *Volevo la luna*, p. 255.

49. FG, APCI, Palmiro Togliatti, Carte Botteghe Oscure, PCI, fascicolo 27, p. 12.

50. Zhihua Shen and Yafeng Xia, "Hidden Currents during the Honeymoon," p. 91.

51. *Nasledniki Kominterna*, p. 222.

52. FG, APCI, Palmiro Togliatti, Carte Botteghe Oscure, PCI, fascicolo 27.

53. V. Vidali, *Diario del XX Congresso* (Milan: Vangelista, 1974), p. 162; see in English *Diary of the Twentieth Congress* (Westport, CT: Lawrence Hill; and London: Journeyman Press, 1984).

54. RGASPI, f. 495, op. 221, d. 106, ch. 1, ll. 161–70. In his recollections of the meeting with Khrushchev in 1958, Amendola does not mention the question; see Amendola, *Il rinnovamento del PCI*, pp. 150–51.

55. C. Spagnolo, *Sul memoriale di Yalta: Togliatti e la crisi del movimento comunista internazionale (1956–1964)* (Rome: Carocci, 2007), pp. 192–94.

56. FG, APCI, Palmiro Togliatti, Carte Botteghe Oscure, PCI, fascicolo 34, pp. 1–24.

57. FG, APCI, Fondo Berlinguer, Movimento operaio internazionale, conferenza degli 81 partiti comunisti e operai, Moscow 1960.

58. L. Longo, *Opinione sulla Cina* (Milan: La Pietra, 1977), p. 27, 36, 47–48. RGASPI, f. 495, op. 221, d. 1, c. 22, ll. 66–90.

59. FG, APCI, Conferenza di Mosca dei PC e operai November 1960, microfilm 0474, pp. 2628–43.

60. FG, APCI, Directorate, minutes, 9 December 1960.

61. Agosti, *Palmiro Togliatti*, p. 517.

62. Barca, *Cronache dall'interno del vertice del PCI*, vol. 1, pp. 265 and 269.

63. M. L. Righi, ed., *Il PCI e lo stalinismo: Un dibattito del 1961* (Rome: Editori Riuniti, 2007), pp. 29–32.

64. M. Congiu, "Gli appunti di Imre Nagy a Snagov (1956–57)," *Studi storici* 2011, no. 1, pp. 127–54.

65. *Il PCI e lo stalinismo*, pp. 105–20; Barca, *Cronache dall'interno del vertice del PCI*, vol. 1, pp. 276–79.

66. *Il PCI e lo stalinismo*, pp. 280–99.

67. On the subject of communist language, see Andreucci, *Da Gramsci a Occhetto*, pp. 303–9.

68. F. Bettanin, M. Prozumenshchikov, A. Roccucci, and A. Salacone, eds., *L'Italia vista dal Cremlino: Gli anni della distensione negli archivi del Comitato Centrale del PCUS, 1953–1970* (Rome: Viella, 2015), doc. 28, pp. 160–69.

69. FG, APCI, Directorate, minutes, 7 December 1961.

70. FG, APCI, USSR, 1962, microfilm 0503, pp. 481–82.

71. *L'Italia vista dal Cremlino*, doc. 29, pp. 169–71.

72. On the conquest of space as the last Soviet myth, see S. Pivato and M. Pivato, *I comunisti sulla luna: L'ultimo mito della rivoluzione russa* (Bologna: Il Mulino, 2017).

73. Togliatti, *La politica nel pensiero e nell'azione*, p. 1756. In English, see *On Gramsci and Other Writings*, pp. 210–34, especially p. 234.

74. Togliatti, *La politica nel pensiero e nell'azione*, pp. 1700–1701.

75. Togliatti, *La politica nel pensiero e nell'azione*, p. 1729.

76. M. Maggiorani, *L'Europa degli altri: Comunisti italiani e integrazione europea (1957–1969)* (Rome: Carocci, 1998).

77. G. Calchi Novati, "Mediterraneo e questione araba nella politica estera italiana," in F. Barbagallo, ed., *Storia dell'Italia Repubblicana*, vol. 2 (Turin: Einaudi, 1994), pp. 195–251; A. Varsori, *L'Italia nelle relazioni internazionali dal 1943 al 1992* (Rome and Bari: Laterza, 1998), pp. 117–29.

78. Formigoni, *Storia d'Italia nella guerra fredda*, pp. 221–23; G. Monina, *Lelio Basso, leader globale: Un socialista nel secondo Novecento* (Rome: Carocci, 2016), pp. 124–25.

79. G. Scirocco, *Politique d'abord: Il PSI, la guerra fredda e la politica internazionale (1948–1957)* (Milan: Edizioni Unicopli, 2010), pp. 224–25.

80. Westad, *The Cold War*, p. 281. A. Fursenko and T. Naftali, *Khrushchev's Cold War: The Inside Story of an American Adversary* (New York and London: Norton, 2006), p. 138 et seq.

81. A. Brogi, *L'Italia e l'egemonia americana nel Mediterraneo* (Florence: La Nuova Italia, 1996); E. Bini, *La potente benzina italiana: Guerra fredda e consumi di massa tra Italia, Stati Uniti e Terzo Mondo (1945–1973)* (Rome: Carocci, 2013); E. Bini, "Fueling Modernization from the Atlantic to the Third World: Oil and Economic Development in ENI's International Policies, 1950s–1960s," in A. Beltran, E. Boussière, and G. Garavini, eds., *Europe and Energy from the 1960s to the 1980s* (Brussels: Peter Lang, 2016), pp. 41–59.

82. Togliatti, *Discorsi parlamentari*, vol. 2, 13 June 1956, pp. 928–29.

83. Togliatti, *Discorsi parlamentari*, vol. 2, 5 June and 15 October 1957, pp. 960 and 988.

84. Togliatti, *Discorsi parlamentari*, vol. 2, 15 October 1957, p. 994.

85. S. Segre, "Italia atlantica o mediterranea?" *Rinascita*, 1 December 1957.

86. Togliatti, *Discorsi parlamentari*, vol. 2, 29 January 1958, p. 1006.

87. Brogi, *Confronting America*, p. 226.

88. Imlay, *The Practice of Socialist Internationalism*, pp. 417–22, 440–44; G. Garavini, *Dopo gli imperi: L'integrazione europea nello scontro Nord-Sud* (Florence: Le Monnier, 2009), pp. 68–70.

89. *Rinascita* 15, nos. 11–12 (November and December 1958).

90. A. Giovagnoli, "Pio XII e la decolonizzazione," in A. Riccardi, ed., *Pio XII* (Rome and Bari: Laterza, 1984), pp. 179–209.

91. Formigoni, *Storia d'Italia nella guerra fredda*, p. 251; R. Gualtieri, *L'Italia dal 1943 al 1992* (Rome: Carocci, 2006), pp. 141–42.

92. Togliatti, *Discorsi parlamentari*, vol. 2, 15 October 1959, pp. 1099–1101.

93. On Fanfani's views of international politics, but also on their evident limits, see the essays by A. Giovagnoli and A. Riccardi in A. Giovagnoli and L. Tosi, eds., *Amintore Fanfani e la politica estera italiana* (Venice: Marsilio, 2010).

94. A. Roccucci, "Coesistenza pacifica tra diseguali: Italia e Unione Sovietica dalla morte di Stalin alla visita di Gronchi a Mosca" in *L'Italia vista dal Cremlino*, pp. 30–31.

95. B. Bagnato, ed., *I diari di Luca Pietromarchi: Ambasciatore italiano a Mosca (1958–1961)* (Florence: Olschki, 2002), pp. 260–61.

96. *IX Congresso del partito comunista italiano* (Rome: Editori Riuniti, 1960), pp. 39–40.

97. *L'Italia vista dal Cremlino*, doc. 20. On Gronchi and Pella's talks in Moscow, see A. Salacone, *La diplomazia del dialogo: Italia e URSS tra coesistenza pacifica e distensione (1958–1968)* (Rome: Viella, 2017), pp. 93–105.

98. *L'Italia vista dal Cremlino*, doc. 24.

99. FG, APCI, microfilm 477, pp. 283–85, note for the Secretariat, 28 July 1961.

100. Spagnolo, *Sul memoriale di Jalta*, p. 81.

101. F. De Felice, "Nazione e sviluppo: Un nodo non sciolto," in *Storia dell'Italia repubblicana*, vol. 2, 1, p. 118; L. Magri, *Il sarto di Ulm: Una possibile storia del PCI* (Milan: Il Saggiatore, 2009), pp. 187–90; in English, *The Tailor of Ulm* (London: Verso, 2011), pp. 173–76.

102. Brogi, *Confronting America*, pp. 253–54; Forgacs and Gundle, *Mass Culture and Italian Society from Fascism to the Cold War*.

103. G. Corsini, "L'elezione di Kennedy e l'inquietudine americana," *Rinascita*, December 1960; G. Corsini, "I cento giorni del Presidente Kennedy," *Rinascita*, July–August 1961.

104. D. W. Ellwood, *Una sfida per la modernità: Europa e America nel lungo Novecento* (Rome: Carocci, 2012), pp. 198 and 202.

105. M. Connelly, *A Diplomatic Revolution: Algeria's Fight for Independence and the Origins of the Post-Cold War Era* (Oxford, UK, and New York: Oxford University Press, 2002).

106. O. A. Westad, *The Global Cold War: Third World Interventions and the Making of Our Times* (Cambridge, UK: Cambridge University Press, 2005), p. 66 et seq.; A. Hilger, "Communism, Decolonization and the Third World," in *The*

Cambridge History of Communism, vol. 2, pp. 322–31; A. Hilger, "Mondi diversi, storie intrecciate: Gli stati socialisti e il Terzo Mondo durante la guerra fredda," in *Globalizzazioni rosse*, pp. 133–54.

107. T. Rupprecht, *Soviet Internationalism after Stalin: Interaction and Exchange between the USSR and Latin America during the Cold War* (Cambridge, UK: Cambridge University Press, 2015).

108. Tonelli, *A scuola di politica*, p. 175 et seq. For an autobiographical reconstruction, see G. Cervetti, *Compagno del secolo scorso: Una storia politica* (Milan: Bompiani, 2016).

109. J. Lill, *Völkerfreundschaft im Kalten Krieg? Die Politischen, Kulturellen und Wirtschaftlichen Beziehungen der DDR zu Italien 1949–1989* (Frankfurt am Main: Peter Lang, 2001); M. Martini, *La cultura all'ombra del Muro: Relazioni culturali tra Italia e DDR (1949–1989)* (Bologna: Il Mulino, 2007); T. Malice, "Transnational Imaginations of Socialism: Political Town Twinning between Italy and the German Democratic Republic in the 1960s and 1970s," unpublished doctoral thesis, University of Bologna, 2019.

110. D. Bernardini, *Scampoli rossi: Ricordi di un comunista impenitente* (Rome: Slavia, 2017), pp. 72–79.

111. T. Dragostinova and M. Fidelis, "Introduction: Beyond the Iron Curtain: Eastern Europe and the Global Cold War," *Slavic Review* 77, no. 3 (2018), pp. 577–87.

112. S. Lorenzini, "The Socialist Camp and Economic Modernization in the Third World," in *The Cambridge History of Communism*, vol. 2, pp. 343–51; S. Lorenzini, *Una strana guerra fredda: Lo sviluppo e le relazioni Nord-Sud* (Bologna: Il Mulino, 2017), pp. 81–84; P. Muehlenbeck, *Czechoslovakia in Africa, 1945–1968* (London: Palgrave Macmillan, 2016).

113. J. Friedman, *Shadow Cold War: The Sino-Soviet Competition for the Third World* (Chapel Hill: University of North Carolina Press, 2015), pp. 71–73.

114. RGANI, f. 81, op. 1, d. 306.

115. M. Galeazzi, *Il PCI e il movimento dei paesi non allineati (1955–1975)* (Milan: Franco Angeli, 2011), pp. 41–49.

116. *Nasledniki Kominterna*, p. 450.

117. FG, APCI, Directorate, minutes, microfilm 22, 3 October 1958.

118. RGANI, f. 81, op. 1, d. 306, ll. 47–50.

119. G. Siracusano, *"Pronto per la rivoluzione": I comunisti italiani e francesi e la decolonizzazione in Africa centro-occidentale (1958–1968)* (Rome: Carocci, 2023).

120. FG, APCI, Esteri, microfilm 468, meeting of 1 March 1960 to discuss the policy of the PCI towards the Arab countries, pp. 2295, 2299, 2301.

121. S. Mazov, *A Distant Front in the Cold War: The USSR in West Africa and the Congo 1956–1964* (Stanford, CA: Stanford University Press, 2010): R. Ledda, "Unità dell'Africa e lotta anticoloniale," *Rinascita*, December 1960; G. C. Pajetta, "L'assassinio di Lumumba," *Rinascita*, February 1961.

122. FG, APCI, Esteri, microfilm 468.

123. Togliatti, *Discorsi parlamentari*, vol. 2, 27 September 1961, p. 1216.

124. R. Ledda, "Posta al Cairo l'esigenza di riassestare l'economia mondiale," *Rinascita*, 28 July 1962; R. Ledda, "I sottosviluppati rifiutano la vocazione 'agricola,'" *Rinascita*, 4 August 1962. See Garavini, *Dopo gli imperi*, p. 39.

125. G. Calchi Novati, *L'Africa d'Italia: Una storia coloniale e postcoloniale* (Rome: Carocci, 2011), pp. 355–69; Labanca, *La guerra d'Etiopia* (Bologna: Il Mulino, 2015), pp. 219–30.

126. On the positions of the French and Algerian communists in the war in Algeria, see A. Ruscio, *Les communistes et l'Algérie: Des origines à la guerre d'indépendance* (Paris: La decouvérte, 2019); A. Drew, *We Are No Longer in France: Communists in Colonial Algeria* (Manchester, UK: Manchester University Press, 2014).

127. FG, APCI, Estero, Algeria, 1961, microfilm 483, pp. 2387–88, 2391.

128. P. Borruso, *Il PCI e l'Africa indipendente: Apogeo e crisi di un'utopia socialista (1956–1989)* (Florence: Le Monnier, 2009), p. 70.

129. Friedman, *Shadow Cold War*, pp. 134–38.

130. P. Togliatti, "Algeria indipendente," *Rinascita*, 7 July 1962.

131. C. Kalter, *The Discovery of the Third World: Decolonization and the Rise of the New Left in France, 1950–1976* (Cambridge: Cambridge University Press, 2016), pp. 90–99.

132. Srivastava, *Italian Colonialism and Resistances to Empire*, p. 213 et seq.

133. P. Goedde, *The Politics of Peace: A Global Cold War History* (Oxford, UK, and New York: Oxford University Press, 2019), pp. 60, 162–67.

134. J. P. Sartre, "La guerra fredda e l'unità della cultura," *Rinascita*, 13 October 1962.

135. R. Rossanda, "Problemi e prospettive dell'Algeria indipendente," *Rinascita*, 13 July 1963; N. Mandela, "J'accuse," *Rinascita*, 29 June 1963; K. N'Krumah, "La ricchezza dell'Africa," *Rinascita*, 10 August 1963.

136. FG, APCI, Estero, 1963, microfilm 489, notes by Maurizio Valenzi for a discussion on Italy's policies towards the Third World, pp. 2766–69.

137. FG, APCI, Directorate, minutes, 31 October 1962.

138. Spagnolo, *Sul Memoriale di Yalta*, p. 232.

139. *X Congresso del partito comunista italiano: Atti e risoluzioni* (Rome: Editori Riuniti, 1963), pp. 38–45.

140. P. Togliatti, "Riconduciamo la discussione ai suoi termini reali," *Rinascita*, 12 January 1963.

141. Togliatti, *La politica nel pensiero e nell'azione*, pp. 930–31, 935.

142. Friedman, *Shadow Cold War*, pp. 103–4.

143. P. Togliatti, "Sull'accordo pel divieto delle esplosioni atomiche," *Rinascita*, 24 August 1963.

144. FG, APCI, Directorate, minutes, 12 September 1963.

145. FG, APCI, Directorate, minutes, 11 October 1963.

146. P. Togliatti, "Verso il socialismo in occidente?" *Rinascita* 20, no. 42 (26 October 1963).

147. FG, APCI, Central Committee, 24 October 1963, tape recording. *L'unità*, 26 October 1963. *Il Partito comunista italiano e il movimento operaio internazionale 1956–1968* (Rome: Editori Riuniti, 1968), pp. 168–98.

148. Friedman, *Shadow Cold War*, pp. 117–18.

149. FG, APCI, Esteri, 1964, Yugoslavia, microfilm 520, 15–21 January 1964, pp. 1393–1401.

150. FG, APCI, Palmiro Togliatti, Carte Marisa Malagoli, viaggio in Yugoslavia (14 January–1 February 1964), pp. 7–15 and 16–25; FG APCI, Esteri, 1964, Yugoslavia, microfilm. 520, pp. 15–21, January 1964, 1402–14. For the Yugoslav account of affairs, see Galeazzi, *Il PCI e il movimento dei paesi non allineati*, pp. 102–3.

151. J. J. Byrnes, *Mecca of Revolution: Algeria, Decolonization, and the Third World Order* (Oxford, UK, and New York: Oxford University Press, 2016).

152. Borruso, *Il PCI e l'Africa indipendente*, pp. 84–89.

153. FG, APCI, Esteri, 1964, Algeria, microfilm. 520, information provided by comrade Maria Antonietta Macciocchi on the mission of the PCI delegation to Algeria, pp. 124–56.

154. Friedman, *Shadow Cold War*, pp. 137–38.

155. FG, APCI, Esteri, 1964, Cuba, microfilm 492, pp. 2555–66, 12 August 1963.

156. *L'unità*, 19 January 1964; O. Pappagallo, *Il PCI e la rivoluzione cubana: La via latino-americana al socialismo tra Mosca e Pechino (1959–1965)* (Rome: Carocci, 2009), pp. 206–11.

157. FG, APCI, Palmiro Togliatti, Carte della scrivania, August 1964.

158. *Rinascita*, 1 February 1964.

159. FG, APCI, USSR, 1964, microfilm 0520, pp. 2435–39.

160. FG, APCI, Directorate, minutes, 1964, microfilm 028, 26 February 1964, pp. 490–98.

161. FG, APCI, Directorate, minutes, 2 April 1964.

162. FG, APCI, USSR, 1964, microfilm 0520, pp. 2514–20.

163. *L'Italia vista dal Cremlino*, doc. 46, p. 235.

164. FG, APCI, Directorate, minutes, 9 April 1964.

165. FG, APCI, Central Committee series, microfilm 28, 22 April 1964.

166. FG, APCI, Directorate, minutes, 12 May 1964.

167. FG, APCI, Estero, 1964, microfilm 0520, 22 May 1964.

168. RGASPI, f. 495, op. 221, d. 1, ch. 2, l. 164.

169. FG, APCI, Directorate, minutes, 2 July 1964.

170. FG, APCI, USSR, 1964, microfilm 0520, pp. 2621–26.

171. FG, APCI, USSR, 1964, microfilm 0520, pp. 2649–65. For a detailed reconstruction, see A. Höbel, "Il PCI nella crisi del movimento comunista internazionale tra PCUS e PCC (1960–1964)," *Studi storici*, 2005, no. 2, pp. 515–72.

172. RGASPI, f. 495, op. 221, d. 106, ch. 1, ll. 139–40.

173. Spagnolo, *Sul memoriale di Yalta*, pp. 27–46.

174. Togliatti, *La politica nel pensiero e nell'azione*, pp. 1842–54. In English, see "The Yalta Memorandum" in *On Gramsci and Other Writings*, pp. 285–97.

(Translator's note: Where possible, direct quotes from the memorandum follow the published 1979 translation.)

175. Spagnolo, *Sul memoriale di Yalta*, pp. 240–43. Fiocco, *Togliatti, il realismo della politica*, pp. 431–36.

176. Maggiorani, *L'Europa degli altri*, p. 165 et seq.

177. Togliatti, *La politica nel pensiero e nell'azione*, p. 1854.

178. The coupling together of the two documents is clearly present in communist memory; see G. Boffa, *Memorie dal comunismo: Storia confidenziale di quarant'anni che hanno cambiato il volto all'Europa* (Florence: Ponte alle Grazie, 1998), p. 128.

179. P. Togliatti, "Promemoria sulle questioni del movimento operaio internazionale e della sua unità," *Rinascita*, 5 September 1964. See A. Höbel, *Il PCI di Luigi Longo (1964–1969)* (Naples: Edizioni scientifiche italiane, 2010), pp. 54–57.

180. *L'Italia vista dal Cremlino*, doc. 48, p. 241.

181. A. Cossutta, *Una storia comunista* (Milan: Rizzoli, 2004), p. 93 et seq.

182. N. Pedrazzi, *L'Italia che sognava Enver: Partigiani, comunisti, marxisti-leninisti; Gli amici italiani dell'Albania popolare (1943–1976)* (Salento Books), pp. 252–70.

183. Among the various publications of memoirs, see G. Pajetta, *La lunga marcia dell'internazionalismo* (Rome: Editori Riuniti, 1978), pp. 135–41; E. Macaluso, *Togliatti e i suoi eredi* (Soveria Mannelli, Italy: Rubbettino, 1988); Boffa, *Memorie dal comunismo*, p. 133.

Chapter 5

1. Westad, *The Cold War*, pp. 325–38.

2. Among the memoirs that call to mind the sense of loss in the leading group of the PCI after Togliatti's death, see above all R. Rossanda, *La ragazza del secolo scorso* (Turin: Einaudi, 2005).

3. FG APCI, Fondo Berlinguer, Movimento Operaio Internazionale, fascicolo 15, 29 October 1964.

4. FG, APCI, Directorate, minutes, 12 February 1965.

5. Höbel, *Il PCI di Luigi Longo*, pp. 161–62.

6. FG, APCI, Directorate, minutes, 21 May 1965.

7. O. Pappagallo, *Verso il nuovo mondo: Il PCI e l'America Latina (1945–1973)* (Milan: Francoangeli, 2017), p. 149.

8. FG, APCI, Directorate, minutes, 25 December 1965.

9. Barca, *Cronache dall'interno del vertice del PCI*, vol. 1, pp. 369–70.

10. FG, APCI, Directorate, minutes, 23 December 1965.

11. Brogi, *Confronting America*, pp. 256–67.

12. Barca, *Cronache dall'interno del vertice del PCI*, vol. 1, p. 368; Ingrao, *Volevo la luna*, pp. 312–15; Höbel, *Il PCI di Luigi Longo*, pp. 179–80, 195.

13. Cerchia, *Giorgio Amendola: Gli anni della Repubblica*, pp. 300–301.

14. M. Di Maggio, *Alla ricerca della terza via al socialismo: I PC italiano e francese nella crisi del comunismo (1964-1984)* (Naples: Edizioni Scientifiche Italiane, 2014), pp. 76-79.

15. M. B. Young, S. Quinn-Judge, "The Vietnam War as a World Event," in *The Cambridge History of the Cold War, Vol. 3: Endgames? Late Communism in Global Perspective, 1968 to the Present*, ed. J. Fuerst, S. Pons, and M. Selden (Cambridge, UK: Cambridge University Press, 2017), pp. 50-71; Westad, *The Global Cold War*, pp. 192-94.

16. FG, APCI, Estero, USSR, 1966, microfilm 537, pp. 1016-24. FG, APCI, Estero, 1966, microfilm 537, pp. 1044-48. See C. Galluzzi, *La svolta: Gli anni cruciali del partito comunista italiano* (Milan: Sperling & Kupfer, 1983), pp. 79-83.

17. Formigoni, *Storia d'Italia nella guerra fredda*, pp. 332-41.

18. L. Brezhnev, *Rabochie i dnevnikovye zapisi v 3-kh tomakh*, vol. 1 (Moscow: IstLit, 2016), doc. 35, pp. 151-53.

19. FG, APCI, Directorate, minutes, 27 December 1966; FG, APCI, Estero, USSR, 1966, microfilm 537, pp. 555-57; Galluzzi, *La svolta*, p. 98.

20. J. Hershberg, *Marigold: The Lost Chance for Peace in Vietnam* (Washington: Woodrow Wilson Center Press, and Stanford, CA: Stanford University Press, 2012). See A. Melloni, "La politica internazionale della Santa Sede negli anni Sessanta," in *Il filo sottile: L'Ostpolitik vaticana di Agostino Casaroli*, ed. A. Melloni (Bologna: Il Mulino, 2006), pp. 26-32.

21. Galluzzi, *La svolta*, pp. 93, 128-29, 159, et seq.

22. Höbel, *Il PCI di Luigi Longo*, pp. 398, 446; Formigoni, *Storia d'Italia nella guerra fredda*, pp. 349-50; V. Lomellini, "Prove di pacifismo all'italiana: La critica alla Guerra del Vietnam e la genesi dell' 'altra America'; Un punto di incontro tra Pci e Dc?" *Ricerche di storia politica* 1 (2019), pp. 37-48.

23. FG, APCI, Estero, 1967, microfilm 545, pp. 2106-14.

24. FG, APCI, Directorate, minutes, 24 January 1967.

25. *L'Italia vista dal Cremlino*, doc. 57, p. 286.

26. FG, APCI, Estero, USSR, microfilm 546, pp. 154-65.

27. *L'unità*, 24 February 1967.

28. Maggiorani, *L'Europa degli altri*, p. 249 et seq.

29. Galluzzi, *La svolta*, p. 154.

30. Letter of W. Brandt, note on the talks of Galluzzi and Segre with Leo Bauer, FG, APCI, 1967, Partiti Esteri, FRG, microfilm 058, pp. 1157-60; reports on the meeting between the Delegation of the PCI and the Delegation of the SPD, FG, APCI, 1967, microfilm 058, pp. 1161-72; Galluzzi, *La svolta*, pp. 171-74.

31. M. Di Donato, *I comunisti italiani e la sinistra europea (1964-1984)* (Rome: Carocci, 2015), pp. 56-66.

32. See A. Iandolo, "The Rise and Fall of the 'Soviet Model of Development' in West Africa, 1957-1964," *Cold War History* 2012, no. 4, pp. 683-704.

33. *L'unità*, 11 July 1967. See L. Riccardi, *Il "problema Israele": Diplomazia italiana e PCI di fronte allo Stato ebraico* (Milan: Guerini, 2006), pp. 253 et seq.; C. Brillanti,

Le sinistre italiane e il conflitto arabo-israelo-palestinese 1948–1973 (Rome: Sapienza Università Editrice, 2018), pp. 190–92, 222–23.

34. R. Ledda, "La Resistenza palestinese," *Rinascita*, 3 May 1968.

35. Galeazzi, *Il PCI e il movimento dei paesi non allineati*, pp. 173–74; Borruso, *Il PCI e l'Africa indipendente*, pp. 100–104.

36. A. Getachew, *Worldmaking after Empire: The Rise and Fall of Self-Determination* (Princeton, NJ: Princeton University Press, 2019), ch. 5.

37. Höbel, *Il PCI di Luigi Longo*, pp. 440–41.

38. L. Longo, "I tre fronti della lotta antimperialista," *Rinascita*, 24 November 1967.

39. R. Rossanda, "Il punto di vista di Cuba," *Rinascita*, 29 September 1967; L. Pavolini, "Cultura e rivoluzione nel terzo mondo," *Rinascita*, 26 January 1968; L. Foa, "Le attese deluse del terzo mondo,' *Rinascita*, 23 February 1968.

40. *L'unità*, 27 and 31 March 1968.

41. M. Bracke, *Quale socialismo, quale distensione? Il comunismo europeo e la crisi cecoslovacca del '68* (Rome: Carocci, 2008), p. 142. The report of the talks from the Czechoslovak side is published in *The Prague Spring 1968*, ed. J. Navratil (Budapest and New York: Central European University Press, 1998), doc. 29, pp. 126–28. See Boffa, *Memorie dal comunismo*, p. 151.

42. *Prager Fruehling: Das internationale Krisenjahr 1968; Dokumente* (Cologne, Weimar, and Vienna: Boehlau Verlag, 2008), doc. 77, p. 531.

43. FG, APCI, Directorate, minutes, 10 May 1968.

44. FG, APCI, 1968, Estero, USSR, microfilm 553, pp. 216–37; FG, APCI, Directorate, minutes, 17 and 26 July 1968; *The Prague Spring 1968*, doc. 56, p. 257; Pajetta, *Le crisi che ho vissuto*, pp. 124–27.

45. Galluzzi, *La svolta*, pp. 202–4.

46. FG, APCI, Directorate, minutes, 23 August 1968.

47. *L'unità*, 28 August 1968.

48. T. Baris, "La 'Primavera di Praga' e il Partito comunista italiano," in *Praga 1968: La "Primavera" e la sinistra italiana*, ed. F. Anghelone and L. Scoppola Iacopini (Rome: Bordeaux edizioni, 2014), pp. 180–82; Boffa, *Memorie dal comunismo*, p. 154.

49. A. Cossutta, "*Note sul viaggio a Mosca*," 12 September 1968, 971–80; FG, APCI, Directorate, minutes, 18 September 1968. See also Höbel, *Il PCI di Luigi Longo*, pp. 536–37.

50. FG, APCI, Directorate, minutes, 18 September 1968.

51. G. Amendola, "Il nostro internazionalismo," *Rinascita*, 6 September 1968.

52. P. Ingrao, "La democrazia socialista è forza della rivoluzione," *Rinascita*, 13 September 1968.

53. FG, APCI, Directorate, minutes, 4 October 1968.

54. FG, APCI, Directorate, minutes, 31 October 1968.

55. FG, APCI, Estero, USSR, 1968, microfilm 058, pp. 1015–45; FG, APCI, Fondo Berlinguer, Movimento Operaio Internazionale, fascicolo 59. The Italian delegation

was composed of Berlinguer, Cossutta, Bufalini, Galluzzi, and Colombi. For the report from the Soviet side of the meeting see *Istochnik*, May 1994, pp. 77–86.

56. FG, APCI, Directorate, minutes, 16 November 1968.

57. FG, APCI, Directorate, minutes, 30 January 1969; FG, APCI, Estero, USSR, 1969, microfilm 58, pp. 839–46; *L'Italia vista dal Cremlino*, doc. 69, pp. 346–51.

58. Barca, *Cronache dall'interno del vertice del PCI*, vol. 1, p. 432; F. Barbagallo, *Enrico Berlinguer* (Rome: Carocci, 2006), p. 23–24, 103.

59. *XII Congresso del Partito comunista italiano: Atti e risoluzioni* (Rome: Editori Riuniti, 1969), p. 82.

60. Bracke, *Quale socialismo, quale distensione?*, pp. 192–97.

61. Di Donato, *I comunisti italiani e la sinistra europea*, pp. 78–79.

62. FG, APCI, Directorate, minutes, 16 April 1969.

63. FG, APCI, Fondo Berlinguer, Movimento Operaio Internazionale, fascicolo 81.

64. A. Chernyaev, *Moya zhizn' i moë vremya* (Moscow: Mezhdunarodnye otnosheniya, 1995), p. 271.

65. FG, APCI, Directorate, minutes, 20 December 1969.

66. FG, APCI, Directorate, minutes, 31 October 1968.

67. *XII Congresso del Partito comunista italiano*, pp. 749 and 758.

68. See the essays by L. Baldissara and E. Taviani in R. Gualtieri, ed., *Il PCI nell'Italia repubblicana* (Rome: Carocci, 2001).

69. Romero, *Storia della guerra fredda*, pp. 196–98.

70. Hobsbawm, *Interesting Times*, p. 227.

71. *L'Italia vista dal Cremlino*, doc. 72, p. 361.

72. *XII Congresso*, pp. 423–24.

73. On the "Manifesto" affair, see Bracke, *Quale socialismo, quale distensione?* pp. 230–33; V. Casini, "Gli anni della contestazione: Il Sessantotto e la questione del 'Manifesto,'" in *Alessandro Natta intellettuale e politico: Ricerche e testimonianze* (Rome: Ediesse, 2019), pp. 63–80.

74. L. Cominelli, *L'Italia sotto tutela: Stati Uniti, Europa e crisi italiana degli anni Settanta* (Florence: Le Monnier, 2014), p. 126 et seq.

75. L. Barca, *Cronache dall'interno del vertice del PCI*, vol. 2, *Con Berlinguer* (Soveria Mannelli: Rubbettino, 2005), p. 493.

76. "Nota su nostra politica europeistica," FG, APCI, USSR, microfilm 058, p. 891.

77. "Gli attuali sviluppi della lotta contro la NATO e per il superamento dei blocchi militari" (1969), FG, APCI, Central Committee Commissions, microfilm 305, pp. 403–33.

78. FG, APCI, Directorate, minutes, 31 March–1 April 1970.

79. FG, APCI, Directorate, minutes, 8 January 1971.

80. G. Panvini, "Thirdworldism in Italy," in *Marxist Historical Cultures and Social Movements during the Cold War*, ed. S. Berger and C. Cornelissen (London: Palgrave Macmillan, 2019), pp. 289–308.

81. FG, APCI, Estero, 1970, microfilm 071, pp. 281–88.

82. FG, APCI, Estero, 1971, microfilm 162, pp. 18–22 and 26–36.
83. FG, APCI, Estero, 1970, microfilm 071, pp. 302–5.
84. FG, APCI, Estero, 1971, microfilm 162, pp. 1151–58.
85. Formigoni, *Storia d'Italia nella guerra fredda*, pp. 388–91.
86. A. Santoni, *Il PCI e i giorni del Cile: Alle origini di un mito politico* (Rome: Carocci, 2008).
87. Renato Sandri, note to President Allende, FG, APCI, Estero, 1970, microfilm 70, pp. 1445–58.
88. FG, APCI, Estero, 1971, microfilm 53, pp. 1284–90.
89. FG, APCI, Directorate, minutes, 8 September 1971.
90. FG, APCI, Directorate, minutes, 29–30 September 1971.
91. G. Amendola, *I comunisti italiani e l'Europa* (Rome: Editori Riuniti, 1971).
92. FG, APCI, Directorate, minutes, 31 January–1 February 1973.
93. FG, APCI, Fondo Berlinguer, Movimento Operaio Internazionale, fascicolo 109; FG, APCI, Directorate, attachments, 28 March 1973; Barca, *Cronache dall'interno del vertice del PCI*, vol. 2, p. 547.
94. FG, APCI, Directorate, minutes, 18 March 1973.
95. See A. Rubbi, *Il mondo di Berlinguer* (Rome: Napoleone, 1994), pp. 32–33; FG, APCI, writings and speeches of Berlinguer, 26 January 1974, microfilm 073, pp. 384–99; Di Maggio, *Alla ricerca della terza via al socialismo*, pp. 246–52.
96. FG, APCI, Directorate, minutes, 19 February 1974.
97. FG, APCI, Estero, Chile, 1973, microfilm 48, p. 304.
98. "La proposta del compromesso storico, 12 October 1973," in E. Berlinguer, *La passione non è finita*, ed. M. Gotor (Turin: Einaudi, 2013), pp. 42–54.
99. Santoni, *Il PCI e i giorni del Cile*.
100. "Imperialismo e coesistenza alla luce dei fatti cileni, 28 September 1973," in Berlinguer, *La passione non è finita*, pp. 25–33.
101. Romero, *Storia della guerra fredda*, 221–23.
102. Ch. Maier, "'Malaise': The Crisis of Capitalism in the 1970s," in *The Shock of the Global: The 1970s in Perspective*, ed. N. Ferguson, Ch. S. Maier, E. Mandela, and D. J. Sargent (Cambridge, MA, and London: Harvard University Press, 2010), pp. 25–48.
103. Cominelli, *L'Italia sotto tutela*, pp. 171–72.
104. G. Amendola, "L'Europa nel ciclone," *Rinascita*, 30 November 1973.
105. Formigoni, *Storia d'Italia nella guerra fredda*, pp. 451 and 460.
106. Mazower, *Governing the World*, pp. 303–4.
107. Getachew, *Worldmaking after Empire*, pp. 170–71.
108. *L'unità*, 12 April 1974.
109. FG, APCI, Estero, 1974, microfilm 080, pp. 441–68.
110. On the communist analysis of the 1973 crisis in the Middle East, see L. Riccardi, *L'internazionalismo difficile: La "Diplomazia" del PCI e il Medio Oriente dalla crisi petrolifera alla caduta del muro di Berlino (1973–1989)* (Soveria Mannelli: Rubbettino, 2013), pp. 36–77.

111. FG, APCI, Estero, 1974, microfilm 080, pp. 441–68. See G. Cervetti, *L'oro di Mosca: La testimonianza di un protagonista* (Milan: Dalai, 1993).

112. E. Berlinguer, *La proposta comunista: Relazione al Comitato centrale e alla Commissione centrale di controllo del partito comunista italiano in preparazione del XIV Congresso* (Turin: Einaudi, 1975).

113. Garavini, *Dopo gli imperi*, pp. 222–24.

114. Barca, *Cronache dall'interno del vertice del PCI*, vol. 2, p. 583.

115. Barca, *Cronache dall'interno del vertice del PCI*, vol. 2, p. 591.

116. Rubbi, *Il mondo di Berlinguer*, pp. 18–19.

117. FG, APCI, Directorate, minutes, 4 March 1975.

118. Di Donato, *I comunisti italiani e la sinistra europea*, pp. 125–27.

119. *L'unità*, 5 July 1975.

120. FG, APCI, Estero, Yugoslavia, 1975, microfilm 204, p. 424.

121. "Tendenze e problemi della vita internazionale," *Rinascita*, 7 February 1975.

122. M. Del Pero, "La transizione portoghese," in M. Del Pero, V. Gavin, F. Guirao, and A. Varsori, *Democrazie: L'Europa meridionale e la fine delle dittature* (Florence: Le Monnier, 2010), pp. 95–171.

123. N. P. Ludlow, "The Real Years of Europe? US–West European Relations during the Ford Administration," *Journal of Cold War Studies* 15, no. 3 (Summer 2013): 136–61; A. Varsori, *La cenerentola d'Europa? L'Italia e l'integrazione europea dal 1947 a oggi* (Soveria Mannelli, Italy: Rubbetino, 2010), pp. 291–96.

124. FG, APCI, notes to the Secretariat, 1975, microfilm 206, p. 262. On the PCI and the "Carnation Revolution" in Portugal, see S. Pons, *Berlinguer e la fine del comunismo* (Turin: Einaudi, 2006), pp. 52–55.

125. FG, APCI, Fondo Berlinguer, Movimento Operaio Internazionale, fascicolo 125.

126. Di Donato, *I comunisti italiani e la sinistra europea*, p. 174.

127. Borruso, *Il PCI e l'Africa indipendente*, pp. 136–54; Siracusano, *La fine di un miraggio politico*, pp. 557–67.

128. E. Berlinguer, "Il mondo è più libero," *L'unità*, 9 May 1975.

129. FG, APCI, Fondo Berlinguer, Movimento Operaio Internazionale, fascicolo 132; Rubbi, *Il mondo di Berlinguer*, p. 236; Siracusano, *La fine di un miraggio politico*, pp. 661–64.

130. On the Lomé convention, see Lorenzini, *Una strana guerra fredda*, pp. 250–57; K. Patel, *Project Europe: A History* (Cambridge, UK: Cambridge University Press, 2018), pp. 253–55.

131. Lorenzini, "The Socialist Camp and Economic Modernization in the Third World," in *The Cambridge History of Communism*, vol. 2, pp. 355–56.

132. Pons, *Berlinguer e la fine del comunismo*, pp. 61–65.

133. FG, APCI, Directorate, minutes, 23 April, 24 July, and 26 September 1975.

134. FG, APCI, Fondo Berlinguer, Movimento Operaio Internazionale, fascicolo 129.

135. FG, APCI, Directorate, minutes, 21 November 1975.
136. National Archives and Records Administration (hereafter NARA), RG 59, Kissinger's staff meetings, 12 January 1975.
137. Formigoni, *Storia d'Italia nella guerra fredda*, p. 471.
138. NARA, RG 59, records of Henry A. Kissinger, 12 December 1975.
139. FG, APCI, notes to the Secretariat, microfilm 201, pp. 779–83, 10 January 1975; S. Pons, "L'Italia e il PCI nella politica estera dell'URSS di Brezhnev," in *L'Italia repubblicana nella crisi degli anni Settanta*, ed. A. Giovagnoli and S. Pons (Soveria Mannelli: Rubbettino, 2003), pp. 78–81.
140. *Time*, December 1975.
141. FG, APCI, Estero, 1975, microfilm 308.
142. FG, APCI, Directorate, minutes, 26 September 1975.
143. FG, APCI, Directorate, minutes, 23 October 1975.
144. Formigoni, *Storia d'Italia nella guerra fredda*, p. 471; G. Barberini, *Pagine di storia contemporanea: La Santa Sede alla Conferenza di Helsinki* (Siena: Cantagalli, 2010).

Chapter 6

1. Brogi, *Confronting America*; F. Heurtebize, *Le Péril rouge: Washington face à l'eurocommunisme* (Paris: PUF, 2014); and U. Gentiloni Silveri, *L'Italia sospesa: La crisi degli anni Settanta vista da Washington* (Turin: Einaudi, 2009).
2. Di Donato, *I comunisti italiani e la sinistra europea*, pp. 131–34; S. Pons, *The Rise and Fall of Eurocommunism*, in M. P. Leffler and O. A. Westad, eds., *The Cambridge History of the Cold War*, Cambridge University Press, 2010), pp. 45–65; L. Fasanaro, "Neither in One Bloc nor in the Other: Berlinguer's Vision of the End of the Cold War," in F. Bozo, M.-P. Rey, N. P. Ludlow, and B. Rother, eds., *Visions of the End of the Cold War in Europe, 1945–1990* (New York and Oxford: Berghahn, 2012), pp. 163–76.
3. S. Pons and M. Di Donato, "Reform Communism," in Fürst, Pons, and Selden, eds., *The Cambridge History of Communism: III. Endgames?*, pp. 178–202; and V. Strazzeri, "Forging Socialism through Democracy: A Critical Survey of Literature on Eurocommunism," *Twentieth Century Communism* 2019, no. 17, pp. 26–66.
4. E. J. Hobsbawm, "The Great Gramsci," *New York Review of Books* 21 (1974), no. 5. See R. J. Evans, *Eric Hobsbawm: A Life in History* (London: Little, Brown, 2019), pp. 489–99.
5. "Lottiamo per la costruzione di una società socialista nella libertà, nella democrazia, nella pace," 25th Congress of the CPSU, Moscow, 27 February 1976, in Berlinguer, *La passione non è finita*, pp. 77–82.
6. FG, APCI, Fondo Berlinguer, Movimento Operaio Internazionale, fascicolo 136, FG, APCI, Directorate, minutes, 5 March 1976; Rubbi, *Il mondo di Berlinguer*, p. 102; and M. P. Bradley, "Human Rights and Communism," in Fürst, Pons, and Selden, eds., *The Cambridge History of Communism, III: Endgames?*, pp. 77–82.

7. FG, APCI, Fondo Berlinguer, Varie, fascicolo 28.
8. G. Napolitano, *Intervista sul PCI*, ed. E. J. Hobsbawm (Rome and Bari: Laterza, 1976); in English, *The Italian Road to Socialism*, trans. J. Cammett and V. DeGrazia (Westport, CT: Hill, 1977).
9. Di Donato, *I comunisti italiani e la sinistra europea*, pp. 175–77; Rubbi, *Il mondo di Berlinguer*, p. 125; and "Il PCI, l'Europa e il socialismo," *Rinascita* 30, no. 11 (1976).
10. "Berlinguer conta 'anche' sulla Nato per mantenere l'autonomia da Mosca," *Corriere della Sera*, 15 June 1976, now in Berlinguer, *La passione non è finita*, pp. 83–93.
11. A. Varsori, "Puerto Rico (1976): Le potenze occidentali e il problema comunista in Italia," *Ventunesimo secolo* 7 (2008), pp. 89–121; and D. Basosi and G. Bernardini, "The Puerto Rico Summit of 1976 and the End of Eurocommunism," in L. Nuti, ed., *The Crisis of Détente in Europe: From Helsinki to Gorbachev, 1975–1985* (London: Routledge, 2009).
12. FG, APCI, Fondo Berlinguer, Movimento Operaio Internazionale, fascicolo 140.
13. Pons, *Berlinguer e la fine del comunismo*, pp. 84–90; and Chernyaev, *Moya zhizn' i moë vremya*, p. 345.
14. D. J. Sargent, *Superpower Transformed: The Remaking of American Foreign Relations in the 1970s* (New York: Oxford University Press, 2015), pp. 233–36. See also U. Tulli, *Tra diritti umani e distensione: L'amministrazione Carter e il dissenso in URSS* (Milan: FrancoAngeli, 2013).
15. FG, APCI, notes to the Secretariat, microfilm 0243, 24 September 1976.
16. A. Ciulla, "L'amministrazione Carter e la "questione comunista" in Italia: Elaborazione e azione politica, 1976–1978," *Italia contemporanea* 2020, no. 293, pp. 254–79.
17. R. N. Gardner, *Mission Italy. On the Front Lines of the Cold War* (Oxford, UK: Rowman and Littlefield, 2005), p. 68.
18. Barca, *Cronache dall'interno del vertice del PCI*, vol. 2, pp. 601–3.
19. F. Calamandrei, *Le occasioni di vivere: Diari e scritti 1975–1982* (Florence: La Nuova Italia, 1995), p. 78.
20. A. S. Chernyaev, *Sovmestnyi iskhod: Dnevnik dvukh epokh 1972–1991* (Moscow: Rosspen, 2008), p. 269.
21. S. Segre, *A chi fa paura l'eurocomunismo?* (Rimini and Florence: Guaraldi, 1977).
22. "Notes on the Ceaușescu-Berlinguer Meeting," 19 January 1977, in FG, APCI, notes to the Secretariat, 1977, microfilm 0288.
23. FG, APCI, notes to the Secretariat, 1977, microfilm 0309, 565–66.
24. "Dichiarazione di intellettuali comunisti sulla Cecoslovacchia," *L'unità*, 13 January 1977.
25. FG, APCI, Directorate, minutes, 26 January 1977, microfilm 0288, 69.
26. FG, APCI, Estero, USSR, 1977, microfilm 0297, 1494–95.

27. FG, APCI, Directorate, minutes, 16 February 1977; and Barca, *Cronache dall'interno del vertice del PCI*, vol. 2, pp. 670–71.

28. FG, APCI, Estero, USSR, 1977, microfilm 0297, 1494–95; Chernyaev, *Moya zhizn' i moë vremya*, p. 349; and C. Andrew and V. N. Mitrokhin, *L'archivio Mitrokhin: L'attività segreta del KGB in occidente* (Milan: Rizzoli, 2000), p. 372.

29. L. Fasanaro, *La DDR e l'Italia: Politica, commercio e ideologia nell'Europa del cambiamento (1973–1985)* (Rome: Carocci, 2016), pp. 170–72.

30. RGANI, f. 81, op. 1, d. 311; and FG, APCI, notes to the Secretariat, 1977 microfilm 0299, 235–48.

31. FG, APCI, Fondo Berlinguer, Movimento Operaio Internazionale, fascicolo 149; and FG, APCI, notes to the Secretariat, 1977, microfilm 0304, 480–95.

32. FG, APCI, Fondo Berlinguer, Movimento Operaio Internazionale, fascicolo 151.

33. Rubbi, *Il mondo di Berlinguer*, pp. 108–14.

34. E. Berlinguer, "Austerità: Occasione per cambiare l'Italia: Conclusioni al convegno degli intellettuali," 15 January 1977, in Berlinguer, *La passione non è finita*, pp. 7–22.

35. Saresella, *Catholics and Communists in Twentieth-Century Italy*, pp. 112–13.

36. Di Donato, *I comunisti italiani e la sinistra europea*, pp. 192–93.

37. P. Craveri, *L'arte del non governo: L'inesorabile declino della Repubblica italiana* (Venice: Marsilio, 2016), pp. 324–27.

38. P. Ferrari, *In cammino verso l'Occidente: Berlinguer, the PCI e la comunità europea negli anni '70* (Bologna: Clueb, 2007), p. 230.

39. Barca, *Cronache dall'interno del vertice del PCI*, vol. 2, pp. 708–10.

40. FG, APCI, Fondo Berlinguer, Movimento Operaio Internazionale, fascicolo 148.

41. Di Donato, *I comunisti italiani e la sinistra europea*, pp. 194–205.

42. "Reserved Note for Berlinguer," 4 November 1977, in FG, APCI, notes to the Secretariat, 1977, microfilm 0309, 220–21.

43. Gardner, *Mission Italy*, pp. 114–17, 143–44.

44. Brogi, *Confronting America*, pp. 338–45; and Heurtebize, *Le péril rouge*, pp. 270–76.

45. Barca, *Cronache dall'interno del vertice del PCI*, vol. 2, pp. 716–17.

46. G. Formigoni, *Aldo Moro: Lo statista e il suo dramma* (Bologna: Il Mulino, 2016), pp. 346–43.

47. M. Gotor, *Il memoriale della Repubblica: Gli scritti di Aldo Moro dalla prigionia e l'anatomia del potere italiano* (Turin: Einaudi, 2011).

48. G. M. Ceci, *Il terrorismo italiano: Storia di un dibattito* (Rome: Carocci, 2013); and G. Panvini, *Cattolici e violenza politica: L'altro album di famiglia del terrorismo* (Venice: Marsilio, 2014).

49. A. Moro, *Lettere dalla prigionia*, ed. M. Gotor (Turin: Einaudi, 2008), pp. 7–8, 29, 41, 71.

50. U. Pecchioli, *Tra misteri e verità: Storia di una democrazia incompiuta* (Milan: Baldi & Castoldi, 1995); and Andrew and Mitrokhin, *L'archivio Mitrokhin*, p. 373.

51. S. Pons, "Cold War Republic: The 'External Constraint' in Italy during the 1970s," in A. Varsori and B. Zaccaria, *Italy in the International System from Détente to the End of the Cold War: The Underrated Ally* (London: Palgrave Macmillan, 2018), pp. 34–67.

52. FG, APCI, Fondo Berlinguer, Politica interna, fascicolo 525.

53. "Abbiamo aiutato il paese a superare prove durissime: Dobbiamo rilanciare la nostra politica in tutto il suo significato rinnovatore," *L'unità*, 25 July 1978.

54. A. Tatò, *Caro Berlinguer: Note e appunti riservati di Antonio Tatò a Enrico Berlinguer 1969–1984* (Turin: Einaudi, 2003), p. 80.

55. V. Lomellini, *L'appuntamento mancato: La sinistra italiana e il dissenso nei regimi comunisti (1968–1989)* (Florence: Le Monnier, 2010), p. 113 et seq.

56. Berlinguer, *La passione non è finita*, pp. 94–109.

57. Napolitano, *Dal PCI al socialismo europeo*, pp. 94–109.

58. Rubbi, *Il mondo di Berlinguer*, pp. 135–40.

59. FG, APCI, Directorate, attached documents, 19 October 1978, 67–72, 78–82; FG, APCI, Fondo Berlinguer, Movimento Operaio Internazionale, fascicolo 157.2; Rubbi, *Il mondo di Berlinguer*, pp. 141–57; S. Pons, "Meetings between the Italian Communist Party and the Communist Party of the Soviet Union, Moscow and Rome, 1978–1980," *Cold War History* 3, no. 1 (2002), 157–66.

60. Barca, *Cronache dall'interno del vertice del PCI*, vol. 2, pp. 752–53. See Pons, *Berlinguer e la fine del comunismo*, pp. 135–40.

61. Amendola, "L'impegno del PCI per l'Europa," in *L'unità*, 5 December 1978.

62. Di Donato, *I comunisti italiani e la sinistra europea*, p. 220.

63. *XV Congresso del Partito comunista italiano: Atti e risoluzioni* (Rome: Editori Riuniti, 1979), vol. 1, p. 552.

64. "Una riflessione critica seria e appassionata," *L'unità*, 4 July 1979; *I capisaldi di una strategia di rinnovamento*, 7 July 1979.

65. Sargent, *Superpower transformed*, p. 261 et seq.

66. Maier, *Malaise*, pp. 42–44.

67. Note from Sandri to the Directorate of the PCI, 22 June 1977, in FG, APCI, Estero, 1977, b. 406, fascicolo 203.

68. Speech by Sandri to the Commission for International Cooperation, 19 April 1978, FG, APCI, Estero, 1978, b. 486, fascicolo 83.

69. Speech by Sandri on the renewal of the Lomé Convention, 12 June 1978, FG, APCI, Estero, b. 468, fascicolo 166.

70. FG, APCI, note to the Secretariat, 1978, microfilm 7808, pp. 25–28.

71. Westad, *The Global Cold War*, pp. 203–6.

72. Borruso, *Il PCI e l'Africa indipendente*, pp. 235–39.

73. "Meeting in Moscow of 24/02/1978 with Ponomarëv," in FG, APCI, Estero, USSR, microfilm 7803, pp. 213–16.

74. FG, APCI, Estero, Cuba, 1978, microfilm 7807, pp. 64–66.

75. FG, APCI, Directorate, attached documents, 19 October 1978, microfilm 7812, p. 79.
76. Tatò, *Caro Berlinguer*, pp. 100–105.
77. *XV Congresso del Partito comunista italiano*, vol. 1, pp. 31–34.
78. FG, APCI, Directorate, minutes, 20 February 1979.
79. Rubbi, *Il mondo di Berlinguer*, p. 160.
80. FG, APCI, Directorate, minutes, 19 February 1979.
81. Strazzeri, *Forging Socialism through Democracy* and I. Balampanidis, *From the Communist to the Radical European Left* (London and New York: Routledge, 2019).
82. Calamandrei, *Le occasioni di vivere*, p. 161.
83. FG, APCI, Directorate, minutes, 4 January 1979.
84. E. Berlinguer, *Discorsi parlamentari 1968–1984*, ed. M. L. Righi (Rome: Camera dei Deputati, 2001), pp. 348–50.
85. FG, APCI, Estero, USSR, microfilm 8003, 394–408; Westad, *The Global Cold War*, p. 286.
86. FG, APCI, Directorate, minutes, 27 March 1980.
87. Note by Rubbi for Berlinguer, Pajetta, Bufalini, 12 October 1979, FG, APCI, Estero, Yugoslavia, 1979, microfilm 7911, pp. 0285–88; and account of a conversation of Ottavio Cecchi with Grličkov, FG, APCI, note to the Secretariat, 1980, microfilm 8102, pp. 128–30.
88. "Note on the Berlinguer-Brandt Meeting of 12 March 1980 in Strasbourg," FG, APCI, Estero, Germany-FRG, 1980 microfilm 8005, pp. 252–59; Rubbi, *Il mondo di Berlinguer*, pp. 244–45; and A. Pancaldi, "Brandt e Berlinguer: Ampio colloquio sulla crisi internazionale," *L'unità*, 1 March 1980.
89. Rubbi, *Il mondo di Berlinguer*, pp. 182–83; Rubbi, *Appunti cinesi* (Rome: Editori Riuniti, 1992), pp. 101–50.
90. FG, APCI, Estero, China, 1980, microfilm 8005, pp. 200–207.
91. FG, APCI, Directorate, minutes, 6 May 1980.
92. FG, APCI, Directorate, minutes, 9 September 1980.
93. A. Roccucci, "Il Concilio Vaticano II e l'elezione di Giovanni Paolo II: Mosca di fronte al a due svolte dell'Ostpolitik," in Melloni, ed., *Il filo sottile*, pp. 262–91.
94. FG, APCI, Estero, USSR, 1980, microfilm 8101, 137–48; and Pons, "Meetings between the Italian Communist Party and the Communist Party of the Soviet Union."
95. Lomellini, *L'appuntamento mancato*.
96. FG, APCI, Estero, Poland, 1980, microfilm 8012, pp. 97–98; and Chernyaev, *Sovmestnyj iskhod*, p. 429.
97. E. Serventi Longhi, "Solidarity and Italian Labor Movement Culture: CGIL Intellectuals and the Revision of the CGIL's International Relations (1980–1982)," in A. Guiso and A. Tarquini, eds., *Italian Intellectuals and International Politics, 1945–1992* (London: Palgrave Macmillan, 2019), pp. 243–47. See also Pajetta, *Le crisi che ho vissuto*.
98. FG, APCI, Directorate, minutes, 5 February 1981.

99. E. Scalfari, "Dove va il Pci? Intervista a Berlinguer," *La Repubblica*, 28 July, 1981, republished under the title "Che cos'è la questione morale" in Berlinguer, *La passione non è finita*, pp. 133–55; see also FG, APCI, Directorate, minutes, 10 September 1981; Napolitano, *Dal Pci al socialismo europeo*, pp. 166–69.

100. Tatò, *Caro Berlinguer*, pp. 187–92.

101. FG, APCI, Directorate, minutes, 5 February 1981.

102. FG, APCI, Centro Studi di Politica Internazionale, b. 2630.

103. "Pace e sviluppo cardini per un nuovo assetto mondiale," *L'unità*, 6 October 1981.

104. FG, APCI, Directorate, minutes, 26 November 1981, microfilm 8205.

105. A. Tatò, ed., *Conversazioni con Berlinguer* (Rome: Editori Riuniti, 1984), p. 271.

106. J. Fürst and S. V. Bittner, "The Aging Pioneer: Late Soviet Socialist Society, Its Challenges and Challengers," in Fürst, Pons, and Selden, eds., *The Cambridge History of Communism: Vol. 3, Endgames?* p. 295 et seq.

107. Tatò, *Caro Berlinguer*, pp. 227–41.

108. FG, APCI, Directorate, minutes, 22 December 1981.

109. *L'unità*, 30 December 1981.

110. *L'unità*, 12 January 1982.

111. FG, APCI, Directorate, minutes, 18 January 1982. For a reconstruction of the "break" between the PCI and Moscow, see Pons, *Berlinguer e la fine del comunismo*.

112. Chernyaev, *Moya zhizn' i moë vremya*, pp. 431–32.

113. Chernyaev, *Sovmestnyi iskhod*, pp. 468–69.

114. Fond Gorbacheva, f. 3, op. 1, k. 15064.

115. *L'unità*, 12 January 1982.

116. Brogi, *Confronting America*, p. 367 et seq.

117. FG, APCI, Estero, France, 1982, microfilm 8210, pp. 183–86; FG, APCI, Directorate, minutes, 2 April 1982.

118. Di Donato, *I comunisti italiani e la sinistra europea*, p. 265 et seq.

119. *XVI Congresso del Partito comunista italiano: Atti risoluzioni documenti* (Rome: Editori Riuniti, 1983), pp. 24–25. Cf. Gualtieri, *L'Italia dal 1943 al 1992*, pp. 224–25.

120. "Note on the Arguments of Grličkov, Minić, and Moissov (Belgrade, 18–19 February 1981)," FG, APCI, notes to the Secretariat, microfilm 8103, pp. 39–49.

121. FG, APCI, Fondo Berlinguer, Movimento Operaio Internazionale, fascicolo 174; Rubbi, *Il mondo di Berlinguer*, pp. 247–71.

122. Rubbi, *Il mondo di Berlinguer*, pp. 281–95.

123. Garavini, *Dopo gli imperi*, p. 308.

124. FG, APCI, Fondo Berlinguer, Movimento Operaio Internazionale, fascicolo 174.

125. FG, APCI, notes to the Secreteriat, 1980, microfilm 8012, pp. 64–73.

126. Salati to the Secretariat, FG, APCI, Estero, Algeria, 1982, microfilm 507, 3166–73; see Borruso, *Il PCI e l'Africa indipendente*, pp. 118–19.

127. FG, APCI, notes to the Secretariat, microfilm 8207, pp. 200–206, 5 July 1982.
128. Lorenzini, *Una strana guerra fredda*, pp. 262–66.
129. Riccardi, *L'internazionalismo difficile*, pp. 503–7.
130. Rubbi, *Il mondo di Berlinguer*, pp. 295–308.
131. A. Reichlin, "Begin non Israele" in *Rinascita*, 1 October 1982. See Riccardi, *L'internazionalismo difficile*, pp. 534–35.
132. FG, APCI, Estero, Algeria, 1983, microfilm 8301, pp. 22–30.
133. FG, APCI, notes to the Secretariat, 1983, microfilm 8302, pp. 26–34.
134. FG, APCI, notes to the Secretariat, microfilm 8302, 18 February 1983.
135. FG, APCI, Directorate, attachments to the minutes, 1983, microfilm 8403, 16 August 1983, pp. 115–22; see Rubbi, *Appunti cinesi*, pp. 169–203.
136. Cossutta, *Una storia comunista*, pp. 124–25.
137. Berlinguer, *Discorsi parlamentari*, pp. 298–304.
138. FG, APCI, notes to the Secretariat, 1983, microfilm 8311, pp. 103–15.
139. "Acuta tensione tra Usa e Urss, Berlinguer: Una più forte iniziativa di pace per fermare la terribile spirale dei missili," *L'unità*, 26 November 1983.
140. FG, APCI, Directorate, minutes, 5 January 1984.
141. "Obiettivi: Pace, sviluppo, riforme: Così il PCI affronta l'appuntamento delle elezioni europee; L'intervento del compagno Berlinguer," *L'unità*, 12 January 1984.
142. FG, APCI, notes to the Secretariat, 1983, microfilm 8405, pp. 22–42.
143. E. Di Nolfo, ed., *La politica estera italiana negli anni ottanta* (Venice: Marsilio, 2003).
144. FG, APCI, notes to the Secretariat, 1983, microfilm 8405, pp. 1–21, 12 December 1983; see Fasanaro, *La DDR e l'Italia*, pp. 190–94.
145. FG, APCI, Directorate, minutes, 15 December 1983.
146. M. D'Alema, *A Mosca l'ultima volta: Enrico Berlinguer e il 1984* (Rome: Donzelli, 2004).
147. "L'intervento di Enrico Berlinguer," *L'unità*, 28 April 1984.
148. "L'Europa, la pace, lo sviluppo: Intervista a 'Critica marxista' di Enrico Berlinguer," *Critica Marxista* 1984, no. 1–2, pp. 5–19.
149. Pons, *La rivoluzione globale*, pp. 384–87.
150. C. S. Maier, "Thirty Years After: The End of European Communism in Historical Perspective," in Fürst, Pons, and Selden, eds., *The Cambridge History of Communism, Vol. 3, Endgames?*, pp. 535–58.

Epilogue

1. M. S. Gorbachev, *Zhizn' i reformy*, 2 vols. (Moscow: Novosti, 1995), vol. 1, pp. 255–56.
2. A. S. Chernyaev, *Shest' let s Gorbachëvym* (Moscow: Progress-Kul'tura, 1993), pp. 15–16.
3. A. Rubbi, *Incontri con Gorbaciov: I colloqui di Natta e Occhetto con il leader sovietico* (Rome: Editori Riuniti, 1990), p. 26.

4. A. Brown, *The Gorbachev Factor* (Oxford, UK: Oxford University Press, 1996), p. 75; J. Lévesque, *The Enigma of 1989: The USSR and the Liberation of Eastern Europe* (Berkeley: University of California Press, 1997), pp. 19–21.

5. FG, APCI, Secretariat, 1985, microfilm 8505, pp. 150–56.

6. FG, APCI, Directorate, minutes, 20 March 1985.

7. Boffa, *Memorie dal comunismo*, pp. 222–23.

8. Cervetti, *Compagno del secolo scorso*, pp. 303–4.

9. G. Petracchi, "L'Italia e la Ostpolitik," in *La politica estera italiana negli anni ottanta*, pp. 271–93; S. Tavani, "L'Ostpolitik italiana nella politica estera di Andreotti," in M. Barone and E. Di Nolfo, eds., *Giulio Andreotti: L'uomo, il cattolico, lo statista* (Soveria Mannelli, Italy: Rubbettino, 2010), pp. 243–304.

10. Rubbi, *Incontri con Gorbaciov*, p. 78 et seq.

11. FG, APCI, Secretariat, 1986, microfilm 8605, pp. 132–57.

12. FG, APCI, Directorate, minutes, 4 February 1986.

13. On the significance of the Chernobyl catastrophe for Gorbachev's glasnost, see Gorbachev, *Zhizn' i reformy*, vol. 1.

14. FG, APCI, Directorate, Esteri, 1986, microfilm 8905, pp. 9–15.

15. R. Service, *The End of the Cold War 1985–1991* (London: Macmillan, 2015), pp. 209–18; R. English, *Russia and the Idea of the West: Gorbachev, Intellectuals, and the End of the Cold War* (New York: Columbia University Press, 2000), p. 223.

16. Rubbi, *Incontri con Gorbaciov*, pp. 120–21.

17. FG, APCI, Estero, Algeria, minutes of Natta's meetings with Vidoje Žarković, Sherif Messadia of the Algerian FLN, and Al-Qaddumi of the PLO, 27 June 1986, microfilm 8607, pp. 45–49.

18. FG, APCI, Estero, China, report of Natta's visit to China (13–18 October 1985), microfilm 0579, pp. 1425–42.

19. FG, APCI, minutes of the meeting of the PCI delegation with Hu Yaobang, Rome, 21 June 1986, microfilm 8607, pp. 23–29.

20. Ch. Jian, "China's Changing Policies toward the Third World and the End of the Global Cold War," in *The End of the Cold War and the Third World: New Perspectives on Regional Conflict*, ed. A. Kalinovsky and S. Radchenko (London and New York: Routledge, 2011), pp. 101–21.

21. Chernyaev, *Shest' let s Gorbachëvym*, p. 141.

22. FG, APCI, Directorate, minutes, 22 October 1987.

23. *V Politburo TsK KPSS: Po zapisami Anatoliya Chernyaeva, Vadima Medvedeva, Georgiya Shakhnazarova (1985–1991)* (Moscow: Al'pina Biznes Books, 2006), p. 273.

24. A. Possieri, *Il peso della storia: Memoria, identità, rimozione dal PCI al PDS 1970–1991* (Bologna: Il Mulino, 2007), pp. 173–74, 198.

25. FG, APCI, Directorate, minutes, 16–17 November 1987.

26. Napolitano, *Dal PCI al socialismo europeo*, p. 233.

27. Fond Gorbacheva, f. 3, op. 1, k. 7125.

28. Rubbi, *Incontri con Gorbaciov*, p. 196; Napolitano, *Dal PCI al socialismo europeo*, p. 230.

29. FG, APCI, Estero, USSR, minutes taken by Renato Sandri of the meeting between the delegation of the CPSU and that of the PCI, Moscow, 29 March 1988.
30. *V Politburo TsK KPSS*, p. 312.
31. Service, *The End of the Cold War*, pp. 298–300.
32. Boffa, *Memorie dal comunismo*, p. 224.
33. Fond Gorbacheva, f. 2, op. 1, k. 1163.
34. FG, APCI, Esteri, 19 July 1988 and 23 December 1988.
35. FG, APCI, Directorate, minutes, 13–14 October 1988.
36. *V Politburo TsK KPSS*, p. 420; Service, *The End of the Cold War*, pp. 356–57.
37. *V Politburo TsK KPSS*, p. 375.
38. Westad, *The Global Cold War*, p. 364 et seq.; S. Savranskaya, "Gorbachev and the Third World," in *The End of the Cold War and the Third World*, pp. 21–45.
39. J. Mark, B. C. Iacob, T. Rupprecht, and L. Spaskovska, *1989. A Global History of Eastern Europe* (Cambridge, UK, and New York: Cambridge University Press, 2019), pp. 40–41.
40. Patel, *Project Europe*, p. 166 et seq.
41. FG, APCI, Estero, USSR, 11 January 1989.
42. F. Di Palma, ed., *Perestroika and the Party: National and Transnational Perspectives on European Communist Parties in the Era of Soviet Reform* (New York and Oxford, UK: Berghahn, 2019).
43. Conversation with Brandt, January 1989, FG, APCI, Giorgio Napolitano, microfilm 8904, pp. 284–89; and note on the meetings in Bonn with the delegation of the SPD, 23 February 1989, FG, APCI, Antonio Rubbi, microfilm 8904, pp. 243–47.
44. FG, APCI, Estero, USSR, minutes of Occhetto's meeting with Gorbachev, Moscow 28 February 1989.
45. Chernyaev, *Shest' let s Gorbachëvym*, p. 282.
46. FG, APCI, Directorate, minutes, 6 March, 1989.
47. FG, APCI, Directorate, minutes, 28 April 1989.
48. FG, APCI, Directorate, minutes, 5 July 1989.
49. S. Kotkin, *Armageddon Averted: The Soviet Collapse 1970–2000* (Oxford, UK, and New York: Oxford University Press, 2008); see also S. Pons and F. Romero, eds., *Reinterpreting the End of the Cold War: Issues, Interpretations, Periodizations* (London: Frank Cass, 2005).
50. S. Kotkin, *Uncivil Society: 1989 and the Implosion of the Communist Establishment* (New York: Modern Library, 2010).
51. P. Fassino, *Per passione* (Milan: Rizzoli, 2003), pp. 183–88.
52. FG, APCI, Directorate, minutes, 14–15 November 1989.
53. Chernyaev, *Sovmestnyi iskhod*, p. 818.
54. A. Varsori, *L'Italia e la fine della guerra fredda: La politica estera dei governi Andreotti (1989–1992)* (Bologna: Il Mulino, 2013).
55. Rubbi, *Incontri con Gorbaciov*, pp. 284–86.
56. Rubbi, *Incontri con Gorbaciov*, p. 295.

57. Fond Gorbacheva, f. 2, op. 1, k. 8161.
58. Lévesque, *The Enigma of 1989*, pp. 210–11.
59. Boffa, *Memorie del comunismo*, p. 233.
60. "La relazione di Occhetto al Comitato centrale," *L'unità*, 24 July 1990.
61. Notes of Giuseppe Boffa on the meeting with Gorbachev, 15 November 1990, FG, APCI, Estero, USSR.
62. Chernyaev, *Shest' let s Gorbachëvym*, p. 379.
63. A. Occhetto, *La lunga eclissi: Passato e presente del dramma della sinistra* (Palermo: Sellerio, 2018). For a reading dating back to the period, see G. Vacca, *La sfida di Gorbaciov: Guerra e pace nell'era globale*, with the collaboration of G. Fiocco (Rome: Salerno, 2019).
64. Pons and Di Donato, *Reform Communism*, pp. 178–202.
65. Napolitano, *Dal Pci al socialismo europeo*, p. 228.
66. Patel, *Project Europe*, pp. 271–72.

Index

Adenauer, Konrad, 195
Afghanistan, 285–89, 300, 322
Al Fatah, 237
Algeria, 178, 220–21, 237, 254, 255, 301, 304, 316; coup d'état in, 211; French left's view of, 179, 186, 189; independence won by, 190, 191, 198; Italian communists aligned with, 302; as mediator, 253
Alicata, Mario, ix, 169, 172, 174, 212
Allende, Salvador, 238, 242–43
Amendola, Giorgio, ix, 84, 96, 155, 163, 181, 191–92, 202, 204, 236, 255, 257, 262, 265, 285; bourgeois background of, 58; Bretton Woods dissolution viewed by, 239; at Brussels Conference (1974), 242; Christian Democrats opposed by, 275; "democratic centralism" criticized by, 174–75; de-Stalinization viewed by, 157; European integration backed by, 239–40, 278; internationalism avoided by, 230; national vs. internationalist language viewed by, 172; in occupied France, 85; in party leadership, 109, 154, 169; peaceful coexistence viewed by, 226; during Prague Spring, 228, 231; Salerno turn backed by, 110; Soviet links backed by, 215; Togliatti contrasted with, 173; Yom Kippur War viewed by, 245

Andreotti, Giulio, 264–65, 314, 328, 331
Andropov, Yuri, 298, 305, 307
Angola, 253, 254
Aquila, Giulio (Gyula Sas), 20, 26
Arafat, Yasser, 198, 237, 303–4
Atlantic Alliance, xiii, 138, 146, 151, 176
Austria, 81
Austro-Hungarian Empire, 11

Badoglio, Pietro, 96–99
Bahr, Egon, 219, 240
Bandung Conference (1955), 157, 166
Barbusse, Henri, 60
Barca, Luciano, 147–48, 155–56, 171, 213, 249, 266, 277
Barre, Mohammad Siad, 281–82
Basso, Lelio, 177
Bauer, Leo, 219
Bauer, Otto, 72–73
Bavarian Republic, 11, 14

379

Bay of Pigs invasion (1961), 198
Begin, Menachem, 304
Belgium, 117
Ben Bella, Ahmed, 190, 196, 197, 211
Bendjedid, Chadli, 302
Beriya, Lavrentiy, 147–48
Berlinguer, Enrico, ix, 169, 192, 201, 202, 212–13, 219, 255, 266–68; Afghanistan invasion condemned by, 286; Brandt and, 271; China visited by, 288–89, 304; Chinese politics viewed by, 170, 195, 218; as communist youth leader, 228; *Corriere della sera* interview with, 262, 274; death of, 307, 322; democracy praised by, 269; Eurocommunism and, 264-69, 275–77; European integration embraced by, xiii, 236, 240–42, 249, 260–61, 283–84, 306; fall of, 298–311, 321; Gorbachev likened to, 318; "historic compromise" and, 242–43, 249–50, 275–76, 279, 292, 294; as humanistic socialist, 248–50, 252–53, 308; Italian exceptionalism viewed by, 294; Kissinger criticized by, 257; Latin America visited by, 301–2; legacy of, 308, 310; Leninist influence on, 276; Middle East conflict and, 303; missile negotiations sought by, 307; Moro linked to, 272–73; Napolitano's criticism of, 293; during Prague Spring, 225, 230, 231; "second Cold War" viewed by, 287–88, 292; Soviet financial support opposed by, 248; Soviet future viewed by, 296–97; Soviet intransigence criticized by, 226–27; Soviets' Africa policy viewed by, 282; Soviets and Eastern Europe cultivated by, 307; Soviets faulted by, 289, 295, 296; "third way" backed by, 278–79, 296; two camps thesis rejected by, 239; US faulted by, 289; in Vietnam, 217; Vietnam peace viewed by, 254
Berlin Wall, 171, 326, 327
Berti, Giuseppe, ix, 4, 79, 85, 96
Bianco, Vincenzo, 85, 94, 96
Bierut, Bolesław, 121
Blackmer, Donald, 266
Blagoeva, Stella, 80, 83, 85, 87
Boffa, Giuseppe, 314, 329
Bogomolov, Aleksandr, 101, 102
Bordiga, Amadeo, ix, 10, 12, 19, 23, 31, 41, 54, 55; Gramsci distinguished from, 4–5, 27–28; intransigence of, 17, 20; as orthodox Marxist, 4; Stalin challenged by, 29; Togliatti influenced by, 57; Wilson disparaged by, 8
Boumedienne, Houari, 220, 302
Brandt, Willy, xi, 229, 240, 250, 300, 302, 306, 324; Berlinguer and, 271, 276, 288, 305; Italian communists linked to, 219; Ostpolitik launched by, 235; Socialist International led by, 271, 281
Brazil, 48
Bretton Woods system, 239, 240
Brezhnev, Leonid, 245, 266–67, 277, 285, 298, 299; Berlinguer and, 230, 241–42, 261, 269, 282; Longo and, 216, 218, 223; Togliatti's meeting with, 202
Brezhnev doctrine, 226, 263, 328
Briand-Kellogg Pact (1928), 46
Browder, Earl, 85, 103
Brutents, Karen, 287
Brzezinski, Zbigniew, 265, 266, 271
Bufalini, Paolo, ix, 169, 212, 227, 249, 268, 285, 288, 295–97, 303; Afghanistan invasion viewed by, 286; authoritarianism denounced by, 224; bipolarism rejected by, 252; détente viewed by, 240, 257

Bukharin, Nikolai, 15, 21, 32, 42, 47, 55; antifascism stressed by, 20, 26; fall of, 49, 53; Gramsci linked to, 33–34; Stalin's split with, 41, 52; struggle for peace rejected by, 45–46; Trotsky vs., 27, 30
Bulgaria, 143

Cabral, Amilcar, 198, 253
Cairo Conference (1962), 189
Calamandrei, Franco, 266, 286
Cambodia, 283
Cameroon, 187
Carrillo, Santiago, 202, 253, 267, 268
Carter, Jimmy, 265, 266, 267, 272, 277
Castro, Fidel, 190, 212, 220, 282, 301
Catholics, 81, 95, 140, 150, 154, 177, 179, 193, 215, 217, 257, 269–70; anticommunist, 104, 115–16, 131, 151; neutralist, 108, 138; Polish workers' movement and, 290–91; progressive, 237; waning influence of, 246
Ceaușescu, Nicolae, 225–26, 266, 307
Central Intelligence Agency (CIA), vii
Cervetti, Gianni, 248, 295, 314
Charter for Peace and Development (1981), 294, 301
Chernayev, Anatoly, 266, 287, 291, 298, 313, 320, 323, 325, 328
Chernenko, Konstantin, 313
Chernobyl nuclear accident (1986), 315
Cheysson, Claude, 254–55, 280
Chiang Kai-shek, 45
Chiaromonte, Gerardo, 304
Chile, 199, 238–39, 242–45
China, 8, 89, 163, 201; Algerian revolutionaries linked to, 190; Berlinguer's overtures to, 300; British decline and, 32, 33, 45; cultural revolution in, 219; Indian border disputes with, 192; Italian policy toward, 197–98, 288–89; Korean war and, 145; nonviolent transformation rejected by, 185, 192; perestroika viewed by, 316; during Prague Spring, 228; revolution in, 31, 45, 46, 86, 142, 143, 158; Soviet alliance with, 183; Soviet tensions with, 168, 169–70, 194, 195, 205; student protests in, 326; Third World influence of, 199; Tito's view of, 196–97; Togliatti's stance toward, 174, 193, 198, 205; Vietnam War and, 283
Christian Democrats, 126, 130, 145, 155, 177, 182, 264–65, 267, 273–75, 308; anticommunism of, 134–35; Berlinguer's overtures to, 242; in Chile, 238, 245; divisions within, 179; electoral strategy of, 279; neutralism of, xiii, 108; in Portugal, 252; secularization and, 246, 269–70
Churchill, Winston, 102, 109
Cicalini, Antonio, 143
Cocchi, Armando, 82
Codovilla, Victorio, 76
Colombi, Arturo, 147, 148, 169, 201
Cominform, 126, 133, 151; Asian communism and, 143; decline of, 149, 155; founding of, 122, 123; ideological splits exposed by, 125, 127; socialist bloc and Western communists linked by, 135; Togliatti and, 142, 145, 146; Yugoslavia in, 128, 132
Comintern, vii, ix, x, 9–10, 12; antifascist turn of, 65; birth of, 8; dissolution of, 93, 137; eroding power of, 71; internationalism of, 15–16, 17; Italian Communists criticized by, 54
Comitato di Liberazione Nazionale Alta Italia (CLNAI), 104, 109
Committee of National Liberation (CLN), 97, 98
Confederazione Generale Italiana del Lavoro (CGIL), 84

Conference of Helsinki (1975), 256, 257, 267, 328, 330
Conference of Non-Aligned Countries, 188
Conference on the Mediterranean (1968), 221
Congo, 188
Convention of Lomé (1975), 255
Corsini, Gianfranco, 181
Corvalán, Luis, 238, 239, 243
Cossutta, Armando, ix, 225, 227, 249, 295, 297, 305
Craxi, Bettino, 276, 292, 305, 307, 308, 314, 331
Croce, Benedetto, 100
Cuba, 194, 199, 238, 281, 288, 323; in Angolan civil war, 254; Bay of Pigs invasion of, 198; missile crisis in, 190, 192; revolution in, 186; Yugoslavia and, 196, 211, 212
Cucci, Aldo, 143
Cunhal, Álvaro, 252, 253
Czechoslovakia, 52, 116, 117, 129, 135, 198; Charter 77 dissidents in, 267; Soviet invasion of, 222–34, 241, 244, 264

D'Alema, Massimo, 325, 328
Dawes Plan, 27, 33
De Gasperi, Alcide, xiii, 116, 117–18, 131, 138, 145, 150, 153, 176–77
de Gaulle, Charles, 179, 180, 195
De Martino, Francesco, 228
Deng Xiaoping, xi, 170, 282, 288–89, 316, 326
Díaz, José, 76, 87
Đilas (Djilas), Milovan, 105, 119, 128
Dimitrov, Georgi, 51, 63, 67–68, 82–84, 101, 120; Browder criticized by, 103; Comintern led by, 62, 86–87; death of, 145; Spanish Civil War and, 74–76; Stalinism embraced by, 78; Togliatti and, 73–74, 81, 85–86, 88, 95, 98–99, 103; Trieste annexation to Yugoslavia proposed by, 106
Di Vittorio, Giuseppe, ix, 84, 107, 133, 159
Dobrynin, Anatoly, 315
Donini, Ambrogio, 96
D'Onofrio, Edoardo, 96, 143, 145, 147, 169
Dozza, Giuseppe, 85
Dubček, Alexander, 222, 223, 224, 229
Duclos, Jacques, 76, 167, 168, 186
Dunn, James, 129

East Germany, 182, 184, 219, 268, 323, 326
Eastman, Max, 9, 34–35
Ebert, Friedrich, 6
Egypt, 187–88, 220, 221
Ehmke, Horst, 253
Eisenhower, Dwight D., 178
Engels, Friedrich, 5
Eritrea, 281–82
Ethiopia, 68–71, 189, 220, 281–82, 287, 301
Eurocommunism, 259–69, 275–77, 282, 285–87, 294, 305, 311
Euromissile crisis, 279, 284, 285, 291, 292, 305, 306, 320
European Community, 189, 215, 235–36, 239, 247, 255, 259, 268, 280, 332; Berlinguer's view of, 240, 249, 264; enlargement of, 246; Italy in, xiii, 216; sovereignty guaranteed by, 284; Togliatti's view of, 205
Executive Committee of the Communist International (ECCI), 51, 61

Fanfani, Amintore, 179, 180, 217
Fanon, Frantz, 191
Finland, 117
Ford, Gerald, 256
Forlani, Armaldo, 282
Fortichiari, Bruno, 23

France: as colonial power, 178, 179, 189–90; communists in, x, 17, 63, 112, 116, 117, 134, 136–38, 162, 189, 212, 226, 285, 320, 323; Czechoslovakia invasion denounced by, 224; financial crisis in, 30; Hungarian invasion and, 167–68; left-wing consensus and frictions in, 240, 271; in Suez crisis, 161; US policy toward, 149
Franco, Francisco, 115–16, 195, 251, 256
Franke, Egon, 219

Galluzzi, Carlo, 216, 218, 219, 225, 235
Gardner, Richard, 266, 271, 272
Germany, 10, 11–12, 16, 32, 219; Austria annexed by, 81; communists in, 17, 19, 22–26, 51, 117; emigrants from, 72; factory councils in, 6; labor strength in, 13–14, 15; in League of Nations, 33, 45; "March action" in, 18; partition of, 143, 171; Poland invaded by, 84; postwar economy in, 27, 31; reunification of, 328, 329, 331; sectarianism in, 57; social democrats in, 61; Soviet Union invaded by, 86–87, 89
Ghana, 187, 211
Gierek, Edward, 290
Giolitti, Antonio, 160, 247
Giolitti, Giovanni, 145
Giustizia e Liberta, 61
Gomułka, Władysław, 121, 143, 164, 165, 171
Gorbachev, Mikhail, xi, xiv, 312–31
Gramsci, Antonio, ix, xii, 36, 47, 54, 63, 88, 206; American power stressed by, 33, 68; Bolshevik victory in civil war viewed by, 13; Bolshevik repression accepted by, 22; Bordiga opposed to, 4–5, 27–28; capitalist stabilization viewed by, 30–31; Comintern's criticism of, 25; criticism of both Trotsky and Stalin expressed by, 35; fascism viewed by, 55–56; German revolution viewed by, 13–14; hegemony interpreted by, 38–39, 43; legacy of, 260; Lenin's backing of, 15; Lenin's death and, 24; Lenin's "dictatorship of the proletariat" viewed by, 5; Lenin's meeting with, 21; in Moscow, 18–20; October Revolution viewed by, 4; "passive revolution" interpreted by, 66, 161; postwar order viewed by, 5–11, 22–25, 31–32; prison notebooks of, xii, 88–89, 140, 161; "socialism in one country" and, 27–28; Soviet relations with Mussolini and, 26–27; Soviet Republic viewed by, 7; "statolatry" interpreted by, 59; Togliatti contrasted with, 37–40, 44; Togliatti's posthumous defense of, 88–89; Versailles peace viewed by, 11–12; Wilson viewed by, 7–9
Gramsci, Gennaro, 55–56
Great Britain, 9, 69, 112, 224, 271; Bolsheviks' view of, 31; general strike in, 29, 30, 32; Soviet split with, 45; in Suez crisis, 161
Greece, 85, 100, 107, 112, 122, 129, 220, 234, 246
Grieco, Ruggero, ix, 23, 51, 53, 56, 67, 79, 96; Bordiga criticized by, 29; colonialism viewed by, 49; Mussolini's proposals viewed by, 26; war resistance backed by, 70
Gromyko, Andrei, 247
Gronchi, Giovanni, 180
Guevara, Ernesto (Che), 190, 198, 199
Guinea, 187, 253, 254
Guinea-Bissau, 253, 254

Helsinki Accords (1975), 330
Hilferding, Rudolf, 44

Hiroshima, 120
Hitler, Adolf, x, 59–62, 64–65, 71–75, 81, 83–85, 112, 124
Hobsbawm, Eric, xi, 54, 74, 150, 260
Hoffmann, Stanley, 266
Honecker, Erich, 241, 242, 307
Hoxha, Enver, 207
Hua Guofeng, 288
Humbert-Droz, Jules, 18, 37, 50
Hungary, 6, 7, 143, 225, 298, 326; failed revolution in, 11, 14; popular revolts in, 158–65; Russian Revolution and, 10; Soviet invasion of, 158–66, 168, 171, 175, 290
Hu Yaobang, 288, 304, 316

Ibárruri, Dolores, 87
India, 8, 186, 192
Indonesia, 158, 186
Ingrao, Pietro, ix, 163, 167, 169, 201–2, 226, 228, 286–87, 325; in Cuba, 198, 201; radicalism of, 192, 213, 227, 249; at the Cominform Secretariat of November 1950, 145; working-class mobilization stressed by, 215
International Monetary Fund (IMF), 263
Iotti, Nilde, 169, 292
Iran, 283, 285
Iraq, 303
Israel, 220, 303
Iurenev, Konstantin, 25

Jaruzelski, Wojciech, 295, 298
Jaurès, Jean, 120
John Paul II, Pope, 290, 303, 328
John XXIII, Pope, 180, 193
Johnson, Lyndon B., 216
Jospin, Lionel, 299

Kádár, János, 269, 321
Kaganovich, Lazar', 69

Kamenev, Lev, 35
Kania, Stanislaw, 290
Kapp, Wolfgang, 13
Kardelj, Edvard, 102, 105, 122, 128
Katayama, Sen, 10
Kautsky, Karl, 77
Kellogg-Briand Pact (1928), 46
Kennan, George F., 129
Kennedy, John F., 180, 197, 205
Kerzhentsev, Platon, 28, 36
Khrushchev, Nikita, 159, 160, 170, 175–76, 185–86, 200; anti-Semitism of, 163–64, fall of, 202, 211, 212; Stalin denounced by, 150, 155, 156–57, 158, 171
Kirilenko, Andrei, 230
Kirov, Sergei, 72
Kissinger, Henry, 245, 246, 256–57, 263–67, 271, 283
Knorin, Vilhelm, 62
Kolarov, Vasil, 18, 51
Korea, 144
Kosygin, Aleksei, 218, 230
Kostov, Trajčo, 143
Kostylev, Mikhail, 105, 106, 111, 124, 126, 129, 133; as ambassador, 102; Togliatti's secret meeting with, 130, 131
Kozlov, Frol, 174
Kozyrev, Semën, 200, 201
Kreisky, Bruno, 306
Kun, Béla, 11, 18
Kuusinen, Otto, 18, 62

Lange, Peter, 266
La Pira, Giorgio, 177, 216
La Palombara, Joseph, 265
League of Nations, 7–10, 33, 45, 46, 69
Lebanon, 303
Ledda, Romano, 220, 294–95
Le Duan, 220
Lenin, Vladimir, xi, 13, 16, 19, 25, 77, 166; death of, 22, 54; evolutionary

Marxism rejected by, 4; Gramsci influenced by, 36–37, 38; Gramsci's meeting with, 21; Italian revolution urged by, 15; as mythic figure, 24; socialism and democracy distinguished by, 5; state capitalism launched by, 39; Terracini attacked by, 18; "testament" of, 34–35, 37; Third International sought by, 3
Leonetti, Alfonso, 55
Lessons of October (Trotsky), 27
Lettere di Spartaco (Togliatti), 85, 86
Libya, 49, 303
Liu Shaoqui, 170
Lithuania, 15, 179
Litvinov, Maksim, 26, 68, 76, 83, 114
Livorno Conference (1921), 16–17
Locarno Treaty (1925), 33, 46
Lomé Convention (1976), 280, 303
Longo, Luigi, ix, 58, 77, 104, 121–23, 147–48, 163, 174, 185–87, 207, 213–14; Algiers visited by, 198; arrest in France of, 85; extralegal options viewed by, 145, 146; rapprochement with French communists, 212; Moscow visited by, 200; nuclear war viewed by, 170; in party leadership, 169; polycentrism mistrusted by, 216; Prague Spring endorsed by, 223–24, 227–28, 229; in Resistance in the North, 96; as Stalinist, 54, 55; "three fronts" strategy embraced by, 221; Tito approached by, 218
López Portillo, José, 302
Löwenthal, Richard, 271
Lumumba, Patrice, 188
Lyon Congress (1926), 28, 41, 48–49, 52, 57, 70

Macaluso, Emanuele, 268, 296
Magnani, Valdo, 143
Magri, Lucio, 181, 213, 233
Makar, Aleksandr, 2

Malenkov, Georgii, 153, 155
Mandela, Nelson, 191, 198
Manuilsky, Dmitri, 18, 20, 37, 42, 56, 62, 78, 80, 86, 96, 98, 101; antifascism viewed by, 73, 81; German communists' split viewed by, 50, 51; Gramsci criticized by, 27; as inquisitor, 79; Togliatti criticized by, 83
Mao Zedong, 89, 143, 164–67, 170, 193, 316
Marchais, Georges, 241, 242, 252, 255, 267, 277, 323
Marković, Ante, 306
Marshall Plan, xiii, 118–21, 124, 126, 135
Martini, Rigoletto, 82
Marty, André, 76
Marx, Karl, 4–5
Mattei, Enrico, 177, 198
Matteotti, Giacomo, 25, 26, 31
Mazowiecki, Tadeusz, 326
Mengistu Hailé Mariam, 281–82
Mitterrand, François, 250, 288, 292, 299, 306
Mlynář, Zdeněk, 222, 267
Mollet, Guy, 179
Molotov, Vyacheslav, 67, 69, 83, 96, 97, 99, 101, 112; antimonarchist intransigence in Italy backed by, 98; at Marshall Plan conference, 119; Ribbentrop's pact with, 86; as Stalinist head of the Comintern, 57; Yugoslavs mistrusted by, 130–31
Molotov-Ribbentrop Pact, 86
Mondini, Teresa, 96
Montagnana, Rita, 96
Moro, Aldo, 216, 220–21, 238, 246, 249, 256, 257, 265, 272–75
Morocco, 185
Moskvin (Trilisser), Mikhail, 73, 78
Mozambique, 253
Münzenberg, Willi, 49, 60

Mussolini, Benito, 19, 20, 25, 56, 65, 75, 85; empire proclaimed by, 71; imperialist attack to Ethiopia by, 70, 189; fall of, 94, 95; Soviet talks with, 26–27; as totalitarian dictator, 42

Nagasaki, 120
Nagy, Imre, 159, 171
Naimark, Norman, 134
Napolitano, Giorgio, ix, 240, 257, 276, 292–93, 296–97, 305, 315–19, 321, 324, 325; Berlinguer criticized by, 293; Europe viewed by, 317, 325; Gorbachev viewed by, 331; as moderate leader, 172, 249, 262, 285, 299, 331; relationship with Berlinguer of, 262; Socialist International viewed by, 327–28; Suslov's criticism of, 269; US visa denied to, 266; visit to the US of, 276
Nasser, Gamal Abdel, 158, 186, 188, 196, 220, 237
NATO (North Atlantic Treaty Organization), 163, 205, 235, 236, 283, 292, 305; Italy in, 138, 240, 249, 256, 263, 277; reunified Germany in, 328, 331
Natta, Alessandro, ix, 192, 234, 257, 304, 313–16, 319, 320, 325
Nazis, 57, 64, 68
Negarville, Celeste, ix, 84, 87, 157
Negrín, Juan, 78, 82
Nehru, Jawaharlal, 158, 166, 178
Nenni, Pietro, 70, 177, 217
neoliberalism, 310, 316
New Deal, 139, 181
New Left, 222, 225, 233, 234, 236
Nicaragua, 301
Nigeria, 187
Nin, Andrés, 77
Nixon, Richard M., 235, 239, 251
Nkrumah, Kwame, 191, 211
Noce, Teresa, ix, 147

Norway, 224
nuclear weapons, 120, 143, 144, 153–54, 166, 193, 310

Occhetto, Achille, 213, 318, 320–30
Operation Marigold, 217
Ordine Nuovo group, 10, 18, 19, 41; factory councils linked to, 12; Lenin's view of, 15, 25; sectarianism of, 17
Orlov, Aleksandr, 77
Ortega, Daniel, 31
Ostpolitik, 219–20, 235, 236, 249

Pajetta, Giancarlo, ix, 109, 147, 169, 172, 213, 224, 225, 249, 268, 282, 285, 288, 295, 296, 304; Arafat and, 237; Chilean coup viewed by, 243; moderate tendencies of, 191–92, 227; in Moscow, 157; in Resistance, 104, 163; in Vietnam, 212
Pajetta, Giuliano, 186, 216
Palestine, 221, 237, 257, 303, 316
Palestine Liberation Organization (PLO), 303
Palme, Olof, 250, 270, 305, 306
Pankhurst, Sylvia, 10
Papandreou, Andreas, 307
Partisans of Peace (World Peace Council), 138, 149, 182
Pavone, Claudio, 94
peaceful coexistence, 175–77, 192, 193, 196, 213–15, 226, 233, 320
Pecchioli, Ugo, 199, 225, 285
Pertini, Sandro, 303, 307
Pieck, Wilhelm, 63
Pietromarchi, Luca, 180
Pilsudski, József, 16, 30
Pinochet, Augusto, 243
Pintor, Luigi, 233
Podgorny, Nikolai, 218, 230
Poland, 31, 48, 143, 163–64, 285; communist party dissolved in, 78–79; coup d'état in, 30, 295, 296, 305;

elections in, 325; German invasion of, 84; partition of, 83; popular revolts in, 158; "round table" in, 321; Polish-Soviet war, 15–16; Vatican linked to, 179; workers' protests in, 267, 290–92, 296
Pollitt, Harry, 62
Ponomarev, Boris, 163, 174, 200, 202, 212, 230, 247–48, 277, 315
Popular Front, 63, 71, 76–79, 86–88, 123, 129–31
Portillo, José Lopez, 302
Portugal, 31, 234, 246, 251–54, 257, 323
Prague Spring (1968), xiii, 222–34, 241–42, 267, 277, 296, 303, 313, 327
Prison Notebooks (Gramsci), xii, 88–89, 140, 161
Problems of Peace and Socialism, 184–85
Procacci, Giuliano, 74
Prunas, Renato, 97
Prussia, 57
Purman, Leon, 56
Pyatnitsky, Osip, 18, 56, 62

Radek, Karl, 18, 23
Rajk, László, 143
Rákosi, Mátyás, 18, 20, 111
Ravazzoli, Paolo, 55
Ravera, Camilla, ix, 84
Reagan, Ronald, 292, 315, 320
Reale, Eugenio, ix, 97, 111, 112, 119, 121, 122, 124; communist party abandoned by, 160; Greek civil war viewed by, 130; Trieste crisis and, 105–6
Red Brigades, 273–74
Reichlin, Alfredo, 199, 213, 262, 304, 316
Roasio, Antonio, ix, 87
Robotti, Paolo, 81, 169
Rochet, Waldeck, 212
Rockefeller, David, 265
Rodano, Franco, 261

Rolland, Romain, 60
Romania, 218, 227, 323
Roosevelt, Franklin D., 108
Rossanda, Rossana, 213, 233, 274
Roy, M. N., 55
Rubbi, Antonio, 288–89, 303, 305, 313, 315, 323, 328
Ruivo, Mário, 252–53
Russian Revolution, 7, 8

Sadat, Anwar, 237
Sakharov, Andrei, 315
Salati, Remo, 302
"Salerno turn," 100–103, 110, 112, 114, 184
Sandri, Renato, 199, 280–81
Santos, Marcelino dos, 253
Sartre, Jean-Paul, 191
Sas, Gyula (Giulio Aquila), 20, 26
Scalfari, Eugenio, 293
Scelba, Mario, 145, 154
Schlesinger, Arthur, 181
Schmidt, Helmut, 250, 264, 300
Schucht family, 85, 88
Schucht, Yulya, 83
Scoccimarro, Mauro, ix, 30, 54, 84, 96, 157, 163
Secchia, Pietro, ix, 110, 121, 132, 133, 144–49, 169, 239; de-Stalinization opposed by, 163; European violence foreseen by, 126–28, 129–30; intelligence role of, 135; Khrushchev's speech viewed by, 157; mass mobilization urged by, 123; on Moscow mission, 126, 128; as radical, 54–55; as Resistance leader, 96, 101, 104; Togliatti slighted by, 154
Second International, 3, 4
Segre, Sergio, 219, 252, 262, 265, 266, 270–71, 288; PCI international strategy explained by, 247; German social democrats linked to, 235; PCI Westpolitik backed by, 251

Senghor, Leopold, xi, 281
Seniga, Giulio, 154
Sereni, Emilio, ix, 58, 85, 109, 138
Serrati, Giacinto Menotti, 18, 20
Sforza, Carlo, 89
Shevlyagin, Dimitry, 118
Silone, Ignazio, 55
Six-Day War (1967), 220, 242, 304
Socialist International, 281, 300–301, 327–28
Solidarność, 290–91, 321, 325
Somalia, 187, 220, 281
Souvarine, Boris, 72–73
Soviet Union, ix; centrality of, 41–58; collapse of, xvi; Italian communists' faith in, xi, xv; Italian emigrants in, x, 79; "revolution from above" in, 50
Spadolini, Giovanni, 303
Spain, 31, 256; Civil War in, ix, 73–78, 82–83, 86, 115–16; right-wing government in, 234
Spano, Velio, ix, 70, 97, 162–64, 185, 186
Spartacists, 6
Spinelli, Altiero, 284
Stalin, Joseph, 27-30, 30, 34, 38, 98, 100; antifascist policy and, 61, 67–68; Bordiga vs., 28–29; Bukharin's split with, 41, 52; capitalist encirclement viewed by, 60; Central and Eastern Europe policy of, 113, 114, 115, 138, 158; Comintern dissolved by, 86, 93; Comintern radicalized and purged by, 50, 52, 77; death of, xiii, 150; French left viewed by, 126; Hitler's pact with, x, 83–85, 112, 124; Italian elections viewed by, 132; legacy of, 153; Lenin's "testament" and, 35–36; Marshall Plan opposed by, 120; modernization pursued by, 58–59; as mythic figure, 115, 156; radicalism and brutality of, 39, 45, 53, 65, 111, 170; religion viewed by, 144; sacralized politics and, 139; social democracy and fascism linked by, 48, 59; Soviet defense and internationalism linked by, 46, 54, 62; Spanish communists criticized by, 83; Spanish Republicans backed by, 76; sphere of influence strategy of, 102, 122, 135; Secchia's meeting with, 126-28; Tasca reprimanded by, 51; Tasca's judgement of, 52; Tito's split with, 135; Togliatti aligned with, 43, 46–47, 65, 72–73, 127, 156, 206; Togliatti's dissent from, 147–48; Togliatti viewed by, 111; Trieste crisis and, 106-7; war's inevitability theorized by, 69, 146–47; writings of, 141; xenophobia of, 78; at Yalta, 105
Stalingrad, Battle of (1942–43), 93, 94
Suez crisis (1956), 160, 161, 177
Sukarno, Akmed, 158, 211
Suslov, Mikhail, 163, 171, 187, 200, 268, 277, 285, 298; anti-Soviet views rejected by, 174; Berlinguer and, 228, 269; during Prague Spring, 225-26, 227–28, 230; struggle for peace backed by, 142
Sweden, 271
Syria, 220, 221, 303

Tarrow, Sidney, 265–66
Tasca, Angelo, ix, 14, 21, 47, 55, 57, 63, 80; anticommunist turn of, 64; expulsion of, 54; generational split noted by, 12; Gramsci criticized by, 31; as party representative at the Comintern, 49-50; Stalin criticized by, 52; Stalin's attack on, 50; Togliatti's split with, 51-52
Tatò, Antonio, 261, 276, 283, 293, 296, 318–19

Terracini, Umberto, vii, ix, 23, 54, 55, 85, 147, 157, 236; antifascism backed by, 67; Lenin's reprimand of, 18; dissent on the Molotov-Ribbentrop Pact expressed by, 84; Soviet foreign policy criticized by, 124–25
terrorism, 245, 273–74, 278
Thälmann, Ernst, 53
Thorez, Maurice, 63, 76, 86, 109, 162, 167, 201; in exile, 84; Stalin and, 102, 126, 128
Tienanmen Square massacre (1989), 326, 327
Tito, Josip Broz, 101, 143, 145, 171, 188, 212, 220, 251, 256, 264, 267, 277; Chinese polemics viewed by, 196, 199–200; death of, 301; international organization discussed with Stalin by, 111; Italian communists linked to, 156–58; Soviet tensions with, 218; Stalin's split with, 135; Trieste crisis and, 105, 106, 107
Togliatti, Palmiro, x, xii, 19, 34, 36, 46, 74-75, 121, 214, 221; Amendola contrasted with, 173; American hegemony viewed by, 118, 137; antifascism of, 73-74; assassination attempt against, 133; authority asserted by, 172–73; Berlin wall backed by, 171; Bukharin linked to, 45; catastrophism avoided by, 69, 104, 112, 119, 131, 134, 144–45, 148, 151, 160, 170, 193, 204; Chinese criticism of, 192; Chinese influence viewed by, 201–2; Cold War rhetoric of, 158–61; colonial revolution viewed by, 49; Cominform and, 132–33; as Comintern official, 72, 79, 81, 86-87; contradictory ideas of, 54–55, 57; coup d'état feared by, 105; "course on adversaries" by, 63–66; death of, 211; decolonization viewed by, 158, 177–78, 190, 197, 321; de-Stalinization and, 156–63, 173, 204; "destiny of humankind" viewed by, 192–93; détente backed by, 176, 177, 179, 180, 188; dissimulation strategy of, 53–54; fascism viewed by, 20, 42–43, 47–48, 62, 63–65, 71, 84, 85, 107–8, 175–76; French left and, 63; Gramsci's thought and Marxism-Leninism integrated by, 141–42; Gramsci contrasted with, 37–40, 44; Gramsci's prison writings edited by, 140; hegemonic ambitions of, xiii, 33, 44; Kostylev's secret meeting with, 130–31; mass party project of, 103–4, 115, 116, 133, 143, 149, 162; national unity invoked by, 93–94, 101, 108–9, 111–12, 119; nuclear war viewed by, 153–54, 166, 193; as "old guard" member, 51–52; as party leader after Gramsci's arrest, 41–43; as party representative at the Comintern, 29–30, 33–34, 37; peaceful coexistence and "new civilizations" linked by, 177–78; polycentrism viewed by, 157, 161–62, 165–66, 168, 174, 183, 200, 205, 206; "progressive democracy" viewed by, 113–14, 120, 131; as realist, 56–57, 70, 81–82, 87, 100, 102, 108, 131; Secchia's split with, 110, 148, 154–55; Sino-Soviet split viewed by, 194-96, 199–202, 205–6; social democracy denounced by, 142, 144, 161; "socialist camp" leadership viewed by, 165; "Salerno turn", 98-101; Soviets criticized by, 203; Soviet system viewed by, 59, 65–66; Spanish Civil War and, ix, 76–78, 82–83; Stalinism embraced by, 43, 46–47, 65, 72–73, 156; Stalinist terror and, 77-82; Stalin's meetings with, 98–99, 143–44, 146–47;

Togliatti, Palmiro (*continued*)
  Stalin's dismissiveness toward, 111; Stalin's plans for the Cominform rejected by, 145–49; strategy after Mussolini's fall, 95–103; "structural reforms" backed by, 181, 250; struggle for peace backed by, 45, 67–68, 73, 124, 126, 149, 192; Tasca's split with, 51; Tito's meeting with, 196–97; Trieste crisis and, 105–7, 109, 112; "war of position" viewed by, 134, 141, 144, 149–50, 152, 161, 182; war's inevitability viewed by, 60, 61, 68–69, 134, 145, 149–50, 152; Yalta memorandum of, 202–7, 211, 212, 288, 305, 312
Tortorella, Aldo, 262
Touré, Sékou, 187, 188
Treaties of Rome, 176
Treaty of Versailles, 10, 11
Trentin, Bruno, 181
Tresso, Pietro, 55
Treves, Claudio, 5, 32
Trilateral Commission, 265, 271
Trotsky, Leon, xi, 24, 30–36, 45, 64, 157; antifascism stressed by, 19–20; Gramsci linked to, 21; "socialism in one country" opposed by, 27; stabilization theory opposed by, 29
Truman, Harry, 118, 129
Tunisia, 49, 185
Turati, Filippo, 5

Ukraine, 14
United Arab Republic, 221

Valenzi, Maurizio, 186
Varga, Eugen, 62
Vidali, Vittorio, ix, 76–77, 78, 168, 169, 198
Vidić, Dobrijove, 306

Vietnam, 205, 211–18, 226, 227, 236, 238, 251, 283
Vyshinsky, Andrei, 96–99, 129

Wałęsa, Lech, 291
Wang Ming, 62
Warsaw Pact, 223–24, 225, 227, 256, 329, 331
Wilson, Woodrow, 5–9, 16
Workers' Party of Marxist Unity (POUM), 77
World Communist Conference (1969), 229–30
World Federation of Trade Union (WFTU), 159
World Peace Council (Partisans of Peace), 138, 149, 182
The Wretched of the Earth (Fanon), 191

Yata, Ali, 186
Yemen, 287, 301
Yom Kippur War (1973), 244–45, 249
Yudin, Pavel, 128–29
Yugoslavia, 100, 117, 119, 128, 129, 131, 158, 164, 169, 189, 211, 227, 255, 281, 304; Italian overtures to, 288, 316; Italian reformers aligned with, 251; transnational goals of, 101, 104, 134, 196–97; in Trieste crisis, 105–7, 109, 112, 132; Western communists upbraided by, 122, 123

Zagladin, Vladim, 287, 291, 298–99, 315, 318, 319
Zetkin, Clara, 26
Zhdanov, Andrei, 121–22, 124, 126, 127
Zhivkov Todor, 241
Zhou Enlai, 164, 166, 196
Zinoviev, Grigory, 15, 20, 29, 30, 32, 35, 38

STANFORD-HOOVER SERIES ON **AUTHORITARIANISM**

Edited by Paul R. Gregory and Norman Naimark

The Stanford–Hoover Series on Authoritarianism is dedicated to publishing peer-reviewed books for scholars and general readers that explore the history and development of authoritarian states across the globe. The series includes authors whose research draws on the rich holdings of the Hoover Library and Archives at Stanford University. Books in the Stanford–Hoover Series reflect a broad range of methodologies and approaches, examining social and political movements alongside the conditions that lead to the rise of authoritarian regimes, and is open to work focusing on regions around the world, including but not limited to Russia and the Soviet Union, Central and Eastern Europe, China, the Middle East, and Latin America. The Stanford–Hoover Series on Authoritarianism seeks to expand the historical framework through which scholars interpret the rise of authoritarianism throughout the twentieth century.

Mark Harrison, *Secret Leviathan:*
Secrecy and State Capacity under Soviet Communism
2023

David Brandenberger, *Stalin's Usable Past: A Critical*
Edition of the 1937 Short History of the USSR
2024